ANGOLA

REPÚBLICA DE ANGOLA

BUSINESS AND INVESTMENT OPPORTUNITIES YEARBOOK

VOLUME 1
STRATEGIC, PRACTICAL INFORMATION AND OPPORTUNITIES

International Business Publications, USA
Washington DC, USA -Angola

ANGOLA

BUSINESS AND INVESTMENT OPPORTUNITIES YEARBOOK
VOLUME 1 STRATEGIC, PRACTICAL INFORMATION AND OPPORTUNITIES

UPDATED ANNUALLY

We express our sincere appreciation to all government agencies and international organizations which provided information and other materials for this yearbook

Cover Design: International Business Publications, USA

2016 Edition Updated Reprint International Business Publications, USA
ISBN 1-4387-7610-1

For customer service and information, please contact:

in the USA: **International Business Publications, USA**
                     P.O.Box 15343, Washington, DC 20003
                     Phone: (202) 546-2103, Fax: (202) 546-3275.
                     E-mail: rusric@erols.com

Printed in the USA

For additional analytical, business and investment opportunities information,
please contact Global Investment & Business Center, USA
at (202) 546-2103. Fax: (202) 546-3275. E-mail: rusric@erols.com

ANGOLA

BUSINESS AND INVESTMENT OPPORTUNITIES YEARBOOK

VOLUME 1
STRATEGIC, PRACTICAL INFORMATION AND OPPORTUNITIES

TABLE OF CONTENTS

For additional analytical, business and investment opportunities information,
please contact Global Investment & Business Center, USA
at (202) 546-2103. Fax: (202) 546-3275. E-mail: rusric@erols.com

**For additional analytical, business and investment opportunities information,
please contact Global Investment & Business Center, USA
at (202) 546-2103. Fax: (202) 546-3275. E-mail: rusric@erols.com**

For additional analytical, business and investment opportunities information,
please contact Global Investment & Business Center, USA
at (202) 546-2103. Fax: (202) 546-3275. E-mail: rusric@erols.com

**For additional analytical, business and investment opportunities information,
please contact Global Investment & Business Center, USA
at (202) 546-2103. Fax: (202) 546-3275. E-mail: rusric@erols.com**

STRATEGIC AND DEVELOPMENT PROFILES

al (and largest city)	Luanda 8°50′S 13°20′E8.833°S 13.333°E
Official language(s)	Portuguese
Recognised regional languages	Kongo, Chokwe, South Mbundu (Umbundu) , North Mbundu (Kimbundu)
Demonym	Angolan
Government	Presidential republic
- President	José Eduardo dos Santos
Independence	from Portugal
- Date	November 11, 1975
Area	
- Total	1,246,700 km^2 (23rd) 481,354 sq mi
- Water (%)	negligible
Population	
- 2009 estimate	18,498,000
- census	5,646,177
- Density	14.8/km^2 (199th) 38.4/sq mi
GDP (PPP)	2009 estimate
- Total	$105.888 billion
- Per capita	$6,116
GDP (nominal)	2009 estimate
- Total	$68.755 billion
- Per capita	$3,971
HDI (2007)	▲0.564 (medium) (143rd)
Currency	Kwanza (AOA)
Time zone	WAT (UTC+1)
- Summer (DST)	not observed (UTC+1)
Drives on the	right
Internet TLD	.ao
Calling code	+244

STRATEGIC PROFILE

Located on the Atlantic Coast of southern Africa, Angola is bordered by Namibia to the south and Zambia and Zaire to the east and north. Angola's 1,600 km-long coastline and its four major ports make it a natural trans-shipment point for the entire region.

Land Area: 486,213 square miles
Population: 16 million
Capital City: Luanda
Languages: Portuguese (official) , Umbundu, Kimbundu, Kikongo, Tchokwe, Ovambo
Religions: Roman Catholic (51%) , Protestant (17%) , non-Christian (32%)
Climate: Tropical in the north, subtropical in the south
Time: One hour ahead of GMT

For additional analytical, business and investment opportunities information, please contact Global Investment & Business Center, USA at (202) 546-2103. Fax: (202) 546-3275. E-mail: rusric@erols.com

FACTS ABOUT THE GOVERNMENT

National Legislature: National Assembly with 220 seats
Last Elections: 1992 (legislative and presidential)
Next Elections: Will take place after the end of the peace process
Main Political Parties: The Popular Movement for the Liberation of Angola (MPLA) and the National Union for the Total Independence of Angola (UNITA)

ECONOMIC DATA

Currency: Readjusted Kwanza (Kzr)
GNP Growth: Nine percent
Exports: Over $5 billion worldwide
Major Exports: Oil, diamonds, minerals, coffee, fish, timber, cotton, sisal and other agricultural products
Imports: Over $1.5 billion worldwide
Major Imports: Food, beverages, vegetable products, capital goods, transportation and electrical equipment
Major Import Sources: The United States, Portugal and France
Roads: 46,575 miles
Railways: Benguela (810 miles) , Luanda (334 miles) , Moçâmedes (563 miles)
Major Ports: Luanda, Lobito and Namibe
Airports: International airport in Luanda; 13 other airports

GEOGRAPHY

Location: Southern Africa, bordering the South Atlantic Ocean, between Namibia and Democratic Republic of the Congo
Geographic coordinates: 12 30 S, 18 30 E
Map references: Africa

Area:
total: 1,246,700 sq km
land: 1,246,700 sq km
water: 0 sq km

Area—comparative: slightly less than twice the size of Texas

Land boundaries:
total: 5,198 km
border countries: Democratic Republic of the Congo 2,511 km of which 220 km is the boundary of discontiguous Cabinda Province, Republic of the Congo 201 km, Namibia 1,376 km, Zambia 1,110 km

Coastline: 1,600 km

Maritime claims:
exclusive economic zone: 200 nm
territorial sea: 12 nm

For additional analytical, business and investment opportunities information,
please contact Global Investment & Business Center, USA
at (202) 546-2103. Fax: (202) 546-3275. E-mail: rusric@erols.com

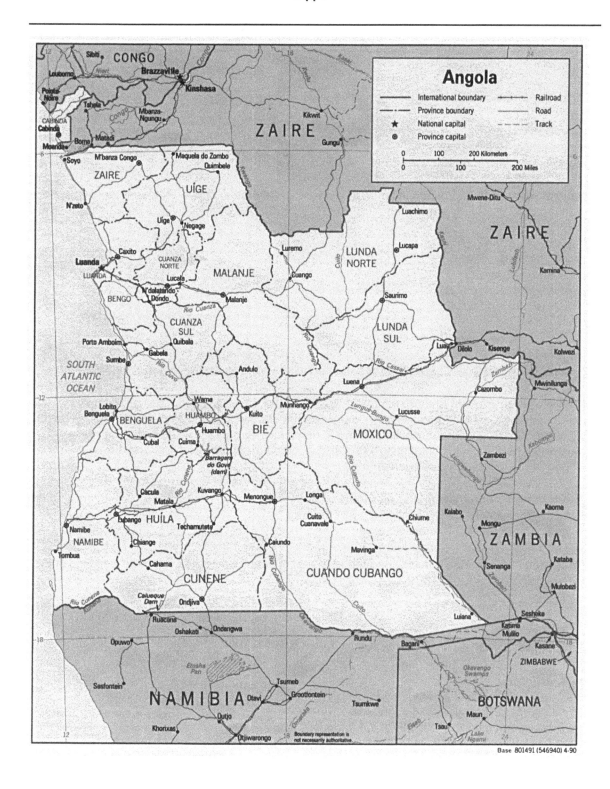

For additional analytical, business and investment opportunities information,
please contact Global Investment & Business Center, USA
at (202) 546-2103. Fax: (202) 546-3275. E-mail: rusric@erols.com

Climate: semiarid in south and along coast to Luanda; north has cool, dry season (May to October) and hot, rainy season (November to April)

Terrain: narrow coastal plain rises abruptly to vast interior plateau

Elevation extremes:
lowest point: Atlantic Ocean 0 m
highest point: Morro de Moco 2,620 m

Natural resources: petroleum, diamonds, iron ore, phosphates, copper, feldspar, gold, bauxite, uranium

Land use:
arable land: 2%
permanent crops: 0%
permanent pastures: 23%
forests and woodland: 43%
other: 32%

Irrigated land: 750 sq km
Natural hazards: locally heavy rainfall causes periodic flooding on the plateau

Environment—current issues: the overuse of pastures and subsequent soil erosion attributable to population pressures; desertification; deforestation of tropical rain forest, in response to both international demand for tropical timber and to domestic use as fuel, resulting in loss of biodiversity; soil erosion contributing to water pollution and siltation of rivers and dams; inadequate supplies of potable water

Environment—international agreements:
party to: Biodiversity, Desertification, Law of the Sea
signed, but not ratified: Climate Change

Geography—note: Cabinda is separated from rest of country by the Democratic Republic of the Congo

PEOPLE

Population: 11,177,537

Age structure:
0-14 years: 45% (male 2,545,006; female 2,473,732)
15-64 years: 52% (male 2,938,178; female 2,909,844)
65 years and over: 3% (male 143,074; female 167,703)

Population growth rate: 2.84%
Birth rate: 43.11 births/1,000 population
Death rate: 16.35 deaths/1,000 population

Net migration rate: 1.6 migrant(s) /1,000 population

Sex ratio:
at birth: 1.05 male(s) /female
under 15 years: 1.03 male(s) /female
15-64 years: 1.01 male(s) /female
65 years and over: 0.85 male(s) /female
total population: 1.01 male(s) /female

Infant mortality rate: 129.19 deaths/1,000 live births

Life expectancy at birth:
total population: 48.39 years
male: 46.08 years
female: 50.82 years

Total fertility rate: 6.12 children born/woman
Nationality:
noun: Angolan(s)
adjective: Angolan
Ethnic groups: Ovimbundu 37%, Kimbundu 25%, Bakongo 13%, mestico (mixed European and Native African) 2%, European 1%, other 22%
Religions: indigenous beliefs 47%, Roman Catholic 38%, Protestant 15%
Languages: Portuguese (official) , Bantu and other African languages

Literacy:
definition: age 15 and over can read and write
total population: 42%
male: 56%
female: 28%

GOVERNMENT

Country name:
conventional long form: Republic of Angola
conventional short form: Angola
local long form: Republica de Angola
local short form: Angola
former: People's Republic of Angola

Data code: AO

Government type: transitional government, nominally a multiparty democracy with a strong presidential system

Capital: Luanda

Administrative divisions: 18 provinces (provincias, singular—provincia) ; Bengo, Benguela, Bie, Cabinda, Cuando Cubango, Cuanza Norte, Cuanza Sul, Cunene, Huambo, Huila, Luanda, Lunda Norte, Lunda Sul, Malanje, Moxico, Namibe, Uige, Zaire

Independence: 11 November 1975 (from Portugal)
National holiday: Independence Day, 11 November (1975)

For additional analytical, business and investment opportunities information,
please contact Global Investment & Business Center, USA
at (202) 546-2103. Fax: (202) 546-3275. E-mail: rusric@erols.com

Constitution: 11 November 1975; revised 7 January 1978, 11 August 1980, 6 March 1991, and 26 August 1992
Legal system: based on Portuguese civil law system and customary law; recently modified to accommodate political pluralism and increased use of free markets
Suffrage: 18 years of age; universal

Executive branch:

chief of state: President Jose Eduardo DOS SANTOS (since 21 September 1979); Vice President Manuel Domingos VICENTE (since 26 September 2012); note - the president is both chief of state and head of government

head of government: President Jose Eduardo DOS SANTOS (since 21 September 1979); Vice President Manuel Domingos VICENTE (since 26 September 2012)

cabinet: Council of Ministers appointed by the president

elections: president indirectly elected by National Assembly for a five-year term (eligible for a second consecutive or discontinuous term) under the 2010 constitution; note - according to the 2010 constitution, ballots are cast for parties rather than candidates, the leader of the party with the most votes becomes president; following the results of the 2012 legislative elections DOS SANTOS became president (eligible for a second term)

election results: NA; as leader of the MPLA, Jose Eduardo DOS SANTOS became pesident following legislative elections on 31 August 2012; DOS SANTOS was inaugurated on 26 September 2012 to serve the first of a possible two terms under the 2010 constitution

Legislative branch:

unicameral National Assembly or Assembleia Nacional (220 seats; members elected by proportional vote to serve five-year terms)

elections: last held on 31 August 2012 (next to be held in 2017)

election results: percent of vote by party - MPLA 71.8%, UNITA 18.7%, CASA-CE 6.0%, PRS 1.7%, FNLA 1.1%, other 0.7%; seats by party - MPLA 175, UNITA 32, CASA-CE 8, PRS 3, FNLA 2

Judicial branch: Supreme Court or Tribunal da Relacao, judges of the Supreme Court are appointed by the president

Political parties and leaders: Popular Movement for the Liberation of Angola or MPLA [Jose Eduardo DOS SANTOS] ruling party in power since 1975; National Union for the Total Independence of Angola or UNITA [Jonas SAVIMBI], largest opposition party engaged in years of armed resistance before joining the current unity government in April 1997; Social Renewal Party or PRS [leader NA]; National Front for the Liberation of Angola or FNLA [leader NA]; Liberal Democratic Party or PLD [leader NA]
note: about a dozen minor parties participated in the 1992 elections but won few seats and have little influence in the National Assembly

For additional analytical, business and investment opportunities information,
please contact Global Investment & Business Center, USA
at (202) 546-2103. Fax: (202) 546-3275. E-mail: rusric@erols.com

Political pressure groups and leaders: Front for the Liberation of the Enclave of Cabinda or FLEC
note: FLEC is waging a small-scale, highly factionalized, armed struggle for the independence of Cabinda Province

International organization participation: ACP, AfDB, CCC, CEEAC, ECA, FAO, G-77, IBRD, ICAO, ICRM, IDA, IFAD, IFC, IFRCS, ILO, IMF, IMO, Intelsat, Interpol, IOC, IOM, ITU, NAM, OAS (observer) , OAU, SADC, UN, UNCTAD, UNESCO, UNIDO, UPU, WCL, WFTU, WHO, WIPO, WMO, WToO, WTrO

Diplomatic representation in the US:
chief of mission: Ambassador Antonio dos Santos FRANCA "N'dalu"
chancery: 1615 M Street, NW, Suite 900, Washington, DC 20036
telephone: (202) 785-1156
FAX: (202) 785-1258

Diplomatic representation from the US:
chief of mission: Ambassador Joseph G. SULLIVAN
embassy: number 32 Rua Houari Boumedienne, Miramar, Luanda
mailing address: international mail: Caixa Postal 6484, Luanda; pouch: American Embassy Luanda, Department of State, Washington, DC 20521-2550
telephone: [244] (2) 345-481, 346-418
FAX: [244] (2) 346-924

Flag description: two equal horizontal bands of red (top) and black with a centered yellow emblem consisting of a five-pointed star within half a cogwheel crossed by a machete (in the style of a hammer and sickle)

ECONOMY

Angola"s high growth rate in recent years was driven by high international prices for its oil. Angola became a member of OPEC in late 2006 and its current assigned a production quota of 1.65 million barrels a day (bbl/day). Oil production and its supporting activities contribute about 85% of GDP. Diamond exports contribute an additional 5%. Subsistence agriculture provides the main livelihood for most of the people, but half of the country"s food is still imported. Increased oil production supported growth averaging more than 17% per year from 2004 to 2008. A postwar reconstruction boom and resettlement of displaced persons has led to high rates of growth in construction and agriculture as well. Much of the country"s infrastructure is still damaged or undeveloped from the 27-year-long civil war. Land mines left from the war still mar the countryside, even though peace was established after the death of rebel leader Jonas SAVIMBI in February 2002. Since 2005, the government has used billions of dollars in credit lines from China, Brazil, Portugal, Germany, Spain, and the EU to rebuild Angola"s public infrastructure. The global recession that started in 2008 temporarily stalled economic growth. Lower prices for oil and diamonds during the global recession slowed GDP growth to 2.4% in 2009, and many construction projects stopped because Luanda accrued $9 billion in arrears to foreign construction companies when government revenue fell in 2008 and 2009. Angola abandoned its currency peg in 2009, and in November 2009 signed onto an IMF Stand-By Arrangement loan of $1.4 billion to rebuild international reserves. Consumer inflation declined from 325% in 2000 to about 10% in 2012. Higher oil prices have helped Angola turn a budget deficit of 8.6% of GDP in 2009 into an surplus of 12% of GDP in 2012. Corruption, especially in the extractive sectors, also is a major challenge.
GDP (purchasing power parity):

For additional analytical, business and investment opportunities information,
please contact Global Investment & Business Center, USA
at (202) 546-2103. Fax: (202) 546-3275. E-mail: rusric@erols.com

$130.4 billion (est.)
country comparison to the world: 66
$120.3 billion (est.)
$115.7 billion (est.)
note: data are in 2012 US dollars
GDP (official exchange rate):

$118.7 billion (est.)
GDP - real growth rate:

8.4% (est.)
country comparison to the world: 14
3.9% (est.)
3.4% (est.)
GDP - per capita (PPP):

$6,500 (est.)
country comparison to the world: 144
$6,100 (est.)
$6,100 (est.)
note: data are in 2012 US dollars
GDP - composition by sector:

agriculture: 10.2%
industry: 61.4%
services: 28.4% (est.)
Labor force:

8.468 million (est.)
country comparison to the world: 56
Labor force - by occupation:

agriculture: 85%
industry and services: 15% (est.)
Unemployment rate:

NA%
Population below poverty line:

40.5% (est.)
Household income or consumption by percentage share:

lowest 10%: 0.6%
highest 10%: 44.7% (2000)
Investment (gross fixed):

13.3% of GDP (est.)
country comparison to the world: 142
Budget:

revenues: $56.07 billion
expenditures: $42.26 billion (est.)
Taxes and other revenues:

For additional analytical, business and investment opportunities information,
please contact Global Investment & Business Center, USA
at (202) 546-2103. Fax: (202) 546-3275. E-mail: rusric@erols.com

47.2% of GDP (est.)
country comparison to the world: 20
Budget surplus (+) or deficit (-):

11.6% of GDP (est.)
country comparison to the world: 6
Public debt:

17.1% of GDP (est.)
country comparison to the world: 135
18.1% of GDP (est.)
Inflation rate (consumer prices):

10.3% (est.)
country comparison to the world: 200
13.5% (est.)
Central bank discount rate:

25% (31 December 2010 est.)
country comparison to the world: 2
30% (31 December 2009 est.)
Commercial bank prime lending rate:

16% (31 December 2012 est.)
country comparison to the world: 21
18.76% (31 December 2011 est.)
Stock of narrow money:

$12.93 billion (31 December 2012 est.)
country comparison to the world: 72
$11.58 billion (31 December 2011 est.)
Stock of broad money:

$44.65 billion (31 December 2012 est.)
country comparison to the world: 69
$36.55 billion (31 December 2011 est.)
Stock of domestic credit:

$27.12 billion (31 December 2012 est.)
country comparison to the world: 73
$22.18 billion (31 December 2011 est.)
Agriculture - products:

bananas, sugarcane, coffee, sisal, corn, cotton, cassava (manioc), tobacco, vegetables,
plantains; livestock; forest products; fish
Industries:

petroleum; diamonds, iron ore, phosphates, feldspar, bauxite, uranium, and gold; cement; basic
metal products; fish processing; food processing, brewing, tobacco products, sugar; textiles; ship
repair
Industrial production growth rate:

5% (est.)
country comparison to the world: 59

**For additional analytical, business and investment opportunities information,
please contact Global Investment & Business Center, USA
at (202) 546-2103. Fax: (202) 546-3275. E-mail: rusric@erols.com**

Current account balance:

$17.09 billion (est.)
country comparison to the world: 21
$15.92 billion (est.)
Exports:

$71.95 billion (est.)
country comparison to the world: 50
$65.8 billion (est.)
Exports - commodities:

crude oil, diamonds, refined petroleum products, coffee, sisal, fish and fish products, timber, cotton
Exports - partners:

China 36.3%, US 18.5%, India 10.6%, Taiwan 8%, Canada 6.9% (est.)
Imports:

$22.32 billion (est.)
country comparison to the world: 74
$19.75 billion (est.)
Imports - commodities:

machinery and electrical equipment, vehicles and spare parts; medicines, food, textiles, military goods
Imports - partners:

China 36.3%, Portugal 16.5%, South Korea 11.3%, Netherlands 9%, China 8.8%, US 8.1%, South Africa 4.9%, Brazil 4.5%, France 4.2% (est.)
Reserves of foreign exchange and gold:

$34.63 billion (31 December 2012 est.)
country comparison to the world: 48
$27.01 billion (31 December 2011 est.)
Debt - external:

$19.65 billion (31 December 2012 est.)
country comparison to the world: 81
$18.78 billion (31 December 2011 est.)
Stock of direct foreign investment - at home:

$115.5 billion (31 December 2012 est.)
country comparison to the world: 36
$101.9 billion (31 December 2011 est.)
Stock of direct foreign investment - abroad:

$8.196 billion (31 December 2012 est.)
country comparison to the world: 55
$6.346 billion (31 December 2011 est.)
Exchange rates:

kwanza (AOA) per US dollar -
95.54 (est.)

**For additional analytical, business and investment opportunities information,
please contact Global Investment & Business Center, USA
at (202) 546-2103. Fax: (202) 546-3275. E-mail: rusric@erols.com**

93.74 (est.)
91.91 (est.)
79.33 (2009)
75.02 (2008)
Fiscal year:

calendar year

ENERGY

Electricity - production:

4.08 billion kWh (est.)
country comparison to the world: 123
Electricity - consumption:

3.659 billion kWh (est.)
country comparison to the world: 125
Electricity - exports:

0 kWh (est.)
country comparison to the world: 156
Electricity - imports:

0 kWh (est.)
country comparison to the world: 155
Electricity - installed generating capacity:

1.155 million kW (est.)
country comparison to the world: 121
Electricity - from fossil fuels:

56.9% of total installed capacity (est.)
country comparison to the world: 143
Electricity - from nuclear fuels:

0% of total installed capacity (est.)
country comparison to the world: 40
Electricity - from hydroelectric plants:

43.1% of total installed capacity (est.)
country comparison to the world: 51
Electricity - from other renewable sources:

0% of total installed capacity (est.)
country comparison to the world: 105
Crude oil - production:

1.84 million bbl/day (est.)
country comparison to the world: 17
Crude oil - exports:

1.757 million bbl/day (est.)
country comparison to the world: 9

For additional analytical, business and investment opportunities information,
please contact Global Investment & Business Center, USA
at (202) 546-2103. Fax: (202) 546-3275. E-mail: rusric@erols.com

Crude oil - imports:

0 bbl/day (est.)
country comparison to the world: 153
Crude oil - proved reserves:

15 billion bbl (1 January 2013 est.)
country comparison to the world: 16
Refined petroleum products - production:

37,310 bbl/day (est.)
country comparison to the world: 89
Refined petroleum products - consumption:

79,430 bbl/day (est.)
country comparison to the world: 87
Refined petroleum products - exports:

31,050 bbl/day (est.)
country comparison to the world: 67
Refined petroleum products - imports:

41,480 bbl/day (est.)
country comparison to the world: 75
Natural gas - production:

734 million cu m (est.)
country comparison to the world: 69
Natural gas - consumption:

733 million cu m (est.)
country comparison to the world: 96
Natural gas - exports:

0 cu m (est.)
country comparison to the world: 56
Natural gas - imports:

0 cu m (est.)
country comparison to the world: 154
Natural gas - proved reserves:

310 billion cu m (1 January 2012 est.)
country comparison to the world: 39
Carbon dioxide emissions from consumption of energy:

24.2 million Mt (est.)
country comparison to the world: 80

COMMUNICATIONS

Telephones - main lines in use:

303,200 (2011)

For additional analytical, business and investment opportunities information,
please contact Global Investment & Business Center, USA
at (202) 546-2103. Fax: (202) 546-3275. E-mail: rusric@erols.com

country comparison to the world: 115
Telephones - mobile cellular:

9.491 million (2011)
country comparison to the world: 78
Telephone system:

general assessment: limited system; state-owned telecom had monopoly for fixed-lines until 2005; demand outstripped capacity, prices were high, and services poor; Telecom Namibia, through an Angolan company, became the first private licensed operator in Angola's fixed-line telephone network; by 2010, the number of fixed-line providers had expanded to 5; Angola Telecom established mobile-cellular service in Luanda in 1993 and the network has been extended to larger towns; a privately owned, mobile-cellular service provider began operations in 2001
domestic: only about two fixed-lines per 100 persons; mobile-cellular teledensity about 50 telephones per 100 persons in 2011
international: country code - 244; landing point for the SAT-3/WASC fiber-optic submarine cable that provides connectivity to Europe and Asia; satellite earth stations - 29 (2009)
Broadcast media:

state controls all broadcast media with nationwide reach; state-owned Televisao Popular de Angola (TPA) provides terrestrial TV service on 2 channels; a third TPA channel is available via cable and satellite; TV subscription services are available; state-owned Radio Nacional de Angola (RNA) broadcasts on 5 stations; about a half dozen private radio stations broadcast locally (2008)

Internet country code:.ao

Internet hosts:
20,703

country comparison to the world: 116
Internet users:

606,700 (2009)
country comparison to the world: 114

TRANSPORTATION

Railways:
total: 2,952 km (limited trackage in use because of land mines still in place from the civil war) (1997 est.)
narrow gauge: 2,798 km 1.067-m gauge; 154 km 0.600-m gauge

Highways:
total: 76,626 km *paved:* 19,156 km *unpaved:* 57,470 km (1997 est.)

Waterways: 1,295 km navigable
Pipelines: crude oil 179 km
Ports and harbors: Ambriz, Cabinda, Lobito, Luanda, Malongo, Namibe, Porto Amboim, Soyo
Merchant marine:
total: 10 ships (1,000 GRT or over) totaling 48,384 GRT/78,357 DWT
ships by type: cargo 9, oil tanker 1
Airports: 252

Airports—with paved runways:
total: 32
over 3,047 m: 4 *2,438 to 3,047 m:* 9 *1,524 to 2,437 m:* 12 *914 to 1,523 m:* 6
under 914 m: 1
Airports—with unpaved runways:
total: 220
over 3,047 m: 1 *2,438 to 3,047 m:* 5 *1,524 to 2,437 m:* 32
914 to 1,523 m: 100 *under 914 m:* 82

MILITARY

Military branches: Army, Navy, Air and Air Defense Forces, National Police Force
Military manpower—military age: 18 years of age
Military manpower—availability:
males age 15-49: 2,544,203
Military manpower—fit for military service:
males age 15-49: 1,280,377
Military manpower—reaching military age annually:
males: 111,168
Military expenditures—dollar figure: $1 billion
Military expenditures—percent of GDP: 25%

TRANSNATIONAL ISSUES

Disputes—international: none

Illicit drugs: increasingly used as a transshipment point for cocaine and heroin destined for Western Europe and other African states

For additional analytical, business and investment opportunities information,
please contact Global Investment & Business Center, USA
at (202) 546-2103. Fax: (202) 546-3275. E-mail: rusric@erols.com

IMPORTANT INFORMATION FOR UNDERSTANDING ANGOLA

GEOGRAPHY AND LOCATION

A total area of 1,246,700 square kilometers (including Cabinda Province) makes Angola the seventh largest state in Africa, but it is also one of the most lightly populated. The country is bordered to the north and east by Zaire, to the east by Zambia, and to the south by Namibia. The 7,270-square-kilometer enclave of Cabinda, which is separated from the rest of Angola by a strip of Zairian territory, is bordered on the north by Congo.

TERRAIN

Angola has three principal natural regions: the coastal lowland, characterized by low plains and terraces; hills and mountains, rising inland from the coast into a great escarpment; and an area of high plains, called the high plateau (*planalto*) , which extends eastward from the escarpment

The coastal lowland rises from the sea in a series of low terraces. This region varies in width from about 25 kilometers near Benguela to more than 150 kilometers in the Cuanza River Valley just south of Angola's capital, Luanda, and is markedly different from Angola's highland mass. The Atlantic Ocean's cold, northwardflowing Benguela Current substantially reduces precipitation along the coast, making the region relatively arid or nearly so south of Benguela (where it forms the northern extension of the Namib Desert) , and quite dry even in its northern reaches. Even where, as around Luanda, the average annual rainfall may be as much as fifty centimeters, it is not uncommon for the rains to fail. Given this pattern of precipitation, the far south is marked by sand dunes, which give way to dry scrub along the middle coast. Portions of the northern coastal plain are covered by thick brush.

The belt of hills and mountains parallels the coast at distances ranging from 20 kilometers to 100 kilometers inland. The Cuanza River divides the zone into two parts. The northern part rises gradually from the coastal zone to an average elevation of 500 meters, with crests as high as 1,000 meters to 1,800 meters. South of the Cuanza River, the hills rise sharply from the coastal lowlands and form a high escarpment, extending from a point east of Luanda and running south through Namibia. The escarpment reaches 2,400 meters at its highest point, southeast of the town of Sumbe, and is steepest in the far south in the Serra da Chela mountain range.

The high plateau lies to the east of the hills and mountains and dominates Angola's terrain. The surface of the plateau is typically flat or rolling, but parts of the Benguela Plateau and the Humpata Highland area of the Huíla Plateau in the south reach heights of 2,500 meters and more. The Malanje Plateau to the north rarely exceeds 1,000 meters in height. The Benguela Plateau and the coastal area in the immediate environs of Benguela and Lobito, the Bié Plateau, the Malanje Plateau, and a small section of the Huíla Plateau near the town of Lubango have long been among the most densely settled areas in Angola.

DRAINAGE

Most of the country's many rivers originate in central Angola, but their patterns of flow are diverse and their ultimate outlets varied. A number of rivers flow in a more or less westerly course to the Atlantic Ocean, providing water for irrigation in the dry coastal strip and the potential for hydroelectric power, only some of which had been realized by 1988. Two of Angola's most important rivers, the Cuanza and the Cunene, take a more indirect route to the Atlantic, the

For additional analytical, business and investment opportunities information, please contact Global Investment & Business Center, USA at (202) 546-2103. Fax: (202) 546-3275. E-mail: rusric@erols.com

Cuanza flowing north and the Cunene flowing south before turning west. The Cuanza is the only river wholly within Angola that is navigable--for nearly 200 kilometers from its mouth- -by boats of commercially or militarily significant size. The Congo River, whose mouth and western end form a small portion of Angola's northern border with Zaire, is also navigable.

North of the Lunda Divide a number of important tributaries of the Congo River flow north to join it, draining Angola's northeast quadrant. South of the divide some rivers flow into the Zambezi River and thence to the Indian Ocean, others to the Okavango River (as the Cubango River is called along the border with Namibia and in Botswana) and thence to the Okavango Swamp in Botswana. The tributaries of the Cubango River and several of the southern rivers flowing to the Atlantic are seasonal, completely dry much of the year.

CLIMATE

Like the rest of tropical Africa, Angola experiences distinct, alternating rainy and dry seasons. In the north, the rainy season may last for as long as seven months--usually from September to April, with perhaps a brief slackening in January or February. In the south, the rainy season begins later, in November, and lasts until about February. The dry season (*cacimbo*) is often characterized by a heavy morning mist. In general, precipitation is higher in the north, but at any latitude it is greater in the interior than along the coast and increases with altitude.

Temperatures fall with distance from the equator and with altitude and tend to rise closer to the Atlantic Ocean. Thus at Soyo, at the mouth of the Congo River, the average annual temperature is about 26°C, but it is under 16°C at Huambo on the temperate central plateau. The coolest months are July and August (in the middle of the dry season) , when frost may sometimes form at higher altitudes.

POPULATION

As of late 1988, the last official census in Angola had been taken in 1970. As a result, most population figures were widely varying estimates based on scanty birth and death rate data. According to the United States Department of Commerce's Bureau of the Census, Angola's 1988 population was about 8.2 million. The United States Department of State gave a 1986 figure of 8.5 million, while the United Nations (UN) Economic Commission for Africa estimated the mid-1986 population at 8.9 million.

The Angolan government estimated the 1988 population at almost 9.5 million The government figure, however, may have included Angolan refugees in neighboring countries. According to the U.S. Committee for Refugees, a private agency, in mid-1987 more than 400,000 Angolan refugees resided in Zaire and Zambia. There were about 50,000 Cuban soldiers and civilians and about 2,000 military and civilian advisers and technicians from the Soviet Union and the German Democratic Republic (East Germany) stationed in Angola. There were also about 10,000 South African refugees, most associated with the antigovernment African National Congress (ANC) ; 70,000 Namibian refugees, most associated with the South West Africa People's Organization (SWAPO) ; and 13,200 Zairian refugees. There was no officially reported immigration or emigration.

In spite of warfare, poor health care, and the large number of Angolans in exile, the population was growing steadily in the late 1980s. Like population estimates, however, growth rate calculations varied considerably. According to a 1987 estimate by the United States Central Intelligence Agency (CIA) , the growth rate was 3.6 percent. The UN 1986 estimate of 2.7 percent was a good deal lower, while the government, whose demographic estimates typically exceeded those of Western governments and international organizations, announced a 1986 growth rate of almost 4.9 percent. The CIA figured the infant mortality rate in 1987 at 167 per 1,000, and the United States Bureau of the Census calculated the death rate at 21 per 1,000.

According to UN figures, Angola had a very young population. In 1986 the UN estimated that about 46 percent of the population was under age fifteen (see fig. 4) . At the other end of the age scale, only 4.8 percent of the population was sixty years of age or older. The government estimated the median age at 17.5 years. Life expectancy in 1987, according to United States government sources, was forty-one for males and forty-four for females.

The 1970 census showed the most densely settled areas of Angola to be the plateau, those coastal zones including and adjacent to the cities of Luanda, Lobito, Benguela, and Moçâmedes (present-day Namibe) , and the enclave of Cabinda. The most densely settled province in 1970 was Huambo. The other large area of relatively dense settlement included much of Cuanza Norte Province and the southern part of Uíge Province. This area was the major center for coffee cultivation and attracted a number of Europeans and migrant workers. Except for Zaire Province in the far northwest, the most thinly populated areas of Angola lay in its eastern half.

Since the start of the independence struggle in the early 1960s, an almost continuous process of urbanization has taken place. This process was accelerated in the 1980s by the UNITA insurgency, which induced hundreds of thousands of Angolans to leave the countryside for large towns. Angola's urban population grew from 10.3 percent in 1960 to 33.8 percent in 1988 (according to government statistics) . Much of the growth occurred in Luanda, whose population more than doubled between 1960 and 1970, and which by 1988 had reached about 1.2 million. Other towns had also acquired larger populations: Huambo grew from less than 100,000 residents in 1975 to almost 1 million in 1987, and Benguela's population increased from 55,000 to about 350,000 over the same period.

After independence in 1975, there were a number of changes in the structure of the population. The first was the exodus of an estimated 350,000 white Portuguese to their homeland. Yet, by 1988 there were an estimated 82,000 whites (representing 1 percent of the population) , mostly of Portuguese origin, living in Angola.

The second change was brought about by large-scale population movements, mostly among the Ovimbundu who had migrated in the 1950s and 1960s to work on coffee plantations in northwestern Uíge Province. Panic-stricken by the onset of civil war in 1975, most Ovimbundu workers fled to their ethnic homelands in the central provinces. Another large-scale population movement occurred as many of the Bakongo who had fled to Zaire during the nationalist struggle returned to Angola.

The third and most striking population shift, most notable in the late 1970s and 1980s, had been the flight of increasing numbers of internal migrants out of the central provinces, where the effects of the UNITA insurgency had been most destructive. Most of this massive migration had been toward urban areas. From 1975 to 1988, millions of rural civilians were displaced, including more than 700,000 forced from their villages since 1985 by armed conflict. Many of these migrants relocated to ramshackle displacement camps, many of which were run by West European private voluntary organizations. Although these camps were less vulnerable to attacks by UNITA guerrillas, conditions in them were poor. Food and water were in short supply, and health care was limited.

Many of the displaced persons living in Benguela Province were Ovimbundu from the plateau regions of eastern Benguela and Huambo provinces. The officially registered displaced population of 21,478 in Benguela Province (1988 figure) lived in nine camps and one transit center, but there were probably thousands more living with family members in the province's urban areas, including Lobito and Benguela.

The estimated 116,598 displaced persons living in several camps in Cuanza Sul Province had been forced to flee from the province's eastern rural areas or from the plateau regions of Benguela, Huambo, and Bié provinces because of intense guerrilla activity. Because access to many rural areas was limited and sometimes impossible, most of these displaced persons were forced to rely on other local populations and some limited and sporadic outside assistance. Most displaced persons fled from the more fertile and wetter highlands to the less hospitable coastal zone and would be expected to return to their homes when the security situation improved.

In 1988, however, the majority of displaced persons had become integrated into the larger urban population, especially around Luanda. Many displaced persons who sought refuge in urban areas did so through family or other relations to circumvent government registration procedures and so avoid taxation, conscription, or forced resettlement. Consequently, the exact numbers of these people could not be computed. In Luanda much of the destitute population, estimated at 447,000 and mostly consisting of displaced persons, lived in vertical shantytowns (large apartment blocks in the center of the city with inadequate or nonexistent water sources or sanitary facilities) or in huge, maze-like neighborhoods known as *musseques*, the largest of which housed an estimated 400,000 people.

GOVERNMENT OF ANGOLA

The Government of National Unity is dominated by the MPLA. Unita, the rebel group, was expelled from the government in September 1998.

Other major parties include Frente Nacional para a Libertação de Angola (FNLA) (Angolan National Liberation Front) ; Partido da Aliança da Juventude, Operários e Campesinos de Angola (PAJOCA) (Angola Youth, Worker, Peasant Alliance Party) ; Fórum Democrátrico Angolano (FDA) (Angolan Democratic Forum) , Partido Renovador Democrático (PRD) (Democratic Renewal Party) ; Partido Democrático para Progreso/Aliança Nacional Angolano (PDPANA) (Democratic Progress Party/Angolan National Alliance) .

GOVERNMENT STRUCTURE

PEOPLE'S ASSEMBLY:

The People's Assembly is the highest governmental body in Angola and represents the sovereign will of the Angolan people. It promotes the i mplementation of the objectives of the state, legislates and makes decisions on basic questions relating to the State's life.

The Assembly's jurisdiction includes making changes in the constitutional law, approving laws, and drafting the Nationa l Plan and the general state budget. The People's Assembly also monitors, at supreme level, the actions of the government and of the other State organs.

The president of the People's Assembly is the President of the Republic.

The People's Assembly has 229 deputies elected by popular vote and is the only body with constituent power elected for a 3-year period. The People's Assembly elects committees consisting of deputies for carrying out ongoing activities or specific tasks. These committees are responsible for preparing for the People's Assembly sessions and for the Permanent Committee sessions, developing opinions, and producing studies concerning subjects within their juri sdiction. These committees also submit bills, draft resolutions and monitor the activities of the

For additional analytical, business and investment opportunities information,
please contact Global Investment & Business Center, USA
at (202) 546-2103. Fax: (202) 546-3275. E-mail: rusric@erols.com

sectors within their jurisdiction. Based on the country's political-administrative divisions, there are also representative organs of communes, distr icts and villages.

The Provincial People's Assemblies have 55 to 85 deputies.

COUNCIL OF MINISTERS:

The Council of Ministers is the State's higher administrative body within the Angolan government.

The members of the Council of Ministers are the President of the Republic, the ministers and the state secretaries. The Council of Ministers is the executive body of the People's Assembly, and its work consists of guiding the State's entire administrative apparatus.

This body organizes and directs the implementation of the State's domestic and foreign policy in accordance with the decisions made by the People's Assembly and by its Permanent Committee. Among other powers, it directs, coordinates and checks on the activity of the ministries and the other central organs of State administration.

Orientation of each sector of the national economy is up to the ministries or other central bodies of State administration. The ministries and other central bodies are led by members of the Council of Ministers, in accordance with the principles of individual leadership and personal responsibility to the President of the Republic. The President of the Republic is the head of government and is assisted by the Prime Minister.

SENIOR ANGOLAN GOVERNMENT OFFICIALS

Pres., **Jose Eduardo DOS SANTOS**
Vice Pres., **Manuel Domingos VICENTE**
Min. of Agriculture, Rural Development, & Fisheries, **Afonso Pedro CANGA**
Min. of Assistance & Social Reintegration, **Joao Baptista KUSSUMUA**
Min. of Commerce, **Rosa Escocio PACAVIRA DE MATOS**
Min. of Culture, **Rosa Maria MARTINS DA CRUZ E SILVA**
Min. of Defense, **Candido Pereira dos Santos VAN DUNEM**, *Maj. Gen.*
Min. of Economy, **Abraao Pio dos Santos GOURGEL**
Min. of Education, **Pinda SIMAO**
Min. of Energy & Water, **Joao Baptista BORGES**
Min. of Environment, **Maria de Fatima Monteiro JARDIM**
Min. of External Relations, **Georges Rebelo CHIKOTI**
Min. of Family & Women Promotion, **Maria Felomena de Fatima Lobao TELO DELGADO**
Min. of Finance, **Armando MANUEL**
Min. of Former Combatants & Veterans of War, **Kundi PAIHAMA**
Min. of Geology, Mines, & Industry, **Joaquim da Costa DAVID**
Min. of Health, **Jose Vieira DIAS VAN-DUNEM**
Min. of Higher Education, Science, & Technology, **Maria Candida Pereira TEIXEIRA**
Min. of Hotels & Tourism, **Pedro MUTINDE**
Min. of Interior, **Angelo de Barros Veiga TAVARES**
Min. of Justice & Human Rights, **Rui Jorge Carneiro MANGUEIRA**
Min. of Parliamentary Affairs, **Rosa Luis de Sousa MICOLO**
Min. of Petroleum, **Jose Maria Botelho de VASCONCELOS**
Min. of Planning, **Job GRACA**
Min. of Public Admin., Employment, & Social Security, **Antonio Domingos da Costa Pitra NETO**
Min. of Social Communication, **Jose Luis DE MATOS**
Min. of Telecommunications & Information Technology, **Jose Carvalho DA ROCHA**

Min. of Territorial Admin., **Bornito de Sousa Baltazar DIOGO**
Min. of Transport, **Augusto da Silva TOMAS**
Min. of Urban Affairs & Construction, **Waldemar Pires ALEXANDRE**
Min. of Youth & Sports, **Goncalves Manuel MUANDUMBA**
Min. in the Office of the Presidency, Civil Affairs, **Edeltrudes Mauricio Fernandes GASPAR DA COSTA**
Min. in the Office of the Presidency, Military Affairs, **Manuel Helder "Kopelipa" VIEIRA DIAS**
Sec. of the Council of Ministers, **Frederico Manuel dos Santos e Silva CARDOSO**
Governor, National Bank of Angola, **Jose de Lima MASSANO**
Ambassador to the US, **Alberto do Carmo BENTO RIBEIRO**
Permanent Representative to the UN, New York, **Ismael Abraao GASPAR MARTINS**

US ANGOLA RELATIONS

Angola – United States relations are diplomatic relations between the Republic of Angola and the United States of America. These relations were tense during the Angolan Civil War when the U.S. government backed UNITA rebels, but have warmed since the Angolan government renounced Marxism in 1992.

After the government renounced Marxism, the US recognized the Angolan government. United States Secretary of State Colin Powell visited Angola and Gabon in September 2002 and among other subjects, discussed petroleum.

U.S. assistance to Angola amounted to 188 million USD in 2003, much of it in the field of health services and disease control. USAID's food for peace program gave over 30 million USD to Angola's population in 2005. Angola is currently the second biggest trading partner in Sub-Saharan Africa of the U.S., primarily because of oil; Angola produces .0014 billion barrels (220,000 m^3) of oil per day, second only to Nigeria in all of Africa. This is expected to rise to .002 billion barrels (320,000 m^3) per day by 2008. A 2005 visit by Angolan President José Eduardo dos Santos to Washington, D.C. was a sign of warm relations between the two nations. In May 2007 the Council on Foreign Relations said, "Few African countries are more important to U.S. interests than Angola."

CURRENT INITIATIVES

The United States established diplomatic relations in 1993 with Angola, which had become independent from Portugal in 1975. Post-independence, Angola saw 27 years of civil war among groups backed at various times by countries that included the United States, the Soviet Union, Cuba, China, and South Africa. Angola has had two presidents since independence. The first president came to power in 1975; upon his 1979 death, the second president assumed power. Multiparty elections were held in 1992 under a process supervised by the United Nations, but the results were disputed and civil war continued until the 2002 death of one holdout guerilla leader.

Angola has a strong and capable military. Although the country is sub-Saharan Africa's second-largest oil producer and has great agricultural potential, two-thirds of the population live in poverty. U.S. foreign policy goals in Angola are to promote and strengthen Angola's democratic institutions, promote economic prosperity, improve health, and consolidate peace and security. The United States has worked with Angola to remove thousands of landmines and help war refugees and internally displaced people return to their homes.

For additional analytical, business and investment opportunities information,
please contact Global Investment & Business Center, USA
at (202) 546-2103. Fax: (202) 546-3275. E-mail: rusric@erols.com

In 2009 Secretary Clinton declared Angola a "strategic partner" of the United States, one of three that the Obama Administration has identified on the African continent (the other two are Nigeria and South Africa). The U.S. – Angola Strategic Partnership Dialogue (SPD) was formalized with the signing of a Memorandum of Understanding in Washington in July 2010.

U.S. ASSISTANCE TO ANGOLA

U.S. assistance seeks to focus on preventing major infectious diseases, strengthening health systems, increasing access to family planning and reproductive health services, and building capacity within nongovernmental organizations working in health advocacy and health service delivery. U.S. assistance also promotes stabilization and security sector reform.

BILATERAL ECONOMIC RELATIONS

Angola is the second-largest trading partner of the United States in sub-Saharan Africa, mainly because of its petroleum exports. U.S. imports from Angola are dominated by petroleum, with some diamonds. U.S. exports to Angola include machinery, aircraft, poultry, and iron and steel products. Angola is eligible for preferential trade benefits under the African Growth and Opportunity Act. The United States and Angola have signed a trade and investment framework agreement, which seeks to promote greater trade and investment between the two countries.

Angola's Membership in International Organizations

Angola and the United States belong to a number of the same international organizations, including the United Nations, International Monetary Fund, World Bank, and World Trade Organization. Angola also is an observer to the Organization of American States.

USAID's development program in Angola in FY 2007 was consistent with the country's status as a developing country at a pivotal juncture in its development and reconstruction. In FY 2006, the program budget was $25.5 million and focused on civil society strengthening, improved governance, and democratization; market-oriented economic analysis and economic reform policy; agricultural sector productivity; maternal and child health; HIV/AIDS prevention, education and voluntary counseling; and workforce development. Angola also launched a major program to fight malaria through the President's Malaria Initiative (PMI).

The Governing Justly and Democratically objective strengthens constituencies and institutions required for democratic governance by strengthening civil society organizations and promoting local government decentralization; fostering an independent media, government transparency, accountability, and capability, and improved dialogue between citizens and government; and laying the groundwork for free and fair elections. The Investing in People objective aims to improve maternal and child health and prevent the spread of HIV/AIDS and other infectious diseases by helping communities and institutions to provide necessary health services and to conduct HIV/AIDS prevention programs. The PMI is the largest health program and expands efforts to scale up proven preventive and treatment interventions toward achievement of 85% coverage among vulnerable groups and 50% reduction in morbidity due to malaria. The Economic Growth objective fosters economic policy and financial sector reform; credit access for micro-, small-, and medium-sized enterprises; and expanded trade and investment.

To assist with economic reform, in FY 2007 the State Department provided $2.2 million to work on land tenure, economic policy, and the financial sector. An additional $143,000 in grants was provided to community development projects and non-governmental organization (NGO)-sponsored democracy and human rights projects. $152,000 in International Military Education

**For additional analytical, business and investment opportunities information,
please contact Global Investment & Business Center, USA
at (202) 546-2103. Fax: (202) 546-3275. E-mail: rusric@erols.com**

and Training (IMET) funds was provided for English language training to the Angolan Armed Forces. Professional training for law enforcement personnel at the International Law Enforcement Academy (ILEA) in Gaborone, Botswana continued. The Safe Skies for Africa program provided around $800,000 in equipment and training to the Angolan civil aviation authority. As part of its public diplomacy program, the Embassy provided nearly $434,000 in English language training, educational exchanges and fellowships, and information resource services. The State Department provided $6 million for ongoing landmine, small arms, and munitions destruction projects throughout the country. These projects have played a major role in clearing agricultural land and opening critical road networks and increasing access in those areas of the country most impacted by landmines.

At the same time, the energy-based U.S. trading relationship continues to expand and spark other ties. One offshoot has been the development of a Sister City relationship between Lafayette, Louisiana and Cabinda and between Houston, Texas and Luanda. The Catholic University of Luanda has close links with a number of American institutions and has received support from the Angola Educational Assistance Fund, a U.S. non-profit organization organized by Citizens Energy of Boston. Sonangol has a longstanding program of educating its professionals in U.S. universities, complementing Chevron's policy of U.S. training for its own growing pool of Angolan professionals.

PRINCIPAL U.S. OFFICIALS

- Ambassador--Christopher J. McMullen
- Deputy Chief of Mission—Francisco Fernandez
- USAID Director—Randall Peterson
- Defense Attaché—LTC Chris Grieg

For additional analytical, business and investment opportunities information,
please contact Global Investment & Business Center, USA
at (202) 546-2103. Fax: (202) 546-3275. E-mail: rusric@erols.com

STRATEGIC INFORMATION AND BUSINESS OPPORTUNITIES

US ASSISTANCE TO ANGOLA

Angola remains in the throes of a complex and delicate transition from war to peace. U.S. national interests in Angola are in the consolidation of peace, a successful democratic transition, the promotion of U.S. economic interests and Angola's meaningful economic integration into the region. Currently, the U.S. obtains nearly 7% of its petroleum from Angola; this level is expected to increase to 10% within eight years. Angola is the United States' second largest investment site in sub-Saharan Africa, with over $4 billion invested to date. With increased stability, Angola will play a more significant role in the southern African economy, which is expected to be an engine of growth for the continent. Without internal stability, large quantities of food and/or other forms of humanitarian assistance may be required.

THE DEVELOPMENT CHALLENGE.

In 1994, the Lusaka Protocol was signed and Angola emerged from over 20 years of fighting with 500,000 dead, 3.5 million internally displaced persons, and more than 300,000 refugees in neighboring countries. Millions of land mines had been laid, most of the country's infrastructure was destroyed, and the economy largely collapsed. What few civil society organizations remained were weak and ineffective.

Four years later, the expected peace and prosperity has not yet been fully realized. Renewed conflict in some parts of the country between the National Union for the Total Independence of Angola (UNITA) and the Government of the Republic of Angola (GRA) is creating additional internally displaced persons, particularly in rural areas. This reverses the progress that had been achieved between 1996 and 1998 through the emergency humanitarian assistance provided by the international community. Angola's nascent democracy remains fragile and imperfect. This climate of national emergency has led to the increased centralization of GRA authority. Nevertheless, the revitalization of civil society continues despite the renewed conflict, albeit at a slower pace than in the 1997-98 period. Angolans have begun to recognize the need to network for more effective representation of their interests before the government. Thus Angola's transition continues.

OTHER DONORS.

The World Bank, the European Union and the U.N. specialized agencies are the leading multilateral donors. The United States is the largest bilateral donor. At present, the U.S. government channels its humanitarian assistance through U.S. private voluntary organizations (PVOs) and universities, international organizations and U.N. specialized agencies. Residual emergency food assistance is now being channeled through the World Food Program, but if the new crisis deepens, the United States may become more directly involved in food distribution programs.

Activities in food production will include assistance for seed multiplication, trials of improved varieties, and better post-harvest storage practices. Child survival activities will include immunizations for children and training of health workers and communities in topics such as nutrition and sanitation. Mine awareness education, assistance to vulnerable groups including war-traumatized children, and prosthetics for land mine victims will also go forward. Modifications to activities will be made on a case-by-case basis, depending upon the extent of the conflict. Emergency measures to assist newly displaced persons, now numbering over 500,000, will most likely be required for the year 2000.

USAID's democracy and governance portfolio will continue to focus on civil society through the strengthening of NGOs and the media. Most of these programs are implemented in Luanda or safe provincial capitals. USAID plans to continue supporting local administration, and such institutions as political parties and the National Assembly. Support for human rights, especially those of women, will continue. In light of the conflict, USAID may develop reconciliation activities to respond to new needs. The democracy portfolio will help build foundations for future elections.

While most of the program will continue to be implemented through U.S. and international NGOs, USAID will explore opportunities to help the government build its institutional capacity to provide social services in those areas for which program performance can be monitored effectively. The GRA requires international oil companies working in Angola to provide "Social Responsibility Funds" for community development activities; USAID will continue discussions with the oil companies on joint implementation of activities through these funds.

SELECTED PROJECTS

INCREASED RESETTLEMENT, REHABILITATION AND FOOD-CROP SELF-RELIANCE OF WAR-TORN ANGOLAN COMMUNITIES, 654-SO01

STATUS: Continuing
PROPOSED OBLIGATION AND FUNDING SOURCE: FY 2000: $1,500,000 DFA; $4,500,000 CS; $7,455,000 P.L. 480 Title II
INITIAL OBLIGATION: FY 1996 **ESTIMATED COMPLETION DATE:** 2000

Summary: USAID's assistance to post-war Angola began in 1995 with a strictly emergency, humanitarian focus. As stability began to return to Angola in 1997 and the prospects for lasting peace improved, USAID's activities expanded to include non-emergency humanitarian assistance. These transitional activities targeted food security and child survival, and were concentrated in the Planalto region (high need, high population, high impact) . In many cases, these were natural extensions of emergency activities, and took advantage of existing infrastructure. In addition to resettled persons, beneficiaries include vulnerable groups affected by the war, such as traumatized children and land mine victims in need of prosthetics. The food security activities underway aim to increase production, improve farming techniques, and reduce constraints on farmers. The child survival activities will improve local health centers' ability to respond to needs of isolated rural populations, provide immunizations and vitamin A to children, and strengthen preventive efforts that will reduce demands on an over-extended health system.

Key Results: Key intermediate results include: (1) Increased levels of food security in communities with significant resettled populations; (2) Improved health status in areas covered by NGO partner programs; and (3) Rehabilitation of war victims and other vulnerable groups.

Performance and Prospects: Through September 1998, USAID's implementing partners, mostly U.S. PVOs, reported that implementation remained on track. Of the 108,000 internally displaced persons receiving assistance from Catholic Relief Services in one province, 62,386 returned to their home communities, 28,257 were resettled in other nearby communities, and

For additional analytical, business and investment opportunities information,
please contact Global Investment & Business Center, USA
at (202) 546-2103. Fax: (202) 546-3275. E-mail: rusric@erols.com

17,357 will be further assisted by the World Food Program and an Angolan NGO. The Christian Children's Fund was able to reunite about 52% of its targeted population of demobilized child soldiers with their families.

A seed distribution program implemented by CARE reached over 100% of the target beneficiaries. Its vegetable seed program, which reintroduced seeds that had not been available for 15 years, exceeded targets by 50%. Africare distributed 60-pound kits of basic crop seeds and essential hand tools to 4,000 farmers, and provided complementary, community-based, practical training. Africare also trained public health assistants and technicians who vaccinated 155,400 women and children and reached over 48,000 Angolans with health and nutrition education. Three new child survival grants were signed in September 1998, and implementation has begun.

With the return of hostilities between government and UNITA forces in December 1998, the movement of the entire international community away from emergency support and into rehabilitation activities could be in jeopardy. USAID and its partners had planned to undertake longer-term food security programs. Now USAID may once again be compelled to focus resources on emergency humanitarian relief. To the extent possible, however, USAID still will undertake transitional food production and child survival activities in those geographic zones not affected by the fighting, including areas that have received an influx of displaced persons.

Possible Adjustments to Plans: Several options are under consideration to concentrate future resources in geographic zones of greater stability to protect prior investments and ensure that USAID can meet its targets. The extent of the modifications required will depend upon the length and intensity of the conflict. If the conflict remains localized, USAID will redirect non-emergency activities towards stable regions. If the conflict intensifies, USAID will develop new emergency activities to address humanitarian needs.

Other Donor Programs: Sweden and Norway are among the leading bilateral donors providing assistance to Angola. Many donors are involved in emergency activities, with the World Food Program and the U.N. Humanitarian Assistance Coordination Unit as the main partners. Of the approximately $56 million raised by the 1998 U.N. consolidated appeal, the United States contributed about $30 million. The European Union and UNICEF are strong supporters of child survival activities and other health programs in Angola.

Principal Contractors, Grantees or Agencies: USAID funds the activities of key U.S. and international organizations including Africare, Christian Children's Fund, Catholic Relief Services, CARE, Save the Children, Norwegian People's Aid, UNICEF, World Vision, Vietnam Veterans of America Foundation, and the World Food Program.

INCREASED NATIONAL RECONCILIATION THROUGH STRENGTHENED DEMOCRATIC AND POLITICAL INSTITUTIONS, 654-SO02

STATUS: Continuing
PROPOSED OBLIGATION AND FUNDING SOURCE: FY 2000: $3,000,000 DFA
INITIAL OBLIGATION: FY 1996 **ESTIMATED COMPLETION DATE:** 2000

Summary: USAID recognizes that the development of a more open and participatory political system is a pre-condition for Angola's emergence from the anarchy of the past 35 years. The prolonged conflict had prevented Angolans from working together toward common objectives and left political and civil society institutions extremely weak. USAID thus initiated a set of activities designed to promote the development of stable, efficient formal institutions, including strengthening Parliament and political parties.

Activities were also developed to strengthen civil society institutions, prevent human rights abuses, and promote a free and democratic press, intending to facilitate Angola's successful transition to peace and prosperity. Together, these interventions have aimed to strengthen the skills of the political leadership and ordinary citizens to support the creation of a free and democratic political system. USAID assistance, provided through U.S. PVOs and universities, ranges from training community-based organizations in rural areas to implementing civic education and human rights programs and to addressing needs of such government institutions as the legislature and political parties.

Key Results: The expected intermediate results include: (1) Creating reconciliation opportunities among diverse groups of Angolans; (2) Citizens exercising their democratic rights and responsibilities; (3) Accountable governance within Parliament and three provincial administrations; and (4) Strengthened foundation for the participation of citizens and political parties in free, fair and peaceful elections.

Performance and Prospects: USAID has made progress on its democracy/governance (D/G) work with grassroots organizations and civil society. Given the weakness of civil society in Angola, USAID has focused on training local non-governmental organizations (NGOs) and community-based organizations (CBOs) in organizational and leadership skills. A first round of 18 NGOs completed their training in 1998 under a grant to the U.S. PVO PACT. A second group of 18 began training in November 1998; their trainers include some of the previously-trained NGO leaders. Initial evaluation results are encouraging, demonstrating significant management improvements among the trained NGOs. Human rights training by the U.S. PVO World Learning continues, while an Angolan NGO has been teaching women farm workers to organize to defend their rights. Applications from NGOs for human rights training have increased by 50% since 1997. The Mississippi Consortium for International Development signed an agreement with the Ministry of Education to include civic education topics in its training for primary school teachers. USAID also is training NGOs to integrate women's needs into their programs more effectively.

Because of the civil war, Angolan civil society has been isolated from its neighbors and their experiences. During this past year, USAID organized an exchange with NGO communities in Mozambique. Angolan delegates to Mozambique gathered ideas on how to energize civil society, and signed agreements with Mozambican civil society organizations, journalists, and children's rights groups to continue their collaboration. USAID also sponsored a workshop to enable Angolan NGOs to participate in the USAID-funded Southern Africa Regional Democracy Fund.

Assistance to the legislature also got off to a promising start in 1997 and 1998. The International Republican Institute (IRI) conducted the first-ever parliamentary training program for the National Assembly; 160 out of the 220 members participated. In addition, IRI provided training to over 200 national party leaders and activists. The National Democratic Institute administered three seminars to strengthen the capacity of local and provincial administrators to respond to needs of their communities; these seminars were widely attended and acclaimed by the local press. New challenges are anticipated in 1999, as the factional split in the UNITA delegation to the National Assembly may make it more difficult for the legislature to leverage a greater share of power from the executive branch.

Possible Adjustments to Plans: Most of the democracy and governance activities are organized in Luanda with participants from around the country, and thus are expected to continue. Human rights training will also continue as planned. However, some of the plans to implement activities in areas beyond the capital may not materialize because of insecurity in

For additional analytical, business and investment opportunities information,
please contact Global Investment & Business Center, USA
at (202) 546-2103. Fax: (202) 546-3275. E-mail: rusric@erols.com

certain provinces. Further, municipal elections envisioned for 1999 have been postponed, thus the support intended for this event also will be deferred. The focus on the legislature and strengthening political party development may change in light of the weakened role of the National Assembly and the renewed conflict. The emphasis of USAID assistance may move to constituent relations or organizational development, investments that will prove valuable when peace finally comes to Angola.

Other Donor Programs: USAID remains the lead donor in D/G activities in Angola. Donor coordination has been particularly strong in this sector. The United States and Sweden spearheaded a donor roundtable in 1998, at which ideas were exchanged on innovative approaches to preventing human rights abuses, techniques to bolster women's power in political processes, and the organization of grassroots party support. The meeting was attended by eleven bilateral and multilateral donors as well as several NGOs. Sweden has provided funding for democracy and governance activities, while the UN provides assistance for human rights activities. A donor coordination group on gender equity was recently initiated; this group will share information, pool resources, and monitor gender related activities.

Principal Contractors, Grantees or Agencies: The National Democratic Institute, PACT, International Republican Institute, Voice of America, World Learning, Mississippi Consortium for International Development, America's Development Foundation.

IMPORTANT OPPORTUNITIES FOR INVESTMENTS

AGRICULTURE, FORESTRY & FISHERIES

In the past Angola has proved to be a world power in terms of agricultural production and at one point was the world's fourth largest coffee producer though this is not the case anymore. Some of the farmers and agriculturist have estimated that only 3% of their arable land is cultivated now. Therefore the potential in Angola is enormous, although the success of the sector depends directly upon the outcome of the civil conflict.

The government in Angola has made the rehabilitation of coffee plantations a priority. In this regard Angola has made efforts and has taken up assistance from the UN agency for the World Food Programme .This aid is important for the development of the sector and the country has received assistance from the EU in the form of seeds and farming equipment. The Ministry of Agriculture in Angola, is in the process of reforming its legislation in order to ensure that its policies are carried out with greater commitment in the interests of guaranteeing food self sufficiency for the people. Among new laws proposed in 2005 are those concerning land, agrarian development, co-operative law, forests and seeds Many of the natural forests arc yet to be exploited. Plantations of eucalyptus, cypress and pine which once formed the basis of a small export industry add to a rich agricultural heritage.

From 1975, the timber production in the country has fallen drastically. There are now as many as nearly 150,000 hectares of eucalyptus, cypress and pine plantations waiting to be rehabilitated. Several of the valuable tree species including rosewood, ebony, African sandalwood mahogany, tola and mulberry, are found in the northern forests which have remained untapped since independence.The coastline in Angola is rich in shellfish and a variety of other fish species. An attempt is currently being made to rehabilitate and modernize the domestic fishing industry. The fishing fleet has been built through donor assistance. Refrigeration facilities at the southern ports of Tombwe and Namibe have been overhauled and a new production line at the Tombwe canning factory has been installed with EU assistance. The prices of fish were deregulated, thus

For additional analytical, business and investment opportunities information, please contact Global Investment & Business Center, USA at (202) 546-2103. Fax: (202) 546-3275. E-mail: rusric@erols.com

encouraging the development in this sector. The government with assistance from the World Bank, has set up the Angolan Support Fund for Fisheries Development.

TOURISM INDUSTRY :

Angola has a tropical climate, beaches, rivers, mountains, wildlife and cultural attractions all factors giving it a excellent opportunity for growth in the tourism industry. But still, development of this sector has not yet begun in earnest. The visas are still difficult to obtain for the region . Even as the wildlife resources have severely depleted in the region, many species in Angola are still roaming free like from elephants to the rare giant palanca. There is a huge geographical variety right from the tropical beaches to inland mountains and lakes, is sure to be a major draw card.There are a lot of traditional crafts present in Angola some of them in ivory, wood, ceramics and metal, quite different to styles found elsewhere in Africa. Other aspects of Angolan culture such as dance, music and night life add to the Angolan attraction. Angola has much to offer in its cuisine .There is fish, shellfish and meat cooked with strong spices, some of the country's specialties.The hotel industry of Angola requires coming up further as the demand far exceeds supply. The restructuring of existing hotels is underway and also there is plenty of opportunities for construction of new ones.

ELECTRICITY INDUSTRY

The Angolan electricity industry has a tremendous potential for growth. Despite the global financial meltdown, the current growth demand for electricity is estimated at 12.0 per cent per annum. The national programme for reconstruction is expected to remain a significant driving force. In 2004, the Capanda dam started its operation almost doubled the country's electricity capacity and began a new era for the Angolan electricity industry.

The surge in the economic growth has led to the rise in the country´s electricity industry. Angola has a huge potential in the generation of the hydro electricity, which is still currently underdeveloped. Thus the underdeveloped industry has put additional pressure on the Angolan government to help rebuild it through a reconstruction programme - the Angolan government is expected to channel $8.4 billion towards the industry.

The current electricity industry reformation is expected to significantly reduce investment barriers. Investment laws in Angola give foreign and domestic investors equal access to investment incentives and enable the participation of private investor in public infrastructure projects such as electricity supply. Though the environmental regulations are becoming tighter, potentially increasing the risk in investment and thus adding to the requirements for investing in both existing and new power plants.

MINERALS

Diamonds: Angola was the fifth biggest producer of diamonds of the world in the year of 2006 and the main geologists of the world estimate that the alluvial backups of Angola can total up the 130 millions of carats. The country has at least six gold-mines of kimberlitos virgin and these gold-mines are among the ten biggest of the world, an estimate of 180 millions of carats in the value of several billions of dollars.

With substantial golden deposits, iron, phosphates, manganese, copper, leads, quartz, plaster, marble, black granite, beryl, zinc and numerous strategic minerals, Angola was described as one of the most greatest world treasures among the countries in development

OIL

Angola is exporting about 90% of its crude oil primarily to China and the US.US imported nearly 496,000 bbl/d of crude oil in 2007 from Angola (507,000 total oil imports),making it the sixth largest supplier of crude oil to the United States after Nigeria. For most of 2007, Angola was the second largest exporter of crude oil to China after Saudi Arabia —occasionally surpassing the kingdom. The monthly records show that China imported around 650,000 bbl/d of Angolan crude in the December of 2007 as compared to US imports of 440,000 bbl/d for the same month. Other export destinations include Europe and Latin America, mainly Brazil—the fellow lusophone country is increasing political and economic links with Angola, specifically in the oil sector.

ECONOMY & ECONOMIC DEVELOPMENT

Economy of Angola	
Currency	Angolan kwanza (AOA)
Fiscal year	Calendar year
Trade organisations	AU, WTO
Statistics	
GDP	$99.01 billion (est.)
GDP growth	7.9% (est.)
GDP per capita	$9,000 (est.)
GDP by sector	agriculture: 9.6%; industry: 65.8%; services: 24.6% (est.)
Inflation (CPI)	13.3% (est.)
Population below poverty line	40.5% (est.)
Labour force	7.977 million (est.)
Labour force by occupation	agriculture: 85%; industry and services: 15% (est.)
Average gross salary	10,000 (2011)
Main industries	petroleum; diamonds, iron ore, phosphates, feldspar, bauxite, uranium, and gold; cement; basic metal products; fish processing; food processing, brewing, tobacco products, sugar; textiles; ship repair
Ease of Doing Business Rank	172nd
External	
Exports	$51.65 billion (est.)
Export goods	crude oil, diamonds, refined petroleum products, coffee, sisal, fish and fish products, timber, cotton
Main export partners	China 35.65%, United States 25.98%, France 8.83%, South Africa 4.13% (2009)
Imports	$18.1 billion (est.)
Import goods	machinery and electrical equipment, vehicles and spare parts; medicines, food, textiles, military goods
Main import partners	Portugal 18.71%, China 17.39%, United States 8.51%, Brazil 8.22%, South Korea 6.72%, France 4.51%, Italy 4.28%, South Africa 4.02% (2009)
Gross external debt	$17.98 billion (31 December 2010 est.)
Public finances	
Public debt	20.3% of GDP (est.)
Revenues	$40.41 billion (est.)
Expenses	$37.38 billion (est.)
Economic aid	$383.5 million
Foreign reserves	$16.89 billion (31 December 2010 est.)

The **Economy of Angola** is one of the fastest-growing economies in the world, with the Economist asserting that for 2001 to 2010, Angolas' Annual average GDP growth was 11.1 percent. It is still recovering from the Angolan Civil War that plagued Angola from independence in 1975 until 2002. Despite extensive oil and gas resources, diamonds, hydroelectric potential, and rich agricultural land, Angola remains poor, and a third of the population relies on subsistence agriculture.

Since 2002, when the 27-year civil war ended, the country has worked to repair and improve ravaged infrastructure and weakened political and social institutions. High international oil prices and rising oil production have led to a very strong economic growth in recent years[but corruption and public-sector mismanagement remain, particularly in the oil sector, which accounts for over 50 percent of GDP, over 90 percent of export revenue, and over 80 percent of government revenue.

The Angolan economy is highly dependent on its offshore oil sector. Positive growth rates are attributable to the regional oil boom which is centred on developing Angola's large oil reserves. However, ordinary Angolans languish in poverty with one of the lowest GDP per capita rates in the world while oil revenues are ploughed into fighting the Unita rebels in the south and east of the country.

Angola has a rich subsoil heritage, from diamonds, oil, gold, copper, as well as a rich wildlife (dramatically impoverished during the civil war), forest, and fossils. Since independence, oil and diamonds have been the most important economic resource. Smallholder and plantation agriculture have dramatically dropped because of the Angolan Civil War, but have begun to recover after 2002. The transformation industry that had come into existence in the late colonial period collapsed at independence, because of the exodus of most of the ethnic Portuguese population, but has begun to reemerge (with updated technologies), partly because of the influx of new Portuguese entrepreneurs. Similar developments can be verified in the service sector.

Overall, Angola's economy has undergone a period of transformation in recent years, moving from the disarray caused by a quarter century of civil war to being the fastest growing economy in Africa and one of the fastest in the world, with an average GDP growth of 20 percent between 2005 and 2007.

In the period 2001–2010, Angola had the world's highest annual average GDP growth, at 11.1 percent. In 2004, China's Eximbank approved a $2 billion line of credit to Angola. The loan is being used to rebuild Angola's infrastructure, and has also limited the influence of the International Monetary Fund in the country.

China is Angola's biggest trade partner and export destination as well as the fourth-largest importer. Bilateral trade reached $27.67 billion in 2011, up 11.5 percent year-on-year. China's imports, mainly crude oil and diamonds, increased 9.1 percent to $24.89 billion while China's exports, including mechanical and electrical products, machinery parts and construction materials, surged 38.8 percent.

The Economist reported in 2008 that diamonds and oil make up 60 percent of Angola's economy, almost all of the country's revenue and are its dominant exports. Growth is almost entirely driven by rising oil production which surpassed 1.4 million barrels per day (220,000 m^3/d) in late 2005 and was expected to grow to 2 million barrels per day (320,000 m^3/d) by 2007. Control of the oil industry is consolidated in Sonangol Group, a conglomerate which is owned by the Angolan government. In December 2006, Angola was admitted as a member of OPEC. The economy grew 18% in 2005, 26% in 2006 and 17.6% in 2007. However, due to the global recession the economy contracted an estimated −0.3% in 2009. The security brought about by the 2002 peace settlement has led to the resettlement of 4 million displaced persons, thus resulting in large-scale increases in agriculture production.

Although the country's economy has developed very significantly since achieving political stability in 2002, mainly thanks to the fast-rising earnings of the oil sector, Angola faces huge social and economic problems. These are in part a result of the almost continual state of conflict from 1961 onwards, although the highest level of destruction and socio-economic damage took place after the 1975 independence, during the long years of civil war. However, high poverty rates and blatant social inequality are chiefly the outcome of a combination of a persistent political authoritarianism, of "neo-patrimonial" practices at all levels of the political, administrative, military, and economic apparatuses, and of a pervasive corruption.

The main beneficiary of this situation is a social segment constituted since 1975, but mainly during the last decades, around the political, administrative, economic, and military power holders, which has accumulated (and continues accumulating) enormous wealth. "Secondary beneficiaries" are the middle strata which are about to become social classes. However, overall almost half the population has to be considered as poor, but in this respect there are dramatic differences between the countryside and the cities (where by now slightly more than 50% of the people live).

An inquiry carried out in 2008 by the Angolan Instituto Nacional de Estatística has it that in the rural areas roughly 58% must be classified as "poor", according to UN norms, but in the urban areas only 19%, while the overall rate is 37%. In the cities, a majority of families, well beyond those officially classified as poor, have to adopt a variety of survival strategies. At the same time, in urban areas social inequality is most evident, and assumes extreme forms in the capital, Luanda. In the Human Development Index Angola constantly ranks in the bottom group.

According to The Heritage Foundation, a conservative American think tank, oil production from Angola has increased so significantly that Angola now is China's biggest supplier of oil. Growing oil revenues have also created opportunities for corruption: according to a recent Human Rights Watch report, 32 billion US dollars disappeared from government accounts from 2007 to 2010.

Before independence in 1975, Angola was a breadbasket of southern Africa and a major exporter of bananas, coffee and sisal, but three decades of civil war (1975–2002) destroyed the fertile countryside, leaving it littered with landmines and driving millions into the cities. The country now depends on expensive food imports, mainly from South Africa and Portugal, while more than 90 percent of farming is done at family and subsistence level. Thousands of Angolan small-scale farmers are trapped in poverty.

The enormous differences between the regions pose a serious structural problem in the Angolan economy. This is best illustrated by the fact that about one third of the economic activities is concentrated in Luanda and the neighbouring Bengo province, while several areas of the interior are characterized by stagnation and even regression.

One of the economic consequences of the social and regional disparities is a sharp increase in Angolan private investments abroad. The small fringe of Angolan society where most of the accumulation takes place seeks to spread its assets, for reasons of security and profit. For the time being, the biggest share of these investments is concentrated in Portugal where the Angolan presence (including that of the family of the state president) in banks as well as in the domains of energy, telecommunications, and mass media has become notable, as has the acquisition of vineyards and orchards as well as of touristic enterprises

For additional analytical, business and investment opportunities information, please contact Global Investment & Business Center, USA at (202) 546-2103. Fax: (202) 546-3275. E-mail: rusric@erols.com

Despite its abundant natural resources, output per capita is among the world's lowest. Subsistence agriculture provides the main livelihood for 85% of the population. Oil production and the supporting activities are vital to the economy, contributing about 45% to GDP and 90% of exports. Growth is almost entirely driven by rising oil production which surpassed 1.4 million barrels per day (220×10^3 m³/d) in late-2005 and which is expected to grow to 2 million barrels per day (320×10^3 m³/d) by 2007. Control of the oil industry is consolidated in Sonangol Group, a conglomerate which is owned by the Angolan government. With revenues booming from oil exports, the government has started to implement ambitious development programs in building roads and other basic infrastructure for the nation.

In the last decade of the colonial period, Angola was a major African food exporter but now imports almost all its food. Because of severe wartime conditions, including extensive planting of landmines throughout the countryside, agricultural activities have been brought to a near standstill. Some efforts to recover have gone forward, however, notably in fisheries. Coffee production, though a fraction of its pre-1975 level, is sufficient for domestic needs and some exports. In sharp contrast to a bleak picture of devastation and bare subsistence is expanding oil production, now almost half of GDP and 90% of exports, at 800 thousand barrels per day (130×10^3 m³/d). Diamonds provided much of the revenue for Jonas Savimbi's UNITA rebellion through illicit trade. Other rich resources await development: gold, forest products, fisheries, iron ore, coffee, and fruits.

Exports in 2004 reached US$10,530,764,911. The vast majority of Angola's exports, 92% in 2004, are petroleum products. US$785 million worth of diamonds, 7.5% of exports, were sold abroad that year. Nearly all of Angola's oil goes to the United States, 526 kbbl/d (83.6×10^3 m³/d) in 2006, making it the eighth largest supplier of oil to the United States, and to the People's Republic of China, 477 kbbl/d (75.8×10^3 m³/d) in 2006. In the first quarter of 2008, Angola became the main exporter of oil to China.

The rest of its petroleum exports go to Europe and Latin America. U.S. companies account for more than half the investment in Angola, with Chevron-Texaco leading the way. The U.S. exports industrial goods and services, primarily oilfield equipment, mining equipment, chemicals, aircraft, and food, to Angola, while principally importing petroleum. Trade between Angola and South Africa exceeded USD 300 million in 2007. From the 2000s many Chinese have settled and started up businesses.

PETROLEUM

Angola produces and exports more petroleum than any other nation in sub-Saharan Africa, surpassing Nigeria in the 2000s. In January 2007 Angola became a member of OPEC. By 2010 production is expected to double the 2006 output level with development of deep-water offshore oil fields. Oil sales generated USD 1.71 billion in tax revenue in 2004 and now makes up 80% of the government's budget, a 5% increase from 2003, and 45% of GDP.

Chevron Corporation produces and receives 400 kbbl/d (64×10^3 m³/d), 27% of Angolan oil. Elf Oil, Texaco, ExxonMobil, Agip, Petrobras, and British Petroleum also operate in the country.

Block Zero provides the majority of Angola's crude oil production with 370 kbbl/d (59×10^3 m³/d) produced annually. The largest fields in Block Zero are Takula (Area A), Numbi (Area A), and Kokongo (Area B). ChevronTexaco operates in Block Zero with a 39.2% share. SONANGOL, the state oil company, Total, and ENI-Agip own the rest of the block. ChevronTexaco also operates Angola's first producing deepwater section, Block 14, with 57 kbbl/d (9.1×10^3 m³/d).

The United Nations has criticized the Angolan government for using torture, rape, summary executions, arbitrary detention, and disappearances, actions which Angolan government has justified on the need to maintain oil output.

Angola is the third-largest trading partner of the United States in Sub-Saharan Africa, largely because of its petroleum exports. The U.S. imports 7% of its oil from Angola, about three times as much as it imported from Kuwait just prior to the Gulf War in 1991. The U.S. Government has invested USD $4 billion in Angola's petroleum sector.

DIAMONDS

Angola is the third largest producer of diamonds in Africa and has only explored 40% of the diamond-rich territory within the country, but has had difficulty in attracting foreign investment because of corruption, human rights violations, and diamond smuggling. Production rose by 30% in 2006 and Endiama, the national diamond company of Angola, expects production to increase by 8% in 2007 to 10 million carats annually. The government is trying to attract foreign companies to the provinces of Bié, Malanje and Uíge.

The Angolan government loses $375 million annually from diamond smuggling. In 2003 the government began Operation Brilliant, an anti-smuggling investigation that arrested and deported 250,000 smugglers between 2003 and 2006. Rafael Marques, a journalist and human rights activist, described the diamond industry in his 2006 *Angola's Deadly Diamonds* report as plagued by "murders, beatings, arbitrary detentions and other human rights violations." Marques called on foreign countries to boycott Angola's "conflict diamonds".

IRON

Under Portuguese rule, Angola began mining iron in 1957, producing 1.2 million tons in 1967 and 6.2 million tons by 1971. In the early 1970s, 70% of Portuguese Angola's iron exports went to Western Europe and Japan. After independence in 1975, the Angolan Civil War (1975–2002) destroyed most of the territory's mining infrastructure. The redevelopment of the Angolan mining industry started in the late 2000s

INDUSTRIAL DEVELOPMENT

MANUFACTURING

Prior to the war, Angola's manufacturing sector had:

- 4000 manufacturing entities
- 200,000 people employed
- $650 million worth of goods produced

With the end of the war, a resurgence of industry to pre-war levels is possible. Both food processing and light industry are likely investment candidates.

FOOD PROCESSING INCLUDES

beer
sugar
wheat flour
cooking oil
molasses

For additional analytical, business and investment opportunities information, please contact Global Investment & Business Center, USA at (202) 546-2103. Fax: (202) 546-3275. E-mail: rusric@erols.com

salt
soft drinks

Light Industry includes:

textiles
soap
shoes
matches
paint
plastic bottles
glues

HEAVY INDUSTRY

Accounts for 15% of Angola's industrial output and includes:

cement production
oil refining
tire production
steel tube production
vehicle assembly

US firms that are leaders in these industries and have the potential to develop these markets include: Rubbermaid, Proctor & Gamble, Colgate-Palmolive, Shaw Industries, Burlington Industries, Goodyear Tire & Rubber, and Cooper Tire & Rubber.

AGRICULTURAL DEVELOPMENT IN ANGOLA

AGRICULTURE

The agricultural sector fell from 13 per cent of GDP in 1998 to 6.7 per cent in 2000 as a result of falling agricultural output and the increasing importance of the oil sector.

At least 75 per cent of national food requirements are imported and this is likely to continue until the government succeeds in stabilising the currency, freeing farmgate prices and providing rural areas with farm inputs, basic transport and essential commodities.

Of the major crops, only coffee is produced in exportable volumes, while the cultivation of sisal and cotton has virtually ceased. Following the May 1991 cease-fire, there were programmes to rehabilitate coffee plantations with French and UN financial assistance while the government planned to privatise 33 state-owned coffee plantations in order to revive the industry. Several overseas companies are reportedly interested in rehabilitating sugar, cotton and sisal estates.

Livestock farming has been disrupted by insecurity, the neglect of veterinary services and recurrent droughts which have affected much of the south and centre of Angola.

Potentially one of the richest agricultural countries in southern Africa, Angola's climatic diversity provides for both tropical and semi-tropical crops. Prior to 1975 Angola was self sufficient in food production and was a major exporter of agricultural produce, particularly coffee and sisal. Today only 3% of its arable land is under cultivation.

**For additional analytical, business and investment opportunities information,
please contact Global Investment & Business Center, USA
at (202) 546-2103. Fax: (202) 546-3275. E-mail: rusric@erols.com**

However Angola's highlands, which have been called some of the richest in the world by development experts could grow a wide variety of tropic and semi-tropic crops, such as cassava, maize, sorghum, bananas, sugar cane, cotton, sisal citrus and other fruits, yams, millet, beans, rice, palm oil, coffee, sunflowers, timber and tobacco. In 1974, Angola was Africa's second largest coffee producer and the world's fourth largest coffee producer. Rehabilitation of coffee plantations is a priority for the government. Initial finance is being provided by France, while the UN World Food Program is paying for a food-for-work program in an attempt to halt the exodus of workers from coffee estates. Sugar, cotton and sisal estates have also piqued the interest of several large overseas corporations.

In 1986 the government liberalized the farm prices and made efforts to improve equipment supplies and services to the agricultural sector. In 1991 Angola negotiated with British, Portuguese and American companies to sell the large state-owned coffee plantations, and planned to privatize the medium and small-size plantations among Angolan nationals. While there were no barriers to 100% foreign ownership of a large plantation, overall foreign ownership was limited to 30% to 40% of coffee production.

Foreign aid has been vital to agricultural development. The then-European Community provided grants for seeds, tools, machinery and vehicles in the 1980s. In 1990 the EC approved funding for the rehabilitation of the Chivinguiro agricultural complex, including transport infrastructure, teacher training and import of agricultural equipment.

United Nations agencies have also been instrumental in helping Angola's agricultural sector. The Food and Agriculture Organization (FAO) supplied $6.9 million in 1990 for food security and planning, sawmill training and assistance for displaced persons. The United Nations Development Program (UNDP) provided $1.8 million toward seed production. In its $212 million 1995 Consolidated Inter-Agency Appeal for Angola, the UN has requested $34.7 million in food aid and an additional $22.8 million in food production and basic rural capacity assistance. UN programs designed to help promote agricultural production include distribution of seeds, tools and fertilizers.

The World Food Program estimated in December 1993 that 2 million Angolans would need food aid in the first half of 1994; however, the current cease-fire has improved the food situation. WFP now estimates that it will reduce the number of its recipients to 1.4 million in 1995 as many feeding programs are now being transformed into agriculture development programs.

In 1994 agriculture and fishery production increased by 12%. Under a new agricultural strategy, Angola has trimmed most price controls and set up a rural credit program to help farmers. With only 3% of its arable land under cultivation, Angola's agriculture potential is vast.

Woods International of the UK was granted a forestry concession of two million cubic meters of eucalyptus in February 1990, which will be harvested for cellulose production. The firm will invest some US$ 5 million and employ 600 Angolan nationals.

Agriculture, livestock and fisheries accounted for 12 per cent of GNP in 1994. An estimated 72% of the population resides in rural areas.

BASIC FACTS ABOUT AGRICULTURE

☐ Prior to the war, Angola was self-sufficient in most food crops and a top producer of commercial crops, such as: coffee and sisal (natural cord fiber) , palm oil, bananas and sugar cane.

For additional analytical, business and investment opportunities information,
please contact Global Investment & Business Center, USA
at (202) 546-2103. Fax: (202) 546-3275. E-mail: rusric@erols.com

☐ Prior to the war, Angola was the world's 4th largest coffee producer.

☐ Angola's highlands are called some of the richest in the world by development experts. With only 3% of its arable land under ultivation, Angola's agricultural potential is vast.

☐ Agriculture and fishing production increased in 1994 by 12%. These two sectors currently account for 12% of total GDP.

☐ Under a new agricultural strategy, Angola has removed most price controls and set up a rural credit program to help farmers.

With a diverse climate, opportunities abound for commercial farming of a wide variety of tropic and semi-tropic crops, including:

- bananas
- beans
- cassava
- citrus and other fruits
- coffee
- cotton
- maize
- millet
- palm oil
- rice
- sisal
- sorghum
- sugar cane
- sunflowers
- timber
- tobacco
- yams

FORESTRY: PRIVATE SECTOR

Forestry remains promising and this is where labour-intensive jobs, particularly suitable for ax-combatants, can be created through logging wood and wood processing prior to export. For Angola to be competitive in this sector, the labor and transportation costs must be low enough to result in a fair return on investment. The manufacture of paper and furniture and other higher value added products can be derived from forestry. Paper manufacturing is very capital intensive and may not become a profitable business for Angola especially because paper can be sourced cheaply from Brazil and perhaps South Africa. Furniture-making for local consumption and export is a possibility, especially if Portuguese decor can be combined with Italian finishing. In Ghana for instance, Italian companies have entered into joint ventures with Ghanaians and are producing furniture with an excellent finish.

Note: This sector analysis is excerpted from a private sector strategy prepared in collaboration with the European Union and the United Nations Development Program for Angola's donors' conference held in Brussels, Belgium on September 25-26, 1995.

LIVESTOCK: PRIVATE SECTOR

Livestock which is concentrated mainly in southern and central Angola has dwindled as a result of the prevalence of the tsetse fly and the poor quality of natural pastures in northern Angola. Modern ranching, which was introduced by the Portuguese, was nationalized after independence and has been hampered by the war and the drought in the sub-region. It is therefore not uncommon for Angola to face a shortage of meat in many cities.

One incontestable assumption is that given its present situation, livestock cannot become a basis for trade for Angola in the short-run. At most it may be developed for local consumption and become part of its small trading activities with Zaire and Zambia; since Namibia has enough livestock for its home consumption. Some of the issues that have to be addressed are whether to encourage small businesses and the informal sector to enter the livestock market or whether to revitalize modern ranching.

Attempts would have to be made to cost various plans of action such as (i) the arrest of tsetse flies and other diseases that prey on livestock; (ii) the development of feed for livestock and; (iii) the rehabilitation of pastures. Meat processing is clearly an area that can benefit from horizontal integration, but its prospects will depend on the setting up of refrigerated compartments that can be easily transported by road and rail and on adequate storage facilities in the cities. It is unlikely that the Government will enter into modern ranching and this therefore creates an opportunity for the private sector. However, there may be good prospects for rearing poultry and birds for local consumption, since this is ideal for small business development. This sector could be a good entry point for co-operatives following the example of Zeh Noh in Japan.

Note: This sector analysis is excerpted from a private sector strategy prepared in collaboration with the European Union and the United Nations Development Program for Angola's donors' conference held in Brussels, Belgium on September 25-26, 1995.

FRUITS, VEGETABLES & OIL SEEDS: PRIVATE SECTOR

There may be some potential for the production of fruits, vegetables, oil seeds and specialty products such as green products, big-technology, the cut flower industry, seasonings and food colorings. This is where foreign direct investment could play a crucial role. Also the involvement of agri-business based NGOs can help establish effective linkages from the exploitation of raw material to the final production and processing, for Angola to become an major actor in the agri-business sector in the sub-region. Research and extension services will have to be revived to support agricultural production and agri-business.

Note: This sector analysis is excerpted from a private sector strategy prepared in collaboration with the European Union and the United Nations Development Program for Angola's donors' conference held in Brussels, Belgium on September 25-26, 1999.

COFFEE

In the past Angola has enjoyed a competitive advantage in coffee production and it represents one activity in which Angola has the potential to become a major player. Two significant factors that can assist Angola here is firstly, coffee is a small holder crop that can create a rural middle-class and rural stability, thus easing over-crowding in the urban areas. Secondly, the institutional memory for growing coffee still exists. If indeed Angola wants to compete in the production of coffee, it must carve out a niche by producing special varieties of coffee such as organic, mild or low caffeine coffee because the trend in demand for coffee is in the specialty category. One advantage here is that due to the war, farming lands in Angola have been left fallow and thus ecologically sound (this was the case with El Salvador and Nicaragua) and they could therefore join the bandwagon of green products grown on a truly sound ecological environment, that are enjoying tremendous success with market entry particularly in Europe.

This activity could also serve as a good entry point for co-operatives. The Government would, however, have to ensure that there is institutional support for the production of coffee, providing seeds and inputs, and establishing transportation hubs near government or private buying posts. Buying agents will also have to work closely with co-operatives. In addition, financial support through small credit schemes, should be made available to small growers. Since coffee prices are relatively high at the moment, Angola is well poised to make a strategic move in this direction. One word of caution though is that coffee production requires three years to reach full capacity and Angola's entry into this market should not be based solely on the currently high prices.

AGRICULTURAL DEVELOPMENT: OPPORTUNITIES IN COFFEE PRODUCTION

- Prior to the war, Angola was the world's 4th largest coffee producer with outputs totaling 200,000 tons each year.
- In 1995-96, Angola more than doubled its coffee output thus demonstrating that this once rich export sector is making a recovery.
- Coffee production during the 1996-97 season is forecasted at 8,000 tons and is projected to reach 120,000 tons by 1998-99.
- Angola recently submitted a plan to the International Coffee Organization that would overhaul the sector over the next two years.
- The government has put in place technical support teams to assist coffee producers.
- Under its privatization program, the government plans to liquidate all 33 state-owned coffee companies and to invite international investors to bid for the largest plantations.
- The Angolan government has already begun discussions with international investors from the US, Germany, Italy, Portugal and South Africa who are interested in developing this potentially lucrative sector.

ENERGY

Angola's economic performance is largely determined by the level of oil production which accounts for over 90 per cent of exports. Production was estimated to have increased from 800,000 barrels per day (bpd) in 1999 to 840,000bpd in 2000. This is expected to exceed 1 million bpd by 2002. Oil reserves are estimated at 5.4 billion barrels and gas reserves are estimated at 700 billion cubic metres. There is considerable international interest in Angolan oil, with companies such as Agip, Chevron and Texaco investing more than US$8 billion in the sector.

Although the offshore oil industry has been immune to the civil war, the downstream sector has remained small due to the war-ravaged infrastructure. The country's only refinery, owned by Fina Petroleos de Angola (a consortium of Sonangol (36 per cent), TotalFinaElf (61 per cent) and private investors (3 per cent)) , is decrepit and has a capacity of just 36,000bpd. An upgrading and expansion of refining facilities in Angola would give considerable added value to the country's oil exports.

Oil fields are located mainly in the northern enclave of Cabinda (jointly operated by Cabinda Gulf Oil and Sonangol, the state-owned concessionaire) . The remaining offshore area is divided into 13 blocks, eight of which are allocated to foreign operators.

The state-owned Empresa Nacional de Electricidade (ENE) is responsible for the generation and supply of electricity in Angola. Civil war has damaged the electricity transmission network and the government estimates it will need US$500 million to recover electricity capacity. Around US$200 million has already been allocated to Angola's six dams, only three of which are working.
In April 2000, the Angolan and Namibian governments agreed on bilateral co-operation on the development of a hydroelectric facility on the Cunene River. However, there is concern over how this would affect over 30,000 Himba who regard the area as their ancestral land and farm around the site of the proposed reservoir.

The Russian Alrosa diamond company has proposed a hydroelectric project on the Chicapa River to provide a source of power for its planned US$40 million investment in diamond mining infrastructure in Angola.

OIL SECTOR GROWTH: OPPORTUNITIES FOR THE FUTURE

The Angolan government is considering building a 150,000 b/d capacity refinery and has undertaken preliminary discussions with potential international investors. Also planned is the refurbishment and expansion of Angola's 35,000 b/d capacity refinery.

In addition to offshore production, onshore oil exploration opportunities abound in the Soyo and Cabinda areas of Angola. The government has prepared data to encourage exploration and development of new regions and is preparing for onshore licensing.

The Angolan government has announced plans to invite international participation in downstream operations. Angola has abundant and largely untapped, natural gas resources. The government plans to convert gas to liquid petroleum gas for local consumption. In 1995, Angola produced 3.8 billion cubic meters of gas, but more than half was flared.

ANGOLA'S OIL INDUSTRY: THE ENGINE OF ANGOLA'S ECONOMY

- Angola is the second largest producer of oil in Sub-Saharan Africa, with production worth $4.5 billion annually.
- Angola produces 700,000 barrels of oil per day. Production will reach upwards of 780,000 barrels a day in 1997 and 870,000 barrels a day in 1998.
- Oil output is expected to reach one million barrels a day by the year 2000.
- Observers believe Angola could triple its oil production over the next 15 to 20 years.
- Total recoverable reserves is nearly 4 billion barrels.
- Angola provides 5.5 percent of all US oil imports.
- US petroleum exports from Angola increased 10.9 percent in 1995, with the US importing some 367,000 barrels per day. The Department of Energy's Monthly Review cited this increase as one of the largest among US oil supplier countries.
- Nine new oil fields came onstream during 1996.

**For additional analytical, business and investment opportunities information,
please contact Global Investment & Business Center, USA
at (202) 546-2103. Fax: (202) 546-3275. E-mail: rusric@erols.com**

- Angola boasts exploration success rates of 67 percent. Most of the discoveries have been made by US firms (Chevron & Texaco) .

US Oil Companies Operating in Angola

Chevron (California)

- Operating in Angola for over 40 years.
- Its Cabinda concession is Angola's largest production area - accounting for 59.5 percent of Angola's total output in 1994.
- Developing four recently-discovered offshore fields with 300 million barrels of recoverable oil.
- Intends to increase its oil production in Angola by 100,000 barrels per day (bpd) to 500,000 bpd.
- Plans to invest $700 million a year through the year 2000 on exploration and development.

Halliburton (Texas)

- Recently was awarded a $200 million contract to develop Cabinda's oil well services.
- US Export-Import Bank guaranteed an $86.6 million in loans for this contract.
- The further development of the Cabinda concession area will benefit all oil companies operating there.

Mobil (Virginia)

- In 1996, in conjunction with Texaco, signed a production sharing agreement for Block 20 of Angola's offshore oil site.
- **Offshore Pipeline International (Texas)**
- Lists Angola as its most important international market.
- Recently won a $70 million contract from Chevron's Angola operations.

Texaco (Texas)

- Operating in Angola for over 25 years.
- Planning to invest some $600 million between 1994-98 to develop new oil fields.

Other Important US Firms Operating in Angola's Oil Sector:

- Amoco Overseas Exploration Company (Texas)
- Apache International, Inc. (Texas)
- Citizens Energy Corporation (Massachusetts)
- Exxon Exploration Company (New Jersey)
- Global Marine Drilling Company (Texas)
- Occidental International Exploration and Production Co. (California)
- Pecten International Co. (Texas)

Angola is an important player in regional in energy production. Angola is responsible for coordinating energy policy for the Southern African Development Coordination Conference (SADCC) and SADC's energy secretariat is based in Luanda.

The oil industry is jointly run by foreign oil companies and the state oil firm Sonangol. In contrast to all other sectors of the economy, the oil sector expanded rapidly throughout the 1980s. Oil accounts for 42% of Angola's GDP and 90% of Angola's total exports. Oil production is expect to increase from the 1995 average of 637,000 bpd to 700,000 bpd in 2000 as increased exploration activity offshore and expansion plans for existing operations begin to take effect.

In the early 1990s, the government negotiated with foreign oil companies for several new onshore and offshore exploration permits to expand oil production. An oil exploration agreement was signed in December 1989 between the state company Sonangol and foreign companies, Total, Petrofina and British Petroleum, covering an offshore area south of the Cuanza river. In August 1991 Angola was negotiating a barter agreement with South Africa to allow South Africa to sell Angolan crude in exchange for foodstuffs and mining equipment. In August 1995 Sonangol entered a joint venture agreement with Global Marine Drilling Company to provide offshore drilling and other services to the oil industry in Angola. The Ministry of Energy and Oil is developing plans to use gas production in petrochemical projects.

Angola has made increasing hydroelectric power generation a priority. Several large and powerful rivers cross the country and offer enormous hydroelectric potential. The Portuguese and South Africans built dams in the north, central and southern parts of the country before 1975. Current generating capacity already exceeds local demand and output continues to increase. Electrical energy production increased by 17.6% in 1994.

ANGOLA'S OIL INDUSTRY

The Engine of Angola's Economy:

☐ Angola is the second largest producer of oil in sub-Saharan Africa.

☐ Angola provides 7% of all U.S. oil imports.

☐ Angola produces 637,000 barrels of oil a day. Production will reach 700,000 barrels a day by the year 2000.

☐ Total recoverable reserves is nearly 4 billion barrels.

☐ New discoveries are adding reserves faster than existing reserves are being depleted.

☐ Oil accounts for 42% of Angola's GDP.

☐ Crude oil accounts for 90% of Angola's total exports and more than 80% of government revenues.

☐ The U.S. purchases some 70-80% of all oil exports from Angola.

☐ U.S. exports of equipment for the oil sector account for 37% of all imports to Angola.

FOREIGN INVESTMENT IN ANGOLA'S OIL SECTOR

Angola's oil sector is run jointly by foreign oil companies and the Angolan government. U.S. firms have significant concessions.

Angola's oil industry is an attractive investment opportunity, offering foreign companies:

☐ favorable geology;

☐ low operating costs;
☐ a constructive business approach from the Angolan government.

Total foreign investment in oil exploration and production:

☐ 1980-86 $2.7 billion
☐ 1987-90 $2 billion
1993-97 $4 billion (estimated)

HYDRO-ELECTRIC POWER

With numerous powerful rivers crossing the country, Angola has tremendous potential for generating electricity.

Angola is part of an international consortium to develop power stations along its border with Namibia.

Electrical energy production increased by 17.6% in 1994.

Angola could very well be a regional exporter of hydro-electric energy.

The main project is the 520 MW Capanda dam, presently under construction in Malange province. Once it is completed, Angola's generating capacity is expected to double. The project will generate around 2,400 million KW a year, well in excess of Angola's requirements, making it a likely future regional exporter of hydro-electric energy. In October 1991 Angola agreed to join Namibia in investigating proposals for a hydroelectric plant on their Cunene River border.

Other hydroelectric projects include the second phase rehabilitation of the Lomaum Dam, and the expansion of capacity at Namibia's Ruacana power plant, which involves the release of more water from Angola's Gove Dam.

ENERGY: PRIVATE SECTOR

Angola's hydro-electric potential is tremendous. Since it has a large surplus of commercial energy, it will no doubt have a clear advantage in exporting electricity to neighboring countries. 83% of Angola's 1991 electricity production was generated from its hydro-electricity plants. "As of 1992 installed generating capacity had reached 500 mw, of which some 300mw was hydroelectric, but available generating capacity was only just under 300 mw because of damage to power plants and the poor condition of transmission and distribution lines." Despite all this capacity, electricity production has fallen sharply and it is not uncommon for the capital, Luanda, to experience power outages. (Economic Intelligence Unit)

Many of the problems that cause the irregular supply of power can be attributed to the sabotage of the transmission lines by the UNITA forces. This has led to the deterioration of the electricity infrastructure due to poor maintenance, shortage of foreign-exchange allocations for spare parts and insufficient investment. To make matters worse, electricity companies are making large losses due to a shortage of skilled personnel, lack of commercial autonomy, "uneconomic government-set electricity tariffs," illegal connections by the consumers and inefficient revenue collections systems. (Economic Intelligence Unit) . These are the immediate problems that have to be addressed to boost Angola's electricity supply.

The Capanada hydroelectric dam on the Kwanza river is expected to double Angola's generating capacity. The Government of Angola's long term goal is to connect its three main regional electricity systems and investment in cross-border grid linkages to export electricity to Namibia and Zaire. (Economic Intelligence Unit)

FISHERIES DEVELOPMENT IN ANGOLA

The fishing industry is also undergoing a process of reconstruction. Prior to the war, annual catches were nearly 600,000 tons. Although the annual catch sizes shrunk to some 35,000 tons during the war, the annual catch size since then has continued to rise. In 1993 the catch was 122,000 tons and 1994's catch estimate was even higher. Angola is building up its fishing fleet using money provided by the KU, Spain, Italy and the Arab Bank for African Economic Development (BADEA) . Portugal's Banco Espirito Santo e Commercio de Lisboa provided a $6 million loan to the BNA in 1990 to help rehabilitate the fishing sector.

EU assistance helped to overhaul refrigeration facilities at the southern ports of Tombwe and Namibe and to install a new production line at the Tombwe canning factory. Fish prices have been deregulated to encourage industry development and the Angolan government, with the help of the World Bank, has set up the Angolan Support Fund for Fisheries Development to support the industry. In 1994, the Angola government registered 16 new foreign investment proposals in the fishing sector.

Basic Facts

- Angola's 1,600 kilometer coastline is rich with mackerel, tuna and sardines.
- Pre-war annual catches were nearly 600,000 tons.
- Although the annual catch shrunk to some 35,000 tons during the war, the annual catch size since then has continued to increase. In 1993, the catch was 122,000 tons and 1994's catch was even higher.
- Fish prices have been deregulated and the Angolan government, with the help of the World Bank, has set up The Angolan Support Fund for Fisheries Development to support the industry.
- In 1994, the Angolan government registered 16 new foreign investment proposals in the fisheries sector.

FISHERIES: PRIVATE SECTOR

In Fisheries, lack of maintenance has meant that very few trawlers are operational. Foreign trawlers operate off the coast and in the fishing reserves in Angola waters. For this to become a profitable activity, maintenance facilities will have to be set up and the Government will havc to adopt a policy of cultivating particular species of fish. Value added products such as smoked, salted fish and canned fish for export to the rest of Africa, especially land-locked countries in the sub-region, appear to be viable business opportunities in the medium-term. In the short-term, small businesses run by the Angolan fishermen who are given loans to purchase boats, generators and to set up basic processing activities may seem the way forward for achieving food security.

MANUFACTURING & INDUSTRY

INDUSTRY AND MANUFACTURING

The industrial sector, including diamond mining, oil production and other ancillary services, accounted for approximately 70.4 per cent of GDP in 2000 compared to 53 per cent of GDP in 1998 and employs around 12 per cent of the workforce.

For additional analytical, business and investment opportunities information, please contact Global Investment & Business Center, USA at (202) 546-2103. Fax: (202) 546-3275. E-mail: rusric@erols.com

Production is centred on food processing, brewing, sugar, textiles and tobacco products. Also important are light manufacture, electrical goods (eg radio production), construction materials, steel production, motor vehicles, detergents, bicycles and chemicals.

Activity is concentrated in Luanda, Lobito and Huambo. Output has been sluggish due to shortages of foreign exchange, poor management and a low-paid labour force.

About 60 per cent of total production is accounted for by nationalised industries. The government has embarked upon a privatisation programme involving some 200 state-owned enterprises in a variety of industrial sectors.

ENVIRONMENT

There have been a number of offshore oil spills in recent years, most caused by operations run by the US company Chevron. In 2000, the company awarded compensation to 120 fisherman whose fish stocks were destroyed and 70 villagers who fell victim to serious poisoning as a result of leakage from oil wells.

Prior to the war, Angola had about 4,000 manufacturing enterprises which employed 200,000 people and produced $650 million worth of goods. There is potential to significantly expand food processing and light industry. Angola currently produces beer, soft drinks, sugar, wheat flour, pasta, cooking oil,, molasses and salt. With an infusion of capital, technology and training, the food processing sector could revive quickly.

Light industry production includes textiles, shoes, matches, soap, paint, plastic bottles and glues. Heavy industry accounts for about 15% of Angola's manufacturing output and includes cement production, oil refining, tire production, steel production and vehicle assembly.

The government plans to privatize some of the state-run enterprises. A recently privatized cement plant tripled its production.

Industrial development projects include the construction of three pharmaceutical plants in Luanda, Benguela and Dondo; the rehabilitation of the Somar fish processing factory in Namibe; and the installation of a television assembly line.

Proposed projects include the expansion of the Luanda steel complex; the construction of a shipyard and seaport in Cabinda province; the installation of a local assembly line for military trucks; and the construction of a brewery.

FOOD PROCESSING: PRIVATE SECTOR

In 1990, food, beverages and tobacco were the main activities in the manufacturing industry, accounting for 34% of manufacturing value-added. Some of the activities include: breweries and soft drinks plans, grain mills and bakeries, vegetable oil processing, sugar refining, cigarette manufacture, the canning of fish, meat and fruit. (The Economic Intelligence Unit) This is one area small businesses can intervene. Apparently, the industrial production of foods such as sugar, molasses, alcohol, cassava flour, margarine and canned meat and fruit have stopped completely. Possibilities also exist for the production of fruit juices and flavoured drinks.

Given the dependence of Angola's population on food aid, the Government should therefore promote re-investment in food production. Prior to re-entering the sugar industry, Angola should assess its comparative advantage. In most countries, the sugar industry is subsidized by local price support and by accessibility to preferential sugar quotas. Under these circumstances. the costs of reestablishing this industry must be weighed against benefits like employment creation foreign exchange savings/earnings.

An examination should be made of the potential for value added products such as the revival and/or establishment of a dairy grid because not only is this suitable for small-holders but it also has health advantages as milk for instance, will improve the diet of the population, especially malnourished children in Angola. For this to be sustainable, surrounding support services such as refrigerated facilities, packaging as well as logistics and distribution will have to developed and/or revived.

LIGHT INDUSTRY: PRIVATE SECTOR

One of the main areas in which Angola had a strength and may be reactivated because it requires basic levels of skills and it creates employment, especially for the women. While it is true that Angola still has great potential to grow cotton, a choice will have to be made on whether to go into textile production or the garment industry.

These mere presence of cotton, as a raw material, does not automatically give Angola a competitive advantage in the textile industry. This is because there are two stages of production to be examined: first, turning the cotton into yarn and second, turning the yarn into cloth. While it may not be difficult for Angola to produce yarn that can be used for local consumption, the second stage may prove rather expensive for Angola because in order to compete effectively, the capital costs of the equipment, specialty dyes and finishing material may be over-bearing for an Angolan of foreign investor. In addition, the output in the textile industry has fallen, the production capacity will have to be addressed and Angola may have to seriously consider exiting the textile industry for the purposes of export.

What may make sense for Angola is to encourage other foreign investors, for example from Taiwan and other Far East countries, that have exceeded their quota, to set up finishing plants in Angola for the mass production of uniforms and clothes for export and so take advantage of Angola's quota. Mauritius and the Dominican Republic have taken this option and are doing very well with job-creation through value-added finishing.

Other light industrial activities that existed and could easily be revived include: footwear, wood products and furniture, soaps and detergents, plastic products, glass, paint and glue, (The Economic Intelligence Unit) .

HEAVY INDUSTRY

Heavy Industry is 15% of Angola's industrial output and includes:

- ☐ cement production
- ☐ steel tube production
- ☐ oil refining
- ☐ vehicle assembly
tire production

Heavy Industry: Private Sector

This sector is dominated by oil refining although some of the activities include metal products, building material, agricultural tools and equipment, electrical goods, chemicals and tyres, as well as the assembly of radio and televisions, shipbuilding and repair. There has been a 31% fall in the production of heavy industry since the renewed outbreak of war, with the exception of the production of petroleum products. Although the revival of some of the heavy industries fall into the medium and long-term plans for Angola's economic development, in the short-term, given the country's present needs, the revival of the production of building materials, agricultural tools and equipment are vital to the revitalization of the productive life of the communities in the various provinces in Angola

MANUFACTURING & INDUSTRY: PRIVATE SECTOR

The manufacturing sector in Angola has enormous potential because of the abundance of raw materials such as petroleum and iron ore. However, the manufacturing sector declined during the war. In the mid-1980s, 80% of the industrial work force were employed in state-owned enterprise. It is hoped that once progress is made with privatization, this equation may reverse in favor of the private sector.

ANGOLA'S MINERAL RESOURCES

MINING

The mining and hydrocarbons sectors together accounted for 58.7 per cent of GDP in 1998 and employed 4 per cent of the workforce. Prior to the civil war, Angola was a major producer of iron ore, gold and copper. However, the major disruptions to the country's infrastructure and economy throughout the war has meant that the country's considerable base metal and gold potential have been barely exploited.

After a campaign was launched by European human rights organisations to stop the use of diamond sales to finance rebel armies, De Beers announced in October 1999 that it would no longer buy Angolan diamonds, and the UK government joined the campaign to block unofficial trade in Angolan diamonds in November 1999. However, with diamond smuggling rife throughout Africa, these moves were merely gestures by the international community which continues to permit a flow of arms into Angola.

Diamonds (mostly of gemstone quality) were the country's second-largest foreign exchange earner - as well as providing a source of revenue for the rebel Unita armies until all purchases of Angolan diamonds were banned by De Beers. Before this, Angola was the fourth-largest diamond producer in the world, producing some US$600 million of rough diamonds per year. The government controlled only 20 per cent of the trade, bringing in only US$12 million to government coffers every month. Diamond exports were severely reduced by lower production and, especially, by smuggling, with revenue going to Unita to finance arms purchases. According to unofficial estimates, Unita made around US$400 million a year from illegal diamond mining.

Most diamonds are mined under contract to Endiama, by Roan Selection Trust and Portugal's SPE.

De Beers of South Africa and Endiama signed a partnership agreement on 5 June 1996 to prospect new kimberlites and alluvials in a variety of concessions owned by Endiama. There are over 600 undeveloped kimberlite pipes, Catoca, in Linda Sul province, being the world's largest, spread over 660ha. In July 1996 Sociedade Mineira de Catoca started investigating the commercial viability of mining Catoca's kimberlite pipes. In May 1998 Endiama and the South African De Beers announced the discovery of two new kimberlites in the Lunda Sul province.

For additional analytical, business and investment opportunities information, please contact Global Investment & Business Center, USA at (202) 546-2103. Fax: (202) 546-3275. E-mail: rusric@erols.com

With Endiama's blessing, Unita established its own legal mining company, Sociedade Geral das Minas (SGM) , and was under government pressure to reach agreement on the allocation of the country's diamond concessions.

Angola also has deposits of phosphates (Cabinda site, estimated 100 million tonnes; Kindonakasi, estimated 50 million tonnes) , gold (at Cassinga and Lombige) , copper, lead and zinc (in Tetelo and Alto Zambeze) . There are deposits of marble and black granite (in southern Angola) .

Angola has substantial deposits of diamonds, iron ore, phosphates, manganese, copper, lead and zinc as well as strategic/base metals, chromium, beryl, kaolin, quartz, gypsum, marble and black granite. The government is encouraging foreign companies to participate in joint venture or production sharing agreements in the mining sector. To promote private investment, the Angolan government has abolished the state monopoly of mineral rights so that mining ventures can be held privately.

Before 1975 Angola was the world's fourth largest producer of diamonds, but dropped to seventh place during the war as official production were prey to large-scale theft and smuggling and transportation problems. About three-quarters of diamond production is of gemstone quality stones. Mining, including hydrocarbons, accounted for 45 per cent of GNP in 1991. In 1992 diamond exports earned US$ 250 million, up from US$ 190 million in 1991. By 1994, diamond production as part of GDP increased 537% over 1993 levels.

In Angola, diamonds are found in gravel near rivers, in conglomerates called colonda and in untapped volcanic pipes called kimberlites. Since independence, Angola has primarily focused on extracting diamonds from alluvial sites in the north-eastern province of Lunda Norte. Alluvial reserves have an estimated 40 million to 130 million carats while the reserves in Angola's six known kimberlite pipes, among the 10 biggest in the world, total 180 million carats. These reserves alone could be worth several billion dollars.

In 1986 the government established Empresa Nacional de Diamantes de Angola (Endiama) to oversee and develop the diamond mining industry. Endiama decided to open diamond mining to foreign companies, using production sharing agreements similar to those of the oil sector. The first such arrangement was signed in 1986 with a Zambian firm to work alluvial deposits along the Cuango river.

In 1989 Endiama signed a declaration of intent with De Beers and in 1991 Endiama and De Beers finalized marketing and loan agreements whereby Angolan diamonds from the Cuango basin would be sold through De Beers' Central Selling Organization (CSO) . De Beers provided a $50 million loan for Endiama to expand diamond production in the Cuango region. In 1995 Endiama entered an agreement with a joint Brazilian and Russian venture to mine one of the kimberlite pipes. The project is expected to produce 940 thousand carats a year for the first nine years of operation with revenue projected to total $48S million. After that, annual production is estimated to increase to 5 million carats per year for 30 years with an annual revenue of some $300 million.

In addition, in September, 1995 the Government of Angola announced that it had entered into a long-term agreement with IDAS RESOURCES to explore and develop some of the largest and richest diamond deposits in Angola

DIAMONDS - BASIC FACTS

- Prior to 1975, Angola was the fourth largest producer of diamonds in the world.

- During the war, Angola fell to seventh place as a diamond producer. With peace, Angola should be able to resume its pre-war status.

- Currently, official and unofficial diamond production are estimated to be worth $700 million per year.

- Angola recently announced changes to its production program. The new goal is to produce more than 2 million carats of diamonds annually.

- Alluvial reserves of diamonds are estimated at 40 million to 130 million carats.

- In addition, there are untapped diamond reserves in volcanic pipes called kimberlites. Of Angola's six major known kimberlites, diamond reserves are estimated at 180 million carats – among the ten largest reserves in the world. Experts estimate that several more kimberlites are yet to be discovered.

- The estimated worth of these reserves is some several billion dollars.

- A joint Brazilian and Russian venture to mine one of these kimberlite pipes is expected to produce 6.5 million carats worth $485 billion during the first nine years of operation. After that, annual production is estimated to increase to 5 million carats per year for 40 years with an annual revenue of some $300 million. The venture also plans to open a diamond processing mill in mid-1997.

- In 1996 DeBeers, the South African diamond giant, was awarded three permits to mine in the Lunda Norte province of Angola. DeBeers plans to spend $50 million on exploration.

- DiamondWorks, a Canadian mining interest, expects to begin commercial production of alluvial diamonds from Angola in mid-1997.

Mining Equipment:
Caterpillar, Bechtel, Harnischfeger, Ingersoll-Rand

Mining Production:
Cyprus Amax Minerals, Asarco, Vulcan Materials, Freeport-McMoran, Burlington Resources, Louisiana Land and Exploration, Diamond Fields Resources

ANGOLA'S MINING SECTOR: OTHER MINERALS

Iron ore deposits have been identified at Kassala-Kitungo and at Cassinga. However, production at Cassinga ceased as a result of low world prices and the destruction of the railway to the coast during the civil war. The state iron ore company, Ferrangol, was established in 1981 to oversee government plans for the rehabilitation of the Cassinga mine. Rehabilitation work was largely completed by 1986, but mining did not resume pending rehabilitation of transportation systems. The deposits at Kassala-Kitungo are estimated to be 92 million tons.

Angola has substantial, largely untapped deposits of:

- beryl
- black granite
- chromium
- copper
- gypsum
- iron ore
- lead

- marble
- numerous industrial/strategic base metals
- phosphates
- platinum
- quartz
- zinc

To promote private investment, the Angolan government has abolished the state monopoly of mineral rights so that the mining ventures can now be privately held.

MINING: PRIVATE SECTOR

The major profitable activity in the mining sector for the moment is petroleum, which is dominated by the international oil companies under concessions and joint venture arrangements with SONANGOL. Some petroleum products are being produced and this will remain a lucrative sector for the development of the plastics and the petro-chemical industries, especially for export in the sub-region. Joint ventures and small business development should be promoted in this sector. It is not certain that Angola will have an advantage in refining petroleum. This is certainly a matter to be taken up with the oil and chemical companies for advice on Angola's capacity to refine petroleum.

Local consumption of refined petroleum products is low and heavily biased towards distillates like gasoil, jet fuels, kerosene and butane. A small refinery owned jointly by the Government of Angola, Petrofina and a few minor shareholders which is in operation just outside Luanda, meets domestic consumption, except for butane. Surpluses of fuel oil, gasoil and jet oil are exported. Plans are underway for the establishment of a second and much larger refinery in the south, possibly in a joint venture with foreign investors.

This is contingent upon the re-establishment of peace in the country and an improvement in prospects for export. (Economic Intelligence Unit)
The diamond industry is not as lucrative for the Government since most of the diamondiferous lands are within territories controlled by UNITA forces. The war has resulted in a decline in outputs. Diamond smuggling will continue to remain a major problem until such time as the Government can gain control of those areas and pass a strict policy with stiff penalties imposed on violators in order to deter smuggling.

Prospects for kimberlite mining that is less prone to smuggling than alluvial mining should be considered but this requires heavy capital investment that only foreign companies can provide under a management contract or in a joint venture with ENDIAMA, the state-owned company managing Angola's diamond industry. There is also scope for developing small business in the diamond-cutting industry, and in the artisanal exploration for gem-stones or industrial diamonds. Angola must however diversify from both petroleum and diamond mining in the medium-to-long terms in order to achieve sustainable development.

OIL AND GAS INDUSTRY PROFILE

Angola is sub-Saharan Africa's second largest oil producer and was the eighth largest supplier of crude to the United States in 1999. Major offshore oil finds have made Angola a leading area for hydrocarbon exploration in sub-Saharan Africa.

ENERGY OVERVIEW

Proven Oil Reserves: 5.4 billion barrels
Oil Production : 766,000 barrels per day (bbl/d) , all of which is crude oil
Oil Consumption : 34,000 bbl/d
Crude Oil Exports : 732,000 bbl/d
Refining Capacity: 39,000 bbl/d
Natural Gas Reserves: 1.6 trillion cubic feet
Natural Gas Production : 20.5 billion cubic feet (bcf)
Natural Gas Consumption : 20.5 bcf
Electric Generation Capacity: 617 megawatts
Electricity Generation : 1.9 billion kilowatthours (75% hydroelectric, 25% thermal)

OIL AND GAS INDUSTRIES

Organization: State-owned Sociedade Nacional de Combustiveis de Angola (*Sonangol*) oversees offshore and onshore oil operations in Angola.
Major Oil Fields (production bbl/d) : Takula-Block Zero (135,158 bbl/d) , Numbi-Block Zero (66,713 bbl/d) , Kokongo-Block Zero (37,330 bbl/d) , Pacassa-Block 3 (70,577 bbl/d) , Cobo/Pambi- Block 3 (51,304 bbl/d)
Major Refineries: Fina Petroleos De Angola - Luanda (39,000 bbl/d)
Major Oil Terminals: Luanda, Malango (Cabinda) , Palanca, Quinfuquena
Foreign Oil Company Involvement: Ajoco, BHP, BP-Amoco, Chevron, Daewoo, Engen, ENI-Agip, ExxonMobil, Falcon Oil, Gulf Energy Resources, INA-Naftaplin, Lacula Oil, Marathon Oil, Mitsubishi, Naftgas, Naphta, Neste, Norsk Hydro/Saga, Occidental, Ocean Energy, Pedco, Petrobras, Petrofina, Petrogal, Petro-Inett, Petronas, Phillips, Prodev, Ranger, Shell, Statoil, Teikoku, Texaco, TotalFinaElf

ENVIRONMENTAL OVERVIEW

Total Energy Consumption : 0.1 quadrillion Btu* (0.03% of world total energy consumption)
Energy-Related Carbon Emissions : 3.7 million metric tons of carbon (0.06% of world carbon emissions)
Per Capita Energy Consumption : 8.8 million Btu (vs. U.S. value of 350.7 million Btu)
Per Capita Carbon Emissions : 0.3 metric tons of carbon (vs. U.S. value of 5.5 metric tons of carbon)
Energy Intensity : 9,900 Btu/$1990 (vs. U.S. value of 13,400 Btu/$1990) **
Carbon Intensity : 0.35 metric tons of carbon/thousand $1990 (vs.U.S. value of 0.21 metric tons of carbon/$1990) **
Sectoral Share of Energy Consumption : Transportation (50.1%) , Industrial (37.3%) , Residential (16.1%)
Sectoral Share of Carbon Emissions : Transportation (42.3%) , Industrial (41.3%) , Residential (16.5%)
Fuel Share of Energy Consumption : Oil (65.4%) , Natural Gas (20.5%)
Fuel Share of Carbon Emissions : Natural Gas (63.7%) , Oil (36.3%)

For additional analytical, business and investment opportunities information, please contact Global Investment & Business Center, USA at (202) 546-2103. Fax: (202) 546-3275. E-mail: rusric@erols.com

Renewable Energy Consumption : 170 trillion Btu* (6% increase from 1996)
Number of People per Motor Vehicle (1997) : 50 (vs U.S. value of 1.3)
Status in Climate Change Negotiations: Non-Annex I country under the United Nations Framework Convention on Climate Change (signed June 14, 1992 but not ratified) . Not a signatory to the Kyoto Protocol.
Major Environmental Issues: Overuse of pastures and subsequent soil erosion attributable to population pressures; desertification; deforestation of tropical rain forest (in response to both international demand for tropical timber and to domestic use as fuel) , loss of biodiversity; soil erosion contributing to water pollution and siltation of rivers and dams; inadequate supplies of potable water
Major International Environmental Agreements: A party to Conventions on Biodiversity, Desertification and Law of the Sea

* The total energy consumption statistic includes petroleum, dry natural gas, coal, net hydro, nuclear, geothermal, solar and wind electric power. The renewable energy consumption statistic is based on International Energy Agency (IEA) data and includes hydropower, solar, wind, tide, geothermal, solid biomass and animal products, biomass gas and liquids, industrial and municipal wastes. Sectoral shares of energy consumption and carbon emissions are also based on IEA data. **GDP based on EIA International Energy Annual 1998

GENERAL BACKGROUND

Angola has been in a state of nearly constant civil war since it achieved independence from Portugal in 1975. More than 500,000 people have been killed in the strife, Africa's longest running conflict in the post-colonial era. After a brief period of cease-fire, hostilities resumed in the latter half of 1998 between the government Forcas Armadas de Angola (FAA) and forces of the National Union for the Total Independence of Angola (UNITA) .

Angola's civil war has ravaged the non-mineral sectors of the country's economy, destroyed much of its infrastructure, and displaced an estimated 2.5 - 4 million people. The capital, Luanda, continues to experience chronic water and power outages, and insecurity reigns throughout much of the interior. In April 2000, the United Nations Security Council voted unanimously to tighten sanctions against UNITA in response to violations of the Council's three previous sanctions resolutions on UNITA. Angola's President Eduardo dos Santos has promised to hold national elections in 2001.

The Angolan economy is highly dependent on its offshore oil sector, which accounts for over 40% of Gross Domestic Product (GDP) and as much as 90% (approximately $3.5 billion annually) of government revenues. Angola maintains positive GDP growth rates due to the strength of its oil sector, which has very few linkages to other sectors of the economy. In spite of Angola's rapidly rising oil production, most of Angola's 12 million people live in poverty. In 1999, inflation measured approximately 250%, mainly due to the government decision to print money to finance its military expenditures. Revenue from petroleum exports provides the principle source of funding for the Angolan government's war effort, while UNITA has relied on the sale of diamonds to fund its activities. In recent months, government forces pushed UNITA out of the diamond-rich Cuango River valley and its strongholds in Andulo, Bailundo and Jamba, cutting UNITA's main source of funding to pay for its military operations.

In July 2000, the World Bank approved a Second Social Action Fund Credit of $33 million to support increased Angolan government spending on social and poverty-oriented programs. In April 2000, Angola signed a nine-month economic monitoring program agreement with the International Monetary Fund (IMF) that requires Angola to undertake a sustained program of economic reforms before it is considered for a formal loan agreement. Under the agreement with the IMF, Angola has promised to allow outside auditors to examine the way it spends oil money. In 1999, Angola successfully introduced a floating exchange-rate regime.

Within the framework of the Angola-United States Bilateral Consultative Commission (BCC) , the U.S. Department of Energy plans to work with the Angolan energy ministry to streamline the country's energy sector and to facilitate the development of its infrastructure. In 1999, the United States ran a $2.2 billion trade deficit with Angola.

Angola is active militarily in the Central West African sub-region and is a member of the Southern Africa Development Community (SADC) . Under a security pact linking Angola, the Democratic Republic of Congo (DRC) and the Republic of Congo, Angola has provided troops to support government forces against rebel groups operating in the two Congos.

OIL

Angola is sub-Saharan Africa's second largest oil producer behind Nigeria, with the majority of its crude production located offshore Cabinda. Crude reserves are also located onshore around the city of Soyo, offshore in the Kwanza Basin north of Luanda, and offshore of the northern coast. Angola's crude oil generally is of high quality. The crude has an API gravity ranging from 32° to 39.5° and sulfur content from 0.12% to 0.14%.

Angola's national oil company, Sonangol, was established in 1976. A hydrocarbon law passed in 1978 made Sonangol sole concessionaire for exploration and production. Associations with foreign companies are in the form of joint ventures (JVs) and production sharing agreements (PSAs) .

Angola is attracting considerable international investment attention in the oil sector. In late 1999, Sonangol announced that more than $18 billion in foreign oil investment was being lined up over the next four years. The top foreign oil companies operating in Angola are Chevron, TotalFinaElf, and Texaco.

Foreign oil companies operating in Angola are expected to pay a non-recoverable "signature bonus" generally worth millions of dollars for the right to operate one of Angola's oil exploration blocks. In 1999, a total of $900 million in payments for Blocks 31-33 helped to finance the government's military operations. Government financing of arms purchases and oil-backed loans typically bypass the Central Bank and Ministry of Finance and are routed through the state oil company, Sonangol, and the Office of the Presidency. In 1999, according to international banking officials, a $900-million windfall in oil earnings was not recorded in the country's published budget.

The Angolan province of Cabinda faces a situation similar to the Niger Delta states in Nigeria. Cabinda produces about 70% of Angola's oil and accounts for nearly all of its foreign exchange earnings. Political tensions are high in some areas of Cabinda as separatist groups such as FLEC (Front for the Liberation of the Enclave of Cabinda) -Renovata demand a greater share of oil revenue for the province's population of 250,000. FLEC-Renovata wants Cabinda to control 30% of the province's production. The province receives about 10% of the taxes paid by Chevron and its partners operating offshore Cabinda.

PRODUCTION AND EXPORTS

Crude oil production, which has more than quadrupled since 1980, averaged 766,000 barrels per day (bbl/d) in 1999. The Angolan government expects that oil production will increase to 1 million bbl/d by the end of 2001 and to 1.4 million bbl/d by 2003. Block Zero (Area A, Area B, and Area

For additional analytical, business and investment opportunities information,
please contact Global Investment & Business Center, USA
at (202) 546-2103. Fax: (202) 546-3275. E-mail: rusric@erols.com

C) , located offshore the enclave of Cabinda, accounts for nearly 70% of Angolan crude oil production. The Chevron subsidiary, Cabinda Gulf Oil Company (CABGOC) , is the operator of the fields located offshore Cabinda, with a 39.2% share in the JV. Other partners include Sonangol (41%) , TotalFinaElf (10%) and ENI-Agip (Agip 9.8%) . Angola's largest producing oil fields are Takula (Area A) , Numbi (Area A) , and Kokongo (Area B) . Total production on Block Zero reached 510,000 bbl/d at the end of 1999, as new wells were commissioned on the Nemba field (Area B) and development was completed on the Lomba field (Area B) . CABGOC and its partners expect to expand Block Zero production to 600,000 bbl/d by 2001. CABGOC plans to invest nearly $4 billion in field development activities over the next five years. CABGOC will continue to develop Areas B and C, and will develop enhanced recovery projects on older fields in Area A.

The second largest area of production in Angola is Block 3, which is located offshore of the northern coast. The largest fields on Block 3 are Pacassa, Cobo/Pambi, and Palanca. TotalFinaElf is the operator of Block 3 with a 50% interest. Other partners on the block include Ajoco, Agip, Mitsubishi, Sonangol, INA-Naftaplin, and Naftgas.

In January 2000, Chevron announced that production had begun on the Kuito field in Block 14, Angola's first deepwater field. First oil on the Kuito field was achieved only 15 months after the award of the contract, making it the fastest cycle time of any project of its kind in sub-Saharan Africa. Kuito currently is producing at a rate of 80,000 bbl/d and Chevron anticipates that Kuito will reach a peak production level of 100,000 bbl/d later in the year. Chevron is the operator with 31%, while Sonangol holds 20%, Agip 20%, and Petrogal 9%. In July 1999, Chevron announced the start of production on the Banzala oil field, located offshore Angola's Cabinda province.

Blocks 1 and 2, located offshore of the northern Angolan city of Soyo, also are in production. Agip (Safueiro field) and Texaco are the operators on Block 1, while Texaco and TotalFinaElf are operators on Block 2. Approximately 100,000 bbl/d of crude is produced on the Texaco-operated portion (Sections 80-85) of Block 2. Major Block 2 fields include Lombo, Sulele, and Tubarao.

TotalFinaElf is the operator of Angola's onshore production. Production is centered in two areas, Kwanza near Luanda, and the Congo basin near Soyo. Ganda, Pangala, Kitona, and N'Zombo are the major onshore fields.

Canada's Ranger Oil began production from the Kiame field (Block 4) in June 1998. Ranger produced an average of 8,239 bbl/d from Kiame in 1999, but the field is now in the decline phase. The Kiame field has estimated reserves of 8.5 million barrels. Ranger has 100% interest on the Kiame field. Sonangol is the operator (100% share) of the Kiabo field, another Block 4, shallow water field. The Kiame and Kiabo fields are Angola's only fields that are not operated by major foreign oil companies.

Angola's crude oil exports to the United States were 337,000 bbl/d in 1999 (44% of Angola's production for the year) . Angola was the eighth largest supplier (largest non-OPEC supplier outside the Western Hemisphere) of imported crude to the United States in 1999. Angolan crude is also exported to markets in Europe, Asia, and Latin America.

EXPLORATION

In February 2000, Chevron announced the completion of two significant appraisal wells in the Benguela and Belize oil fields in deepwater Block 14. The exploration tests on Benguela and Belize resulted in an average output of 8,400 and 11,000 bbl/d, respectively. Chevron is operator for Block 14 and holds 31% interest. Sonangol (20%) , Agip (20%) , TotalFina Elf (20%) , and Petrogal (9%) hold the remaining interest.

Several significant discoveries have been made on deepwater offshore Block 17, located northwest of Luanda. The Girassol field was discovered in 1996 in 4,500 feet (1,365 meters) of water. Girassol, like the Kuito field, is estimated to contain between 700 million - 1 billion barrels of recoverable reserves. TotalFinaElf, operator with 40% interest in the Block 17 PSA, and its partners ExxonMobil (20%) , BP-Amoco (16.67%) , Statoil (13.33%) , and Norsk Hydro (10%) decided to fast-track the development of the Girassol field, and then experienced delays. Production is expected to begin by the fourth quarter of 2000, and peak production of 200,000 bbl/d is planned by the end of 2001. Additional discoveries have been made on Block 17, including Dalia (1997) , Rosa (1998) , Lirio (1998) , Tulipa (1999) , Orquidea (1999) , Cravo (1999) , Camelia (1999) and Jasmin 1 (2000) . The Dalia and Rosa finds are potentially larger than Girassol and further appraisal on both discoveries is planned. The latest Block 17 find, Jasmin 1, has an expected production capacity of 10,800 bbl/d.

In May 2000, BP Amoco announced the discovery of the Galio field, its third oil discovery on Angola Block 18. The Galio field tested at 4,770 bbl/d. In July 1999, BP Amoco reported that its second significant discovery in Block 18, the Plutonio well, tested at up to 5,700 bbl/d. The first discovery, Platina, tested at 6,500 bbl/d in early 1999. BP Amoco is operator of Block 18 with a 50% stake, while Shell holds the remaining 50%. The Platina and Plutonio wells are expected to contain 500 million barrels of oil. The first of four exploration wells is scheduled to be drilled on Block 18 at the end of 2000.

In June 2000, ExxonMobil announced a deepwater oil discovery on Block 15. The Mondo field, located 230 miles northwest of the capital Luanda, flowed at a test rate of 4,200 bbl/d. ExxonMobil's affiliate Esso, and Sonangol, have announced six other Block 15 discoveries since 1998. The first discovery, Kissanje, was made in February 1998 with initial oil flows of 10,000 bbl/d. The second discovery on Block 15, Marimba, was made in March 1998. Marimba's initial test flow was 6,800 bbl/d. In July 1998, Hungo, with a test flow rate of 15,900 bbl/d was discovered. The October 1998 discovery of the Dikanza field flowed at a test rate of 4,400 bbl/d. In 1999, Esso and Sonangol announced the Chocalho and Xilomba discoveries, which flowed at a test rate of 4,500 bbl/d and 1,400 bbl/d respectively. Total recoverable reserves on Block 15 are estimated to exceed 2 billion barrels. ExxonMobil (40%) , BP Amoco (26.67%) , Agip (20%) , and Statoil (13.33%) are the participants on the Block 15 PSA.

Recent offshore discoveries in Angola have sparked interest in Angola's exploration blocks. Agreements on significant deepwater blocks were finalized in early 1999. BP Amoco was named operator (40%) in a PSA signed for deepwater Block 31. TotalFinaElf (30% interest) was chosen as operator for Block 32, and ExxonMobil (45%) was chosen as the operator on Block 33. Deepwater Blocks 31-33 drew intense international interest because of their potential to become as productive as Brazil's Campos Basin. Other recent agreements include Block 25 (Agip operator) , and two onshore blocks -- Cabinda Central (Ocean Energy operator) and Cabinda Southern (TotalFinaElf operator) . There are also plans to establish new deepwater blocks along Angola's central and southern coasts. Energy Africa is drilling a wildcat well (Mexilhao 1) on Block 7, the first deepwater well in Angola's Kwanza Basin.

In 2000, Angola plans to farm-out the highly prospective Block 34. This block is to be operated by Sonangol with technical assistance from Norway's Norsk Hydro. Angola also may open additional blocks in the very deep offshore Kwanza basin to foreign investment pending the results of an exploration well drilled by Agip toward the end of 2000.

In January 2000, Sonangol announced a joint venture project with the Namibian Petroleum Corporation (Namcor) to conduct petroleum exploration in the offshore Namibe Basin straddling the Angola-Namibia border.

REFINING AND DOWNSTREAM

The Fina Petroleos de Angola refinery in Luanda has current capacity of 39,000 bbl/d. The refinery is a joint venture between Sonangol (36%) , TotalFinaElf (operator, 61%) and private investors (3%) . The refinery is the source of supply for products consumed in Angola, as well as for a small amount of products destined for export.

Three firms, Sonangol, TotalFinaElf, and Sonangalp, a joint venture between Sonangol (51%) and Petrogal (49%) , provide product distribution and marketing in Angola. Angola's small market size and lack of infrastructure have hindered Sonangol's plans to attract additional foreign companies to the country's downstream market.

Angola is developing plans for a new 200,000-bbl/d refinery, tentatively to be located in the central coastal city of Lobito with an estimated cost of $2 billion. The majority of products refined at the new facility (80%) would be exported regionally. Angola has discussed potential partnerships for the construction of the refinery with China, Petrogal, Gabon, and most recently, the Republic of Congo and the Democratic Republic of Congo. In the Republic of Congo, Sonangol is to assist with exploration, production, and marketing of Congolese petroleum.

NATURAL GAS

Angola has estimated natural gas reserves of 1.6 trillion cubic feet. The majority (approximately 85%) of gas produced in Angola is flared, but some is reinjected to aid in crude production. The government is developing strategies to reduce gas flaring and increase commercial usage of natural gas. CABGOC has initiated two zero-flare fields, Nemba and Lomba, and plans to make Kuito the third.

Texaco and Sonangol have agreed to undertake the development of a LNG (liquefied natural gas) project that would convert natural gas from offshore oil fields to LNG for domestic consumption and export. The LNG plant will process natural gas from offshore Blocks 1, 2, 3, 4, 16, as well as from the large new discoveries on Blocks 15, 17, and 18. Sonangol and Texaco each have a 50% interest in the project. Subject to the completion of development studies with Sonangol, Texaco expects to implement the $2.5-billion LNG project in 2005. The preferred site for the plant is next to the existing oil refinery in the capital, Luanda.

ELECTRICITY

Angola has announced plans for a major rehabilitation of its power sector infrastructure. Significant portions of the country's power generation and transmission facilities were damaged during the civil war. Angola intends to mobilize approximately $500 million for a program to recover the productive capacity of the National Electricity Company (ENE) by rehabilitating most of its hydropower stations.

The government already has allocated $200 million for repairs on Angola's six dams. Of the six, only three (Cambambe, Biopo, and Matala) are functioning. Under the plan, Cambambe will receive $70 million, Biopo $3 million, and Matala $20 million for renovation and upgrades. The other three dams (Mabubas, Lumaun, and Gove) have been severely damaged during Angola's civil war. The government plans to create a national grid by linking the three regional electricity sectors and establishing grid linkages with neighboring countries. This project, coupled with the power plant rehabilitation projects, could provide the basis for Angola becoming a regional exporter of electricity.

Recent power outages in the capital Luanda and other urban centers have been attributed to shortages of fuel oil for generator groups operated by ENE. Local analysts estimate that only 15% of Angola's 11 million people have access to electric power.

The Brazilian construction company Odebrecht has signed a contract to restore the energy generating capacity of central Angola, beginning with a renovation of the Biopio gas and thermal power stations. Oderbrecht also is building the 520-megawatt Capanda hydroelectric dam in Malange, 300 kilometers (190 miles) east of Luanda. Completion of the Capanda project will double Angola's electricity generating capacity.

Spain has offered to donate $3 million to rehabilitate the electrical supply network in Cabinda city. According to ENE authorities, implementation of the project consists of three phases and will supply power to the city within 15 months.

In April 2000, Angola and Namibia signed a bilateral cooperation agreement in the field of energy. The two countries are considering the development of a hydroelectric facility on the Cunene River. Both countries would receive electricity from the facility. Two possible sites for the dam are being considered, one at Baynes and the other at Epupa Falls, pending environmental impact studies. Namibia reportedly favors the Epupa site while Angola is pressing for the Baynes site because it would enable Angola to renovate and regulate the Gove dam, which was damaged during the Angolan civil war. The proposal for location of the dam at Epupa Falls has met with opposition from environmental groups and local communities. A central issue is the potential displacement of the Himba people, the traditional inhabitants of the area surrounding the falls. An estimated 3,000 Himba would be displaced if the land they occupy is flooded by the dam, and another 30,000 Himba could be affected by exposure to diseases such as hepatitis and malaria transmitted by mosquitoes breeding in the stagnant water of the reservoir. A feasibility study conducted by a consortium of Namibian, Swedish, Norwegian, and Angolan consultants has concluded that the Epupa Falls dam site would be economically more viable because the Baynes site would require Angola reconstruct the Gove dam and to regulate the flow of the Cunene River at Gove, located upstream from Baynes. Namibia has cited instability in southern Angola and the millions of dollars needed to repair Gove as factors that favor the Epupa Falls site.

The Russian Alrosa diamond company has proposed a hydroelectric project on the Chicapa River to provide a source of power for its planned $40 million investment in diamond mining infrastructure in Angola.

ENVIRONMENT

In early 2000, up to 100 barrels of crude oil was estimated to have leaked from a CABGOC offshore oil well, causing serious pollution of the surrounding waters and coastal areas. Many residents of Futilla village near the Malongo oilfield reportedly fell ill as a result of the pollution. Chevron announced it would take responsibility for the pollution, which resulted in 70 people receiving hospital treatment for poisoning.

In late December 1999, a crude oil discharge at a Chevron-owned treatment tank polluted beaches in Cabinda and killed large quantities of fish. CABGOC reportedly paid compensation to some 160 fishermen for losses suffered as a result of the spill.

**For additional analytical, business and investment opportunities information,
please contact Global Investment & Business Center, USA
at (202) 546-2103. Fax: (202) 546-3275. E-mail: rusric@erols.com**

In November 1999, the Angolan government drafted a bill to prevent ecological disaster caused by oil production in the country. The bill stipulates provisions for the creation of institutions to deal specifically with major environmental disasters.

SERVICES

The service sector is increasingly being seen as a buttress to private sector development in many developing countries. In the case of Angola, this sector which is almost non-existent most be seen as a source of employment creation.

BANKING

CENTRAL BANK

Banco Nacional de Angola (BNA) started functioning in late-1996 as the central bank, ceasing its commercial activities, as part of the government's financial reforms.

MAIN FINANCIAL CENTRE

Luanda

At present the World Bank is assisting the Government of Angola in streamlining its banking laws and regulations. A lot of work is required on the macro-economic framework in which the banking sector operates, rural banks wil} have to strengthened, the separation of functions between Central Bank and commercial banks will have to be made clear and the issue of access to credit for entrepreneurs will also have to be addressed.

b. Business Services: computer, telecommunications, legal, financial, insurance, accountancy, transportation and consulting services are very important to buttress.

Angola's attempt at private sector development. More significantly it also create jobs and builds national capacity. As a result, the development of these services should be given priority by the Angolan Government and should be opened to the private sector.

TELECOMMUNICATIONS: PRIVATE

The government's modernization of the telecommomcations network operated by Empresa Publica de Telecomunicaes (Eptel) was due for completion by mid-1991. The scheme involved the expansion of the Cacuaco standard A earth station (on the outskirts of Luanda) , the installation of new microwave links between the earth station and new telephone and telex exchanges, and the reconstruction of Eptel's headquarters with a $37.7 million credit from the African Development Bank. A Portuguese company Radio Marconi is to undertake two modernization projects involving the telecommunications network and links between Luanda and the provincial capitals.

TELECOMMUNICATIONS OVERVIEW

The following is an outline of the present state of Angolan telecommunications for potential investors. The telecommunications sector offers a number of promising opportunities.

Providers - Angola Telecom remains the sole provider of telecommunications services.

Lines - Angola has a capacity of 53,500 telephone lines in Luanda and 34,700 telephone lines outside Luanda. At present there are 37,032 lines listed as "in use" within Luanda and 22,900 outside Luanda. The ratio of lines to population is 1.9 per 100 in Luanda and .3 outside Luanda. The estimated number of "dead lines" due to the war is 20,000.

Switches:
Terrestrial - There are 3,600 junctions: 600 international and 3,000 domestic. The 53,500 lines in Luanda are all electromechanical. Outside Luanda several different systems are in use. As follows: 26,700 lines are x-bar electromechanical; 8,000 lines are strowger electromechanical; 3,000 lines are manual pmbx.

Cellular - Only Luanda has a cellular phone system. It is analog, not rpt not digital. There are only 100 analog amps channels saturated with a ratio of 1 to 30.

International connections - All international connections are done through the Luanda Funda satellite station which has an IBS Intelsat connection. Angola rents a space segment of 72 mhz. However, about 20 mhz are used to distribute Angolan national television on a countrywide basis. All circuits downs are IDR. Channels are dedicated as follows: Portugal: 226 channels; South Africa: 28 channels; United Kingdom: 21 channels; Italy: 20 channels; Switzerland: 12 channels; USA: 12 channels linking to AT&T.

Domestic connections -
Microwave - these are small connecting stations used to connect urban centers that are geographically close, such as Lubango and Namibe.
Satellite - the Angosat system was to become the national domestic connecting system. It covers most Angolan provincial capitals. The project is known locally as Telecom II. It was being financed by Caisse Francaise. The first phase of the Caisse financed program built stations in Luanda, Cabinda, Benguela, Namibe, Lubango, and Ongiva. Phase II has yet to start, it is under negotiation and should include the remaining provincial capitals.

Suppliers of telecommunications equipment to private users - The total market is around 500 companies. The average number of lines per company is 30. Only about 50 percent of the demand in this area has been met. Only about 10 percent of these firms are still using x-bar switches, most are using electronic switches.

Present Angola Telecom projects - Angola Telecom has three major infrastructure enhancement programs, all using Alcatel equipment. The three programs are: Switches - replacement of all x-bar switching by electronic switches in the major urban centers, including Luanda; Connectors - replacement of interconnectors within the main switching station in Luanda with optic fiber; Cellular - expansion of the Luanda cellular system.

Angola's telecommunications needs - VSAT technology would ideally suit Angola. It could give a national "spread," with small systems. In remote areas particularly, equipment must be able to withstand frequent power fluctuations. In most major towns, the "local" system will have to be wireless. Solar and battery powered equipment will be necessary.

(Source: National Trade Data Bank and Economic Bulletin Board, products of STAT-USA, US Department of Commerce)

For additional analytical, business and investment opportunities information,
please contact Global Investment & Business Center, USA
at (202) 546-2103. Fax: (202) 546-3275. E-mail: rusric@erols.com

BUSINESS OPPORTUNITIES IN THE TOURISM SECTOR

As a result of the long period of political and military instability, the Angolan economy suffers from great structural distortions. The Government of Unity and National Reconciliation is now doing the groundwork to attain the recovery of all the sectors of the economy that can contribute to the socio-economic progress of the country. This will be done through a program of action that aims at the maintenance and rehabilitation of the economic infra-structure, the development of the private sector and attraction of foreign investment.

The consolidation of the peace process opens new horizons to projects in the hotel and resort industry. The national reconstruction program will have as a fundamental component the rehabilitation and/or construction of hotel units and other lodging facilities for technicians and national and foreign cadre in the several provinces of the country.

To the prospects for the hotel industry we must also add the rehabilitation and construction of restaurants and other projects in infra structure for tourism.

Given the lack of financial capability and insufficient internal savings the Ministry of Tourism and Hotel Industry is trying to attract foreign investment, (the ways in which this will take place are to be negotiated) to assist the national private sector in the following projects:

FIRST PRIORITY: CONSTRUCTION OF FIVE STAR HOTELS IN LUANDA

The first short-term priority (1997 to 1998) is the construction of five star hotels in Luanda with 400 to 500 rooms each, and complementary facilities. Click above for a complete listing of properties currently available.

Current hotel room capacity by province

Construction Projects for the Development of Infrastructure in Areas of Interest for Tourism

- Nature Parks
- Mountains and Waterfalls

Construction of Infrastructure for Leisure and Amusement as Tourist Attactions

Golf courses, tennis courts, swimming pools, casinos, night clubs

SERVICE FACILITIES TO SUPPORT TOURISM

- Travel Agencies
- Tourist Transportation
- Highways
- Railways
- Maritime Transportation
- Air Transportation
- Riverine Transportation

Trade in Equipment and Materials for the Development of Hotels and Tourism Facilities

For additional analytical, business and investment opportunities information, please contact Global Investment & Business Center, USA at (202) 546-2103. Fax: (202) 546-3275. E-mail: rusric@erols.com

Priority Areas for Development

Main Tourism Products to be Developed

Steps Taken by the Government to Develop the Hotel and Tourism Industries in Angola

Contact and Related Information for the Hotel and Tourism Industries in Angola

CONSTRUCTION OF FIVE STAR HOTELS IN LUANDA

A-1 Lot Situated on Avenida 4 de Fevereiro, at the foothill of the San Miguel Fort.

Total area:	28,700 sq. meters (approx. 90,000 sq. ft.)
Area for Construction:	14,500 sq. meters (approx. 45,000 sq. ft.)
Number of Floors:	3 to 7
Legal Status:	Confiscated by the Government by Decree 43/76
Acquisition:	Sale of Surface rights for 60 years, which can be extended in accordance with Decree 1/94 (juridical regime for the concession of land in the province of Luanda.)
Price per sq. meter:	USD 80
Total Price*:	USD 2,296,000
State of the Lot:	There are a few unlicensed buildings
Type of Project:	Five Star Hotel

A-2 Lot Situated in Gavelo, between Rua Comandante Gilka Street and Avenida Revolução de Outubro.

Total area:	7,2600 sq. meters (approx. 21,000 sq. ft.)
Area for Construction:	2,034 sq. meters (approx. 6,000 sq. ft.)
Number of Floors:	7
Legal Status:	Confiscated by the Government by Decree 43/76
Acquisition:	Sale of Surface rights for 60 years, which can be extended in accordance with Decree 1/94 (juridical regime for the concession of land in the province of Luanda.)
Price per sq.	USD 80

**For additional analytical, business and investment opportunities information,
please contact Global Investment & Business Center, USA
at (202) 546-2103. Fax: (202) 546-3275. E-mail: rusric@erols.com**

meter:	
Total Price[*]:	USD 580,000
State of the Lot:	There are a few unlicensed buildings
Type of Project:	Four Star Hotel

A-3 Lot Situated on Rua do Conselheiro Aires de Ornellas (Roadway axis)

Total area:	19,000 sq. meters (approx. 60,000 sq. ft.)
Area for Construction:	4,050 sq. meters (approx. 12,000 sq. ft.)
Number of Floors:	11
Legal Status:	Confiscated by the Government by Decree 43/76
Acquisition:	Sale of Surface rights for 60 years, which can be extended in accordance with Decree 1/94 (juridical regime for the concession of land in the province of Luanda.)
Price per sq. meter:	USD 187.50
Total Price[*]:	USD 3,563,830
State of the Lot:	The lot contains the foundation of an unfinished hotel
Type of Project:	Five Star Hotel

A-4 Lot Situated at Via Indrade and Futungo de Belas (In front of Costa do Sol Hotel)

Total area:	32,860 sq. meters (approx. 76,000 sq. ft.)
Arca for Construction:	23,756 sq. meters (approx. 70,000 sq. ft.)
Number of Floors:	3 to 7
Legal Status:	Confiscated by the Government by Decree 43/76
Acquisition:	Sale of Surface rights for 60 years, which can be extended in accordance with Decree 1/94 (juridical regime for the concession of land in the province of Luanda.)
Price per sq. meter:	USD 80
Total Price[*]:	USD 2,628,800

**For additional analytical, business and investment opportunities information,
please contact Global Investment & Business Center, USA
at (202) 546-2103. Fax: (202) 546-3275. E-mail: rusric@erols.com**

State of the Lot:	There are a few precariously built houses
Type of Project:	Four Star Hotel

A-5 Lot Situated at Avenida Revolucção de Outubro (near the airport, on the left)

Total area:	3,900 sq. meters (approx. 12,000 sq. ft.)
Area for Construction:	1,456 sq. meters (approx. 3,500 sq. ft.)
Number of Floors:	7
Legal Status:	Confiscated by the Government by Decree 43/76
Acquisition:	Sale of Surface rights for 60 years, which can be extended in accordance with Decree 1/94 (juridical regime for the concession of land in the province of Luanda.)
Price per sq. meter:	USD 80
Total Price*:	USD 312,000
State of the Lot:	There is some unlicensed construction
Type of Project:	Four Star Hotel

A-6 Lot Situated on Avenida Revolucção de Outubro (near the airport, on the right)

Total area:	3,900 sq. meters (approx. 12,000 sq. ft.)
Area for Construction:	1,456 sq. meters (approx. 4,500 sq. ft.)
Number of Floors:	7
Legal Status:	Confiscated by the Government by Decree 43/76
Acquisition:	Sale of Surface rights for 60 years, which can be extended in accordance with Decree 1/94 (juridical regime for the concession of land in the province of Luanda.)
Price per sq. meter:	USD 80
Total Price*:	USD 312,000
State of the Lot:	There is some unlicensed construction
Type of Project:	Four Star Hotel

**For additional analytical, business and investment opportunities information,
please contact Global Investment & Business Center, USA
at (202) 546-2103. Fax: (202) 546-3275. E-mail: rusric@erols.com**

*Price subject to negotiation

A - 7 Lot situated near the Museum of Slavery (Museu da Escravatura)

There is some space available in this area to build inns and motels linked to the cultural tourism around the Museum of Slavery, declared a world heritage by UNESCO.

A - 8 Other Lots.

Apart from these, other lots may become available, with the same special legal concession regime established for the promotion of tourism in the country.

There are several other cultural and historical sites that may be developed as well, including monuments and sites along the coast, that mark the history of colonization and the slave trade and can be restored and developed.

EXISTING HOTEL UNITS BY PROVINCE

Province	No. of Hotels	No. of Rooms
Bengo	2	40
Benguela	16	484
Bié	5	143
Cabinda	4	124
Cunene	-	-
Huambo	13	444
Huíla	12	398
Kwando Kubango	1	36
Kwanza-Norte	3	83
Kwanza-Sul	7	165
Luanda	22	1306
Lunda Norte	1	12
Lunda Sul	2	107
Malange	3	96
Moxico	4	118
Namibe	4	131

Uige	4	148
Zaire	-	-
Total	103	3835

NATURAL PARKS

The following projects have been selected for joint venture opportunities:

Name	Province	Area Size	Predominant Species
Kissama National Park	Bengo	9,600 km^2	Manatees, Palanca Vermelha Antelopes, Talapoin, Sea Turtles
Cangandala National Park	Malange	600 km^2	Giant Palanca Negra Antelope
Bicuar National Park	Huila	7,900 km^2	Black Buffalo
Iona National Park	Namibe	15,150 km^2	Mountain Zebra and Guelengue, Lion, Zebra
Kameia National Park	Moxico	14,450 km^2	Cacu
Mupa National Park	Cunene	6,600 km^2	Giraffe and Cahama
Cimalavera Regional Nature Park	Benguela	150 km^2	Cabra de Leque (type of goat)

The Angolan wild life is rich and varied, there are elephant herds in several regions. There are also hippopotamus and crocodiles in the rivers and lakes as well as very rare animals such as the palanca preta antelope and the white rhino.

In Angola there is a system of national parks, total reserves, special reserves, partial reserves and hunting areas which are doubtlessly of great tourist potential. Below are some of the more remarkable, which have been placed at the top of the list of priorities by the government:

1. Tourist development of the National Park of Kissama (Bengo)
2. Development of the National Park of Iona (Namibe)
3. Development of the Water Falls (Kwanza- Sul)

TRANSPORTATION

No sector has suffered as severely as transportation from the war. Roads and railways have been seriously damaged. Ports have become run-down and antiquated. Some 120 bridges were destroyed during the 1992-1994 resumption of war. Recognizing the critical needs in the transportation sector the World Bank in 1991 approved a $38 million credit for an Infrastructure Rehabilitation Engineering Project. The Bank also earmarked another $41 million in 1992 for emergency rehabilitation. Although the resumption of the war after the 1992 election put these projects on hold, infrastructure rehabilitation, including rehabilitation of railways, roads and bridges are a major component of the 1995 UN Consolidated Appeal for Angola.

Of Angola's 72,323 kilometers of roads, only 8,317 kilometers are paved. More than 60% of the paved roads need repair. Scores of bridges have been destroyed. The government estimates that it will take 10-15 years to restore the road system to its pre-independence status. UN forces in the country have targeted 13 priority west-east roads for primary rehabilitation. These roads will link provincial capitals and run through valuable sugar cane, coffee, cotton, cattle and iron ore areas. Although road rehabilitation and demining are long processes, there has been progress made. The World Food Program estimates that its convoys can now deliver some 25% of their goods via roads which were previously closed due to war.

RAILWAYS

The Portuguese laid four railway lines during the colonial Into transport minerals and natural resources from inland areas to ports for shipment abroad. Of the 2,9S2 km of track, only about 20% of the lines are operating on a normal basis. The railroads are running at only 3% of their pre-independence levels. The Caminhas de Ferro de Angola is responsible for overseeing the four independent railways comprising the network.

The largest of the four is the 1,347-km Benguela railway, which is 90% foreign-owned. Most of the Benguela railway has been badly damaged by war-related attacks. Following the 1991 cease-fire, an assessment was undertaken to determine the extent of repairs needed to make the railway operable again. The 899-km Mocamedes railway, linking the port of Namibe with Menongue, is only partly operable and would need an estimated $83 million to be fully operational again. The 536-km Luanda railway between Luanda and Malanje is being rehabilitated. The fourth line is the 123-km Amboim railway.

Other plans for the network include a 60-km line linking the Benguela and Luanda railways, a 240-km link between the Benguela and Mocamedes lines and a 250-km line from Mbanza (Congo) to the port at Soyo.

Also under consideration are plans to construct a second rail link with Zaire and to extend the southern line to join up with the Namibian network.

PORTS / SHIPPING

Angola has four main ports: Luanda, Lobito, Malongo and Namibe. Plans to construct roll-on/roll-off container terminals at Luanda and Lobito have been developed but have not been implemented yet. Lobito port currently handles some 500,000 tons of cargo, all domestic. This is far below the 2.5 million tons it serviced prior to the war. At that time Lobito serviced most of the copper exports from Zambia and Zaire via the Benguela railway. Containers are handled at two general cargo quays which have a depth of water of 10 meters.

Luanda's port contains five general cargo berths up to 180 meters long with a depth of water alongside of 10 meters. It can take containers. At Namibe port, Angonave, the national shipping company, operates several ships including both dry bulk carriers and multi-purpose vessels. Cabotang is the state coastal shipping company.

In August 1995 the government put out an international tender for the construction of a seaport in the north-western Cabinda enclave. The port would be equipped with 596 meter-long vertical anti-flood devices and a 200 meter terminal and is expected to take two years to construct.

AIR TRANSPORT

The main airport is the Aeroporto 4 de Fevereiro located four kilometers from the capital, Luanda.

Angola's transport infrastructure has been one of the hardest hit by the war. Access to many parts of the country by road, despite its superb network of roads, has been impossible due to acts of sabotage and insecurity, although the main highways are now open.

Railway services have been halted because of the risk of ambush or mines and damage to lines and the destruction of bridges. Although the main ports have remained unaffected by the war, poor maintenance and insufficient investment has resulted in poor performance. Internal air transportation is relatively well developed with a fairly good network of airports and landing strips which appear to be the safest mode of transportation; given the insecurity of the roads and railway. These will be useful for the transportation of goods for trade within the country and for export. Empresa Nacional de Telecommunicacoes (ENATEL) and Empresa Publica de Telecommunicacoes (EPTEL) are the two state-owned corporations that service the domestic and foreign markets respectively. Cellular telephones seem to be the main mode of communication in Luanda these days. But on the whole, the telephone service in Angola is relatively poor.

ECONOMIC AND FINANCIAL POLICIES[1]

INTRODUCTION

This memorandum describes the government's economic and social program for the period April to December 2000, which was formulated in consultation with the staff of the International Monetary Fund (IMF). The government believes that dissemination and monitoring of the program by the IMF staff and civil society will enhance transparency and increase the credibility of its economic and social policies.

THE ECONOMIC AND SOCIAL CONTEXT

Angola has been ravaged by a civil war that has created vast social, economic, and humanitarian problems. Disruptions in farming and transportation have increased the economy's dependence on oil and led to an exodus of rural population, aggravating urban unemployment and social problems. Severe fiscal pressures have led to three hyper-inflation episodes and sizable domestic and external public sector arrears over the past ten years, and per capita income fell by 30 percent in this period.

Oil production is poised to double over the next five years. In addition, oil prices rose sharply during 1999 and in early 2000, and the government received sizable exploration bonuses from oil companies. The heavy dependence of exports and government revenue on oil receipts has rendered the country particularly vulnerable to fluctuations in world oil prices. Furthermore, even though real GDP growth is estimated at 2.7 percent in 1999, non-oil output remains far below potential, in part because of the war. Inflation is estimated at 135 percent during 1998 and 333 percent in the 12 months ended February 2000.

The increase in oil receipts and the floating of the kwanza in May 1999 permitted an increase in gross official international reserves from the equivalent of less than one week of projected imports of goods and services in early 1999 to about four weeks at the end of the year, and net reserves, which had turned negative in 1998, became positive again. Nevertheless, the combination of

---

[1] The following item is a Memorandum of Economic Policies of the government of Angola. This memorandum describes the policies that Angola is implementing in the framework of a staff-monitored program.

weak macroeconomic policies, volatile oil prices, and limited access to concessional external financing in recent years has led to a heavy external debt burden. The public and publicly guaranteed debt stock amounted to US$9.6 billion at end–1999 (171 percent of GDP), of which US$4.4 billion was in arrears.

Faced with deteriorating economic and social conditions, in March 1999 the government approved a global strategy (Estratégia Global para a Saída da Crise) aimed at addressing these problems in a context of sustained economic growth led by the private sector. The economic recovery is expected to be underpinned by an enhanced domestic security situation and improvements in public sector operations, especially to make the government and public enterprises more efficient and to reorient public spending toward the social sectors and infrastructure. In this vein, important reforms have been introduced to revamp the operations of the government and the parastatals.

The Permanent Commission of the Cabinet (Comissão Permanente do Conselho de Ministros) has been restructured and the functioning of local governments has been reformed. In addition, the government has created working groups with external technical assistance to reform the legal framework of public enterprises (Lei das Empresas Públicas) and the civil service (Estatuto do Gestor Público), and appointed new directors for key public sector enterprises and state-owned banks as a first step to enhance their efficiency and accountability. Furthermore, an Economic and Social Development Fund (FDES) has been created to foster the development of small- and medium-sized private enterprises. To simplify the setting up, registrati

on, and licensing of enterprises, a one-stop window (Guichet Único de Empresa) is being established. In June 1999 the government began implementing a Program of Rehabilitation of Social and Productive Infrastructure, and in July it established a national emergency program of humanitarian assistance to people displaced by the war, funded by budgetary allocations and external grants.

Since May 1999, the National Bank of Angola (BNA) has floated the kwanza, established an interbank foreign exchange market, abolished restrictions on foreign exchange purchases for imports, liberalized commercial bank interest rates, and introduced central bank bills as a first step toward an eventual shift to indirect instruments of monetary control. The National Assembly has approved a new Financial Institutions Law as the basis for strengthening the financial sector. The loss-making agricultural and fisheries credit bank (CAP) has been closed and is being liquidated, and a preliminary diagnostic study on the restructuring and eventual privatization of the two remaining state-owned banks has been completed.

On the fiscal front, the government has broadened the base of the income and sales taxes and lowered the rates. It has also reduced the number of import tariff rates from 43 to 8 and lowered the top rate from 110 percent to 35 percent, thereby reducing the average rate. In February 2000, domestic fuel prices were raised in a range of 972–1,650 percent to eliminate subsidies.

Nevertheless, macroeconomic imbalances remain severe. The resumption of civil war in late 1998 led to an escalation in military spending, but this was partially offset by the sizable increase in oil revenue. As a result, the budget deficit on a **commitment** basis reached 13.1 percent of GDP in 1999 compared with 15.1 percent in 1998 (the surplus on a **cash** basis was 1.1 percent, compared with a deficit of 7.6 percent in 1998). The receipts from oil bonuses in the second half of 1999 permitted a significant accumulation of government deposits in the banking system for the first time in many years. Although monetary aggregates increased rapidly in 1999, much of the increase reflected the increase in foreign currency deposits (which constitute about three-fourths of total bank deposits) and valuation adjustments following the depreciation of the kwanza.

For additional analytical, business and investment opportunities information, please contact Global Investment & Business Center, USA at (202) 546-2103. Fax: (202) 546-3275. E-mail: rusric@erols.com

THE PROGRAM FOR 2000

Rationale. The gravity of the economic and social problems warrants a comprehensive and ambitious adjustment plan action. This staff-monitored program (SMP) is the first step in the formulation of such an adjustment plan and toward normalization of relations with external creditors. The government also hopes that it will pave the way for an eventual Fund arrangement that could catalyze fresh disbursements from other multilateral donors and bilateral debt relief.

Objectives and basic strategy. The central objective of the SMP is to lay the foundation for a decline in inflation to 120 percent by end–2000 and to double digits in 2001, and for an improvement in living standards and social conditions, including the resettlement of displaced individuals and demobilized soldiers. Real GDP is expected to grow by 3¾ percent in 2000, spurred by a further increase in oil production and a recovery of non-oil output (on the back of efforts to rehabilitate infrastructure and to reduce other supply bottlenecks) . Gross official international reserves are targeted to rise from the equivalent of three weeks of projected imports of goods and services at end-March 2000 to four weeks by end–2000. To secure these objectives, the government will strengthen the fiscal stance within the limits dictated by the need for economic and social reconstruction. Furthermore, the implementation of structural reforms will support the stabilization effort and enhance growth prospects over the medium term. Increased priority will be given in the budget to the education and health sectors, and work will begin on the preparation of a poverty reduction strategy in consultation with civil society and the international donor community.

THE FINANCIAL PROGRAM

Fiscal targets. The increase in oil and diamond receipts and the decline in defense spending from its unusually high level in 1999 are expected to permit an increase in social and investment spending in 2000. At the same time, the central government balance on a commitment basis would shift from a deficit of 13.1 percent of GDP in 1999 to a surplus of 1.8 percent in 2000. On a cash basis, the surplus would rise from 1.1 percent of GDP in 1999 to 4.9 percent in 2000.

Revenue measures. Oil revenue is projected to increase by some US$450 million in 2000 spurred by higher oil production and a rise in world oil prices. Efforts to improve the commercialization of diamonds and reduce smuggling will also boost government receipts by at least US$27 million. Furthermore, the tax measures introduced last year, together with others to be taken this year, are also expected to boost tax revenue. To this end, by end–2000 the government will raise the maximum personal income tax rate from 20 percent to 35 percent to match the corporate tax rate and it will also trim exemptions from customs duty and the sales tax.

Customs administration will be improved by strengthening surveillance at border posts and possibly by temporarily outsourcing the management of customs to a private firm while institutional capacity is built up. Internal tax administration also will be strengthened, including through more vigorous and frequent auditing of firms and implementation of other previous technical assistance recommendations for improving tax collections and taxpayer control. In addition, the government will request external technical assistance to formulate a second-generation tax reform by end–2000. Major issues to be considered in that exercise include further simplification of the tax regime; efforts to broaden the tax net to cover the informal sector; a review of the tax and regulatory treatment of mineral resources, with a view to strengthening the linkages between these sectors and the rest of the economy; and an analysis of the scope for introducing a value added tax over the medium term.

Expenditure measures. Total current and capital expenditure commitments will be held to around 43 percent of GDP in 2000. A substantial decline in military spending (which was unusually high in 1999) , and in transfers (in the wake of the elimination of fuel subsidies and

For additional analytical, business and investment opportunities information,
please contact Global Investment & Business Center, USA
at (202) 546-2103. Fax: (202) 546-3275. E-mail: rusric@erols.com

periodic adjustments in water and electricity tariffs) will be offset in part by a significant rise in investment and social outlays, as well as higher interest payments abroad. Spending on education as a share of total spending is budgeted to increase to 12.5 percent in 2000 (from an executed share of 4.8 percent in 1999) , and that of health to 9.3 percent (from an actual share of 2.8 percent in 1999) .

Monetary and exchange rate policies. The central bank will use a monetary anchor to achieve the inflation target and will continue to allow the exchange rate and interest rates to be determined by market forces. Broad money is expected to grow by 128 percent during 2000, and banking system liabilities in local currency by 132 percent, which would allow for growth of credit to the private sector of 133 percent. The program's ceiling on net domestic assets (NDA) of the banking system, which is the operative intermediate target for monetary control, will be enforced at first through ceilings on the NDA of individual banks (this will be replaced eventually by limits on NDA of the **central bank** to be secured by indirect instruments of monetary control) . The program will also include quarterly floors on the net international reserves of the BNA aimed at securing the buildup in gross reserves mentioned earlier.

External debt strategy. Given the urgent need for economic and social rehabilitation, a reduction of Angola's heavy external debt burden is an essential element of the government's medium-term economic strategy. To this end, in 2000 the government will start the process of normalizing relations with its external creditors. The program will include quarterly ceilings on the stock of external payments arrears of the public sector and a subceiling on those arrears to multilateral institutions.

All arrears to multilateral institutions, totaling about US$105 million at end–March 2000, will be cleared by end–September 2000. For budgetary and balance of payments reasons only part of the oil-guaranteed debt and a small amount of bilateral debt falling due can be serviced in 2000. The government will notify bilateral creditors of its intention to seek a Paris Club rescheduling in the context of a successor program supported by an arrangement with the Fund. Once relations with creditors have been normalized, the government will seek to avoid borrowing on nonconcessional terms.

Exchange restrictions. During the program period, the government does not intend to (a) introduce or modify multiple currency practices; (b) impose new restrictions or intensify existing restrictions in the area of payments and transfers for current international transactions; (c) introduce new restrictions on imports or intensify existing restrictions for balance of payments purposes; or (d) enter into new bilateral payments arrangements that are inconsistent with Article VIII of the Articles of Agreement of the Fund.

THE AGENDA OF STRUCTURAL REFORMS

Public sector operations. The government is committed to improving the transparency and efficiency of public sector operations. To this end, it is well on the way to initiating a diagnostic study of the oil sector, and will hire a reputable international auditing firm to initiate an external audit of the BNA's accounts by November 2000. Moreover, an integrated system of public sector financial management (SIGFE) is being implemented to improve budgetary operations, and a new accounting system (SICOES) for public sector operations will be implemented by early 2001.

Payments by the BNA on behalf of the government will be made only against proper authorizations, and every effort will be made to achieve full transparency through universal coverage of government revenues and expenditures in the context of implementation of the 2000 budget and preparation of the 2001 budget. Intra-public sector arrears will be quantified and a timetable for clearing them will be implemented during the year.

Civil service reform. The government is endeavoring to protect the purchasing power of its employees, and at the same time it will accelerate the civil service reform. In that context, the reduction in civilian public employment by 20 percent of the workforce over the period 1999–2001 (through attrition, early retirement, training, and self-employment) is expected to permit an increase in real remunerations of professionals and skilled workers, coupled with efforts to achieve a closer link between pay and performance. On a parallel track, the recent reform of labor market legislation is expected to play an important role in removing obstacles to job creation in the private and parastatal sectors and, as such, to facilitate the absorption of redundant public employees.

Financial sector reforms. The financial reforms are designed to strengthen monetary control, reduce intermediation costs, and deepen the mobilization of financial savings. On April 1, 2000, the BNA reduced legal reserve requirements on demand deposits in local currency from 35 percent to 30 percent. In the context of the technical assistance that is expected to be provided by the IMF's Monetary and Exchange Affairs Department (MAE) later this year, the BNA will review the scope for broadening the coverage of reserve requirements to deposits in other maturities and in foreign exchange, in conjunction with an analysis of the costs of conducting open market operations and remunerating government deposits.

To accommodate the shift to indirect monetary policy, the market for central bank bills (TBCs) and the interbank money market will be deepened, and a market for government securities will be introduced. In May 1999, the BNA authorized commercial banks to grant loans in foreign currency to exporters. The Angolan Payments System will be implemented to improve the payments and check-clearing system. The BNA will gradually eliminate all of its commercial operations, such as the contracting of foreign lines of credit for on-lending to enterprises, and will shift to commercial banks all sales of foreign exchange to the public sector for purposes other than debt service and national security operations.

Bank restructuring and supervision. The main concern in the banking sector is the poor performance of the state-owned banks. The liquidation of the CAP Bank will be completed, and consultants will be hired to make detailed recommendations for the restructuring and recapitalization of the remaining two state-owned banks, with a view to their phased privatization. The central bank will be empowered to enforce existing prudential regulations, which are in line with the Basel Committee core principles, and the regulations for the basic insurance law passed in February 2000 will be approved.

Trade reform. The government will continue to liberalize the trade regime, and consideration will be given to lowering the maximum tariff rate to 30 percent and abolishing the 5 percent customs service fee in 2001 if revenue considerations permit. Meanwhile, efforts at trade reform in 2000 will focus on the elimination of all nontariff barriers and export taxes. Customs procedures will be simplified, and customs exemptions (other than for diplomats, international organizations, or those under contractual agreements for the oil sector) will be eliminated.

Privatization. The government will rely heavily on the private sector to accomplish its economic growth objectives, limiting its own role to that of creating the enabling environment for the private sector to flourish, or providing basic services (such as fuel, electricity, telecommunications, domestic air transport, water, and sanitation) in which the private sector will also be invited to participate.

Consistent with its objective of disengaging from other productive activities, the government will begin to privatize most medium-sized and large public enterprises. To start, it will prepare a policy statement on privatization, which will include a list of all the enterprises it proposes to privatize over the medium term. In 2000, the government will begin to implement a pilot privatization program comprising ten firms. The government also plans to sign performance contracts **(contratos-programas)**, and it will consider the scope for establishing joint ventures and management contracts in order to improve the operations of major public enterprises and strengthen the accountability of managers.

Public utility tariffs. The government's policy is that utility tariffs should fully cover all costs, including a reasonable return on capital, in accordance with formulas agreed previously with the World Bank.

Domestic fuel subsidies were eliminated in February 2000, except for the agricultural, livestock, fisheries, and coastal maritime transport sectors; subsidies to these latter sectors will be kept under review and will be phased out gradually as these sectors recover. Electricity tariffs will be adjusted in April 2000 and will continue to be adjusted periodically to bring them to cost-recovery levels by April 2001 (according to Article 41 of the General Electricity Law, these tariffs must be enough to cover operating costs, taxes, amortizations, capital recovery, and a rate of return established under the criteria specified in that law). Water services are being provided by local governments, which will continue to adjust water tariffs periodically to recover costs. Petroleum prices will be adjusted periodically in line with movements in international oil prices and the exchange rate, again in accordance with an approved formula.

SOCIAL POLICIES

Education and health. Education and health indicators point to the need for a major effort to improve the quality of life in Angola. For example, the illiteracy rate is 60 percent, and life expectancy at birth is 45 years for men and 47 years for women. Efforts to increase the delivery of services have received a setback with the war, but the government has made education and health priority areas for spending in the budget, along with national security and infrastructure rehabilitation.

In the budget for 2000, the share of total current expenditure going to these two sectors has been increased, as mentioned earlier. The government is also seeking to reduce regional disparities in the allocation of education and health services, to the extent permitted by security conditions.

Poverty reduction strategy. The government will begin preparing a comprehensive poverty reduction strategy in consultation with civil society, which will be described in detail in a poverty reduction strategy paper. As this process is unlikely to be completed in 2000, in part because of lack of data, an interim poverty reduction strategy paper will be prepared by December 2000 in consultation with civil society, donors, and the IMF and World Bank staff. Pending the preparation and implementation of the poverty strategy, the government will continue to focus its efforts on emergency humanitarian assistance to people affected by the war, reconstruction of rural infrastructure and creation of rural employment opportunities, self-employment opportunities in both rural and urban areas, and smallholder agriculture.

PROGRAM MONITORING

Quantitative and structural benchmarks. To monitor progress in policy implementation under the program, quarterly quantitative benchmarks have been established (as set out in Table 1) with respect to (a) net international reserves of the BNA, (b) net domestic assets of the banking system, (c) net credit to the government by the banking system, (d) the contracting of medium- and long-term nonconcessional debt and short-term debt, and (e) external payments arrears of the public sector, with a subceiling on arrears to multilateral institutions. Structural benchmarks (as set out in Table 2) have also been established to serve as guideposts for the implementation of core reforms. A midterm review of program implementation will take place in September 2000. The program assumes that oil prices, which are highly volatile, will average US$20.7 per barrel in 2000. The quantitative targets under the program will be adjusted for upward or downward deviations from this reference price according to the mechanism described in the Annex to Table 1.

Statistical reporting to the Fund. The government will keep the Fund informed of the progress in the implementation of the SMP. It will report to the Fund fiscal data on a quarterly basis, within 45 days of the end of the March, June, September, and December 2000 quarters; external debt data within 90 days, and balance of payments data within 120 days, respectively, of the quarters ending March, June, September, and December 2000; monetary data on a monthly basis, within 30 days of the end of each month and beginning with the data for January 2000; data on net international reserves of the BNA and the banking system and on bank financing of the government on a monthly basis; and a weekly series on exchange rates starting from the beginning of 2000.

Technical assistance. The government urgently needs technical assistance to increase its capacity for implementing the program. The areas of greatest need include external debt management, tax reform, and treasury operations (including budget management and expenditure control). However, assistance would also be useful in the areas of statistics compilation; monetary control; central bank operations, organization, and strategic planning; bank supervision; and foreign exchange reserve management. The government has discussed its technical assistance needs with Fund and World Bank staff, and will also approach the donor community for assistance. The government will take all necessary steps, including legal and institutional measures and the provision of adequate resources, to enhance the effectiveness of technical assistance.

TECHNICAL MEMORANDUM OF UNDERSTANDING FOR 2000 STAFF MONITORED PROGRAM (SMP)

The net international reserves of the National Bank of Angola (BNA) are defined as gross international reserves of the BNA minus its short-term external liabilities. For programming purposes, the medium- and long-term external liabilities of the BNA are included in its net domestic assets. Consistent with these definitions, the latest preliminary figures for end-1999 and end-March 2000 are shown in Annex 1. The net foreign assets of the banking system comprise the net international reserves of the BNA, as defined above, and the net foreign assets of the commercial banks. The net foreign assets of the commercial banks, in turn, are defined as the difference between the commercial banks' gross foreign assets and their short-term foreign liabilities (at this time, the banks have no medium- and long-term foreign liabilities outstanding).

The net domestic assets of the banking system are defined as the difference between broad money (money and quasi money in local currency plus foreign currency deposits) and the net foreign assets of the banking system.

Net credit to the government by the banking system is defined as gross credit to the government minus government deposits in domestic and foreign currency. Credit to the government includes implicit credits in the form of BNA advances, such as for government debt service, open foreign exchange operations, or credits to the treasury account for unsettled tax liabilities (under the "oil-account" or otherwise).

The stock of arrears on public and publicly guaranteed external debt (excluding moratorium interest) as of December 31, 1999, is estimated at US $4,440 million.

Nonconcessional public and publicly guaranteed external debt is defined to exclude multilateral and bilateral credits (other than official development assistance (ODA)) . Noncessional external borrowing over one year includes financial leases and other instruments giving rise to external liabilities, contingent or otherwise, on noncessional terms.

The targets for the net international reserves of the BNA, the net domestic assets of the banking system, and net banking system credit to the government will be adjusted to reflect deviations of the actual average export price in U.S. dollars of Angolan crude oil from the benchmark price of US $19 per barrel assumed under the program for the period April-December 2000, as explained below and in Annex 2.

For the period April 1-December 31, 2000, the floor on the net international reserves of the NBA will be adjusted upward (downward) and the ceilings on net banking system credit to government and net domestic assets of the banking system will be adjusted downward (upward) to reflect any excess (shortfall) of the actual average export price in U.S. dollars of Angolan crude oil from the benchmark price of US $19 per barrel assumed under the program for the period April-December 2000, as follows:

The adjustment for each quarter will be US $20.4 million for each deviation of 100 cents of U.S. dollars per barrel from the program reference price of US $19 per barrel.[1] In the case of the benchmarks for net domestic assets of the banking system and net banking system credit to the government, the adjustment for each quarter will be obtained by converting the above mentioned dollar amounts into kwanzas using the average notional exchange rate for each quarter under the program, i.e., Kz 6.62 per US$ for Q2 2000, Kz 8.30 per US$ for Q3 2000, and Kz 10.03 per US$ for Q4 2000.

In the case of a **shortfall** in oil export prices from the program reference price, the adjustment will be limited to a maximum notional difference of US $4 per barrel, i.e., the difference between the reference price of US $19 per barrel and the price of US $15 per barrel utilized in the 2000 budget (O.G.E.) .

---

[1] This value corresponds to the difference between the variation of oil receipts of US$34.8 million and the variation in debt service on oil-guaranteed debt of US$14.4 million per quarter for each US$1 per barrel variation in the oil export price of Angolan crude.

TABLE 2. STRUCTURAL BENCHMARKS, APRIL–DECEMBER 2000

	Timing
Eliminate import licensing and quantitative restrictions on imports.	April 30, 2000
Review domestic petroleum prices every quarter and adjust them as necessary in accordance with a formula that takes into account movements in international prices and the exchange rate.	Beginning April 2000
Agree terms of reference for an independent audit of the National Bank of Angola with the IMF's Monetary and Exchange Affairs Department (MAE) .	June 30, 2000
Initiate the diagnostic study of the oil sector.	July 31, 2000

Finalize the first report of the diagnostic study of the oil sector.	September 30, 2000
Submit tender for international auditing firm to conduct independent audit of the National Bank of Angola.	August 31, 2000
Prepare a document describing the government=s policy on privatization of state-owned enterprises and containing a list of enterprises that the government will privatize.	September 30, 2000
Initiate an independent audit of the National Bank of Angola.	November 30, 2000
Secure approval by cabinet of a detailed plan for the restructuring and phased privatization of the two state-owned banks.	November 30, 2000
Complete liquidation of the assets and liabilities of the CAP Bank.	December 30, 2000

Table 3. Proposed Program of Structural Reforms for the Period April–December 2000

	Measure	Implementation Date
1.	Central government operations	
1.1	Launch the international bidding for the selection of consultants to undertake the oil sector study.	April 2000
1.2	Initiate the diagnostic study of the oil sector.	July 2000
1.3	Finalize the first report of the oil sector study, containing an assessment of the current situation of the sector as described in the approved summary terms of reference for the study.	September 2000
1.4	Agree with the IMF and the World Bank staff on the terms of reference and timetable for a diagnostic study of the diamond sector.	December 2000
1.5	Prepare a proposal for reform of the tax system, including a timetable for implementation.	November 2000
1.6	Raise the maximum personal income tax rate to 35 percent.	December 2000
1.7	Eliminate payments by the central bank on behalf of the government that are made without payment orders, as well as the implicit central bank advances to the government resulting from such transactions.	From April 2000
1.8	Identify all off-budget transactions and include them in the budget for 2001.	From April 2000

1.9	Conclude implementation of the Integrated System of Public Sector Financial Management (SIGFE) , including its budget, treasury, and public accounting components.	August 2000
1.10	Put in place procedures for proper recording of grants and counterpart funds in the budget.	September 2000
1.11	Limit subsidies to loss-making enterprises to budgeted amounts.	From April 2000
1.12	Establish a system for timely and comprehensive reporting of external arrears.	October 2000
1.13	Clear all arrears to multilateral financial institutions.	September 2000
1.14	Produce at the treasury complete and reliable records of external debt commitments and cash flows, including oil-guaranteed loans.	August 2000
1.15	Conclude an inventory of domestic public debt and put in place procedures for its management.	September 2000
1.16	Identify and quantify all intra public sector arrears.	May 2000
	Prepare and begin implementing a plan for clearance of all intra-public sector arrears.	June 2000
1.17	Develop an operational plan for paying salaries of government officials through financial institutions affiliated with the new Angolan Payments System (SPA) .	August 2000
2.	Public enterprises	
2.1	Continue to adjust domestic petroleum prices periodically in accordance with the agreed formula to take into account movements in international prices and the exchange rate.	From April 2000
2.2	Adjust electricity and water tariffs in accordance with formulas agreed with the World Bank.	From April 2000
2.3	Reduce accounts receivables of the water and electricity companies to one month of sales revenue.	August 2000
2.4	Present to the IMF and the World Bank a document describing the government's policy on privatization of state-owned enterprises and containing a list of enterprises that the government will privatize.	September 2000
2.5	Initiate a pilot privatization program:	
	☐ select ten enterprises that will be part of the pilot project;	May 2000
	☐ complete asset valuation of five companies; and	September 2000

		launch a public tender for the sale of these five companies and complete asset valuation of the other five companies.	December 2000
2.6		Set up a single office to deal with all aspects of company establishment, registration, and licensing (guichet único de empresa) .	June 2000
3.		Financial sector	
3.1		Complete the liquidation of the assets and liabilities of the CAP Bank.	December 2000
3.2		Begin implementing plan for restructuring and phased privatization of the two state-owned banks:	
		finalize terms of reference for consultants who will formulate restructuring plan;	April 2000
		hire consultants; and	August 2000
		secure approval by the Council of Ministers of a detailed plan for restructuring and privatizing the two banks.	November 2000
3.3		Initiate an independent audit of the National Bank of Angola, to be completed during the first half of 2001, which will be followed by annual audits.	November 2000
3.4		Strengthen bank supervision and fully enforce the Basel Committee Core Principles.	From April 2000
3.5		Gradually eliminate the commercial operations of the central bank in the form of short-term foreign borrowing for on-lending to enterprises.	From April 2000
3.6		Shift from the central bank to commercial banks all sales of foreign exchange to the public sector for purposes other than debt service and national security operations.	From July 2000
3.7		Establish the legal and institutional framework of a market for public debt securities.	September 2000
3.8		Review (in consultation with the IMF's Monetary and Exchange Affairs Department) the scope for broadening the coverage of legal reserve requirements to time and savings deposits and foreign currency deposits, in conjunction with an analysis of the costs of conducting open market operations and remunerating government deposits.	September 2000
3.9		Approve enabling regulations for the basic insurance law.	July 2000
4.		Trade reform and private sector development	

4.1	Eliminate import licensing and other nontariff trade barriers.	April 2000
4.2	Eliminate customs exemptions not contemplated in international accords.	April 2000
4.3	Simplify customs clearance procedures for imports.	April 2000
4.4	Create interagency group to draft a revised commercial code, with a view to fostering private sector development. Submit to the Council of Ministers a timetable for the revision of the code.	April 2000
4.5	Submit revised draft for approval of the Council of Ministers.	December 2000
5.	Social sectors	
5.1	Increase the share of expenditure on education and health to total expenditure from 4.8 in 1999 to 12.5 percent in 2000 in the case of education, and from 2.8 percent in 1999 to 9.3 percent in 2000 in the case of health.	December 2000
5.2	Prepare an interim poverty reduction strategy paper.	December 2000
5.3	Adopt a package of essential services to be provided under the municipal health system.	September 2000
6.	Statistics	
6.1	Compile budget execution reports within 45 days of the quarter's end.	Begin with the report for the period April–June 2000
6.2	Compile the monetary survey within 30 days of the month's end.	Begin with monetary survey for May 2000
6.3	Produce quarterly external debt statistics within 90 days of the quarter's end and quarterly balance of payments statistics within 120 days of the quarter's end.	Begin with the period April–June 2000
6.4	Publish a unified National Statistics Institute (INE) bulletin containing data on prices, production (sectoral and total) , national accounts, external trade, and social data (population composition and geographical distribution, health, education, etc.) .	Within 45 days of the quarters ending September and December 2000

For additional analytical, business and investment opportunities information,
please contact Global Investment & Business Center, USA
at (202) 546-2103. Fax: (202) 546-3275. E-mail: rusric@erols.com

PRACTICAL INFORMATION FOR CONDUCTING BUSINESS

INVESTMENT CLIMATE

OPENNESS TO FOREIGN INVESTMENT

Angola officially welcomes foreign investment and has established the Foreign Investment Institute to provide a point of contact with potential investors. However, common practices, such as non-transparent regulation, arbitrary decision-making, and corruption undermine this declared policy. Current law prohibits investment in defense, public order, security, and central banking functions.

The Foreign Investment Code specifies that foreign investors receive the same treatment as national companies, and are subject to the same tax regime. Repatriation of profits is guaranteed, and prompt indemnification is assured in cases of nationalization or expropriation, according to applicable law. Enforcement of these laws and protections has not been tested, and the court system has not yet demonstrated its impartiality or dedication to rule of law. In practice, power is concentrated to such a degree in the executive branch that arbitrary decisions, such as the recent expulsion of a U.S.-owned firm without due process, are common. Under the current regulatory regime, investors cannot be assured of legal protections.

Several recent cases highlight the gulf between Angolan law and Angolan action. One major multi-national investor was asked to take on an unwanted Angolan business partner, despite the fact that no such provision exists in Angolan law. In another instance, a U.S. firm's expatriate management was expelled from the country without due process. Contracts were subsequently picked up by the largest competing firm, whose management includes high-ranking Angolan government officials. Another U.S. firm states that it was pressured unsuccessfully to pay bribes to guarantee that the firm would be allowed to fulfil its contract. Actions such as these cast doubt on Angola's dedication to the protection of foreign investors.

Issuance of visas does not hinder foreign investors, but difficulty in obtaining employment permits does. Many expatriates, even those involved in humanitarian services, have found it difficult or impossible to obtain valid work permits. Waits of months are common, and in some cases workers have completed their assignments and returned home without ever having received their work permit. These work permits have become a major impediment to foreign investment. The processing of applications is slow and inconsistent. Protests from both the diplomatic and business community have failed to produce improvement.

FOREIGN TRADE ZONES/FREE PORTS

The government has not established foreign trade zones or free ports, but has indicted its intention to create three free-trade zones: one near Luanda, one at Catumbela in Benguela province, and one in Cabinda.

PROTECTION OF PROPERTY RIGHTS

Angola's legal system is widely regarded as moribund, and the laws and procedures as non-transparent and unlikely to offer real protection to investors in the event of a dispute with politically influential persons. The above-cited case, in which the expatriate staff of a U.S. firm was expelled from the country, effectively closing the business, is a case in point.

For additional analytical, business and investment opportunities information,
please contact Global Investment & Business Center, USA
at (202) 546-2103. Fax: (202) 546-3275. E-mail: rusric@erols.com

CORRUPTION

There are serious and continuing problems with corruption at all levels in Angola. Solicitation of bribes is common and blatant. Little has been done to curb such activity. The large spread between the official and parallel market exchange rates for the kwanza provides ample opportunity for illicit actions by government officials and influential private parties. Corruption also arises from a lack of transparency in the budget process, including poor accounting of petroleum income, off-budget inflows and outflows of funds, and ministry procurement orders conducted outside official channels. Monopolistic and arbitrary import regimes provide opportunities for corruption.

LABOR

The Government of Angola estimates that just under one-half of the population is working age. Unskilled labor is plentiful, but skilled labor is scarce. The Government estimates that 14.9 percent of the population is illiterate; the World Bank estimate is 58 percent and reaches 71 percent in some provinces. The average level of education is sixth grade; 13.2 percent of the population have never attended school, and only 18.5 percent have studied through eighth grade.

There are two significant labor organizations in Angola, the UNTA (a government-sponsored and affiliated trade union) , and the CGSILA, a confederation of several "free and independent" unions. CGSILA claims a membership of 80,000 workers in its 10 constituent unions, though this has not been verified. Trade unions can have an impact on policy, such as the December 1997 strikes by school teachers and hospital workers over unpaid salaries. Following the strikes, back salaries were paid. Unions have also succeeded over the years in establishing a strong worker's protection law. There is also an effective Labor Court, which hears cases brought by grieving workers and which frequently rules in their favor.

EFFICIENT CAPITAL MARKETS AND PORTFOLIOINVESTMENT

No capital market or stock exchange exists in Angola. In late 1997, the Ministry of Finance began studying the development of financial markets in Angola. The study is designed to acquaint the relevant authorities with the fundamentals of financial markets and spur thinking about framework legislation for mechanisms such as a regulatory agency and the central bank.

CONVERSION AND TRANSFER POLICIES

There are no restrictions on the total amount of foreign currency brought into Angola (National Bank of Angola Notice 7/97, published in Diario da Republica, Number 51, November 7, 1997) . Currency imported must be declared within 24 hours of arrival at an authorized agency. All national currency (kwanzas) must be purchased from authorized agencies at the official exchange rate (as of June 1998, $1.00 equals 306,000 kwanzas) . No national currency can be exported from Angola.

Obtaining foreign exchange has traditionally been difficult. Foreign exchange is authorized only by the central bank at a foreign exchange sale called a "fixing", held at irregular intervals. The June 1998 fixing was the first in three months. It is legal to maintain accounts in dollars. All imports must be made through the central bank, even if foreign exchange is held in another bank. The process entails buying kwanzas with the dollars at the official (overvalued) rate and depositing those kwanzas with a bank, which applies to the central bank for dollars and permission to import. When a "fixing" takes place, if there is sufficient foreign exchange on offer

**For additional analytical, business and investment opportunities information,
please contact Global Investment & Business Center, USA
at (202) 546-2103. Fax: (202) 546-3275. E-mail: rusric@erols.com**

to cover the requests, the kwanzas are converted back into dollars, and a letter of credit is opened for use in purchasing the imports. This process can take up to four months to complete, during which time the kwanzas on deposit can devalue relative to the dollar.

EXPROPRIATION AND COMPENSATION

According to the Angolan Foreign Investment Code, all foreign investments subject to the code are guaranteed protection equal to Angolan companies and, in the event of expropriation, prompt compensation. Several recent cases call these guarantees into question. In one case, a U.S. firm was forced to close under force majeure when its expatriate management was expelled from Angola. In 1996, the government summarily expelled thousands of traders accused of conducting business illegally. The traders' merchandise was seized and donated to charity.

POLITICAL VIOLENCE

Political violence remains a problem in Angola. Pursuant to the Lusaka Protocol of 1994, which ended the civil war in Angola, the Angolan government is currently extending its administration to areas of the country previously controlled by UNITA. As this process goes forward sporadic conflicts have erupted in many parts of the country. Luanda, however, has not been affected. Many incidents can be attributed to bandits, consisting of well-armed, well-trained individuals or groups who have demobilized or deserted from one of the armies previously involved in the conflict. The peace process has continued to move forward, albeit at a slower pace than planned. Existing landmines continue to plague the Angolan countryside, while there are reports of incidents of new mines being planted.

Separatist forces in the Cabinda enclave, including FLEC-FAC and FLEC-Renovada, have targeted foreigners for kidnapping for ransom. Separatist groups have also been responsible for armed attacks on vehicle convoys on roads outside of the capital, Cabinda City.

BILATERAL INVESTMENT AGREEMENTS

There is no bilateral investment treaty between the United States and the Republic of Angola.

OPIC AND OTHER INSURANCE PROGRAMS

Angola and the United States have signed an OPIC Investment Guarantee Agreement. Angola is "off-cover" for the U.S. Export-Import Bank.

FOREIGN DIRECT INVESTMENT STATISTICS

Precise foreign direct investment statistics are not available, but estimates place current U.S. FDI at over $4 billion. The pace of investment has increased dramatically in the last three years due to giant-class offshore oil discoveries. Estimated annual foreign investment is exceeds $1 billion; the vast majority is in the petroleum exploration and production sector.

TRADE REGULATIONS AND STANDARDS

The Government of Angola is a member of the World Trade Organization. It is reviewing the need for tariff and non-tariff barrier reduction, but lack of resources and personnel continue to impede this effort. Though a member of SADC, Angola has neither signed nor ratified the SADC Trade Protocol, which seeks to facilitate trade by harmonizing and reducing tariffs, and establishing regional policies on trade, customs, and metrology.

ECONOMIC TRENDS

PRINCIPAL GROWTH SECTORS

Real gross domestic product (GDP) grew by 5.7 percent in 1997, driven by the expanding petroleum sector. With a daily production of proximately 720,000 bbls, oil accounts for 93 percent of export revenues and 56 percent of GDP. Total annual production is expected to reach 1 million bbl/day by the year 2000. Petroleum refining will play a minor role until rehabilitation and reconstruction of the economy begins in earnest. The diamond-mining sector could fuel additional economic expansion if increased accountability can be introduced in production and marketing.

The majority of stones produced in Angola are sold outside official channels. In the industrial and services sectors, a lack of transparency, significant government ownership and control of production, corruption, and an overvalued currency all continue to stifle development. Agricultural production continues to suffer from a degraded infrastructure, lack of funds for investment, and, in certain areas, political instability and the presence of minefields. Angola's production of cereal grains is unlikely to meet domestic demand, despite what the UN food program estimates will be an increase in cereals production from 309,000 tons to 510,000 tons. In addition, scarcities of managerial, administrative, and technical talent, plus past failed attempts at collectivist economic planning, have hampered economic performance.

The government's recently adopted economic strategy for 998-2000 is aimed at achieving the following results:

* guaranteeing peace and stability in Angola;
* guaranteeing minimum consumption levels for foodstuffs and other essentials goods;
* ensuring minimum levels of sustained economic growth;
* reducing the deficits in the country's domestic and foreign accounts;
* controlling inflation;
* decreasing unemployment;
* reducing red tape; and
* creating the necessary climate to promote foreign investment;

The 1998 budget, however, contains few programs which will further those goals. Many of the economic assumptions underlying the budget are overly optimistic and will likely worsen Angola's external debt problem. The budget also ignores recommendations to limit external debt, and instead depends on an additional $700 million in external financing and $400 million in donor finance to cover its projected revenue shortfall. The anticipated shift from security spending to enhanced support for social reconstruction has not occurred. On the revenue side, oil production will continue to supply at least 70 percent of the anticipated $3.1 billion receipts. However, the sharp decline in world oil prices that began in early 1998 jeopardizes these estimates, and will force the Angolan Government to curtail outlays by an estimated $700 million to $1 billion. The budget contains none of the key elements the IMF has established as pre-requisites for future structural adjustment financing negotiations.

The government has implemented fiscal and monetary policies inconsistently and with varying results. Budget deficits of up to 30 percent have been the norm for several years and the primary source of disagreement with the IFI's. The Angolan government's funding of fiscal deficits through monetary expansion has driven persistently high inflation. An economic program, begun in 1996, to reduce inflation has been applied inconsistently. The government-set official exchange rate overvalues the kwanza, and a parallel foreign exchange market flourishes at rates up to twice the official exchange rate.

One report estimates that as of 1996, 85 percent of Angolan long- and medium- term debt was in arrears. As a consequence, much of the government's external borrowing requirement is now financed through short-term debt acquired at high rates. These loans are backed by future oil production, since few banks are willing to lend to Angola based only on sovereign debt. Because many of these loans are off-budget, accurate figures of total debt, and accurate estimations of the extent to which future oil production has already been leveraged, are unavailable.

GOVERNMENT ROLE IN THE ECONOMY

Angola was a Soviet-style centrally planned economy until 1991, but is now making the transition to a more market-based system. Nevertheless, the Government continues to intervene in the markets, including fixing prices, mandating quantity and mix of imports, setting a fixed exchange rate, and owning or directing the actions of much of the non-petroleum industrial sector.

While a privatization program has been established, the private sector in Angola is generally not prepared administratively or financially to purchase public corporations. Smaller state-run enterprises have been sold off, but many proved to be economically unviable. Most large companies, including telecommunications, insurance and banks, remain government monopolies.

BALANCE OF PAYMENTS SITUATION

In 1996 total exports were $5.1 billion; total imports were $2.2 billion, resulting in an overall positive balance of $2.8 billion. However, when services and transfers ($3.5 billion) , notably interest payments on debt, are included, the current account registered a deficit of $606 million, or 9.2 percent of GDP.

INFRASTRUCTURE

Neglect and decades of warfare have ravaged Angola's infrastructure. Conditions in almost all sectors - including water, sewer, sanitation, telecommunications, energy, roads, bridges, airports,and medical care -- have deteriorated in recent years. Many roads remain impassable. Despite attempts at improvement, water and electricity distribution networks continue to have serious problems. Nationwide installed generating capacity is only 547 MW, a sizeable portion of which is not functioning due to war damage or lack of repair and maintenance. According to the National Electric Company, only 130,000 of Luanda's estimated 3 million residents are connected to the electrical grid. For those that are, power interruption is so common that any home or business that can afford one has an individual generator.

The Angolan Government estimates that only 38 percent of the population has access to clean water. Water service in Luanda can be off for days or weeks at a stretch. The Government and international financial institutions are trying to improve the performance of the electricity and water companies through financing to upgrade equipment and improve operations.

Telephone service is sporadic due to lack of maintenance and repair. The cellular telephone system is over-subscribed and routinely cannot be accessed during business hours. Many large international companies have installed H.F. trunking systems to minimize use of the domestic telephone system. Telecommunications quality is unlikely to improve significantly until the government relinquishes its monopoly in this sector. There are currently two local Internet providers in Angola, and service is relatively good.

Angola could benefit from its excellent geographic position if its infrastructure were repaired and upgraded. The ports of Luanda, Lobito, and Namibe are all operational, although each will require significant improvements if they are to become primary ports of entry for commerce in southern Africa. A rail line runs east into the interior from each port, though all rail lines were severely damaged during the conflict. An Italian consortium has agreed to rehabilitate the line between Benguela and the border of the DROC, but construction has not begun. Luanda's international airport handles significant volumes of traffic, but expanded services will not be possible until improvements are made, such as the installation of a parallel taxiway and an instrument landing system. Currently there are no direct flights from the U.S. to Luanda, and no U.S. flag carrier serves Luanda.

DOING BUSINESS BASICS

A visit to Angola is highly recommended as personal relations are crucial in doing business in the country. Most Dutch companies rely on a local representative to handle affairs once contact has been established. A few points of advice:

• Agreements are normally only made once a personal relation is established; take therefore time to socialise during the visit. Because of the importance of this, agreements are often made at a late phase during negotiations.

• Angolans are often relatively formal in the first few meetings. Formal clothing in these occasions is highly appreciated.

• Bureaucracy and corruption have diminished but have not fully disappeared.

• The preferred language is often Portuguese as few people have mastered English. It therefore might be advisable to use Portuguese or hire a translator during a visit or correspondence.

• Have direct communication by phone before sending any (general) e-mails.

VISITING ANGOLA

Please be advised of the following:

• Hotels in Angola and also flights are often fully booked long in advance despite of the high prices. Thus it is wise to book early.

• The use of credit cards is limited, even at hotels; therefore take US dollars in cash.

• As there are no taxies available at the airport or in Luanda, try to arrange transport before arrival.

• Consult the ⇨ reisadvies before travelling to Angola

• The application procedure for a business visa takes on average a week and requires among other things an invitation letter from a contact in Angola. Please visit the Consular Affairs pages of the website for further information on obtaining visas for Angola.

INVESTMENT PROCEDURES

Foreign investment in the Republic of Angola is governed by LAW no.11/03 of May 13 ,2003.

The National Private Investment Agency (ANIP) is the entity responsible for promoting, coordinating, implementing and regulating foreign investment policies in Angola.

Foreign investment is defined here as the introduction into and use in national territory of funds, equipment and other goods or technology services. It likewise includes the use of funds transferable abroad, pursuant to prevailing foreign exchange laws, by non-resident individuals/corporations, with a view to creating new enterprises, branches or any form of corporation, as well as the acquisition of the whole or part of an existing Angolan enterprise.

Also considered as foreign investment, are any transaction or dealings by an Angolan enterprise, achieved by majority ownership or any other means linking it directly or indirectly to non-resident individuals/corporations.

On the other hand, within the framework of its foreign investment legislation, only proposals that have met a minimum capital-investment figure of $100,000.00 (one hundred dollars) will be considered. All other cases will be subject to commercial and foreign exchange legislation.

Foreign investments in the oil and diamond sectors, as well as financial institutions, are governed by specific laws.

Foreign investments in the oil industry are governed by Law N° 10/04 and 11/04, of 2004, and in the diamond industry they are governed by Law N° 16/94 of October 7, 1994.

ADVANTAGES TO INVESTING IN ANGOLA

A strong government commitment in applying economic and political reforms, leading to a free-market economy;

Respect for private property and constitutional guarantees for investors;

Increasingly flexible economic legislation;

Existence of a one-stop-shop business and foreign investor aid and support bureau (planned)

Abundant, affordable labor and skilled young people;

Availability of raw materials and energy resources, both traditional and alternatives, such as natural gas;

Strategic location in relation to external markets, especially central and southern Africa;

A dynamic and young entrepreneurial population, eager for knowledge.

FOREIGN INVESTMENT OPERATIONS

For additional analytical, business and investment opportunities information,
please contact Global Investment & Business Center, USA
at (202) 546-2103. Fax: (202) 546-3275. E-mail: rusric@erols.com

The following acts and agreements, among others, constitute foreign investment activities, even though they may not be directly or necessarily related to capital importation operations:

Establishing and expanding branches or other forms of corporate representation of foreign firms, as well as the acquisition of the whole or part of existing enterprises;

Participation or acquisition of interest in the equity of new or existing companies;

Signing or amending consortia agreements or for third party association in capital stock;

Total or partial takeovers of commercial or industrial establishments and agricultural enterprises;

Management of building complexes (tourism-related or not) and the purchase of real estate in national territory as part of foreign investment projects;

Capital increases, shareholder/partner loans and, in general, profit-sharing venture-related loans.

FOREIGN INVESTMENT CATEGORIES

Foreign investments may be made according to any of the following categories:

PRIOR DECLARATION CATEGORY

Investments of between US$ 100,000 (one hundred thousand US dollars) , for foreign investors and US$ 5,000,000 (five million US dollars) are subject to this category.

CONTRACTUAL CATEGORY

This category encompasses investments of over US$5,000,000 (five million US dollars) .

INVESTMENT PROPOSAL PRESENTATION

An investment proposal is submitted by filling out the respective printed form, available at the ANIP. An investment proposal must be accompanied by the following documents:

Power of attorney to act before the National Private Investment Agency (ANIP) by the person signing the proposal, when not signed directly by the proponent;

Certified copy of legal documents identifying and verifying the usual place of residence of the proponent, in the case of individual persons;

Certified copy of legal incorporation and commercial registry documents of the proponent, in the case of corporate entities;

In the case of companies incorporating: draft incorporation papers of corporation to be formed; certificate of company name availability, issued by the competent agency, dated as of one month prior to the date of submission; and, if applicable, draft articles or agreements of association.

In the case of acquisition of stakes in already-existing corporations: certified copy of incorporation papers and commercial registration of the corporation in which an interest is acquired; certified copy of resolution passed by relevant corporate bodies of the corporation in which an interest is acquired, approving transaction;

In the case of operations involving capital increases, loans, advances, and loans from shareholders/partners: certified copy of the respective of resolution passed by relevant corporate bodies;

In the case of signing of partnership or association agreements, to purchase commercial, industrial or agricultural estate or real estate and exploration of building complexes: draft or final agreements.

In the case of investment in real estate: certified copy of respective land registry title deed, issued in the past three months.

Whenever an investment project includes the incorporation or transfer of patented technology, a certified copy of the respective patents registration.

In the case of investments under prior approval or contractual categories, the proposal should be accompanied by a technical, economic and financial feasibility study on the project.

FOREIGN INVESTMENT PROCEDURAL CATEGORIES

Under the Prior Declaration Category, the decision to reject a proposal may only be based on strictly legal criteria, and must be expressly stated. Rejection of a proposal must be communicated in writing by the ANIP to the proponent, stating its grounds. If there are no grounds for an express rejection of the proposal, the ANIP shall issue a declaration certifying acceptance of the proposal.

Under both the Prior Approval Category and the Contractual Category, an Evaluation Committee coordinated by the ANIP is responsible for assessing the technical, economic and financial merits of a project.

Foreign Investment Procedural Categories

Category	US$ 000's	Approval Period	Approval Bodies
Prior Declaration	From 100 to 5,000	15 days	ANIP
Contractual	Over 5,000	30 days	Cabinet

Under the Contractual category, those investment proposals with amounts below that stipulated, and which will contribute to the development and globalization of the Angolan economy, will adhere to this category independent of their value.

Guarantees are offered to the foreign investors, who will enjoy certain special privileges including:

Entitlement to transfer funds abroad after taxes are paid and in accordance with foreign exchange legislation;

Dividends and profits, to which they are entitled, based on respective share in investment project;

Product of the liquidation of investments, including capital gains;

All amounts owed to the investor, as per acts and agreements or contracts which are recognized under the law as of a foreign investment nature;

Indemnity in the event of expropriation or nationalization of assets of the foreign investment, according to rules and regulations, with recourse to arbitration.

Access to local bank loans, as well as abroad.

The Angolan government guarantees, devoid of any discrimination, just and equitable treatment of all registered businesses, as well as in relation to imported goods, pursuant to foreign investment legislation.

AREAS PRIORITIZED FOR FOREIGN INVESTMENT

In order to bring foreign investment into the country's overall development, the government has defined a policy of preference on foreign investment, which will increase the export of goods while replacing or reducing imports. These are the fields on which the government is focusing:

Agriculture & livestock, and food products;

Mining;

Fisheries & byproducts;

Light industry, especially when associated to widespread consumer items, namely in the agricultural field;

Industrial materials for construction and public works that will permit the construction of social housing, in order to improve the living standards of the Angolan population.

INCENTIVES TO INVESTMENT OFFERED BY ANGOLA

The Angolan Government has set out as its primary objectives the creation of an environment conducive to the good performance of businesses, by undertaking certain actions. Among which are: The production of goods for direct consumption, such as those derived from the farming and fishing industries. The production of goods for export. Activities engaged in by micro or small and medium enterprises. Industries, especially those contributing significantly to objectives and social development and actions, including a focus on restructuring industrial enterprises leading to better use of installed equipment.

TAX INCENTIVES

Exemption from Real Estate Tax (SISA) on the acquisition of a property destined exclusively for use in an investment project;

For additional analytical, business and investment opportunities information,
please contact Global Investment & Business Center, USA
at (202) 546-2103. Fax: (202) 546-3275. E-mail: rusric@erols.com

Acceleration to double of amortizations/depreciations and incorporations with regard to assets belonging to an investment project, as of the year subsequent to its operational phase;

Exemption from import duties on raw materials and equipment acquired exclusively for use in an investment project;

Exemption from consumption tax on goods exported, when exports are made by a manufacturer or entity duly recognized as an exporter.

FINANCIAL BENEFITS

Specially-reduced annual interest rates on credit lines in relation to the priority status of a project;

Annual grants to create permanent employment during the first four years following the initial phase of a project;

Grants for mining, for enterprises with core activities aimed at increasing exports, and thus reducing imports;

Grants for setting-up or transferring businesses, with a view to supporting infrastructure-related public works, usually up to a maximum of 30% of total investment.

OTHER SUPPORT FOR INVESTORS

Industrial Development Hubs

The PDIs (Industrial Development Hubs) are one of the underpinnings of the Angolan Re-Industrialization Program, which is aimed at boosting the industrial sector, converting it into the economy's main engine.

The PDIs are strategic parcels of land previously set aside and equipped with basic industrial infrastructure - energy, water, telecommunications, road and/or railroad access, among others.

Businesses willing to establish themselves in these areas may, among other incentives, be entitled to reduced land prices, tax benefits, incentives and government grants.

The main designated PDIs are: Luanda (Viana) , Benguela (Catumbela) and Cabinda (Fútila) . These areas offer great potential for raw materials and subsidiaries, labor and infrastructures.

PDIs are usually managed by public limited corporations dedicated to industrial development (SODI - Sociedades de Desenvolvimento Industrial) . SODIs are national and regional venture-capital companies, mainly owned and managed by the state (51% through IDIA- Angolan Industrial Development Institute) , provincial governments, banks, insurance companies and national and foreign economic institutions.

PATIA - Program for the Technological Upgrade of Angolan Industry

Since Angola needs to acquire technology to reactivate its production, while coordinating that with the country's specifics on a professional training level and the limitations of the consumer market, the Ministry of Industry has established a new initiative called PATIA (Program for the Technological Upgrade of Angolan Industry) .

**For additional analytical, business and investment opportunities information,
please contact Global Investment & Business Center, USA
at (202) 546-2103. Fax: (202) 546-3275. E-mail: rusric@erols.com**

The PATIA was created with a view to developing partnerships between national and foreign corporations. The latter corporations must be operating in Angola with a view to contributing to its development and must be using equipment that has a useful lifetime of between 15 to 20 years.

MIGA - Multilateral Investment Guarantee Agency

MIGA was created as a member of the World Bank Group and offers credit guarantee insurance for investments related to growth, privatization, financial restructuring and upgrade, direct holdings in capital stock, loans, technical assistance, management contracts, franchising and licensing. Its ultimate goal is to reduce political risks.

The political risk insurance offers cover against three situations: expropriations, war and civil unrest, and currency transfer. This guarantee applies to up to 90% of an investment's value for a period of from 15 to 20 years.

World Bank Credit Guarantee

The Bank offers these specific guarantees:

Partial Risk Guarantee: covering debt-servicing defaults on a loan to a private sector project caused by a government's failure to meet its contractual obligations vis-à-vis a private project.

Partial Credit Guarantee: covering debt-servicing defaults on a specific tranche of a loan or a bond. Such guarantees allow public sector projects to extend maturities and lower spreads, as well as offering incentives for the renewal of medium-term loans.

INVESTMENT OPPORTUNITIES

Potentially one of Africa's richest sub-Saharan countries, Angola offers great opportunities for investment in various sectors.

Moreover, Angola is also blessed with large regions naturally favorable to the building of industrial and farming parks in the Luanda, Bengo, Benguela, Huíla, Cabinda, and Kuanza South areas.

Also in place is a young, dynamic and skilled entrepreneurial sector that owns some underdeveloped property, eager for partnerships that will give them access to new technology and know-how.

Likewise, and in the process of privatization, a meaningful public sector in the banking, transportation, energy and water fields already exists in Angola.

AGRICULTURE & LIVESTOCK.

The FAO estimates over three million hectares of arable land exist. There are also large areas for pasture, especially in the southern part of the country.

Traditional sustainable crops - cassava, beans, and sweet potatoes are found in the country's north, with corn in the central provinces, and small corn and sorghum in the southern areas. We would also mention other crops such as banana, rice, sugar cane, palm oil, cotton, coffee, sisal (hemp) , tobacco, sunflower, citrines, and other fruits and vegetables.

Coffee, which up to 1973 was Angola's major export, is well worth looking at, as it could once again become a very important factor in the Angolan economy.

With the idea of launching an agri-business policy, as part of the government's social and economic program for 2000, it was decided that the main effort should focus on those zones defined in the agricultural program, and on the production of the following basic staples: cereals, roots and tubercles, beans, fruits, vegetables, oil seeds, and specialty products such as green products, small ruminants, cattle breeding and meat processing, pig farming and the rearing of poultry and other birds.

Areas of interest in existence for private investment:

Waterworks Maintenance & Management;
Consultant Engineering ;
All kinds of Production /Marketing Technical & Material Assistance;
Agricultural Mechanization & Technical Assistance;
Industrial Poultry Breeding;
Cattle & Pig Breeding;

MAIN IRRIGATED AREAS

Provinces	Zones	Area (ha)	Crops
BENGO	Bom Jesus	1,300	Roots and tubercles, cereals, horti-fruiters
	Caxito	3,000	Roots and tubercles, cereals, horti-fruiters
CABINDA	Vale do Yabi (Yabi Valley)	5,000	Roots and tubercles, fruiters, cattle breeding
KWANZA NORTH	Mucuso	315	Roots and tubercles, cereals, horticultural crops
	Lucala	250	Roots and tubercles, cereals, horti-fruiters
LUANDA	Vale do Bengo Kiminha/Funda	25,000	Roots and tubercles, cereals, horti-fruiters
BENGUELA	Cavaco	4,1	Roots and tubercles, cereals, horti-fruiters and tobacco
	Catumbela	4,5	Roots and tubercles, cereals, horti-fruiters
HUÍLA	Humpata	1,000	Roots and tubercles, cereals, horti-fruiters
	Matala	3,000	Roots and tubercles, cereals, horticultural crops, fruiters, cattle breeding
	Chibia	1,000	Roots and tubercles, cereals, horti-fruiters
NAMIBE	Carunjamba, Giraul, Bero and Curoca	600	Grapes (wine) and citrines Tubercles, cereals, horticultural crops, industrial crops, cattle breeding
CUNENE	Manquete Xangongo Quiteve/Humbe (Ombandja) Cova do Leão (Kahama)		Tubercles, cereals, horticultural crops, cattle breeding, olives

FISHING

Angola boasts one of Africa's richest coastlines, especially in the country's south. There the cold Benguela current creates a special environment for a great variety of fish, principally mackerel, sardines, tuna, and shellfish.

The government's immediate objectives are to reactivate productive fishing processes, increase fish-conservation activities, and renew catch capacities, as well as increase and rationalize existing cold-storage capabilities. It also plans to revamp and equip naval shipyards, dock areas and fishing ports, while improving the commercial distribution of fish on a national level. Providing technical assistance to entrepreneurs, management training, and scientific investigation is also slated.

Previously state-owned, various small fishing enterprises have already been divested to the private sector as part of a privatization program. Currently, preparation for the privatization of larger enterprises is underway.

MINING

Angola has substantial deposits of diamonds, iron ore, gold, phosphates, manganese, copper, lead, zinc, tin, tungsten, marble, and granite, among others.

In the wake of the country's Independence, these activities have become restricted to the mining of diamonds in the Lunda North and Lunda South zones in the northeast, and, on a much smaller scale, the extraction of marble and granite in the southwest.

Angola is one of the world's major producers of diamond gems, and after oil, diamonds are the country's most important export.

Any increase in production will depend upon the recovery of the main mining areas in the Cuango River Valley. In fact, various foreign companies are interested in this sector.

The prospect of strong growth in the mining sector (oil, diamonds, and other minerals) is bound to generate the interest of foreign companies, both upstream and downstream.

ENERGY

Angola boasts substantial energy resources, having vast oil deposits, abundant hydroelectric potential and natural gas reserves.

Crude oil, which in 1973 became its prime export and having been on the increase since then, is the mainstay of the Angolan economy.

Angola is the second largest oil producer in sub-Saharan Africa (after Nigeria) with a production of 1 million barrels a day having been projected for 2000/2001.

After Independence, among other measures, the government created the Oil Ministry, adopted legislation specific to the sector, and set up a state enterprise called SONANGOL – Sociedade Nacional de Combustíveis de Angola. This was done as a means to defining a clear national oil policy. The state took over all oil fields and gave SONANGOL the exclusive concession for their exploration and production. Simultaneously, it was authorized to go into partnership with foreign enterprises in order to obtain both the financial and technical resources needed.

In 1996, a series of newly-discovered oil wells resulted in an increase in production, pushing Angola to a more prominent status as an oil-producing country.

Recognition of its vast energy potential led to Angola being appointed the Energy Sector Coordinator for the SADC.

Some 80% of energy production is hydroelectric. Supply is assured by three major schemes, linked to three important hydro basins - those of the Kuanza, Catumbela and Cunene rivers.

The remaining 20% comes from electrical power plants, with investments having been made to increase output capacity for Luanda, which is responsible for more than half the country's electricity consumption.

MANUFACTURING

Before Independence, the manufacturing sector carried some impact. It accounted for 16% of GDP in 1973, essentially contributed by foodstuffs and other consumer goods. In 1975, production had decreased by some 75%, with 43% of manufacturing companies forming part of the public sector by 1987. Ten years later, in 1997, manufacturing accounted for 4.4% of GDP, primarily reflecting the oil refining, drinks, and cement sectors.

In response to the above situation, the Angolan Government started to take remedial steps by approving, in 1994, the Master Program for the Reindustrialization of Angola (PDRA) , whose chief objective was to re-energize the private-manufacturing sector, focusing on the following:
- Private-sector participation
- Upgrading industrial equipment
- Training human resources
- Attracting foreign direct investment
- Promoting the export of national finished products
- Concentrating manufacturing activities in industrial development areas (PDI)

At the same time, and because most Angolan industrial equipment is over 25 years old, the PATIA program (mentioned in Section II) was created. Another incentive to make the Angolan industrial sector expand is the putting in place of privatization policies. We would highlight the enactment of Law 8/98 of September 11, 1998 – Basic Industrial Law, whose main objective was to promote a standard industrial policy and create a favorable atmosphere for entrepreneurs, as well as to motivate the development of national resources.

Civil Construction & Public Works

In 1998, the construction sector accounted for 4.8% of GDP, with several foreign companies operating on the market. The country offers great opportunities in terms of public works.

As to infrastructure, such as roadways and railways, there is an urgent need for the rehabilitation of highways, bridges, railways, and dams, etc., in order to ensure connections between the country's provinces.

There is also an enormous need for social infrastructure, such as school compounds, and housing and hospital complexes.

TRADE & SERVICES

Services present exciting prospects, since trade and tourism are expanding. The transportation and communication sectors point to high potential, while banking and insurance began coming to the fore, especially after 1991.

In 1999, 10 banks were in existence, of which four were private ones and two the representative offices of foreign banks. Only a single state-controlled insurance company operates - Empresa Nacional de Seguros de Angola. Studies are, however, being performed to look into ending its monopoly.

Ensuring the availability of essential consumer goods, hindered by low national production, calls for the setting up and development of a solid commercial structure, integrating the production, import, transportation, and distribution segments.

Angola is potentially a country ripe for the development of the tourism sector, offering the following:

☐ 1,650 km. of coastline, a long summer season and beautiful, natural sandy-beaches with excellent conditions for swimming and water sports.

☐ Rich and varied fauna with a system of parks and natural reservations.

☐ Fantastically beautiful, poster-inspiring, landscapes boasting mountains and waterfalls.

☐ Rivers with waterfalls, rapids, and lakes - some navigable.

National game parks and natural reserves constitute hubs of attraction for investment.

PROTECTED AREAS IN ANGOLA

NATIONAL PARKS & NATURAL RESERVES

Name	Province	Area (km²)	Main Species
Quissama National Park	Bengo	9,960	Manatee, Red Palanca, Pacaça
Bikuar National Park	Malange	630	Black Giant Palanca, Red Palanca
Kangandala National Park	Huíla	7,900	Elephant, Buffalo
Iona National Park	Namibe	15,150	Zebras, Guelengue, Lion, Ostrich
Kameia National Park	Moxico	14,450	Cacu, Boi-Cavalo
Mupa National Park	Cunene	6,600	Giraffe, Cahoma
Chimalavera Nat. Park	Benguela	100	Cabra de Leque
Luando Natural Reserve	Malange/Bié	8,280	Black Giant Palanca
Ilhéu Natural Bird Reserve	Luanda	2	Migratory Birds
Moçâmedes Natural Reserve	Namibe	4,450	Ostrich, Cabra de Leque
		5,950	Elephants, Palanca, Southwestern Palanca
		8,400	Elephants, Palanca.
		400	Southwestern P., Rhino, Black Bufalo

Reserve	Kuando Kubango		
Mavinga Natural Reserve	Kuando Kubango		
Luiana Natural Reserve	Kuando Kubango		
Bufalo Natural Reserve	Benguela		

About 50% of the hospitality sector's infrastructure needs to be revamped. Of 105 hotels of varying categories, only half are active, and even so, these are all located along the country's coastal areas.

INVESTMENT OPPORTUNITIES - PRIVATIZATIONS

Law 10/94 of August 31, 1994 establishes the general rules governing the privatization of state-owned small, medium and large companies, and other state properties. An exception is housing owned by the state, regulated by Law 19/91 of May 21, 1991.

Under this law, privatization can be either total or partial. It encompasses both the transfer of the ownership and/or divestment of operations, assets, or capital stock of the companies to be privatized.

Before privatization takes place, an appraisal is performed by a duly accredited entity.

Privatization goes ahead in the following manner, either individually or cumulatively:

☐   Divestment of assets

☐   Divestment of company stock or shares

☐   Capital increase

Privatization takes place, as a rule, through an IPO, albeit bidding may be restricted in exceptional cases.

Organization of an IPO and the ensuing process are controlled by a negotiating committee appointed for each case, composed of a representative of each of the following:

☐   Ministry of Finance (coordinator)

☐   Entity overseeing company management

☐   Office Managing the Entrepreneurial Restructuring Program (GARE)

☐   Institute of Foreign Investment (whenever foreign investment is potentially available)

☐   The company

The Minister of Finance is responsible for ratification of the evaluation, as well as of the results approved by the negotiating committee, independent of an enterprise's size. Final approval for execution of the privatization operation has to be given by the Cabinet in the case of large enterprises, and by the Minister of Finance in the case of small- and medium sized companies.

TRANSFER OF OPERATIONS AND MANAGEMENT AGREEMENTS

The same rules governing the divestment of state enterprises and other state-owned assets are applicable to agreements to reassign business operations. A management agreement per se is not considered a privatization operation, and its validity is subject to the following cumulative conditions:

☐ A favorable opinion by GARE, to whom management should have previously sent the agreement

☐ Ratification of the management agreement by the Minister of Finance

PRIVATE ENTERPRISE RESTRICTIONS

Law 13/94 of September 2, 1994 - Economic-Activity Sector Restrictions - establishes those areas of activity prohibited to private enterprise. It safeguards them in unconditional or comparative exclusivity as the state's reserve, and they can only be operated with its intervention and/or participation.

The description "reserved for the state" is taken to mean a series of economic activities whose ownership or management can only be exercised provided the state or other entities belonging to the public sector intervene or participate in them.

There are three types of reserved areas:

Exclusive Reserve

This group covers areas where economic activity can only be exercised exclusively by the public sector:

☐ Production, distribution, and commercialization of military materiel

☐ Banking, as far as the functions of a central and issuing bank are concerned

☐ Administration of ports and airports

☐ Telecommunications, as far as the basic national network and fundamental services infrastructures are concerned

Controlled Reserve

This includes the following economic activities that can be exercised by companies arising out of partnerships with public-sector entities, but where it is mandatory that the latter shall have a majority controlling position in the new enterprise:

Scheduled international air passenger and cargo transportation

Scheduled domestic air passenger transportation
Regular postal service
Long-distance maritime transportation

Qualified Reserve

Companies or entities not belonging to the public sector, when based on temporary concession contracts, can conduct the following economic activities:
- Basic sanitation
- Production, transportation and distribution of electrical energy for public consumption
- Uptake, treatment and distribution of water for public consumption through fixed networks
- Operation of port and airport services
- Rail freight
- Coastal shipping
- Public transportation
- Chartered air transportation of passengers and cargo (national)
- Supplementary postal and telecommunications services

The exploration of all natural resources, which according to the Constitution are the property of the state, can only be made under a concessionary or some other arrangement provided it does not involve the transfer of ownership.

LAND CONCESSIONS

According to principles defined under the Constitution, all land is at the outset the property of the state. Furthermore, the state is solely responsible for establishing the conditions under which land can be the subject of a concession, while protecting the country's national interests and development. It also demands proven capacity from a petitioner to develop land efficiently, as well as the offering of guarantees to the people who originally lived on and cultivated it.

Land concessions for use and exploration are granted through official licenses issued by the Ministry of Agriculture & Rural Development and the provincial governments concerned. Licenses may be either granted for a limited period (up to 45 years) or be limitless.

In the case of foreign investment being made in land forming part of territorial waters and the continental platform, or for land being used by the rural population, and areas deemed economically or militarily strategic, approval is required by the Cabinet.

Land earmarked for housing, trade, industrial operations, and facilities for social activities do not yet have their own specific legislation. For that reason the disposal of such property must be determined by the Ministry concerned and the respective provincial government on a case-by-case basis.

INCORPORATING COMPANIES

FOREIGN INVESTMENT IN ANGOLA

1. ANGOLAN CORPORATE LEGISLATION

Angolan corporate law is based on legislative texts in use before the country's Declaration of Independence in 1975.

The first Angolan Constitutional Law (1975) safeguarded legislation in use during the colonial period when stating, in article 64, that laws prevailing in Angola would continue to be valid until replaced by newer legislation.

Essentially, corporate legislation is contained in the Commercial Code. This provides information regarding the legal forms of Public Limited Companies *(Sociedades Anónimas - SARL)* , Limited Liability Companies *(Sociedades em nome colectivo)* , and Partnerships *(Sociedades em comandita)* .

During the post-Independence period, very little new legislation was passed changing the Commercial Code or Joint-Stock Company Law.

That is why valid legislation remains almost the same as it was before Independence.

Legislative changes have been focused mainly on the regulation of state-owned enterprises known as State Economic Units (UEEs) , which after 1995 became known as Public Enterprise (EPs) .

In such cases, pre-Independence legislation was entirely repealed and replaced by new laws approved by the Government and National Assembly.

In evidence is Law 9/95, of September 15, 1995, the statute that governs public companies.

1.1   Choice of Investment Vehicle

As per Decree 29/92, of July 3, 1992 and Executive Order 23/93, of October 29, 1993, all foreign investors intending to operate a business in Angola should start by registering with the Ministry of Finance, and obtain a taxpayer number and corporate ID card right from initial date of starting up operations in the country.

Should a foreign investor wish to establish a physical presence in the country, depending on the size of the investment and type of enterprise to be explored, the following options are available: (i) Representative Office, (ii) Branch, or (iii) A legal structure incorporated to operate under Angolan Law.

1.1.1   Representative Office versus Branch versus Angolan-Incorporated Company

Representative Offices

- ☐ Under Decree 7/90, dated March 24, 1990, the activity of a Representative Office is limited to mere representation on behalf and for the account of the foreign entity represented

- ☐ A Representative Office cannot undertake any commercial activities in Angola on its own account

- ☐ Six is the maximum number of employees allowed

Since this type of legal structure is subject to several restrictions, it is not recommended in cases where a foreign investor intends exercising regular economic activity in Angola, or in the case of investments of any sizeable amount.

Branches

For additional analytical, business and investment opportunities information,
please contact Global Investment & Business Center, USA
at (202) 546-2103. Fax: (202) 546-3275. E-mail: rusric@erols.com

A Branch is the most common legal form of representation for a foreign company in Angola, since it allows the foreign investor to exercise commercial activity in Angola on a par with the rights enjoyed by an Angolan company. However, there are several commercial activities reserved exclusively to companies incorporated in Angola and subject therefore to Angolan law.

A branch is not a generally-accepted legal entity per se, although its right to instigate legal proceedings and/or be taken to court under some circumstances entitles it to recognition in law.

Angolan-Incorporated Companies

A company is an entity legally incorporated and set up for business purposes.

In Angola, a foreign investor can opt to choose one of four types of partnerships provided for under law.

For the time being, any type of partnership provided for in law requires a plurality of partners.

2. PROCEDURES REQUIRED FOR COMPANY INCORPORATION/BRANCH OR REPRESENTATIVE OFFICE REGISTRATION

Procedures		Enterprise		Branch	Representative Office
		With FI	Without FI		
1.	Securing Trade Name at the Ministry of Trade (Registry)	♦	♦	B ♦	♦
2.	Securing Authorization by FIA (ANIP) / Prime Minister / Cabinet	♦		♦	
3.	Securing Authorization of Central Bank (BNA)		A ♦	C ♦	
4.	Requesting Authorization from Governor of Central Bank to open Representative Office				♦
5.	Securing Capital Import License(s) issued by the BNA	♦	A ♦	♦	♦
6.	Delivering Company Articles of Incorp. to Notary Office			♦	♦
7.	Securing Notary Deed from Notary Office	♦	♦		
8.	Publishing Company Articles of Incorp. in the Government's Official Gazette (Diário de República)	♦	♦	♦	♦
9.	Securing commercial registration at Company Registry Office	♦	♦	♦	♦

10.	Securing registry at the National Institute of Statistics	♦	♦	♦	
11.	Securing registry at Tax Department / Ministry of Finance	♦	♦	♦	♦
12.	Opening Bank Account – w/national or foreign currency	♦	♦	♦	♦
13.	Depositing a U$ 60,000 surety bond at BNA				♦
14.	Securing a Trading Permit from the Ministry of Trade	♦	♦	♦	
15.	Securing an Import/Export Permit from the Ministry of Trade	♦	♦	♦	
16.	Registering with Social Security / Ministry of Employment & Social Security	♦	♦	♦	♦

A♦ and C♦ - In the case of Foreign Investment (FI) <U$ 100,000 (Advice 6/99 of May 21, 1999 from BNA)
B♦ - In the case of Foreign Investment (FI) (Law)

THE TAX SYSTEM

TAX INCENTIVES LAW

The existence of a General Taxation Law is now standard in many States, representing an instrument to rationalize, structure and stabilize taxation systems.

In fact, when creating a legal framework attractive to private investment, there has to be, along with concerted economic and social policy instruments, an incentives and tax benefits policy.

The incentives and tax benefits to be granted within the framework of this Law constitute an exceptional tax advantage, and when it is approved, the Tax Benefits Code in it, ought to be incorporated in homage to a seamless harmonization of all substantive and procedural tax legislation.

The incentives and tax benefits defined in this Law bear in mind the priorities of reconstruction and development and come within a framework of an integrated policy, where productive investment (agriculture and industry) and human capital (health and education) and in roadway, railway, seaport, airport, telecommunications, energy and water infrastructure, are prioritized.

In these terms, and within the framework of the combined stipulations of paragraph f) of article 90, and of N° 4 of article 92, both of the Constitutional Law, the National Assembly hereby approves the following:

LAW ON INCENTIVES & TAX BENEFITS FOR PRIVATE INVESTMENT

Article 1.Scope of Application

This law regulates the procedures, types and modalities for the granting of incentives and tax benefits within the framework of the law on private investment in Angola.

Article 2.Classification Criteria

Incentives and tax benefits are classified, in agreement with three fundamental criteria:

a)   Sector of activity;

b)   Development zones;

c)   Special economic zones.

Article 3.Objectives

The granting of incentives and tax benefits for investment projects, under the terms of the following articles, is aimed at the realization of the following objectives:

a)   Production of goods of first necessity earmarked for the internal market to satisfy the population's basic necessities;

b)   Prioritized development of under-developed regions, namely those exhibiting high levels of poverty and ongoing unemployment or that do not have infrastructures, or whose infrastructures have been destroyed or need upgrading;

c)   Revamping, implantation or upgrade of infrastructures earmarked for production operations or provision of services;

d)   Improvement of productive capacity or provision of services set up in the country;

e)   Industrial diversification and promotion of the export of manufactured products;

f)   Technological innovation on the level of the production of goods or provision of services and scientific development, when translating to an increase in efficiency, quality of goods and services and productivity;

g)   Increase in productivity of business units;

h)   Creation of jobs for national workers;

i)   Professional training or enhancement of the professional qualification of entrepreneurs and national workers;

j)   Fostering of association between both national and foreign entrepreneurs in different ways;

k)   Increase and diversification in exports;

l)   Increase of incorporation of national raw materials and the value-added of goods produced locally;

m)   Progressive reduction and substitution of imports, namely in sectors of economic activity considered strategic or that, by their very nature, dimension, location or tradition, are of particular importance to the national, regional or local economy;

n)   Increase in foreign currency flowing in and corresponding improvement in balance-of-payments situation.

Article 4.Priority Sectors

Those sectors considered as priority ones, for the purposes of this law, are the following:

a)   Agri-livestock production;

b)   Manufacturing Industries, whose final product incorporates at least 25% of national raw materials and materials, or 30% of value-added, or whose equipment and production process bring about technological advancement and the upgrade of respective industry, (namely, sectors of Agri-industry, Manufacture of composts and fertilizers and foodstuffs industry, Textiles and clothing manufacture, Exploration and manufacture of lumber, Woodwork and furniture, Construction materials, Manufacture of packaging. Metallurgy and heavy engineering, Manufacture of machinery and equipment, tools and accessories, Cellulose and paper-pulp industry, Manufacture of tires and inner tubes, Milling of maize, cassava and wheat, Milk and dairy products, Artifacts and fishing, Husking and roasting of coffee, Manufacture of footwear, Industries for the manufacture of mineral products, IT and telecommunications equipment) ;

c)   Fishing industry and byproducts;

d)   Civil Construction;

e)   Health & Education;

f)   Roadway, Railway, Seaport & Airport Infrastructure, Telecommunications, Energy and Water;

g)   Heavy-duty equipment for loading and passengers.

Article 5.Development Zones

For the purposes of granting incentives and tax benefits for investment operations, the country is organized into the following development zones:

Zone A -   covers the province of Luanda and the chief municipalities of the provinces of Benguela, Huíla and Cabinda

Zone B –   the other municipalities of the provinces of Benguela, Cabinda and Huíla and provinces of Kwanza Sul, Bengo, Uíge, Kwanza Norte, Lunda Norte, Lunda Sul and Zaire

Zone C –   the provinces of Huambo, Bié, Moxico, Kuando-Kubango, Cunene, Namibe and Malange.

Article 6. Criteria for Granting Incentives

1.   The granting of incentives is assigned in relation to:
    a)   The placing of investment projects in sectors classified as priority ones;
    b)   The contribution of an investment project for development zones B and C.

2. The criteria of appreciation referred to in the previous number are not cumulative, merely constituting a simple indicator of reference for the regional or local economy.

Article 7. Requirements

Taxpayers wishing to take advantage of incentives and tax benefits, must cumulatively fulfill the following requirements:

a)   Must have the legal and tax conditions for the exercise of their activity duly in order;

b)   Not be a debtor in relation to the State, Social Security, and not be in arrears in relation to the financial system;

c)   Have an organized accounting system that is adequate to the demands of assessing and monitoring the investment project.

Article 8. Customs Duties

1.   Investment operations are exempt, for the period to be established under the terms of the following number, from the payment of duties and any other customs tariffs, with the exception of stamp duty and charges due for provision of services, on capital goods for the start-up and development of an investment operation, including heavy vehicles and technologies.

2.   The period of exemption referred to in the previous number will be of 3 years in the case of investments realized in Zone A, and of 4 and 6 years respectively, when an investment is realized in Zones B and C.

3.   When used equipment is to be imported, the exemption established in number 1 is substituted, for the period of time provided for in Nº 2, by a reduction of 50%.

4.   Investments are also exempt from the payment of duties and any other customs tariffs, with the exception of stamp duty and charges due for provision of services, on goods that were incorporated or consumed directly in the production of other goods, for a period of 5 years as of the start-up of operations, including tests.

5.   The incentives established in the previous numbers will not be granted when the capital goods, accessories and spare parts, and raw materials are produced in national territory.

Article 9.Industrial Tax

1. Profits arising out of investments, are exempt from the payment of industrial tax, for a period of 8 years, when realized in Zone A, for a period of 12 years, when realized in Zone B, or 15 years, when realized in Zone C.

2. In Zone C and for the same period, equally exempt from the payment of industrial tax due on the price of a contract, the sub-contractors engaged to execute the investment project.

3. The period of exemption is counted as of the start-up of operations of the facility.

Article 10.Expenses Considered as Losses

The following expenses in relation to the investment operations provided for in this law, can, beyond the periods of exemption established under the terms of the previous article, be considered as losses, for the purposes of assessing taxable amounts:

a) Up to 100% of all expenses realized with the construction and repair of roads, railways, telecommunications, water supply and social infrastructure for workers, their families and population in these areas;

b) Up to 100% of all expenses realized with professional training in all spheres of social and productive activity;

c) Up to 100% of all expenses resulting from investment in the cultural sector and/or purchase of works of art produced by Angolan authors or creators, provided that, when classified, they remain in the country and are not sold for a period of 10 years.

Article 11.Capital Gains Tax

1. Companies promoting the investment operations covered by this law, are exempt from the payment of capital gains tax, for the period of time stipulated in number 2 of this article, in relation to profits allocated to shareholders.

2. The exemption provided for in the previous number shall be granted for a period of up to 5 years, in relation to investments realized in Zone A and of up to 10 and 15, in the case of investments realized in Zones B and C, respectively.

Article 12. Real Estate Tax

Companies promoting the investment operations covered by this Law, are exempt from the payment of real estate tax on the acquisition of land and buildings pertaining to a project, and for which purpose they should apply for it at the appropriate tax department.

Article 13.Other Investments

Investments whose value is equal to or more than US$50,000 and lower than or equal to US$250,000, while taking into account their nature, location and importance for the regional or local economy, can benefit from the following tax incentives:

For additional analytical, business and investment opportunities information, please contact Global Investment & Business Center, USA at (202) 546-2103. Fax: (202) 546-3275. E-mail: rusric@erols.com

1. Rate lowered to half for duties and any other customs tariffs, with exception of stamp duty and charges due for services provided, on capital goods imported for construction, supply, and equipment, including vehicles of more than three and a half metric tons (3.5 tonnes) of gross weight and raw materials, namely:

   a) Investments in new enterprises, with a positive impact on the region and that also include construction and/or revamping of economic or social infrastructure;

   b) Investments for expansion, revamping or upgrade of commercial or industrial facilities, especially those destroyed by war;

   c) Investments in priority sectors and/or in Zone C;

   d) Investments guaranteeing the creation of more than 10 exclusively dedicated jobs for national workers.

2. When already-used equipment is to be imported, the rate referred to in number 1 shall be lowered by 75%.

3. The incentives established in the previous number will only be granted when the equipment, accessories and spare parts to be imported are not produced in national territory or, when so produced, they certifiably do not fulfill the requirements inherent to the nature of the project to be put in place.

4. Exempt from payment of industrial tax, for a period of up to 10 years, are:

   a) Investments in new enterprises and the revamping of destroyed or paralyzed enterprises, provided that they are realized in priority areas (Zone C) ;

   b) Investments in the areas of agriculture, livestock and foodstuffs industry;

   c) Investments creating 50 or more exclusively dedicated jobs for national citizens.

5. Exempt from the payment of industrial tax, for a period of up to 5 years are:

   a) Investments in new enterprises, the revamping, enlarging, or upgrading of paralyzed enterprises, realized in Zones A and B;

   b) Investments in sectors of light industry, housing, provision of specialized services, technological development;

   c) Investments creating 30 or more exclusively dedicated jobs for national citizens.

6. Exempt from payment of capital gains tax, are those profits allocated to the shareholders of companies that make investments:

   a) In the provinces of Zones A and B, for a period of up to 5 years;

   b) In the provinces of Zone C for a period of up to 10 years.

Article 14.Medium & Long Haul Transportation

For additional analytical, business and investment opportunities information,
please contact Global Investment & Business Center, USA
at (202) 546-2103. Fax: (202) 546-3275. E-mail: rusric@erols.com

1. Exempt from the payment of customs duties is the importation of new resources, by individual or corporate persons, operating in the medium and long haul transportation of cargo or passengers by means of coastal shipping and vehicles of more than three and a half metric tons (3.5 tonnes) of gross weight.

2. When the exemption concerns used resources, up to three (3) years, the applicable rate is lowered by 50%.

Article 15.Private Education Establishments & Clinics

1. The income from private education establishments integrated in the national educational system, as well as clinics integrated into the national health system, is subject to income tax at the rate of 20%.
2. The rate established in the previous number shall be lowered to 10% whenever the educational establishment and private clinics freely offer 10% of their capacity to students coming from underprivileged backgrounds, under terms that will be eventually regulated

Article 16.Special Economic Zones

Incentives for the investments to be realized in the special economic zones will be defined in a specific law.

Article 17.Legal Obligations

1. Entitlement to standard-type tax incentives, resulting directly and immediately from law, neither releases the taxpayer from the General Taxpayers Register nor from compliance with any other legal obligations and formalities prescribed by the tax administration, with a view to proving their entitlement to the incentive.
2. Exercising entitlement to any of the standard-type tax incentives provided for in this law, takes place when tax obligations have been met, by showing verification of the presuppositions established for the incentive in question.

Article 18.Recognition of Incentives & Tax Benefits

Incentives and tax benefits are automatic, resulting directly and immediately from the law.

Article 19.Prior Consultation

1. Before verifying the presuppositions of the tax incentives provided for in the law, or even before start-up of the project, interested parties can ask the Investment Promotion Agency to officially pronounce on a given taxation situation not yet realized.

2. The official reply made to a formal request, submitted under the terms of the previous number, shall be communicated to the interested party, and be binding on the services, which, once the facts provided for in law have been verified, cannot proceed differently, save in compliance with a court decision.

3. Recourse cannot be had to lodging a complaint or appeal in respect of the official reply referred to in the previous number and does not release the interested parties from requesting recognition of the respective tax benefit, under the terms of the law.

4.   Once a request for recognition has been submitted, and has been preceded by a prior consultation, this shall be attached to the interested party's formal request. The entity authorized to grant recognition must conform with the previous official reply, insofar as the hypothetical situation that is the subject of the prior consultation coincides with the de facto situation that is the subject of the request for recognition, without prejudice to measures of control for the tax benefit demanded by law.

Article 20.Delivery of Processes

Copies of all processes approved must be sent to the Ministry of Finance, by way of the National Departments of Customs and of Taxes.

Article 21.Inspection

Individual or corporate persons, public or private, that are granted incentives and tax benefits, whether automatic or dependent on recognition, are subject to inspection by the Investment Promotion Agency and of any other official entities, under the terms of the law, in order to check observance of the presuppositions on which the granting of incentives and tax benefits depends and of compliance with obligations imposed on taxpayers benefiting from them.

Article 22.Sanctions

Sanctions to impede, suspend or extinguish incentives and tax benefits are only permitted on the grounds of tax-related infringements in respect of the benefits granted.

Article 23.

Extinction of Incentives & Tax Benefits

1. Incentives and tax benefits are extinguished by:
   a)   termination of the period for which they have been granted, when temporary ones;
   b)   verification of the presuppositions of the respective condition resolving them, when so conditioned;
   c)   revocation, in case of non-fulfillment, by virtue of a fact attributable to the taxpayer, of their legal or contractual obligations.

2. The extinction of incentives and tax benefits automatically leads to the general taxation system being reinstated .

3. When incentives and tax benefits involve the acquisition of goods earmarked for investment operations, the respective concession will be invalidated if these goods are divested or given some other destiny without authorization of the National Private Investment Agency (ANIP) , without prejudice to any other sanctions or consequences established in law.

Article 24.Assignment of Incentives & Tax Benefits

1. Entitlement to incentives and tax benefits is assignable, through prior authorization of the Minister of Finance, with the National Private Investment Agency (ANIP) having been heard, provided that the presuppositions on which their concession is based and the obligations arising out of the investment project are maintained, with the proponent having to be notified within eight (8) days following reception of a petition.

For additional analytical, business and investment opportunities information,
please contact Global Investment & Business Center, USA
at (202) 546-2103. Fax: (202) 546-3275. E-mail: rusric@erols.com

Article 25.Transitory System

1. Incentives and tax benefits granted before this law's enactment are subject to that stipulated in prevailing legislation at the date of their concession.
2. The stipulation in the previous number is equally applicable to incentives and tax benefits that have been requested before this law's enactment and whose decision is to be proffered following that date.
3. Investments realized between January 1 and December 31, 2002 can be granted the incentives and tax benefits provided for in this law, provided that by decision of the Investment Promotion Agency, they are considered relevant for national, regional or local economic development, promote the creation of jobs and fulfill any other prerequisites provided for in this law.
4. For the purposes of that stipulated in number 3 of this article, investors must apply for, up to 60 days following the date of this law's enactment, the granting of these incentives and tax benefits.
5. Benefits granted within the framework of that stipulated in the previous number are not cumulative with any others.

Article 26.Doubts & Omissions

Any doubts and omissions arising out of the interpretation and application of this law, are resolved by the National Assembly.

Article 27.Repeal

All legislation contrary to that stipulated in this law, namely, Decree Nº 73/97, of October 24, 1997 is hereby repealed.

Article 28.Enactment

This law comes into force on the date of its publication.
Seen and approved by the National Assembly, in Luanda,
The Speaker of the National Assembly, **Roberto António Víctor Francisco de Almeida**
The President of the Republic, **José Eduardo dos Santos.**

THE FINANCIAL SYSTEM

Reforms put in place in the financial sector have been aimed at reinforcing monetary controls, reducing intervention costs, and increasing savings accounts. All of which are hampered by the limits imposed by the country's current economic situation.

Throughout this process, the monetary authorities (Ministry of Finance and National Bank of Angola) have been active in drafting legislation to attain such goals.

In 1999, the Bank of Angola allowed an exchange-rate flotation of the Kwanza, while creating the Interbank Exchange Market. It likewise abolished restrictions on the acquisition of foreign exchange for imports, liberalized the commercial banks' active and passive interest rates, and introduced its own Central Bank Securities, as a first step in the creation of instruments to indirectly control the country's monetary policy.
In 1999, the Bank of Angola also authorized commercial banks to grant loans in foreign exchange to exporters.

In April 1999, the National Assembly passed the Financial Institutions Law (Law Nº 1/99, of April 23) , seen as the basic instrument laying the groundwork for the financial sector.
This law introduces rules and regulations governing the process of setting up business, supervision, and the turning around of credit institutions and financial entities.
All enterprises entrusted by the public to receive deposits or other reimbursable funds, put to work in turn by these institutions in offering credit, are classified as credit institutions.

Under these provisions, the following are considered credit institutions (i) banks, (ii) finance houses/leasing companies, and (iii) loan cooperatives.

Classified as financial enterprises are those companies that are not credit institutions, whose activities are defined by Law 1/99 (in accordance with a specialization principle) , and that can only operate in conformity with the legal rules and regulations governing such activities.
The following types of activity may operate as financial enterprises:

Financial management and venture capital services, unit trust and annuity management, factoring and strategic alliances, financial brokerage, personal/business investment management, real estate investment, insurance companies, pension funds and asset management, and exchange bureaus.

All credit institutions and financial enterprise dealings, except those as determined under the terms of a special law, are subject to supervision by the Bank of Angola. The minimum capital required for the formation of banks is US$4 million.
At present the following banking institutions are an active part of the Angolan financial system:

COMMERCIAL BANKS

Public Institutions
Banco de Poupança e Crédito
Banco de Comércio e Indústria

Private Institutions
Banco Comercial Angolano

Branches of
Banco de Fomento
Banco Totta & Açores
Banco Português do Atlantico

INVESTMENT BANKS
Private Institutions
Banco Africano de Investimento – African Investment Bank

Equally active are the representative offices for the following institutions:
  Citibank
  Equator Bank
  Banco Espírito Santo
  Banque Paribas

Slated for 2000, is the successful conclusion of the extinction and liquidation of the Caixa de Crédito Agro-Pecuária e Pescas. Completion of the restructuring and capitalization of the other public banks paving the way for a phased-out privatization process is also planned.
The publication of Law 1/2000, of February 3, 2000, opened up the insurance business to private enterprise.

An activity that had been, up until then, exercised solely by ENSA – Empresa Nacional de Seguros de Angola, a state monopoly. Law 1/2000 therefore became the regulatory instrument governing all insurance-related operations and brokers in Angola.

For additional analytical, business and investment opportunities information,
please contact Global Investment & Business Center, USA
at (202) 546-2103. Fax: (202) 546-3275. E-mail: rusric@erols.com

Insurance companies are now supervised by the Institute for the Supervision of Insurance (Instituto de Supervisão de Seguros) , which reports direct to the Ministry of Finance.
The formation of insurance companies with recourse to foreign investment requires that at least 60% of the foreign capital must originate from insurance and financial institutions and at least 30% of the capital has to come from national entities.
Additionally, the Foreign Investment Law applies to the insurance industry's general obligations.

COMMERCIAL REGULATIONS

The Ministry of Commerce is the entity responsible for defining and establishing general commercial policy guidelines in Angola, both within its internal and external scope.

Other important entities carrying out and supervising external trade are the National Bank of Angola, General Customs Directorate, National Board of Stevedores and General Supervisory Bureau.

GENERAL IMPORTATION RULES

All entities (individuals or corporate) , whether private, state-run or cooperative, intending to be involved with import operations must be registered with regional divisions and sub-divisions of the Ministry of Commerce.

Registration as an importer or exporter is made through payment of a bond, organized on a sliding scale. This does not apply to re-export operations, temporary imports and the return of imported goods.

Whether operated by individuals, corporate bodies or cooperatives, those entities involved in farming, livestock-rearing, mining/quarrying or manufacturing industries, hospitality business, railroads, ports, public works concessions and contracts, and civil construction, all belong to a single classification with authorization to import equipment, including maintenance and raw materials essential to performing these activities.

As a general rule, imports of goods into Angola are subject to the prior issue of a license and the subsequent issue of an import registration certificate (Boletim de Registo de Importação - BRI) , which will be issued by the relevant authority based on limits imposed by the national plan and foreign currency available at the time.

When importing spare parts, accessories, pharmaceuticals, or equipment intended for the industrial sector and raw materials valued at or below US$50,000 per quarter, per registered enterprise, no import license is required.

Multiple BRIs should be filled out on the proper form by the importer and are available in the offices and regional bureaus of the Ministry Commerce. Import licenses for goods are valid for 180 days from the date of issue and cannot be extended beyond that period.

Trade agreements follow the usual acceptable international rules while preference is given to the FOB type.

Prior licensing for the import of goods adheres to the following priority listing:

For additional analytical, business and investment opportunities information,
please contact Global Investment & Business Center, USA
at (202) 546-2103. Fax: (202) 546-3275. E-mail: rusric@erols.com

"   1st Priority

Raw materials and subsidiaries, as well as intermediate products for industry;

Equipment intended for productive activities and development;

Individual parts and spare parts;

Fertilizer, seeds and vegetable goods for economic development;

Pharmaceuticals;

Basic products to satisfy the essential needs of the people, in those cases of proven lack of local production;

Other goods directly related to economic progress and public health;

"   2nd Priority

Goods considered of an essential nature that will not compete with local production;

"   3rd. Priority

Goods considered essential to people's well-being;

"   4th Priority

Non-essential and/or luxury types of goods that will not compete with local production;

"   5th Priority

Goods whose local production may or may not directly or indirectly satisfy market needs.

IMPORT RESTRICTIONS & CONTINGENCIES

Restrictions directly related to imports will only be established or enforced when they are indispensably required to ease the adaptation of economic activities and production to new competition scenarios or should difficulties affect the national productive sector of a region or the country, always taking into consideration the multilateral agreements signed by Angola.

The import of goods is free, but importers should be aware of and obey the restrictions pertaining to prohibited products, as set by the Government.

When the import of certain goods is subject to quantitative restrictions the Ministry of Commerce is the entity authorized to allow the concession of a contingent exception, while allotting the initial amount and, whenever feasible, the subsequent pace of increase.

For additional analytical, business and investment opportunities information,
please contact Global Investment & Business Center, USA
at (202) 546-2103. Fax: (202) 546-3275. E-mail: rusric@erols.com

Import restrictions ought to cease as soon as the causes triggering such restrictions are deemed at an end by the supervisory entity.

EXPORT-IMPOT DOCUMENTATION

Commercial Invoice

A minimum of two copies in English or Portuguese is required

Pro-forma Invoice

This is requested from the importer in order that a license can be issued. It must contain an accurate description of goods to be imported, country of origin, name of manufacturer or supplier, itemized description of product and technical specifications, quantities and net weight or measurement unit, unit price, clear description of payment terms & conditions, port of origin, packing list containing full description of the contents and type of packaging of the goods.

Certificate of Origin

This document may, as required under the terms of a letter of credit or other document, be requested by either the importer or bank.

An officer of the exporting company or a representative should sign this document and have it certified by the exporting country's chamber of commerce.

Sanitary Certificate

A sanitary certificate is required for the importation of seeds, plants, animals and animal products. When dealing with perishable consumer goods a phyto-sanitary certificate by a national commerce laboratory and certification by the Health Officer is mandatory.

Bill of Lading

As established by the Angolan National Board of Stevedores and under Decree No. 19/94 of May 20, 1994, presentation of the bill of lading is necessary, which will determine the harbor fee to be levied on the following basis:

US$ 100/ton for a 20-foot container

US$ 200/ton for a 40-foot container

US$ 5 /ton/m3 for bulk/conventional

mport License

The majority of imports must be accompanied by this license. Licenses are granted by the Ministry of Commerce, and should be acquired before the importer places the shipping order.

Certificate of Inspection

For additional analytical, business and investment opportunities information,
please contact Global Investment & Business Center, USA
at (202) 546-2103. Fax: (202) 546-3275. E-mail: rusric@erols.com

All goods imported into Angola must have been inspected prior to embarkation by the Société Géneral de Surveillance (SGS) . This certificate serves as proof of quality, quantity and prices of the goods exported to Angola.

By law, all goods imported into Angola whose value is equal to or higher than US$5,000, or partial shipments, whose CIF value is equal or lower to that amount, when the total value of a shipment reaches or exceeds that figure, must be subjected to prior embarkation inspection.

Specific legislation exists for certain products and it should be noted that seeds, plants, animals and animal products being imported must be accompanied by a sanitary certificate from the country of origin and that pharmaceuticals must be registered in advance with the Angolan Ministry of Health.

CUSTOM TARIFFS AND OTHER TAXES

The Angolan Customs Tariffs' classification used is that of the Customs Cooperation Board. Preparations are under way for transfer to the Harmonized System of Designation and Codification of Goods. A new tariff was introduced in 1990 that replaced specific duties by "ad valorem" duties calculated on the cost, insurance and freight (CIF) of goods.

Imported goods are subject to either the general tariff or maximum tariff.

The general tariff applies to all goods imported with proper certificates of origin (products from the European Market are taxed at levels similar to those coming from commercial-partner countries) . Products are taxed based on their classification as essential, necessary, useful, superfluous or luxury goods. Tariffs generally fluctuate between 2% and 40%, but may reach 80%, or 135%, as in the case of goods made of ivory, platinum or the pelts of endangered species.

The maximum tariff is generally applied when goods are imported without accompanying documentation. The maximum tariff corresponds to twice the regular tariff, and may never be lower than 10%.

Imported essential goods (foodstuffs, medical and surgical equipment) , as well as raw materials, capital equipment, pesticides, parts and accessories for the productive sector, are exempt from customs tariffs.

Goods intended for fairs and exhibitions, automobiles, machinery and equipment can be imported under a temporary authorization, for up to two years, with suspension of all duties.

Besides custom tariffs, importers should take into consideration consumption taxes; these add 10% to the CIF cost of certain goods.

EXPORT AUTHORIZATION

The exportation of goods from Angola requires quantity and quality control, as well as authorization by the regional divisions and sub-divisions of the Ministry of Commerce.

On the other hand, businesses duly authorized to export should present statistical data and information to that Ministry.

For additional analytical, business and investment opportunities information,
please contact Global Investment & Business Center, USA
at (202) 546-2103. Fax: (202) 546-3275. E-mail: rusric@erols.com

TRADE AND INVESTMENT REGULATION AND INCENTIVES

INVESTMENT IN ANGOLA

Most investments still take place in the offshore oil-sector, although investment in other sectors appears to be growing now as well. Angola ranks relatively high on investor security at number 46 worldwide. On the other hand, lengthy bureaucratic processes and other factors still make investing challenging. Lucrative investments are therefore will require patience and will be easier with good contacts. A loyal Angolan business partner is thereby also very important. There is currently no bilateral investment protection agreement (IBO) with Angola.

The Angolan government is aiming to attract more investment with recently introduced tax breaks and the reformed private investment law.

Tax incentives last between 8 to 15 years and include untaxed profit and custom exemption for the import of equipment. There are two factors that influence the applicability and duration of the tax break. Firstly, in which of the three specified investment zones in Angola is invested. Luanda for example is in Zone A and therefore has tax breaks lasting for 8 years, while in Huambo (Zone C) it is 15 years. Secondly, certain areas are considered *priority sectors by the Angolan government. Infrastructure, agriculture and the building industry for example fall within this category.*

Some of the recent legal reforms introduced include:

- the reduction of minimum investment from USD 250,000 to USD 100,000
- the shortening of approbation-period for investments to 15 days
- an investment is approved by issuing a CRIP (Registry Certificate of Private Investment) which also lists the fiscal and customs incentives applicable to the investment

The Angolan investment agency ANIP is now the first point of contact for potential investors. Please refer to their website for complete information on investment in Angola: ➩ http://www/investinangola.org/ingles/default.asp .

IMPORT REGULATIONS OF ANGOLA

A brief guide on the regulations of goods imported in Angola (taxation, documents, etc) , can be requested from the Angolan National Directorate of Customs. Please refer to:
✉ alfandegasdeangola@hotmail.com / tel: (+244) 222 339 490 / 372 600

SUBSIDIES

There are a number of subsidies available from the Dutch and European government institutions that Dutch companies may use for business in Angola. This information can be found at the website of the EVD (part of the Ministry of Economic Affairs) . Please refer to: ➩ http://www.evd.nl/
Important Dutch subsidy programs:

- ORET (Development Related Export Transactions) . Organised via the FMO on behalf of the Ministry of foreign affairs. This subsidy covers up to 50 % of the financing of investments in local infrastructure whereby Dutch or foreign capital goods or services are necessary. Examples are roads, harbours, healthcare, education, etc. For more information, please refer to: ➩ www.fmo.nl / ➩ oret@fmo.nl / ➩ africa@fmo.nl

---

- PESP (Program for Economic Corporation Projects) . Organised by the EVD. The programme provides two thirds of the financing for technical or commercial feasibility studies for a project or investment. These entail activities which eventually will lead to actual export transactions. Dutch companies, in cooperation with Angolan enterprises, can apply for this facility. For more information, please refer to: ➡ www.evd.nl/pesp/➡ pesp@info.evd.nl

Important European subsidy programs:

Please refer to the department of Trade and Industry Support of the Dutch permanent representation with the EU in Brussels. They are willing to inform you how Dutch companies can participate in relevant tenders via the EOF (European Development Fund) . For more information, please refer to:
Hermann Debrouxlaan 48, 1160 Brussel, tel. 00 322 679 1537/34
➡ http://www.eu-nederland.be / ✉ nlbreaob@euronet.be

EXPORT CREDIT FINANCING

At the moment there is no Atradius (formerly NCM) export credit financing available on the medium term for transactions with Angola (EKV-facility) . This might change in due course if Angola manages to come to an agreement with the IMF on restructuring the repayment of the debt. Please refer to: ➡ http://www.atradius.com

LEADING SECTORS FOR U.S. EXPORTS AND INVESTMENT

BEST PROSPECTS FOR NON-AGRICULTURAL GOODS AND SERVICES

USED CLOTHING

Given the population's limited purchasing power, used clothing is in great demand.

USED EQUIPMENT/VEHICLES

Used equipment and vehicles -- particularly trucks -- are in demand.

COMPUTERS AND COMPUTER PERIPHERALS

U.S. products occupy about one-half the growing Angola market for computers and computer peripherals.

AID PROJECTS

The World Bank, USAID, other donors, and many non-governmental organizations (NGOs) are active in Angola. Traditionally, most donor organizations have engaged in emergency relief, provision of food and medicine, mine clearing and community development. As Angola completes it transition to peace and political stability, development assistance will focus more on rehabilitation and reconstruction and will therefore present greater opportunities for sales and investment. The terms of reference for development projects, such as a recently awarded consulting contract for a major water-distribution system rehabilitation project, are published. All bids are awarded competitively.

TELECOMMUNICATIONS

Substantial improvements in this sector are required, and as such represent a long-term opportunity for U.S. firms. Despite Government of Angola support for such schemes, financing of major projects will remain difficult to obtain for the foreseeable future.

BEST PROSPECTS FOR AGRICULTURAL PRODUCTS

Angola has fertile soil and excellent climate for crops as varied as cotton, sugar, and coffee. The near total lack of infrastructure in this sector presents a significant opportunity for U.S. firms. However, related projects, including road building and minefield clearance, must take place before this sector will achieve its potential.

Angola has in recent years been a recipient of U.S. Department of Agriculture PL-480 Title I program foodstuffs, including vegetable oil, beans, rice, wheat, and wheat flour. The explosion in urban population combined with the hurdles faced by the agriculture sector mean that Angola will likely continue to be a large potential market for U.S. commodities.

MARKETING PRODUCTS AND SERVICES

DISTRIBUTION AND SALES CHANNELS

Product distribution in Angola can be problematic because of poor transportation infrastructure. Anti-personnel mines are found on some rural roads, and others become unusable during the rainy season. Banditry, violent crime, and undisciplined police and troops also pose a significant impediment to internal commerce. Some local companies have a network of rural distributors, but many firms opt to reach rural markets through wholesale arrangements with local entrepreneurs.

USE OF AGENTS AND DISTRIBUTORS

Subsidiary or affiliate companies of U.S. organizations operate in several areas including computers/office equipment, petroleum products, and agro-industry. Finding partners or agents and distributors for U.S. products is possible, though financial arrangements can be problematic.

FRANCHISING

There are no restrictions on franchising in Angola.

DIRECT MARKETING

The Angolan business community is aware of only a limited selection of the large range of U.S. products. A U.S. company may market directly through an established importer in Angola, by winning a tender, through investment, or by opening an office in Angola. At present over half of all consumer goods are imported from Portugal; other important suppliers include France and South Africa. Competitive pricing and reliability of supply are essential to enter and stay in the Angolan market.

JOINT VENTURES/LICENSING

The Government of Angola allows joint ventures under the foreign investment law, which also regulates the amount and form of capital invested. If an investment (including setting up a foreign representative office, even if not directly linked to capital importing operations) is valued at more than $250,000 and less than $5 million it is subject to the "Prior Declaration Regime", in which competent authorities (including government ministries and the Foreign Investment Institute) must approve the project. If an investment is valued at more than $5 million and less than $50 million it is subject to the "Prior Approval Regime", in which approval must be granted by both the competent authorities, the Ministry of Planning, the Prime Minister, and, in cases where the investment is over $15 million, the Council of Ministers. If an investment is valued at more than $50 million or involves activities that can only be carried out by concession (such as oil and diamond exploration and production) it is subject to the "Contractual Regime", in which a contract must be established defining project objectives, tax benefits and incentives to be granted, and government monitoring of project development. The contract is subject to the approval of the competent authorities, the Ministry of Planning, the Prime Minister, and the Council of Ministers. Joint ventures must also be licensed by the Ministry of Commerce.

ESTABLISHING AN OFFICE

The Government of Angola officially supports foreign businesses interested in establishing agency, franchise, joint venture, or licensing relationships. The Angolan Foreign Investment Institute distributes "A Summary for Investors" upon request. Other Angolan organizations useful in establishing commercial links with Angola are: the Angola Chamber of Commerce and Industry, and the U.S.-Angola Chamber of Commerce.

ADVERTISING/TRADE PROMOTION

Angola has one government-owned television network and several A.M. and F.M. radio stations, as well as a daily newspaper with a circulation of approximately 10,000 copies per day. A small but vocal alternative press is present in Luanda and accepts advertising. Billboard advertising is also common. Product advertisement can be done through these channels.

SELLING TO THE GOVERNMENT

The Government of Angola solicits bids for supplies and services in local and international publications 15 to 90 days before the bids are due. Bid documents are normally obtained from a specific government ministry, department or agency at a non-refundable fee. Completed bids, accompanied by a specified security deposit, are usually submitted directly to the ministry in question. Bids are often opened in the presence of bidders or their representatives. The Embassy sends TOP cables on major public bids. The bidding process often does not meet minimal standards of objectivity and transparency. Many U.S. firms engaged in selling goods or services to the government have experienced delays ranging from months to years in receiving payment.

PROTECTING YOUR PRODUCT FROM IPR INFRINGEMENT

In Angola, the attribution of intellectual property rights is regulated by: (a) the Ministry of Industry (trademarks, patents, designs) , and (b) the Ministry of Culture (authorship, literary and artistic rights) . Intellectual property is protected via the "Industrial Property Law" (3/92) . Law 4/90 regulates the attribution and protection of copyrights. To the Embassy's knowledge, no court cases testing the strength of these laws involving U.S. intellectual property have been filed. Results from other legal cases involving U.S. investors suggest that a U.S. firm cannot rely on the Angolan judiciary to protect its rights.

Angola is a member of the World International Property Organization (WIPO) and makes use of its international classification of patents and of the international classification of products and services to identify and codify the requests for invention patents and for the registration of trademarks. Each petition for patent that is accepted will be subject to a fee that varies by type of request.

NEED FOR A LOCAL ATTORNEY

A local attorney is required only when preparing "Articles of Association" before registering a company. The U.S. Embassy can provide a list of lawyers or interested parties may seek a lawyer through referrals or other sources of information. The U.S. Embassy strongly recommends the use of a lawyer and the preparation of a binding contract prior to any business dealing, including rental or lease of real property. The lawyer should also conduct due diligence investigations prior to the conclusion of any purchase or other contractual agreement. Oral agreements in Angola are not legally enforceable.

TRADE AND PROJECT FINANCING

BANKING SYSTEM

Angola's central bank, the Banco National de Angola (BNA) , only recently renounced its role as commercial bank. It continues to intervene in the business practices of state-owned commercial banks. Nearly all state-owned banks are undercapitalized and cannot be privatized because their existing structures are not economically viable. A few Portuguese banks operate in Angola but are subject to restrictive regulation in their lending activities.

The Caixa de Credito Agro-Pecuaria e Pescas (CAP) was established in 1991 under a special banking law. It is wholly owned by the Ministry of Finance. In 1996, BNA transferred all its commercial operations to CAP. CAP loans, often on concessionary or even interest-free terms, have been used by the government to provide off-budget financing for parastatal entities. These activities have obscured budgetary accountability and threaten to weaken the banking system. In June 1998 published reports indicate that CAP liquidity problems have significantly delayed clearing checks, and that some enterprises, both state-run and private, no longer accept CAP checks. CAP employs a staff of 1,800 in 4 branches in Luanda and 20 branches in the provinces.

Banco de Comercio e Industria (BCI) is a semi-private bank, with 40 percent of shares owned by the Government of Angola. BCI's loan portfolio is predominately short- and medium-term debt on which it has difficulty collecting. The government has on occasion restricted BCI's lending to all but government programs. In 1997 BCI had 12 branches and 298 employees.

Banco Africano de Investimentos (BAI) , the only investment bank in Angola, was founded in 1997.

Banco de Poupanca e Credito (BPC) reports that 80 percent of its credit activity is addressed to small and medium enterprises (primarily to the trade sector) and 20 percent to large enterprises (principally construction) . Short-term credit accounted for the majority of loans.
BPC has 37 branches and employs 1500 workers.

Banco Fomento Exterior and Banco Totta e Azores, Portuguese commercial banks, operate in Angola. Citibank and Equator Bank have representative offices in Luanda.

FOREIGN EXCHANGE CONTROLS AFFECTING TRADE

The foreign exchange regime is not transparent, and the government sets the official rate. The government has recently imposed limits of foreign exchange transactions, as well as a list of imports for which foreign exchange may be purchased. These policies distort the local market considerably, resulting in inadequate imports, inflated consumer prices, and a flourishing parallel currency exchange market. In July 1998, the rates were $1.00 equals Kzr 365,661 (official) and Kzr 560,000 (parallel market) .

GENERAL FINANCING AVAILABILITY

Local financing for hard-currency-denominated transactions can be problematic; i.e., during shortages of foreign exchange. No local capital market exists, the insurance industry has not yet been privatized, and the few commercial banks in Angola are undercapitalized. Interest-bearing term deposits exist, as do non-interest-bearing on-demand checking accounts. There is no formal government-backed system of deposit protection. Local banks do not issue credit cards, and few businesses accept credit cards.

EXPORT FINANCING AND INSURANCE

Angola has an OPIC Investment Guarantee Agreement. Angola is "off-cover" for the U.S. Export-Import Bank, however Ex-Im will consider lending on a case-by-case basis where the project is secured by future oil production.

AVAILABILITY OF PROJECT FINANCING

Due its poor repayment record, Angola is encountering difficulty in securing project financing for all projects except those guaranteed by oil production. Under the Cabinda Trust arrangement, projects in the petroleum sector can receive financing secured by future oil production. Non-Cabinda Trust loans that are available are often short term and at high interest rates.

TRADE AND INVESTMENT OPPORTUNITIES

Angola needs a much more vibrant and competitive private sector to diversify the economy and promote employment. With its diverse natural resources, climatic variability, and strategic location in Africa, Angola has massive potential to develop a diverse economy based on production and export of agricultural goods, manufactures, and services. 99 Percent of Angola's exports comprise oil and diamonds. At the same time, the country imports a significant proportion of its food requirements, and nearly all its capital and consumer goods. **The government is starting to recognize the importance of attracting private investment, and is taking steps to improve the investment climate.** The government has started to recognize that private sector investment, expertise, and drive are essential to create jobs, deliver services, and diversify the economy from its dependence on the volatile oil and diamond sectors. To reduce the cost of doing business, the government is investing heavily in infrastructure, including roads, railways, and electricity generation and transmission. It is managing its macro-economy reasonably well, although an overvalued exchange rate threatens the competitiveness of local producers of non-oil products. The government has simplified, streamlined, and speeded up its customs services. This has reduced the time required to process customs paperwork to an average of 5 days in 2006 from 25 days in 2000. The government has adopted a new legislation aimed at streamlining the regulatory framework and clarifying land rights. It has also taken steps to improve access to financial services, including microfinance, by allowing new entrants into the market.

For additional analytical, business and investment opportunities information,
please contact Global Investment & Business Center, USA
at (202) 546-2103. Fax: (202) 546-3275. E-mail: rusric@erols.com

Please find below a short description per sector to find out what the opportunities are. These sectors are: the Oil , Banking and Insurance, Mining, Agriculture, Consumergoods, Buiding and Infrastructure, Hotel and Tourism and Water and Energy.

OIL SECTOR

Economy growth is almost entirely driven by rising oil production which surpassed 1.9 million barrels per day in late-2007 and which is 2 million barrels per day. 99 Percent of Angola's exports comprise oil and diamonds. Control of the oil industry is consolidated in ➡ Sonangol Group, a conglomerate which is owned by the Angolan government. In December 2006, Angola was admitted as a member of ➡ OPEC. The vast majority of Angola's exports (95% in 2007) , are petroleum products. U.S. companies account for more than half the investment in Angola, with Chevron-Texaco and French Total leading the way. The oil sector is the major product and source of foreign currency earnings, a modern industry, using up-to-date technology, offering a high degree of profitability. Some figures:

Angola Crude-Oil Production and Projects per breakdown:
Current (2007-08) Angola oil production (total by operator, numbers are approximate)

Chevron	620,000 BOPD
Total	550,000 BOPD
ExxonMobil (Esso)	520,000 BOPD
Sonangol	110,000 BOPD
BP	100,000 BOPD
Total Production	1,900,000 BOPD

Angola – world records setting projects
14.0 billion barrels oil discovered in the past 11 years in the deepwater (proven + potential) ;
Total- operated Girassol FPSO (200,000 BOPD) was world´s Largest FPSO;
Esso-operated Kizomba FPSO (250,000 BOPD) is currently world´s largest FPSO;
Chevron-operated Sanha (Block 0) is world´s first LPG FPSO.

Angola – world class projects
Sonangol estimates expenditures of $40-$50 bln in next 10 years, equivalent to $4-$5 billion per year;
Chevron's Benguela-Belize Compliant-Piled Tower (CPT) in Block 14 installed in 400 meters water is the 5th largest free standing structure in the world and the tallest man-made structure in Africa;
Highly productive deep water wells, e.g. a BP Block 18 well with >28,000 BOPD estimated maximum production capacity (reference Universo Issue #11) .

ANGOLA LNG PROJECT

$4 billion project being constructed near town of Soyo, northern Angola;
Purpose is to commercialize gas currently being flared;
Partners are Sonangol, Chevron, BP, Total and ENI;
Will be on-stream in 2012 producing 5 million tons per year LNG for world markets.
Please refer to our newsletter for the latest developments in this sector.

BANKING AND INSURANCE SECTOR

The financial system is only in its infancy. Barely 5 percent of the population has a bank account. The market, which is still not sufficiently oriented towards the costumer, has everything to give. Only recently, a plan was adopted that foresees the payment of salaries to civil servants to go via bank accounts, or a scheme to issue and accept credit cards, initially Visa. The financial system is daring a frontier moment, producing at the same time a strong growth in the deposit basis and on the other hand an increased competition with the entry of new players that are making banks more aggressive and segmented. In general, the Angolan banking sector is living a renaissance. New banking groups are to start up activities during the next months and more than ten have

For additional analytical, business and investment opportunities information,
please contact Global Investment & Business Center, USA
at (202) 546-2103. Fax: (202) 546-3275. E-mail: rusric@erols.com

already signalled their interest to seek necessary authorisations to be able to operate on the national market. The National Bank of Angola (BNA) will hand out new licences by the dropper to cash in its political triumph.

Hence, Africa's biggest bank by assets, Standard Bank, plans to invest about USD 25 million in Angola to set up a commercial and investment bank and offer retail banking services. Standard Bank, which has applied to the Angolan government to convert its current representative office into a bank, met Angolan President José Eduardo dos Santos in Luanda. According to Standard Bank's chief executive, the bank was looking at developing a universal bank in Angola. The Dutch/Belgium Fortis Bank opened a credit line valued USD 500 million to BPC Bank (Banco de Poupança e Crédito) to finance public investment projects. BPC's management believes that the credit line may reach USD 1 billion. In December 2007, Millennium BCP and Sonangol reached a preliminary agreement whereby Sonangol and a private Angolan bank would take a 49.99 percent stake in Millennium's banking operation in Angola. Consequently, in May 2008 Millennium BCP Bank (Banco Comercial Português), sold 49.9 percent of its Angolan operations to state-owned oil group Sonangol and Banco Privado Atlantico (BPA).

The Angolan Stocks and Securities Exchange (BVDA) will probably open in 2008. The BVDA would like to begin trading shares from as many firms as possible to develop into an international capital market. Some of the companies associated with the Luanda stock exchange are Sonangol, ENSA, Endiama, Port of Luanda, BIC, BAI, BFA, BPC and Millennium Angola banks.

Banking in Angola requires a good knowledge about the country's financial system. Angola is home to many banks, including many privately owned, often international banks, and several governmental banks. These banks cover most banking needs. Banks in Angola can be used by (Dutch) companies, but there are special issues that you need to address when you deal with them. The main banks in Angola are as follows: BFA (Banco de Fomento Angola), BPC (Banco de Poupança e Crédito) BAI (Banco Angolano de Investimento), Banco Totta, BCA (Banco Comercial Angolano), BIC (Banco Internacional de Crédito), BCI (Banco de Comercio e Industria), Banco Atlântico, BANC (Banco Angolano de Negocio e Comercio), BNI (Banco de Negócios Internacionais) and BDA (Banco de Desenvolvimento de Angola).

Please refer to our newsletter for the latest developments in this sector.

MINING SECTOR

Angola is a source of top quality gemstones, and the Lundas region is one of the most important diamond-producing areas in the world. It is estimated that the subsoil contains 35 of the 45 most important minerals in the world trade. The country's diamonds production in 2007 reached 9.7 million carats, estimated at USD 1.3 million. Angola's State-owned National Company of Diamonds (Endiama E.P.) expects to increase its annual production from 9 million to 10 million carats of diamond this year. Therefore in March 2008, the Angolan Government formalised the joint-venture contract involving the state-owned Endiama and the private Angolan firms Genius Mineira, Minara, Nahela and MJIT, for the prospecting of diamonds in the Cafulo region, south-eastern Kuando Kubango province.

Besides, Angolan authorities expressed intentions to revive iron ore exploration and plans to attract investment to iron ore production in order to reduce the country's dependence on oil and diamonds. Hence, more than 10 companies, including BHP Billiton, have expressed interest in a USD 3 billion Angolan project to revive iron ore production and produce steel. The project would revive iron ore mining at the Cassinga mine in southern Angola that was abandoned during Angola's 27-year civil war. The Cassinga iron ore mine in the Huila province produced 40 million tonnes of high-grade iron ore between 1957 and 1975, when it was shut. Cassinga, which lies 650 km inland, has remaining reserves estimated at 34.2 million tonnes of ore containing 44% iron and 1 billion tonnes at 30% iron.

AGRICULTURE SECTOR

The Angolan territory contains natural resources in agriculture and forestry. However, due to irregular rains, lack of enhanced facilities and infrastructure for agricultural activities as well as the lack of industries, the agricultural sector is very weak. But, thanks to its extensive river system and varied environment, as well as arable lands, Angola has enormous potential for the production of tropical and subtropical crops. Certain regions of Angola have ideal climatic conditions for the production of high quality coffee. The Angolan farmers are eager to making partnership with Dutch farmers in Angola. Many project proposals for joint-ventures in agricultural projects have been submitted to both local and international investors, banks and the diplomatic representation. Local banks like BDA (Banco de Desenvolvimento Angolano) and BIC (Banco International de Crédito) are the main promoters and major partners for investors willing to invest in agricultural activities. Agriculture is one of the non-oil sectors that the government wants to rehabilitate, improve and boost. However, it lacks capital, technology and know-how.

CONSUMERGOODS SECTOR

Due to lack of industries, Angola depends very much on imports of foodstuff. The country imports a significant proportion of its food requirements, and nearly all its capital and consumer goods. Major imports partners of the country are Portugal, the U.S., South Africa, Japan, France, Brazil, UK and China. Nevertheless, the government plans to boost the agriculture sector to diminish dependency on food imports, although, investments in supermarkets and food supply are still needed. The Angolan Government will invest over USD 300 million in the construction of 31 supermarkets of the "Nosso Super" Commercial Network (Presild) , in the 18 provinces of the country.The supermarket chain NossoSuper (www.nossosuper.co.ao) is a "joint venture" between Angola Government and a Brazilian company called Construtora Odebrecht.

BUILDING AND INFRAESTRUCTURE SECTOR

The whole country is to rebuilt. Angola's government has embarked on a massive reconstruction of roads, railways, bridges, airports, schools and hospitals and residential housing since the end of a devastating 27-year civil war in 2002. In 2008, approximately 5,000 kilometres of roads will be repaired as part of the special governmental programme for restoring national roads. By March 2008, asphalting works had already been completed on 1,259 kilometres of road. Throughout this year, approximately 4,835 kilometres of roads are expected to be asphalted and repaired.

The refurbishment of Angola's entire road network, estimated in 73,000 kilometers, is being carried out by 50 companies, 25 of which are foreign. Late in March the Minister of Transports announced the construction of Luanda new Harbour. The new Luanda Harbour will be built at "Baia do Dande" with the foundations being laid sometime this year. The new facility will boost current capacity, with 16 to 32 mooring stations and a greater depth. With 32 vessels mooring at higher sea-depth, the new harbour will have different characteristics and greater capacity compared to the current Luanda Port. Apart from the Luanda Harbour, the government plans to rebuild and modernize the ports of Lobito, Cabinda and Porto Amboim. Chinese Firms have been acquiring stakes in infrastructure constructions and rehabilitation, telecommunication and mining countrywide.

Please refer to our newsletter for the latest developments in this sector.

HOTEL AND TOURISM SECTOR

Hundreds of hotels need to be restored or constructed. Beach, river and mountain tourism offering all types of fishing; basic hunting reserves and natural parks available. However, the promotion of tourism in Angola is mainly hampered by the lack of infrastructures. Nevertheless efforts are being carried out by the government to improve the situation by constructing new hotels and rehabilitating some existing touring locations all over the country. Hence, five new hotels were opened in 2007 and 12 are still under construction. Besides, due to 2010 CAN (African Football Cup) to be hosted by Angola, the country is even busy on improving facilities such as new football stadiums, new airports, hotels, restaurants and camping areas. The Ministry of Hotels and Tourism or just MINHTUR, is struggling to attract national and foreign investors to boost the Hotels and Tourism sector. Therefore MINHTUR has created the Angola Institute for Tourism which has the responsibility to execute the general policy of the Angolan tourism. The Angolan Institute for Tourism is also responsible for the approval of all tourism project proposals and for the emission of concessions regarding the exploration, rehabilitation and construction of tourism infrastructures.

WATER AND ENERGY SECTOR

Angola has great hydro electrical potential thanks to its network of large fast-flowing rivers. However, both water and energy distribution is not effective. EPAL, ENE and EDEL companies, are very far from providing quality service to the population countrywide. This is a sector that an investor needs to leap-in. In March 2007 the Minister of Energy and Water, Mr. Botelho de Vasconcelos, said in Hamburg that the Angolan Government intended to invest about USD 2 billions in the national water and energy sector. Angola has concluded infra-structure deals with China, including a recently completed 500 megawatt hydroelectric power plant. In February 2008, the Dutch ⮐ Tahal Group BV signed a contract to build a USD 34 million water supply infrastructure project in Angola. The agreement was signed with Angola's national water company, Empresa Pública de Água (EPAL) . The Angolan government will finance the project. Tahal will build a water supply network distribution system to seven neighbourhoods in a 3,530 km area south of the Luanda province. During the same period the Angolan government invested USD 7.4 million in the construction of a system to treat and distribute potable water, at Chibia District, 45 kilometres south of Lubango City.

BASIC LAWS AND REGULATIONS AFFECTING BUSINESS AND INVESTMENT ACTIVITY IN MINING SECTOR

LAW OF DELIMITATION OF THE SECTORS OF ECONOMIC ACTIVITY LAW NO 13/94

September 2, 1994

Law No 10/88, of July 2nd, called "The Law of Economic Activities", denies the private sector access to a certain number of activities while it delimits those areas of the economy which are not adjusted to the larger option of a development geared to a market economy and consequently a reduction in state direct intervention in the economic life of the country.

It is therefore aimed at reformulating what has been called "State reserve", by considerable reducing its field of application and making it more flexible through the adoption of the concepts and regime of "absolute reserve", "controlled reserve" and "relative reserve".

Furthermore, in accordance with the constitutional principles this law establishes clearly the principle of coexistence of the sectors and their equitable, non - discriminatory treatment.

In that sense, and under the terms of paragraph m of article 89 of the Constitution, the National Legislative Assembly approves the following:

Article 1
(Concept)

For the effects of this law, economic activity is defined as those activities linked to the production and distribution of goods and services in which the exchange of payment is involved and profit oriented.

Article 2
(Sectors of the economy)

Economic activities are performed in the public, private, cooperative and social spheres.

Article 3
(Coexistence of sectors)

The State guarantees the coexistence of the different sectors of the economic activity and the different types of property and management systems it encompasses, providing all of them with equal protection and promotion, and no discrimination, under the terms of the constitution.

Article 4
(Public Sector)

For additional analytical, business and investment opportunities information,
please contact Global Investment & Business Center, USA
at (202) 546-2103. Fax: (202) 546-3275. E-mail: rusric@erols.com

The Public sector encompasses the economic activities pursued by the state and other public entities.

Article 5
(Public sector operation of economic activities)

In the public sector, economic activities may be conducted in the following ways:

a) directly by the state
b) by public corporations
c) by public institutes and other similar public entities
d) by commercial corporations with public capital
e) by commercial corporations and other types of associations where the majority of the capital is public.

Article 6
(Private sector)

The private sector encompasses the economic activities performed by individual or private corporations

Article 7
(Private sector operation of economic activities)

In the private sector, economic activities may be conducted in the following manners:

a) individually, with or without a company
b) by commercial corporations or other types of associations with capitals held mostly by individuals or private corporations.

Article 8
(Cooperative or social sector)

The cooperative or social sector encompasses the economic activities conducted by cooperatives, local communities or families.

Article 9
(State reserve)

1. State reserve is understood to be the group of areas in which economic activities can only be performed with the participation of the state or other entities which under the terms of this law are part of the public sector, either by their ownership or management.

2. State reserve includes absolute reserve, controlled reserve and relative reserve.

Article 10
(Absolute reserve)

1. Absolute state reserve are the set of areas in which economic activities can be exclusively be conducted by the public sector.

2. The following are areas of absolute state reserve:

a) the production, distribution and commercialization of war materiel
b) banking activities related to the functions of the central, issuing bank
c) port and airport management
d) telecommunications in basic national network infrastructure and services.

Article 11
(Controlled reserve)

1. Controlled state reserve are the areas which will be describe below and which can be operated by corporations created through the association of public sector entities, which must hold the majority of the stock, with other entities:

2. The following are areas of controlled state reserve:

a) air transport of passengers and international cargo
b) domestic air transport of passengers
c) regular postal services
d) long distance maritime transportation

Article 12
(Relative reserve)

1. The economic activities in the areas described below can be conducted by corporations or entities which are not integrated into the public sector, through temporary concession contracts.

a) basic sanitation
b) production, transport and distribution of electric power for public consumption
c) collection, treatment and distribution of drinking water through fixed networks
d) exploitation or port and airport services
e) railway services
f) maritime and coastal transport g) collective bus services
h) non regular air transport of passengers and cargo (domestic)
i) complementary postal and telecommunication services.

2. The exploitation of natural resources, which under the terms of the Constitution are the property of the state, can only be undertaken through concessions or other regimes that do not involve the transmission of property.

Article 13
(Doubts and omissions)

Any doubts and omissions which may arise in the interpretation and application of this law shall be decided by the National Legislative Assembly.

Article 14
(Revocation of legislation)

Any legislation contrary to the provision of this law, specifically articles 3, 17, 18 of law No 10/88, of 2 July, is hereby revoked.

**For additional analytical, business and investment opportunities information,
please contact Global Investment & Business Center, USA
at (202) 546-2103. Fax: (202) 546-3275. E-mail: rusric@erols.com**

Article 15
(Regulations)

This regulations applicable to this legislation must be issued by the government within 60 days.

Seen and approved by the National Legislative Assembly
Published.

FOREIGN EXCHANGE LAW LAW NO 5/97

NATIONAL LEGISLATIVE ASSEMBLY
27 June, 1997

Considering, due to the reorganization of the financial system it is imperative that norms and principles which have been valid until the present time, be updated, for they have become obsolete, to reconcile the operation of the financial institutions with the current phase of the economic development in the country.

In that sense, the intention of the law aims is to conduct a profound revision of the above mentioned norms, in order to improve the discipline of foreign exchange operations, as well as establish a basic juridical-legal framework to regulate foreign exchange trade in a manner that takes into account the legitimate interests of the State and other economic entities

In those terms, under the provisions of art 88 of the Constitution the National Legislative Assembly approves the following:

CHAPTER I (GENERAL PROVISIONS)

Article 1
(Objective)

The objective of the following charter is to regulate financial and commercial operations which have and effective or potential effect on the balance of payments.

Article 2
(Scope of application)

This law and its complementary charters and regulations applies to

a) foreign exchange operations b) trade in foreign exchange

Article 3
(Foreign exchange authority)

The National Bank of Angola is the foreign exchange authority in the Republic of Angola. It can delegate power on other entities for specific activities.

Article 4
(Residency)

For additional analytical, business and investment opportunities information,
please contact Global Investment & Business Center, USA
at (202) 546-2103. Fax: (202) 546-3275. E-mail: rusric@erols.com

1. For the effects of the current charter, the following are considered residents in the territory of Angola:

a) individuals that normally reside in the country;
b) corporations with headquarters in the country;
c) branches, agencies or any type of representation in the country of foreign corporations;
d) funds, institutes and public agencies with financial and administrative autonomy, with headquarters in the national territory;
e) national diplomatic officials, consular representatives or similar in the exercise of their office outside of the country, as well as their family members;
f) Angolan nationals, living abroad for more than 90 days and less than a year, who are students or are in the exercise of public functions.

2. For the effects of the current charter, the following are considered non-residents:

a) individuals that normally reside abroad;
b) corporations with headquarters abroad;
c) individuals who have been away from the country for more than a year
d) branches, agencies or any form of representation located abroad of corporations with headquarters in Angola;
e) diplomatic officials, consular representatives or the like, who are serving in Angola, as well as their family members.

3) The National Bank of Angola may decide in special cases, doubts which may arise as to the quality of resident or non resident of a given entity.

CHAPTER II (FOREIGN EXCHANGE OPERATIONS)

Article 5
(Definition)

The following are considered foreign exchange operations:

a) the acquisition or alienation of coined gold, gold bars or any non crafted gold.
b) the acquisition or alienation of foreign currencies
c) the opening and operation of checking accounts in foreign currency in the country by non residents
d) the payment of any transaction in goods, current or capital accounts

Article 6
(Concept of foreign currency)

For the effects of this charter and the complementary legislation and regulations, foreign currency is considered to be the legal tender (bills or coins) of the issuing country and any other means of payment to be made abroad, expressed in the currency or account units that are used in international compensations or payments.

Article 7
(Mandatory brokerage)

For additional analytical, business and investment opportunities information,
please contact Global Investment & Business Center, USA
at (202) 546-2103. Fax: (202) 546-3275. E-mail: rusric@erols.com

Foreign exchange operations can only be performed by a financial institution authorized to perform foreign exchange trade.

Article 8
(Compensation)

Total or partial payment of goods, current account and capital transactions as compensation for credits or debits derived from identical or different transactions must be authorized by the National Bank of Angola.

Article 9
(Opening and operation of accounts)

1) Residents as defined for foreign exchange purposes, may open and operate checking accounts in foreign currency at financial institutions with headquarters in the country.

2) Resident individuals may open and operate checking accounts in foreign currency at financial institutions with headquarters outside the country

3) Non residents as defined for foreign exchange purposes, may open and operate checking accounts in national or foreign currency at financial institutes domiciled in the national territory

4) The National Bank of Angola must define the terms and conditions under which residents and non residents may hold accounts as described in paragraphs 1 and 2 of this article.

CHAPTER III (OPERATION OF FOREIGN EXCHANGE TRADE)

Article 10

1. We understand by the operation of foreign exchange trade the customary execution on their own behalf or for third parties, of foreign exchange operations.

2. The operation of foreign exchange trade must be specifically authorized by the National Bank of Angola under the terms of the applicable legislation.

Article 11
(Special Cases)

The National Bank of Angola may authorizes entities linked to tourism, specifically hotels, travel agents, tour operators and duty free shops, to buy and sell foreign currency, travelers checks or other payment instruments from their respective clients, under the terms and provisions established by the Bank.

Article 12
(Information duty)

Those entities authorized to operate in foreign exchange trade, must submit to the National Bank of Angola, the information, statistics or data which it may request in keeping with the instructions given and within the time limits and conditions set by the Bank.

For additional analytical, business and investment opportunities information,
please contact Global Investment & Business Center, USA
at (202) 546-2103. Fax: (202) 546-3275. E-mail: rusric@erols.com

CHAPTER IV (IMPORT, EXPORT, RE-EXPORT OF GOLD, CURRENCY OR LETTERS OF CREDIT)

Article 13
(Operations in gold)

1. The import, export or re-export of coined gold, gold bars or other non crafted gold is under the exclusive jurisdiction of the National Bank of Angola.

2. The domestic and international transit of coined gold, gold bars or non crafted gold must be authorized by the National Bank of Angola under the conditions and terms it determines.

Article 14
(Imports, export and re-export of currency)

1. The import, export or re-export of legal tender, in bills and coins, national or foreign, as well as travelers checks and other instruments of payment can only be performed by institutions authorized to operate in foreign exchange trade through a special authorization issued by the National Bank of Angola, under its terms and conditions.

2. The provisions in the above paragraph are applicable to the export of national currency not in circulation.

Article 15
(Import, export and re-export of letters of credit)

The import, export and re-export of letters of credit, assigning actions or obligations must be conducted under the terms of the applicable legislation.

Article 16
(Control)

Customs will only clear packages containing gold - coined or not - bills and coins, travelers checks and other instruments of payment as well as letters of credit if the corresponding import, export or re-export upon presentation of the corresponding authorization as issued by the National Bank of Angola.

Article 17
(Circumstancial measures)

In case of difficulties in the balance of payments, as well as disturbances in the operation of financial markets, after informing the Government, the Bank of Angola may establish through a notification, restrictions and other conditions to the operations described in this law.

CHAPTER V (COMPLEMENTARY CHARTERS)

Article 18
(Operations with goods, intangibles* and capital)

We define by the decree the general principles to be followed by import, export and re-export operations as well as operations in current account and capital.

For additional analytical, business and investment opportunities information,
please contact Global Investment & Business Center, USA
at (202) 546-2103. Fax: (202) 546-3275. E-mail: rusric@erols.com

CHAPTER VI (INFRACTIONS AND SANCTIONS)

Article 19
(Transgressions)

The following are considered violations liable to penalties under the terms of this charter:

a) The operations of foreign exchange trade that breach the provisions of article 10 of this law.
b) The performance of operations that breach the provisions of articles 7, 9, 13 and 15 of this law.
c) Any breach against the provisions under the charters mentioned in article 18 of this law.

Article 20
(Sanctions)

1. The penalty for transgressions defined in paragraph a) of the above article of this law will be a fine of between: KzR:300,000,000.00 and KzR: 40,000,000,000,00.

2. The penalty for transgressions defined in paragraphs b) and c) of the above article of this law will be a fine of between: KzR: 600,000,000.00 and KzR: 100,000,000,000.00

3. The penalties defined in the above paragraphs will vary (within their brackets) according to the value of the operation and the objective and subjective severity of the infraction, without prejudice to the provisions of the following article of this law.

4. If there were any alterations in foreign exchange rates, or whenever deemed necessary or timely, the Bank of Angola may propose to the Government an alteration in the value of the fines, either in the minimum or the maximum amounts specified.

Article 21
(Ranking of sanctions)

1. The amount of the fine can never be less than the economic profit realized by the offender.

2. If the agent condemned for a foreign exchange violation, commits a second offense within two years of the previous condemnation, the minimum and maximum limits established in article 20 of this law, will be doubled.

3. The sanctions defined in this charter will be applied with no prejudice to other penal and disciplinary responsibilities provided in other legislation or regulations.

Article 22
(Responsibility of corporations and their directors)

1. Corporations and companies, even if their incorporation is deemed irregular, and non incorporated associations have joint and several liability in the payment of fines and legal costs imposed on their directors, employees or agents for violations punishable under the terms of this law.

2. Those responsible for the administration of corporations, even when irregularly incorporated, and non incorporated associations, who within their capacity did not oppose the illegal practice,

For additional analytical, business and investment opportunities information,
please contact Global Investment & Business Center, USA
at (202) 546-2103. Fax: (202) 546-3275. E-mail: rusric@erols.com

are individually and subsidiarily liable for the payment of the fine and legal costs, even if the corporation has been dissolved or is undergoing settlement procedures.

Article 23
(Accessory sanctions)

The repetition of the violations defined in paragraph a) article 19 of this law as well as those defined in paragraph b) of the same article, as defined in paragraph 2 of the above article may also punished by:

a) Seizure by the State of the assets used or obtained through the illicit activity.
b) Temporary or permanent interdiction from occupying positions in the administration of any institution subject to the supervision of the National Bank of Angola;
c) Interdiction for up to 3 years from performing any foreign exchange operations.

Article 24
(Statute of limitation)

1. Processes for foreign exchange violations will prescribe 5 years after the infraction.

2. Fines and accessory sanctions prescribe in the same period, to be counted form the date of the final sentence.

Article 25
(Fact finding and process)

1) The National Bank of Angola is the agency competent to perform the investigation of foreign exchange violations and institute the process, it may inspect any institution and seize the assets used or gained through the illicit activity

2) Police authorities and other entities or public services must cooperate with the National Bank of Angola when necessary.

3) The application of the fines and other sanctions defined in this charter fall under the jurisdiction of the Governor of the National Bank of Angola

4) The decisions made under the terms of the above paragraph may be appealed under the general provisions of the law.

Article 26
(Disposition of the Fines)

The fines will be paid to the State

Article 27
(Forcible collection of fines)

1. The collection of fines, if there has been no appeal and have not been voluntarily paid, fall under the regulations for tax foreclosures.

2. The copy of the judicial decision is the basis for the foreclosure and should be sent to the competent court for its implementation.

3. In case of appeal and final condemnation, the collection of fines will fall under foreclosure regulations which must be processed within the judicial system.

CHAPTER VII (FINAL AND TRANSITORY PROVISIONS)

1. The regulations provided for under this law must be drafted by the Government, following the proposal to be submitted by the National Bank of Angola within 90 days of its publication.

2. The National Bank of Angola has jurisdiction to define the regulations and procedures to be adopted in foreign exchange operations as well as to publish or transmit instructions, of a technical character or other, necessary for the adequate implementation of the legal framework for those operations.

3. The instructions mentioned in the above paragraph will be valid as of the date of their publication or transmission, except when there are provisions to the contrary.

4. This law is applicable to foreign investment in all areas which are not regulated by a specific legislation.

Article 29
(Revocation)

1. Any legislation contrary to the provisions of this charter, namely Law No9/98, 2 July, is hereby revoked.

2. Any other complementary norms and regulations in force , not in contradiction with this charter will maintain its validity.

Article 30
(Doubts and omissions)

Doubts an omissions that may arise from the interpretation and application of this law shall be resolved by the National Legislative Assembly.

Article 31
(Entry into force)

This law will enter into force on the date of its publication

Seen and approved by the National Assembly in Luanda, 19 February 1997

**Roberto Antonio Victor Francisco de Almeida
the President of the National Assembly**

Enacted on 23 April 1997

Order to publish signed by

**For additional analytical, business and investment opportunities information,
please contact Global Investment & Business Center, USA
at (202) 546-2103. Fax: (202) 546-3275. E-mail: rusric@erols.com**

Jose Eduardo dos Santos
President of the Republic

FOREIGN INVESTMENT LAW

National Assemby Law Number 15/94
September 23, 1994

CHAPTER I - GENERAL PROVISIONS

Article 1 - Scope
Article 2 - Promotion of Foreign Investment
Article 3 - Permissability of Foreign Investment
Article 4 - Definitions
Article 5 - Foreign Investment Operations
Article 6 - Forms of Investment

ARTICLE 1
(Scope)

This Law sets out the foreign investment regime and procedures to be applied in the Republic of Angola.

ARTICLE 2
(Promotion of Foreign Investment)

The Government should promote and provide incentives for foreign investment that is consistent with the country's economic and social development and the general well-being of the population.

ARTICLE 3
(Permissibility of Foreign Investment)

1. Foreign investments are allowed to be made by suitably recognized entities with acknowledged technical and financial capacity, provided the investments are not contrary to:

a) the economic and social developments strategies defined by the competent sovereign bodies

b) the strategic guidelines and objectives set out in the economic policy programs;

c) current law

2. Foreign investment is prohibited in the following areas:

a) defense, internal public order and State security:

b) banking activities involving central bank and issuing bank function;

c) other areas which are considered by law to be absolutely reserved for the State.

For additional analytical, business and investment opportunities information,
please contact Global Investment & Business Center, USA
at (202) 546-2103. Fax: (202) 546-3275. E-mail: rusric@erols.com

ARTICLE 4
(Definitions)

For the purposes of this Law the following definitions shall apply:

a) Foreign investment - the introduction into and utilization in national territory of capital, equipment and other assets or technology, or the use of funds with rights to transfer them abroad, or eligibility to do so, under existing foreign exchange legi slation, by non residents individuals or entities, for the purposes of creating new companies, or groups of companies, branches or other forms of corporate representation of foreign companies, as well as for the total or partial acquiring of existing Ango lan companies of companies.

b) Foreign investor - any non-resident individual or entity, regardless of their nationality,

c) National investor - any resident individual or entity, regardless of their nationality;

d) Competent body - The body referred to in Article 49 of the present Law.

2. Investment by Angolan companies, or those established in Angola, shall also be considered foreign under the terms of part a) of the previous section if, as a result of majority ownership of their capital or any other form, they may be considered, as d irectly linked to non-resident individuals or entities.

3. For the purposes of this Law the terms "resident" and "non-resident" shall be applied to individuals or entities who are considered as such under the foreign exchange legislation.

ARTICLE 5
(Foreign Investment Operations)

Under the terms and for the purposes of the present Law, the following acts and contracts are considered as foreign investment activities, even if they are not directly linked with capital importing operations:

a) setting up and expansion of branches or other forms of corporate representation of foreign companies, creation of new companies that belong exclusively to the investor, and acquiring of all or portion of already existing companies or groups of companie s;

b) the holding or acquisition of an interest in the equity of a new or already existing company or group of companies, regardless of the form this may take;

c) entering into or alteration of consortium or association contracts with third parties by quotas or other capital shares;

d) total or partial takeover of commercial or industrial establishments, by acquiring assets or through contracts involving the transfer of operations;

e) total or partial takeover of agricultural companies, through leasing contracts or any other agreement that implies ownership or engaging in operations on the part of the investor;

f) operation of property complexes, whether or not for purposes of tourism, and regardless of their legal status;

g) realization of supplementary capital contributions, advances from partners and, in general, loans related to profit-sharing;

h) acquiring property in national territory when such acquisition forms part of a foreign investment project.

ARTICLE 6
(Forms of Investment)

1. Foreign investments may be made, singly or cumulatively, in the following ways:

a) transfer of funds from foreign countries;

b) investment of funds from foreign currency bank accounts set up in Angola by non-residents;

c) importing of equipment, accessories and materials;

d) incorporation of credits and other resources into Angola by foreign investors, which are eligible for transfer abroad under the terms of foreign exchange regulations;

e) incorporation of technology.

2. Foreign exchange transactions deriving from the acts enumerated above will be subject to the regulations set out in foreign exchange legislation.

CHAPTER II - RIGHTS AND OBLIGATIONS

Article 7 Foreign Investement Status
Article 8 Rights and Guarantees
Article 9 Obligations
Article 10 Tax regime
Article 11 Recourse to Credit
Article 12 Bank Accounts
Article 13 Labor Force
Article 14 Project Implementation
Article 15 Monitoring
Article 16 Transfer of Contractual Status
Article 17 Dissolution and Liquidation

ARTICLE 7
(Foreign Investment Status)

For all legal purposes, companies constituted under the protection of this Law have the rightful status of Angolan companies, and shall be subject to the application of common Angolan law, except as determined otherwise by this Law or by other specific le gislation.

ARTICLE 8
(Rights and Guarantees)

1. Under the terms of the Constitutional Law and the principles that determine the country's legal, political and economic policies, the Angolan State shall ensure fair, non-discriminatory and

equitable treatment to incorporated companies and assets impo rted under the protection of the Law, guaranteeing them protection and security and shall in no way hinder their management, existence and operations, without prejudice to the exercise of appropriate monitoring.

2. The foreign investor shall be guaranteed rights stemming from the ownership of the resources invested, and specifically the right to transfer abroad the following assets under the terms of the foreign exchange legislation:

a) dividends or profits distributions, after the deduction of legally mandated withholdings and taxed due, taking into consideration the respective interests in the company's equity capital;

b) proceeds of the sale of investments, including gains, after payment of taxes due;

c) any amounts which may be owing to them, after the deduction of respective taxes, as provided for in acts or contracts which constitute foreign investments in the terms of this Law.

3. In the exceptional event that the assets of the foreign investment be expropriated or nationalized, for reasons considered to be of great public interest, the State will ensure rapid, fair and effective indemnification, the amount of which will be det ermined according to the common rules and practice of International Law, or by recourse to arbitration.

4. The State guarantees professional, banking and commercial secrecy for companies constituted under the protection of this Law, regarding activities carried out within the framework of approved projects.

5. Rights and guarantees provided for foreign investments under the terms of this Law are ensured without prejudice to any others that may result from agreements and conventions to which the Angolan State is party.

ARTICLE 9
(Obligations)

Foreign investors shall have the following obligations:

a) to respect current laws and regulations, as well as contractual commitments, and to submit to monitoring by competent authorities, providing them with any requested information;

b) to create funds and reserves and make provisions under the terms of current legislation;

c) to complete a statement of accounts according to the country's established accounting regulations;

d) to comply with regulations relating to environmental protection, sanitation, and the protection and security of workers against occupational diseases and accidents at work, and other eventualities covered by social security legislation;

e) obtain, and currently maintain, insurance cover against workers; professional accidents and occupational diseases, as well as insurance covering civil liability for damages to third parties.

ARTICLE 10
(Tax Regime)

For additional analytical, business and investment opportunities information,
please contact Global Investment & Business Center, USA
at (202) 546-2103. Fax: (202) 546-3275. E-mail: rusric@erols.com

1. Companies covered by this Law shall be subject to compliance with current tax legislation, and have the same tax benefits as those set out for national companies.

2. Investments made under a contractual regime, in the terms of this Law, will also be able to take advantage of the special tax benefits set out in their respective contracts.

ARTICLE 11
(Recourse to Credit)

1. Companies covered under this Law will be able to apply for domestic and foreign loans, within the terms of current legislation.

2. Loans from foreign sources shall be subject to licensing and authorization from the Ministry of Finance and the Central Bank. However, the Central Bank will set the limit above which loans from foreign sources can only be made with its prior authoriz ation.

ARTICLE 12
(Bank Accounts)

Companies covered by this Law may open bank accounts in local or foreign currency in banks domiciled in this country in accordance with current banking and foreign exchange legislation, unless they are covered by some special regime.

ARTICLE 13
(Labor Force)

1. Companies covered by this Law shall promote the employment of Angolan workers and guarantee them the necessary professional training and social benefits identical with those of the foreign workers they employ.

2. Companies covered by this Law which employ a high proportion of Angolan workers, including in positions of management and responsibility, and which provide them with professional training and benefits equivalent to those of their foreign employees, sh all benefit from special fiscal incentives and opportunities.

3. Companies covered by this Law shall be entitled to employ qualified foreign workers; however, they must comply with the respective plan for training national technicians and progressively fill these positions with Angolan workers.

4. Foreign workers contracted under the terms of the previous section will be subject to current law in the Republic of Angola.

ARTICLE 14
(Project Implementation)

1. Implementation of the foreign investment project shall begin within a period set in the respective authorization.

2. In duly justified cases, and by request of the foreign investor, the above-mentioned period may be extended by the competent body.

**For additional analytical, business and investment opportunities information,
please contact Global Investment & Business Center, USA
at (202) 546-2103. Fax: (202) 546-3275. E-mail: rusric@erols.com**

3. Implementation and management of the foreign investment project shall be done in strict conformity with the conditions for its authorization and applicable legislation, and contributions from abroad shall not be used in any way or to any purpose other than that for which it was authorized, nor shall the company alter the objectives for which it had been authorized.

4. Any broadening of the company's objectives to fields of activity not included in its authorization, shall require prior authorization from the competent body.

ARTICLE 15
(Monitoring)

In order to facilitate monitoring of the implementation of the authorized foreign investments, companies must provide information to the competent body, on an annual basis, showing the results and development of their activities, by completing the questio nnaire which the competent body shall send them for this purpose.

ARTICLE 16
(Transfer of Contractual Status)

Total or partial transfer of the contract or corporate status relating to the foreign investment may only occur through prior authorization of the Ministry of Finance, with any existing domestic investors retaining the right of preference in every case.

ARTICLE 17
(Dissolution and Liquidation)

1. Companies constituted under the present Law shall be dissolved in cases provided for under legal and regulatory clauses of the respective contract or incorporation document, as well as those in the following circumstances:

a) the expiry of a pre-determined period of time;

b) the decision of the shareholders;

c) the full achievement of the corporate objective or the impossibility of achieving it;

d) failure to raise the capitol necessary to operate the company;

e) subsequent declaration of its corporate objective as being illegal;

f) the bankruptcy of the company;

g) notable deviation from the company's corporate objective;

h) all other cases provided for under commercial legislation.

2. The dissolution and liquidation of a company constituted under the foreign investment regime shall be subject to current commercial legislation.

CHAPTER III - FOREIGN INVESTMENT PROCEDURES

For additional analytical, business and investment opportunities information,
please contact Global Investment & Business Center, USA
at (202) 546-2103. Fax: (202) 546-3275. E-mail: rusric@erols.com

Section 1 - Types of Procedures

Article 18 - Listing of the Regimes
Article 19 - Exclusion

ARTICLE 18
(Listing of the Regimes)

Foreign investments may be processed under the following regimes:

a) prior declaration regime;

b) prior approval regime;

c) contractual regime.

ARTICLE 19
(Exclusion)

Foreign investment transactions valued at less than the equivalent of two hundred and fifty thousand U.S. dollars shall be excluded from the specific procedures established by this Law, and shall be subject only to the general regime for foreign exchange transactions.

SECTION 2 - PRIOR DECLARATION REGIME

Article 20 - Framework
Article 21 - Submitting the Proposal
Article 22 - Evaluation of the Proposal
Article 23 - Rejection of the Proposal
Article 24 - Acceptance of the Proposal

ARTICLE 20
(Framework)

Investments valued at the equivalent of between two hundred and fifty thousand and five million U.S. dollars shall be subject to the prior declaration regime.

ARTICLE 21
(Submitting the Proposal)

Foreign investment proposals shall be submitted to the competent body, accompanied by the documentation necessary for the (illegible) and legal characterization of the investor and the planned investment.

ARTICLE 22
(Evaluation of the Proposal)

For additional analytical, business and investment opportunities information,
please contact Global Investment & Business Center, USA
at (202) 546-2103. Fax: (202) 546-3275. E-mail: rusric@erols.com

1. Upon receipt of the proposal the competent body shall have a period of forty-five days in which to evaluate it and render a decision.

2. During that period, the competent body shall solicit the opinion of the Ministry responsible for the area of the investment.

ARTICLE 23
(Rejection of the Proposal)

Rejection of the proposal, which shall be formally communicated to the applicant by the competent body, may only be based on reasons of a strictly legal nature.

ARTICLE 24
(Acceptance of the Proposal)

1. In the absence of express rejection of the proposal, upon expiry of the period referred to in No. 1 of Article 22 the proposal shall be deemed to be accepted, which grants the applicant the right to carry out the investment under the precise terms of t he proposal that was submitted.

2. To this effect, the competent body shall issue, within a period of fifteen days, a statement certifying its acceptance of the proposal, a copy of which, certified by the body shall be returned to the applicant.

SECTION 3 - PRIOR APPROVAL REGIME

Article 25 - Framework
Article 26 - Submitting the Proposal
Article 27 - Evaluation of the Proposal
Article 28 - Rejection of the Proposal
Article 29 - Approval of the Proposal

ARTICLE 25
(Framework)

Investments valued at the equivalent of between five million and fifty million U.S. dollars shall be subject to the prior approval regime.

ARTICLE 26
(Submitting the Proposal)

Foreign investment proposals shall be submitted to the competent body, accompanied by the documentation required for the legal, economic, financial and technical identification and characterization of the investor and the planned investment.

ARTICLE 27
(Evaluation of the Proposal)

1. Upon receipt of the proposal, the competent body shall have a period of ninety days in which to evaluate it and give its opinion.

For additional analytical, business and investment opportunities information,
please contact Global Investment & Business Center, USA
at (202) 546-2103. Fax: (202) 546-3275. E-mail: rusric@erols.com

2. During that peiod, the competent body shall analyse and evaluate the proposal, being counselled by the opinion of the evaluation committee to which the Council of Ministers Resolution N' 2/90 of January 6th refers.

ARTICLE 28
(Rejection of the proposal)

1. The rejection of a proposal is within the competence of:

a) the Minister of Planning and Economic Coordination for investments valued at the equivalent of between five and fifteen million U.S. dollars;

b) the Prime Minister for investments valued at between fifteen and fifty million U.S. dollars.

2. The rejection of the proposal, which shall be formally communicated to the applicant by the competent agency, may only be based on:

a) reasons of a legal nature;

b) undersirability of the planned investment in the light of the investment strategy defined by the competent sovereign bodies of the objectives established in the economic and social plans.

ARTICLE 29
(Approval of the proposal)

1. In the absence of express rejection of the proposal upon expiry of the period referred to in N1 of Article 27, it shall be remitted for decision:

a) to the Prime Minister in the case of investments valued at the equivalent of up to fifteen million U.S. dollars;

b) to the Council of Ministers in the case of investments valued at more than the equivalent of fifteen million U.S. dollars.

2. Approval shall take the form of an executive decree in the case of part a) above and a decree in the case of part b) abovc, to be published In the Dirio da Repblica.

SECTION 4 - CONTRACTUAL REGIME

For additional analytical, business and investment opportunities information, please contact Global Investment & Business Center, USA at (202) 546-2103. Fax: (202) 546-3275. E-mail: rusric@erols.com

ARTICLE 30
(Framework)

The following categories of investment shall be subject to the contractual regime:

a) investments valued at greater than the equivalent of fifty million U.S. dollars;

b) regardless of the value, investments involving areas of economic activity in which operations and management may only legally be carried out through a concession;

c) regardless of the value, investments considered to be of special significance to the national economy, whether for structural purposes or by reason of their contribution to the development and internationalization of the national economy.

ARTICLE 31
(Characterization of the Contractual Regime)

1. The contractual regime of foreign investment is essentially characterized by:

a) definition and quantification of the objectives to be undertaken by the foreign investor during the contract period;

b) definition and quantification of the tax benefits and other incentives to be granted and ensured by the Government to the foreign investor, in compensation for accurate and timely compliance with the predetermined objectives.

c) effective and systematic monitoring by the State of the activities involved in carrying out the investment during the contractual period.

2. Investment contracts are administrative in nature, with the parties being the State, represented by the Minister of Planning and Economic Coordination, and the foreign investor.

3. It is permitted to agree in investment contracts that any litigation arising from the interpretation and execution of said contracts be resolved through arbitration.

4. In the cases referred to in section 3 above, arbitration must take place in Angola, and Angolan law will apply to the contract.

ARTICLE 32
(Submitting the Proposal)

Foreign investment proposals shall be submitted to the competent body, accompanied by the documents required for the legal, economic, financial and technical description and characterization of the investor and the planned investments.

ARTICLE 33
(Access to the Regime)

Upon receipt of the proposal, the competent body must decide, within a period of ten days, the appropriateness of the contractual regime, and this decision will be formally communicated to the applicant.

For additional analytical, business and investment opportunities information,
please contact Global Investment & Business Center, USA
at (202) 546-2103. Fax: (202) 546-3275. E-mail: rusric@erols.com

ARTICLE 34
(Evaluation of the Proposal)

1. After determining the appropriateness of the regime as described in the previous article, the competent body shall have a period of thirty days in which to evaluate and give its opinion on the proposal.

2. During that period, the competent body shall analyze and evaluate the proposal, seeking the assistance of the evaluation committee to which the Council of Ministers Resolution N∫ 2/90 of January 6th refers.

ARTICLE 35
(Rejection of the Proposal)

1. Rejection of the proposal is within the competence of:

a) the Minister of Planning and Economic Coordination, for investments which are valued at less than the equivalent of fifteen million U.S. dollars, in the cases mentioned in sections b) and c) of Article :30 of this Law;

b) the Prime Minister, for all the other cases mentioned in Article 30 of this Law.

2. Rejection of the proposal, which shall be formally communicated to the applicant by the competent agency, may only be based on:

a) reasons of a legal nature;

b) undesirability of the planned investment in the light of the development strategy established by the competent sovereign bodies or the objectives set out in the economic and social development plans.

ARTICLE 36
(Negotiations)

1. In the absence of express rejection of the proposal, it shall be submitted to the evaluation and decision of the Ministry of Planning and Economic Coordination, for the purpose of:

a) appointing a negotiation committee;

b) defining negotiating guidelines and instructions. including estimating its duration.

2. The decision referred to in the previous section must be rendered within a period of fifteen days.

3. Without prejudice to the specific circumstances of each particular case, the committee to which part a) of this Article refers shall be coordinated by the competent body and shall include representatives of the Ministry of Finance and the competent Gov ernment agencies involved in the project.

ARTICLE 37
(Approval of the Contract)

1. Upon conclusion of the negotiations, the draft contract shall be remitted by the competent body to the Ministry of Planning and Economic Coordination which, in turn. shall forward it to the Council of Ministers for approval.

2. Approval by the Council of Ministers shall take the form of a resolution to be published in the Diario da Republica.

3. The contract shall be granted in a private document, the original of which is to remain in the archives of the competent body.

SECTION 5 - COMMON PROVISIONS TO THE PROCEDURAL REGIMES

Article 38 - Correction of the Proposals
Article 39 - Complaint Against the Rejection Decisions
Article 40 - Remittance to the Central Bank
Article 41 - Consitution and Modification of Companies
Article 42 - Commercial Registration
Article 43 - Other Registration
Article 44 - Central Bank Information
Article 45 - Competitive Bids and Direct Agreements

ARTICLE 38
(Correction of the Proposals)

In the event that the submitted proposals are either deficient or insufficient in form, the competent body shall notify the applicant, fixing a time limit for the proposal to be corrected or revised.

ARTICLE 39
(Complaint against the Rejection Decisions)

Complaints against rejection decisions that have been made under the terms of Articles 23, 28, 33 and 35, shall be made to the hierarchically higher authority concerned, and shall be filed within a period of 30 days.

ARTICLE 40
(Remittance to the Central Bank)

1. After approval of the foreign investment project under the terms set forth in the previous sections. the competent agency shall remit the documents comprising the plan to the National Bank of Angola, within a period of eight days, for purposes of licen sing the capital transactions.

2. In the event that the prior declaration regime is used, the applicant shall be required to solicit a permit directly from the National Bank of Angola by submitting the statement referred to in N∞ 2 of Article 24 of this Law.

ARTICLE 41
(Constitution and Modification of Companies)

1 In the event that the planned investment implies creating or modifying the status of companies, such acts must be granted by public deed.

2. No deeds relating to activities involving foreign investment operations covered by this Law, or outside its term of effectiveness, may be registered, under penalty of cancellation of the activities in question, without the granting of a license issued by the National Bank of Angola and without the express written approval of the competent body of the Instrument to be granted.

ARTICLE 42
(Commercial Registration)

1. The constitution of companies, end the modification of the Status of existing companies, under the protection of this Law, shall be subject to commercial registration, according to the terms of current legislation.

2. Branches and other forms of representation of foreign companies shall also be subject to commercial registration, which, however, shall be conditional upon the receipt of a license issued by the National Bank of Angola and upon the express written appr oval by the competent body of the instruments to be registered.

ARTICLE 43
(Other Registration)

Upon settlement of capital transactions, and if applicable, upon award of deeds and corresponding commercial registrations, the investment must be registered with the competent body and the National Institute of Statistics, within a period of one hundred and twenty days.

ARTICLE 44
(Central Bank Information)

On a quarterly basis, the National Bank of Angola shall remit information to the competent body on foreign exchange transactions carried out within the framework of the foreign investment.

ARTICLE 45
(Competitive Bids and Direct Agreements)

In cases in which the foreign investment projects are preceded by a competitive bid, public or restricted, or by direct agreement, the procedures established under this Law shall be applied with adaptations as necessary or appropriate.

CHAPTER IV - VIOLATIONS & SANCTIONS

Article 46 - Violations
Article 47 - Sanctions
Article 48 - Descions and Appeals Regarding Sanctions

ARTICLE 46
(Violations)

1 Without prejudice to the provisions of other legal documents, acts of non compliance, malicious or negligent. with the legal obligations to which the foreign investor is liable, constitute violations.

2. Specifically, the following acts shall constitute violations:

a) use of funds originating from foreign sources for purposes other than those which have been authorized;

b) practice of commercial activities outside the scope of the authorized objective;

c) invoicing practices that permit the outflow of capital or which evade the obligations to which the company or association is liable, specifically those of a tax nature;

d) failure to carry out training activities or failure to replace foreign workers with domestic workers, under the conditions and within the time limits provided for in the investment proposal.

ARTICLE 47
(Sanctions)

1. Without prejudice to other sanctions specifically provided for by law the violations referred to in the previous Article shall be subject to the following sanctions:

a) fines ranging from the equivalent of one thousand to one hundred thousand U.S. dollars, with the minimum and maximum to be increased by a factor of three in the event of a repeat violation;

b) loss of tax incentives;

c) revocation of authorization for the investment.

2. Failure to implement the project within the time limits set for it in the authorization or extension is liable to the sanction provided for in line c) of the previous section.

ARTICLE 48
(Decisions and Appeals Regarding Sanctions)

1. The sanctions provided for in lines a) and b) of the previous Article shall be applied by the Ministry of Planning and Economic Coordination when the investment had been approved by the Minister of Planning and Economic Coordination; in cases provided for by line c) and in all cases in which approval was granted by the Council of Ministers, this will decide on the sanctions to be applied.

2. Foreign investors must obligatorily be heard prior to the application of any sanctions.

3. In determining the sanction to be applied, all circumstances surrounding the violation or degree of culpability, the intended benefits and the benefits obtained by committing the violation/ and the damage resulting therefrom, must be taken into conside ration.

4. Foreign investors may file claims against, or appeal, against the sanctions under the terms of current legislation.

CHAPTER V - FINAL & TRANSITORY PROVISIONS

Article 49 - Competent Body
Article 50 - Special Legislation
Article 51 - Previous Investment Projects
Article 52 - Revoking Procedure

ARTICLE 49
(Competent Body)

The body responsible for ensuring the implementation of national policy In the area of foreign investment, as well as for promoting, coordinating, guiding and monitoring foreign investment, is the Foreign investment Bureau, Instituted by decree NC 6/89 of 1st April, under the guidance of the Minister of planning end Economic Coordination, which is responsible for nominating the Bureau's directors.

ARTICLE 50
(Special Legislation)

1 Foreign investments in the areas of oil production and diamond mining and in the area of financial institutions shall be governed by special legislation.

2. Investments referred to in the section above shall benefit from the protection and have the general obligations Covered in this Law.

ARTICLE 51
(Previous Investment Projects)

1. This Law and its regulations do not apply to Investments authorized prior to its coming into effect, which investments shall remain unchanged until their respective termination, to be governed by the provisions of the legislation and the specific terms or contracts by which. their authorization had been granted

2. However, foreign investors may make a request to the competent body to have their already approved projects reviewed and re-approved within the regime of this Law with the decision on this requests falling to the Minister of Planning and Economic Coord ination.

3. Investment plans submitted for analysis and approval up to the time that this Law comes into effect shell be analyzed and decided upon under the terms of this Law, rnaking use of the procedures that have already been applied, with the necessary adaptati ons.

ARTICLE 52
(Revoking Procedure)

1 Law No. 13/88, of 16th June shall be revoked, as shall other legislation contrary to the provisions of this Law.

2. Current regulatory legislation relating to foreign investment insofar ca it Is not contrary to the provisions of this Law and Is not revised, shall continue to be applicable.

ARTICLE 53
(Rules and Statutes)

Rules and statutes repudiating this Law shall be passed by the Council of Ministers, which within a period of ninety days, shall review and bring up to date the current legislation, specifically Decree No. 6189 Of 1st April.

ARTICLE 54
(Disputes and Omissions)

Disputes and omissions resulting from the interpretation and application of this Law shall be resolved by the National Assembly.

ARTICLE 55
(Term of Effectiveness)

This Law shall come into effect fifteen days after its publication in the Diario da Republica.

Reviewed and approved by the National Assembly.
PRESIDENT OF THE NATIONAL ASSEMBLY
FERNANDO JOSE FRANCA VAN-DUNEM

PRESIDENT OF THE REPUBLIC
JOSE EDUARDO DOS SANTOS

REGULATION OF THE FOREIGN INVESTMENT LAW

CHAPTER I GENERAL PROVISIONS

Article 1

(Scope)

This statute regulates the entry into the national territory of capital, capital goods, and other goods, technology, or the use of funds, with the right or possibility of being transferred abroad, with a view to undertaking investment operations defined in Article 5 of Law No. 15/94, of September 23.

Article 2

(Abbreviated expressions)

In the text of this statute, the expressions "G.I.E." and "dollars" shall be understood to refer, respectively, to "Foreign Investment Office" and "dollars of the United States of America."

Article 3

(Applicable legislation)

Foreign investment is governed by the provisions of Law 15/94, of September 23, and the respective regulation, by the foreign exchange legislation, and, in matters not specially regulated, by the commercial and labor legislation in force.

Article 4

(Forms of investment)

1. Foreign investment operations may be made, in isolation or cumulatively, in the following forms:

(a) transfer of funds from abroad;
(b) payment of cash assets into foreign currency bank accounts set up in Angola by non-residents;
(c) import of equipment, accessories, and materials;
(d) incorporating credits and other cash assets of the foreign investor in Angola, which could be transferred abroad in the terms of the foreign exchange legislation;
(e) incorporation of technologies.

2. The Foreign Exchange Office may require of foreign investors the means of proof it deems necessary to verify the value of the capital goods or technologies to be imported for investment purposes.

Article 5

(Lower limit on investment)

Investment operations in an amount less than two hundred fifty thousand dollars are not considered foreign investment operations and as such do not enjoy the status and protection accorded foreign investment; rather, they are subject to the foreign exchange and commercial legislation in force.

Article 6

(Representation offices)

The creation and operation of corporate representatives of foreign companies, under the form of representation offices, shall continue to be governed by the provisions of Decrees 7/90, of March 24, and 37/92, of August 7.

CHAPTER II PROMOTION OF FOREIGN INVESTMENT

Article 7

(Contribution of State Agencies)

The administrative organs of the state shall regularly provide the Foreign Investment Office with information on investment opportunities in their respective areas of oversight.

Article 8

(Contribution of national investors)

For additional analytical, business and investment opportunities information,
please contact Global Investment & Business Center, USA
at (202) 546-2103. Fax: (202) 546-3275. E-mail: rusric@erols.com

Article 9

(Information on investment opportunities)

Any potential investor may request and obtain from the Foreign Investment Office information on investment opportunities in the country, which should be provided free of charge.

CHAPTER III PROCEDURES

Article 10

(Effectuating investment operations)

Foreign investment operations may be effectuated by adopting one of the regimes provided for in the following sections.

SECTION I
Prior declaration regime

Article 11

(Scope)

All investments whose value is between the equivalent of two hundred fifty thousand and five million dollars.

Article 12

(Investment proposal)

1. The investment proposal is submitted by filling out the respective printed form, which is available at the Foreign Investment Office.

2. The investment proposal shall be accompanied by the following documents:

(a) power of attorney to act before the Foreign Investment Office by the person who signs the proposal, when it is not signed by the proponent directly;
(b) certified copy of the legal documents that identify and verify the usual place of residence of the proponent, in the case of natural persons;
(c) certified copy of the legal documents on the incorporation and commercial registry of the proponent, in the case of juridical persons;
(d) in the case of companies incorporating:
-draft incorporation papers of the corporation formed;
-certainty as to the novelty of the planned company name, issued by the competent agency, dated as of the past month as of the date of submission;
-as applicable, draft contract or contracts of association.

For additional analytical, business and investment opportunities information,
please contact Global Investment & Business Center, USA
at (202) 546-2103. Fax: (202) 546-3275. E-mail: rusric@erols.com

(e) in the case of acquisition of corporate interests in already-existing corporations:
-certified copy of the incorporation papers and commercial registration of the corporation in which an interest is acquired;
-certified copy of the decision of the competent corporate bodies of the corporation in which an interest is acquired, approving the transfer;
(f) in the case of operations involving supplementary installments of capital, advances, and loans from partners: certified copy of the respective decision of the competent corporate bodies of the corporation;
(g) in the case of the operations referred to in subsections (c) , (d) , (e) , (f) , and (h) of Article 5, Law 15/94, of September 23: draft of the contract or contracts in question, as the case may be;
(h) in the case of investment in real property: certainty as to the respective property registration, issued in the past three months;
(i) where the investment project includes the incorporation or transfer of patented technology: an authenticated copy of the respective patents.

3. Where national investors participate, they must also attach the proposal, certified copies of the legal documents on their identification and usual place of residence, if natural persons, or a certified copy of the legal documents on incorporation and commercial registration, for corporations.

4. The entirety of the proposal and the documents attached to it shall be submitted in duplicate.

Article 13

(Submission of proposal)

1. Once the proposal is submitted to the Foreign Investment Office, it must immediately issue a receipt, duly dated and signed by the competent official, certifying that the proposal has been received.

2. If the proposal is deficient or insufficient, the Foreign Investment Office shall, within five days, notify the proponent in writing, giving proponent an appropriate time for correction or improvement.

Article 14

(Evaluation of the proposal)

Within five days of receiving the proposal or from the term for correction referred to in paragraph 2 of the previous article, the Foreign Investment Office shall send a copy of it to the organ with oversight responsibility in the area of investment.

Article 15

(Rejection of the proposal)

1. The opinion of the oversight organ and the decision of the Foreign Investment Office to reject the proposal may only be based on strictly legal criteria, and must be expressly stated.

2. The rejection of the proposal shall be communicated in writing by the Foreign Investment Office to the proponent, stating its grounds.

Article 16

(Certification of acceptance of the proposal)

1. If there are no grounds for express rejection of the proposal, the Foreign Investment Office shall issue, within 15 days of the end of the 45-day period referred to in paragraph 1 of Article 22 of Law 15/94, of September 23, a declaration certifying acceptance of the proposal, which shall be delivered to the proponent, accompanied by a complete copy of the proposal certified by the Foreign Investment Office.

2. The documents referred to in the previous paragraph qualify the proponent to effectuate the exchange operations involved in the investment, with the Banks legally authorized for such purpose, and the notarial acts and registrations required with the competent Notaries and Registries.

SECTION II
Prior approval regime

Article 17

(Scope)

Investments whose amount is from five million to fifty million dollars are subject to the prior approval regime.

Article 18

(Investment proposal)

1. The investment proposal shall be submitted to the Foreign Investment Office, using its form, accompanied by the documents necessary for the identification and for the legal, economic, financial, and technical description of the investor and of the planned investment.

2. In addition to the documents referred to in paragraph 2 of Article 12 of this statute, the proposal must be accompanied by the study of the projected investment's technical, economic, and financial feasibility.

3. The proposal in its entirety and the documents that accompany it are to be submitted in triplicate.

Article 19

(Submission of proposal)

1. Once the proposal is submitted to the Foreign Investment Office, it must immediately issue a receipt, duly dated and signed by a competent official, certifying that the proposal was received.

2. In the event that the proposal has deficiencies or insufficiencies, the Foreign Investment Office shall, within five days, give written notice to the proponent, and provide proponent with appropriate time for its correction or improvement.

Article 20

(Evaluation of the proposal)

1. The investment proposal is analyzed and evaluated by the Foreign Investment Office.

2. The purpose of the evaluation will be to assess the technical, economic, and financial feasibility of the foreign investment project and to make an overall or partial assessment, mindful of the cumulative or partial verification of the following aspects:

(a) increase and diversification of exports;
(b) import substitution;
(c) production of raw material for industries and for goods and services to the national economy;
(d) use of national goods and services;
(e) training and use of national workers;
(f) legalization of the project;
(g) benefits induced;
(h) net impact on foreign exchange.

3. The Foreign Exchange Office shall make a decision as to the proposal within 90 days, and shall forward it subsequently to the entities referred to in Articles 28 and 29 of Law 15/94, of September 23, for approval or rejection.

Article 21

(Overall time period for the decision)

The approval or rejection should occur within an overall period of 120 days from the submission of the proposal to the Foreign Investment Office.

SECTION III Contractual regime

Article 22

(Scope)

The following categories of investments are subject to the contractual regime:

(a) investments in an amount greater than or equal to fifty million dollars;
(b) independent of the amount, investments that impact on areas of economic activity whose exploitation and management by law can only be done by concession;
(c) independent of the amount, investments considered of special interest to the national economy, because of the structuring effect or their contributions to the development and internationalization of the national economy.

Article 23

(Submission of the proposal)

The submission of the proposal is governed by the provisions of Article 18 and 19 of this statute.

Article 24

(Admissibility of the regime)

1. The contractual regime is compulsory in the cases referred to in Article 22(a) and (b) of this statute.

2. In the cases contemplated in Article 22(c) , the decision as to admissibility of the regime shall be especially mindful of the cumulative verification of the following aspects:

Article 25

(Evaluation of the proposal)

After the decision as to the admissibility of the contractual regime, the Foreign Investment Office has 30 days to evaluate and decide on the proposal, at the conclusion of which it must forward it to the entities referred to in Articles 35 and 36 of Law 15/94, of September 23, for rejection, if appropriate, or to initiate negotiations.

Article 26

(Negotiations)

1. The negotiations with the proponents and, where appropriate, with the national investors involved in the project, involve the participation, on behalf and in representation of the state, of a negotiations committee; its composition is pursuant to the terms of Article 36(c) of Law 15/94, of September 23.

2. The negotiations committees may request the intervention, collaboration, or opinion of the public or private entities directly or indirectly involved or interested in the project that is the subject of negotiations.

3. The minutes of all the negotiation sessions must be written up.

SECTION IV
Provisions common to the regimes

Article 27

(Monitoring of investment)

For additional analytical, business and investment opportunities information,
please contact Global Investment & Business Center, USA
at (202) 546-2103. Fax: (202) 546-3275. E-mail: rusric@erols.com

1. The Foreign Investment Office shall monitor the implementation of the investments from the economic, financial, legal, and technical points of view, and to this end may request the necessary information of the investors and of any public and private entity.

2. The monitoring functions of the Foreign Investment Office are without prejudice to the specific areas of jurisdiction of the state agencies and of the monetary and foreign exchange authorities.

3. The Foreign Investment Office shall prepare and make public technical instructions on monitoring implementation of the investments.

Article 28

(Information from the Central Bank)

The National Bank of Angola shall forward to the Foreign Investment Office, quarterly, using the printed form designed by the Office, the information on the foreign exchange operations in the area of foreign investment.

Article 29

(Dispute settlement)

Any conflicts that arise from the investments regulated by Law 15/94, of September 23, are resolved, without prejudice to the provision of Article 31(3) and (4) of the same law, pursuant to Angolan common law.

Article 30

(Aspects to consider in dispute settlement)

In judicial, arbitral, or administrative determinations as to acts or situations that represent non-compliance with the obligations set forth in the area of foreign exchange, attention should be given primarily to:

(a) the foreseeable effects of revoking authorization for the investment being carried out;
(b) the possibility of regaining an equilibrium in the installment payments, by changing the objectives and/or incentives or term of the investment;
(c) the deterrent and corrective effect of application of the sanctions provided for by law;
(d) the existence of intent or negligence of the infractors and the respective seriousness of the infraction.

Article 31

(Finding of facts in the proceedings)

1. The finding of facts in the proceedings aimed at hearing and deciding on the infractions set forth at Article 46 of Law 15/94, of September 23, is a responsibility of the Foreign Investment Office.

2. The Foreign Investment Office must initiate a process of inquiry into acts or situations of non-compliance with the provisions of Law 15/94, of September 23, and the respective

complementary legislation, with a view to determining the facts and responsibilities, and the possible application of sanctions.

3. In the course of the fact-finding in the inquiry process, the Foreign Investment Office may propose to the competent entity that it reject the proposal, or the suspension, on a preventive basis, of some or all of the effects of the acts or situations subject to the inquiry.

CHAPTER IV RIGHTS AND OBLIGATIONS

Article 32

(General principle)

1. Pursuant to Article 8(1) of Law 15/94, of September 23, the Angolan state ensures fair, non-discriminatory, and equitable treatment to the companies incorporated and the goods imported under said law, guaranteeing protection and security, and not hindering in any manner their management, maintenance, and operation, without prejudice to the exercise of the appropriate inspection function.

2. Foreign investment operations engaged in without observing the provisions of Law 15/94, of September 23, and the respective complementary legislation, shall have no effect, especially in relation to foreign exchange.

3. Foreign investors must carry out the duties established in Law 15/94, of September 23, and the respective complementary legislation, as a prerequisite for engaging in the foreign exchange operations that are part of the approved proposal, as well as for executing the public documents and for making the commercial registrations effective.

4. In the case of an investment made under the contractual regime, the effective granting of benefits depends on the exact and punctual attainment, by the investors, of the objectives sought.

Article 33

(Dividends and profits)

1. Once the capital of the company is fully paid in, the state guarantees the annual transfer abroad of the dividends and profits, pursuant to generally accepted accounting principles and set forth in the company's chart of accounts, and after deducting the legal and statutory reserves and paying the taxes due, taking account of the magnitude of the investment of the non-resident entities and any contractual limitation in this respect.

2. The Ministry of Economy and Finance shall authorize the transfer once the conditions for authorization of the investment have been met.

3. The annual transfers of dividends and profits may, on an exceptional basis, come to be regulated by the Minister of Economy and Finance, if in view of its large amount they might significantly aggravate balance of payments difficulties.

Article 34

(Export of the product of sale or liquidation)

The export of the product of sale or liquidation of the investments authorized is guaranteed, including the other values, in the terms that come to be agreed upon, and based on the investment made, after having paid the respective taxes and so long as at least six years have elapsed from the date of the initial import of capital.

Article 35

(Compensation for expropriation or nationalization)

1. In the terms of the law, the expropriation or nationalization of the goods or rights that are the subject of foreign investment may only occur, on an exceptional basis, for weighty motives of public interest; the foreign investor is guaranteed the right to fair compensation, in an amount to be determined based on the rules and common practices of international law, with recourse to arbitration.

2. To this end, an Arbitration Committee shall be set up with three members: one representative of the Government of Angola, one representative of the foreign investor, and a third arbitrator to be chosen by the other two or, if there is no agreement on the choice, by an Angolan judge of renowned prestige and qualifications.

3. The provisions in the foregoing paragraphs do not foreclose recourse to international bodies, in the terms of international conventions to which the Angolan state is a party.

CHAPTER V FINAL AND TRANSITORY PROVISIONS

Article 36

(Cases pending)

1. In a period not to exceed 90 days after the entry into force of this statute, the Foreign Investment Office shall screen all the processes pending.

2. In this operation, by the 30th day the Foreign Investment Office shall return to the proponents the letters of Intent or proposals for investment whose value is less than two hundred fifty thousand dollars.

3. The proponents whose processes are susceptible to the treatment provided for in the previous paragraph may, within 15 days after entry into force of this statute, state in writing to the Foreign Investment Office their intent to increase the value of the planned investment.

4. The processes pending with regard to intentions or proposals for investment whose value is from two hundred fifty thousand to five million dollars, 45 days after the entry into force of this statute, shall be considered tacitly authorized; the proponents should then contact the Foreign Investment Office for the purpose contemplated in Article 24(2) of Law 15/94, of September 23.

5. The processes pending with regard to intentions or proposals for investment whose value is from five million to fifty million dollars, if not subsumed under Article 30(c) of Law 15/94, of September 23 shall continue to be processed under the prior approval regime.

6. The processes pending with regard to intentions or proposals for investment whose value is greater than or equal to fifty million dollars, or from five million to fifty million dollars, yet nonetheless subsumed by Article 30(c) of Law 15/94, of September 23, shall continue to be processed under the contractual regime.

7. In the cases provided for in paragraph 5 of this article, the proponents may, within 30 days after the entry into force of this statute, request access to the contractual regime, if they consider that this regime is applicable, in the terms of the law, to their processes.

The Prime Minister, Marcelino JosJ Carlos Moco

The President of the Republic, JosJ Eduardo dos Santos

LEGAL, INVESTMENT AND BUSINESS CLIMATE IN ANGOLA

- A branch has no legal entity and thus, obligations entered into by the branch are binding on the foreign company (if the company fails to comply with the registration requirements, the directors and the company will be jointly liable) . All mandatory regulations (e.g. labour and tax laws) apply to the activities of a branch.

- A branch does not offer the protection of limited liability, and the assets of the operating company are therefore subject to any legal claims arising through the Angolan operations. This could cause serious problems in cases of insolvency or payment of fiscal debts.

- The foreign investment regulation requirements also apply to the registration of a branch in Angola.

- From a legal point of view, a subsidiary has its own legal entity and remains independent of its shareholders.

- For the incorporation of an Angolan company, compliance with the Commercial Law and registration requirements is imposed by Angolan foreign investment regulations.

- A subsidiary company can be set up in different ways. Angolan Commercial Law provides for different kinds of legal structures, of which the most important are Limited Liability Partnerships (Sociedade por Quotas - LDA) and share companies (Sociedade Anonima - SARL) . Both are limited liability company structures and both have to be formed by notarial deed and subsequently registered in the Commercial Registry.

- The minimum capital legally required was established some years ago in Kwanza 50.000. With the strong devaluation of the Kwanza this number is not used for foreign investors for whom an approximate amount of USD 3.000 is used as minimum.

- One of the solutions to consider is to split specific projects and/or contractor services agreements between the incorporated company and the foreign company operating through the branch. Another company could be formed for the rendering of services, in which foreign personnel would be concentrated.

- This would imply that the investing company operates both with a structure established in Angola and with an offshore occasional participation of the mother company, for specific projects or contractual co-operation.

For additional analytical, business and investment opportunities information,
please contact Global Investment & Business Center, USA
at (202) 546-2103. Fax: (202) 546-3275. E-mail: rusric@erols.com

TAXATION

- Companies carrying out industrial and commercial activities in Angola are subject to Industrial Tax (Income Tax) on all profits derived from Angola. If the company has its head office or effective management control in Angola, it is subject to Industrial Tax on its profits derived from Angola and one-third of its gross income earned abroad.

- Under the new tax legislation, all the income obtained abroad by an Angolan company operating overseas will be fully taxable.

- Foreign entities with a permanent establishment in Angola are subject to Industrial Tax only on profits derived from the permanent establishment.

- All companies, regardless of whether they have a permanent place of business in Angola, that perform contracts or subcontracts or render services in Angola, are subject to Industrial Tax if the amounts paid to such companies are considered expenses for Industrial Tax purposes.

- This provision is likely to be changed, as a consequence of the new definition of permanent establishment. This new definition also considers, as permanent establishment, the mere rendering of services, if made by the presence in Angola of hired personnel, for more than 90 days within a year. This implies that those companies that render services will be taxable under the general rules of the Industrial Tax Code.

- The Capital Income Tax imposed on taxable dividends was raised to 10% under the new legislation. An exemption, on the same conditions as the exemption from Industrial Tax, can be obtained from the Minister of Finance for new industries and investment projects in fundamental areas.

- The tax year is the calendar year. Companies other than Angola companies operating abroad must file tax returns together with their financial statements by 31 May in the year following the tax year. Angolan companies operating abroad must file by 31 July. Advance payments of, at least 50% of the prior year s tax liability must be made by 10 December of the tax year. Final payment of tax is due on 15 September of the following year.

PERSONAL INCOME TAX

- All individuals receiving employment income for duties performed in Angola are subject to income tax.

- Under the new legislation, the personal tax liability is clarified. Personal Income Tax will be payable by all Angolan residents and on all the income obtained from an activity in Angola.

- Taxable income includes all employment income, such as wages, salaries, leave payments, fees, gratuities, bonuses and premiums or allowances paid or granted by reason of employment, in cash or in kind.

- Directors fees are ordinarily treated as individual taxable income, regarded in the same way as remuneration income. Under the tax reform, members of any of the boards of Angolan companies will always be considered as residents in Angola for tax purposes.

- Income taxes on employees are satisfied by employer withholding, and employees need not file returns.

- No resident individuals are assessed on only Angolan-source income. The employer or other payer withholds the amount due and is liable for the tax.

EXCHANGE CONTROL

- All the exchange operations are subject to Banco Nacional de Angola supervision.

- All the imported funds (for instance, for start-up expenses) shall be converted into NKz in Angola.

- The contracts signed by a branch or subsidiary must be made in Nkz. However, this obligation does not forbid the parties from entering into a splitting contract in which the head office/mother company is paid directly in another currency and the branch or the subsidiary is paid in NKz.

VISA REQUIREMENTS

All foreign workers performing duties in Angola shall obtain visas after justification is made for their stay. If the workers are hired by an Angolan company or allocated to a permanent establishment of a foreign company, they should also obtain work permits.

NEW RULES TO PROMOTE TRADE AND INVESTMENT

Recognizing the importance foreign participation will play in economic rehabilitation and recovery, the government of Angola has made promotion of trade and investment a high priority. By adopting tough new economic reform measures and entering negotiations with the IMF, the Government is laying the ground work for stable economic growth and development. Angola has an excellent history of cooperation with US firms, particularly in

For additional analytical, business and investment opportunities information,
please contact Global Investment & Business Center, USA
at (202) 546-2103. Fax: (202) 546-3275. E-mail: rusric@erols.com

the oil sector. The oil industry provides a good example of how the US-Angola partnership has benefited both countries.

In September 1994, Angola passed a new foreign investment law to reduce barriers to investment and provide the necessary protections and guarantees to attract new investors. Since then, major US and international companies have begun to participate in Angola's growing economy through infrastructure and natural resources development projects. The government continues to strengthen its commitment to foreign investors by abolishing state monopolies, privatizing state-owned companies and speeding up foreign investment procedures.

The government plans to make available new opportunities to foreign investors, including:

- participation in onshore and downstream oil operations;
- privatization of all 33 state-owned coffee companies;
- rehabilitation and reconstruction contracts worth hundreds of millions of dollars;
- reconstruction of its national power grid at a cost exceeding $800 million;
- modernization of its telecommunications facilities and infrastructure.

THE NEW FOREIGN INVESTMENT LAW:

- Ensures that foreign companies are guaranteed equal treatment;
- Opens nearly all sectors of the economy to foreign investment, including infrastructure development;
- Private commercial banking is now permitted;
- Privatization of state owned companies continues;
- International participation in the mining sector;
- Allows foreign investors to transfer abroad dividends, profits and proceeds of the sale of investments;
- Offers special fiscal incentives to foreign investors who employ a high proportion of Angolans and provide them with professional training and benefits equal to foreign employees;
- Simplifies and speeds up foreign investment procedures;
- Investments less than $5 million no longer need full Cabinet approval.

PROMOTING TRADE AND INVESTMENT

Recognizing the importance foreign participation will play in economic rehabilitation and recovery, the government of Angola has made promotion of trade and investment a high priority. By adopting tough new economic reform measures and entering negotiations with the IMF, the Government is laying the ground work for stable economic growth and development. Angola has an excellent history of cooperation with US firms, particularly in the oil sector. The oil industry provides a good example of how the US-Angola partnership has benefited both countries.

In September 1994, Angola passed a new foreign investment law to reduce barriers to investment and provide the necessary protections and guarantees to attract new investors.

Since then, major US and international companies have begun to participate in Angola's growing economy through infrastructure and natural resources development projects. The government continues to strengthen its commitment to foreign investors by abolishing state monopolies, privatizing state-owned companies and speeding up foreign investment procedures.

The government plans to make available new opportunities to foreign investors, including:

☐ participation in onshore and downstream oil operations;
☐ privatization of all 33 state-owned coffee companies;

☐ rehabilitation and reconstruction contracts worth hundreds of millions of dollars;

☐ reconstruction of its national power grid at a cost exceeding $800 million;

☐ modernization of its telecommunications facilities and infrastructure.

The New Foreign Investment Law:

☐ Ensures that foreign companies are guaranteed equal treatment;

☐ Opens nearly all sectors of the economy to foreign investment, including infrastructure development;

☐ Private commercial banking is now permitted;

☐ Privatization of state owned companies continues;

☐ International participation in the mining sector;

☐ Allows foreign investors to transfer abroad dividends, profits and proceeds of the sale of investments;

☐ Offers special fiscal incentives to foreign investors who employ a high proportion of Angolans and provide them with professional training and benefits equal to foreign employees;

☐ Simplifies and speeds up foreign investment procedures;

☐ Investments less than $5 million no longer need full Cabinet approval.

IMPORTANT LAWS AND REGULATIONS FOR OIL AND GAS SECTOR

PETROLEUM ACTIVITIES LAW
LAW No. 10/04 of 12 November 2004

Law No. 13/78, of 26 August 1978 (General Petroleum Activities Law) constitutes a landmark in Angolan petroleum legislation, setting forth the fundamental principles regulating the exploitation of the country's petroleum potential in the post-independence years, and thanks to which this major sector of the economy has gone from strength to strength.

Although the above Law may still be considered up-to-date in its general outline, in view of factors such as the natural growth of the Angolan oil industry, the consequently greater store of experience which has been built up and the implications of this for the implementation of new concepts and practices in petroleum concessions, it has been decided to revise the Law, in order to enrich and update its contents.

This new Law, which maintains the fundamental principle of state ownership of petroleum resources enshrined in the Constitutional Law, and the regimes of a sole concessionaire and mandatory association for petroleum concessions, also retains a number of other principles contained in Law No. 13/78, of 26 August 1978, which, in view of their importance, shall be maintained fully valid in the Angolan legal system.

In this context, this law envisages to safeguard, *inter alia*, the following principles of economic and social policy for the sector, namely, the protection of the national interest, the promotion of the development of the employment market and the valorisation of mineral resources, the protection of the environment and the rational usage of petroleum resources and the increase of the Country's competitiveness on the international market.

It has also been decided to include in this new Law a number of other issues of recognized importance for the Angolan oil industry, in order to bring it into line with the most recent changes in Angolan petroleum law and in international law.

Now, therefore, under subparagraph (b) of Article 88 of the Constitutional Law, the National Assembly hereby approves the following:

CHAPTER I GENERAL PROVISIONS

Article 1 (Object)

1. This law seeks to establish the rules of access to and the exercise of petroleum operations in the available areas of the surface and subsurface areas of the Angolan national territory, inland waters, territorial waters, exclusive economic zone and the continental shelf.
2. Other petroleum activities, including the refining of crude oil and the storage, transportation, distribution and marketing of petroleum shall be regulated by separate law.

Article 2 (Definitions)

For the purposes of this law, and unless otherwise expressly stated in the text, the words and expressions used herein shall have the following meaning, it being understood that the reference to the singular includes reference to the plural and vice versa:

Affiliate shall mean:

(a) A company or any other entity in which the associate holds, directly or indirectly, the absolute majority of the votes in the shareholders' meeting or is the holder of more than fifty percent of the rights and interests which confer the power of management on such company or entity, or has the power of management and control over such company or entity;

(b) A company or any other entity which holds, either directly or indirectly, the absolute majority of votes at the shareholders' meeting or equivalent corporate body of the associate or holds the power of management and control over the latter;

(c) A company or any other entity in which either the absolute majority of votes in the respective shareholders' meeting or the rights and interests which confer the power of management on said company or entity are, either directly or indirectly, held by a company or any other entity which directly or indirectly holds the absolute majority of votes at the shareholders' meeting or equivalent corporate body of any of the associate or holds the power of management and control over the latter.

Foreign Associate - a corporate entity incorporated abroad and which in its capacity as foreign investor associates itself to the National Concessionaire, in any of the forms set forth in Article 14, paragraph 2. National Associate – a corporate entity which is formed under Angolan law, with registered office in Angola which in such capacity associates itself to the National Concessionaire in any of the forms set forth in Article 14, paragraph 2. Appraisal - the activity carried out following the discovery of a petroleum deposit aimed at better defining the parameters of the reservoir in order to assess its commerciality, including, but not limited to:

drilling of appraisal wells and running deep tests; collecting special geological samples and reservoir fluids; running supplementary studies and acquisition of geophysical and other data, as well as the processing of same data.

Petroleum Bonus – the pecuniary compensation which the associates pay to the National Concessionaire in consideration for executing the Petroleum Operations. National Concessionaire - the entity to which the State grants mining rights. Commercial Discovery - the discovery of a petroleum deposit deemed able to justify development. Mining Rights – the set of powers granted to the National Concessionaire. Development - the activities carried out after the commercial discovery, including, but not limited to:

geological, geophysical and reservoir studies and surveys; drilling of production and injection wells; design, construction, installation, connection and initial testing of equipment, pipelines, systems, facilities, machinery and related activities necessary to produce and operate said wells, to take, save, treat, handle, store, reinject, transport and deliver petroleum, and to undertake repressuring, recycling and other secondary and tertiary recovery projects.

Natural Gas -a mixture essentially comprising methane and other hydrocarbons which are in a petroleum deposit in a gaseous state or which change into such state when produced under normal conditions of pressure and temperature. Licensee - the entity that has been granted a prospecting license under Chapter IV herein. Petroleum Operations - the activities of prospecting, exploration, appraisal, development and petroleum production, carried out under this law. Operator - the entity that carries out petroleum operations in a given petroleum concession.

Exploration -the prospecting activities and the drilling and testing of wells leading to the discovery of petroleum deposits. Petroleum -crude oil, natural gas and all other hydrocarbon substances that may be found in and extracted from, or otherwise obtained and secured from the area of a petroleum concession. Crude Oil - a mixture of liquid hydrocarbons deriving from any petroleum concession which is in liquid state at the wellhead or in the separator under normal conditions of pressure and temperature, including distillates and condensates, as well as liquids extracted from natural gas. Continental Shelf – the sea bed and the subsoil of the submarine zones adjacent to national territory, up to the limits set forth in international conventions or other agreements to which Angola is a party. Production – the set of activities intended to petroleum extraction, including the running, servicing, maintenance and repair of compelled wells, as well as of the equipment, pipelines, systems, facilities and plants completed during development, including all activities related to planning, scheduling, controlling, measuring, testing and carrying out of the flow, gathering, treating, storing and dispatching of petroleum from the underground petroleum reservoirs, to the designated exporting or lifting location, and furthermore, the operations of abandonment of the facilities and petroleum deposits and related activities. Prospecting – the set of operations to be carried out onshore or offshore, through the use of geological, geochemical or geophysical methods, with a view to locating petroleum deposits, excluding the drilling of wells, the processing, analysis and interpretation of data acquired from the respective liftings or of the information available in the archives of the supervising Ministry, or the National Concessionaire, as well as regional studies and maping leading to an appraisal and better knowledge of the petroleum potential of a given area.

Article 3 (State ownership of petroleum deposits)

Petroleum deposits existing in the areas mentioned in Article 1 are an integral part of the public property of the State.

CHAPTER II PRINCIPLES OF ORGANIZATION AND EXECUTION OF PETROLEUM OPERATIONS

Article 4 (Principle of exclusivity of National Concessionaire)

1. The National Concessionaire is Sociedade Nacional de Combustível de Angola, Empresa Pública - (Sonangol, E.P.) , as the holder of mining rights.
2. Mining rights shall be granted to the National Concessionaire under the terms of Article

Article 5 (Non-transferability of mining rights)

The National Concessionaire cannot transfer Its mining rights, whether in all or in part and any actions to that effect shall be deemed null and void.

Article 6 (Conditions for the exercise of Petroleum Operations)

Petroleum operations may only be carried out under a prospecting license or petroleum concession in accordance with this law.

Article 7 (Principles for conducting work)

The licensees, the National Concessionaire and its associates shall conduct and execute, or cause to be executed, the petroleum operations, in a regular and continuous manner and in compliance with applicable laws, regulations and administrative decisions and the good oil industry techniques and practices. Petroleum operations shall be conducted in a prudent manner and shall take into account the safety of persons and facilities, as well as the protection of the environment and the conservation of nature. Holders of the rights granted under this law may freely program, plan and execute, or cause to be executed, the works which they are obliged or authorized to do, using the most appropriate human and technical resources in compliance with the law, the prospecting license, the concession decree and the provisions of the preceding paragraph and Articles 27 and 86.

Article 8 (Powers to issue licenses and concessions)

Prospecting licenses shall be issued by the supervising Minister. The Government shall be responsible for granting concessions for the exercise of mining rights.

Article 9 (Overlapping and conflict of rights)

The granting of rights for the exercise of petroleum operations is not, in principle, incompatible with the prior or subsequent granting of rights for the exercise of other activities relating to other natural resources or uses for the same area. In the event that the exercise of the rights referred to in the previous paragraph is incompatible, the Government shall decide which of the rights shall prevail and under what terms, without prejudice to any compensation which may be due to the holders of the rights thereby overridden as per Article 55. In any case, rights relating to petroleum operations may only be granted with safeguards for the country's interests in respect of defense, safety, the environment, navigation, research, management and preservation of natural resources, particularly of the aquatic biological, living or non living. For the purposes of this Article, the entities with powers for specific sectors under the relevant legislation shall be consulted.

Article 10 (Concession periods and phases)

The duration of concessions shall, as a rule, comprise two periods, divided into phases:

The exploration period, comprising the exploration phase and the appraisal phase; The production period, comprising the development phase and the production phase;

Concessions may cover the production period only.

Article 11 (Definition of concession areas)

The supervising Minister shall have powers to define concession areas, by executive decree, upon obtaining authorization from the Government.

Article 12 (Duration and extension of prospecting licenses and concessions)

The duration of prospecting licenses and of each of the concession periods shall be defined in the respective license and in the concession decree. The maximum duration of a prospecting license is three years.

The duration of the prospecting licenses or of each of the concession periods may exceptionally be extended, upon the request of the licensee or the National Concessionaire. The powers to grant such an extension shall rest with the supervising Minister, who grants or refuses the same in accordance with the reasons invoked and certification checked that the licensee or the National Concessionaire have performed their existing obligations. The application referred to in paragraph 3 shall set forth the facts which have led to the need for an extension. Prospecting licenses shall be deemed granted as from the effective date of the statute granting the same. Concessions shall be deemed granted as from the dates indicated below:

Should the National Concessionaire enter into an association with other entities under Article 14 herein, as from the execution of the relevant contract; Should the National Concessionaire not enter into an association with other entities, as from the effective date of the concession decree.

Article 13 (Obligation for association)

Any company that wishes to carry out petroleum operations in the territory of Angola outside the scope of a prospecting license, may only do so together with the National Concessionaire under the terms of the following Article.

Article 14 (Types of association and risk services agreement)

Subject to the prior consent of the Government, the National Concessionaire may associate with Angolan or foreign entities of recognized capacity, technical knowledge and financial capability. Such association may take the following forms:

Corporation; Consortium; Production Sharing Agreement.

The National Concessionaire shall also be permitted to carry out petroleum operations by means of risk services agreements.

Article 15 (Majority participation of the National Concessionaire)

In the associations referred to in Article 14, subparagraphs 2(a) and (b) where the National Concessionaire holds a participating interest, such interest shall, as a rule, exceed fifty percent. The Government may authorize the National Concessionaire, in duly grounded cases, to hold a participating interest lower than that established in the previous paragraph.

Article 16 (Assignment)

The associates of the National Concessionaire may only assign part or all of their contractual rights and duties to third parties of recognized capacity, technical knowledge and financial capability, after obtaining the prior consent of the supervising Minister by means of an Executive Decree. For purposes of this law, the transfer to third parties of shares representing more than fifty percent of the share capital of the assignor shall be equivalent to the assignment of contractual rights and duties. The authorization referred to in paragraph 1 shall not be necessary in the event of assignment between affiliated companies and provided that the assignor remains jointly and severally liable for the duties of the assignee. The relevant assignment contracts referred to in paragraphs 1 and 3 of this Article shall be submitted to the prior approval of the National Concessionaire. The National Concessionaire shall have the right of first refusal in respect of the assignments referred to in paragraph 1 when the assignee is a non-affiliate of the assignor. In the event that the National Concessionaire waives its right of first refusal, such right shall be immediately transferred to the National Associates which enjoy the special status of national company, pursuant to Article 31, paragraph 3.

Article 17 (Management of Petroleum Operations)

The participation of the National Concessionaire in associations with third parties shall necessarily include the right to take part in the management of petroleum operations, under the relevant contracts.

Article 18 (Obligatory Risk)

The risk of investing in the exploration period shall be borne by the entities which associate themselves with the National Concessionaire. These entities shall not be entitled to recover the capital invested in the event that no economically viable discovery is made.

Article 19 (Operator)

The operator shall be indicated in the relevant concession decree upon proposal of the National Concessionaire, and shall be an entity of recognized capacity, technical knowledge and financial capability. The operator shall be subject to the legislation in force and shall strictly comply with the provisions of the relevant concession decree. Any change of operator shall be subject to the prior consent of the supervising Minister, on the proposal of the National Concessionaire.

Article 20 (Job and service contracts)

The operator shall notify the supervising Ministry and the Ministry of Finance, through the National Concessionaire, of the contracts and sub-contracts entered into with third parties for carrying out petroleum operations, under the terms to be defined by said Ministries.

Article 21 (Rules for the exploitation and recovery of deposits)

1. The mining rights granted hereunder carry the obligation to explore and produce petroleum in a rational manner, in accordance with the most appropriate technical and scientific practices used in the international petroleum industry and in accordance with the national interest.
2. The National Concessionaire and its associates shall be subject to the specific obligations described in the preceding paragraph, together with the general obligations to preserve petroleum deposits or reserves; the breach of such obligations shall be subject to the penalties established by law and regulations.

Article 22 (Safety zones)

The supervising Ministry, after consulting with other relevant bodies, shall establish the limits and the regime of the safety zone adjacent to the site of the equipment and facilities, whether

permanent or temporary, used in the petroleum operations.

Article 23 (Safety and hygiene in the workplace)

1. The petroleum operations shall be carried out in accordance with applicable law and the generally accepted practices in the international oil industry relating to safety, hygiene and health at work.
2. For purposes of the preceding paragraph, the National Concessionaire and its associates shall submit to the supervising Ministry the plans required by applicable law.

Article 24 (Environmental protection)

1. In carrying out their activities, the licensees, the National Concessionaire and its associates shall take the precautions necessary to protect the environment, in order to preserve the same, namely in respect of health, water, soil and subsoil, air, the preservation of biodiversity, flora and fauna, ecosystems, landscape, atmosphere and cultural, archeological and artistic heritage.
2. For purposes of the preceding paragraph, the licensees, the National Concessionaire and its associates shall submit to the supervising Ministry, within the required time frames, the plans required by applicable law, specifying the practical measures which should be taken in order to prevent harm to the environment, including environmental impact studies and audits, plans for rehabilitation of the landscape and structures or contractual mechanisms and permanent management and environmental auditing plans.

Article 25 (Liability)

1. Licensees, the National Concessionaire and its associates shall be obliged to repair the damage they cause to third parties in the course of petroleum operations, unless they can show to have acted without fault.
2. Except as provided in Article 79, paragraph 3, the State shall not be liable for losses or damage of any type or nature, including, but not limited to, losses and damage to property or compensation payable to persons for death or accident, caused by or resulting from any petroleum operation carried out hereunder by the licensees, the National Concessionaire or its associates, or by any entity acting on behalf of the same.
3. The approvals and authorizations which the entities referred to in this Article obtain from the relevant State bodies shall not exempt them from any civil liability in which they may incur.

Article 26 (Promotion of Angolan business community and development)

1. The Government shall adopt measures to guarantee, promote and encourage investment in the petroleum sector by companies held by Angolan citizens and create the conditions necessary for such purpose.
2. The National Concessionaire and its associates shall cooperate with governmental authorities in developing public actions to promote the socioeconomic development of Angola.
3. Before such public actions are undertaken, the parties involved shall agree upon the scope of the projects, the origin of the funds to be used and the recovery of costs related thereto, if applicable.

Article 27 (Use of national products and services)

Licensees, the National Concessionaire and its associates, and any other entities which cooperate with them in carrying out Petroleum Operations shall:

Acquire materials, equipment, machinery and consumer goods of national production, of the same or approximately the same quality and which are available for sale and delivery in due time, at prices which are no more than ten per cent higher than the imported items including transportation and insurance costs and customs charges due;

Contract local service providers, to the extent to which the services they provide are similar to those available on the international market and their prices, when subject to the same tax charges, are no more than ten percent higher than the prices charged by foreign contractors for similar services.

1. For the purposes of the provisions of paragraph 1, Angolan companies shall be mandatorily consulted on the same terms as those used for consulting companies on the international market.
2. The supervising Ministry has the duty of supervising compliance with the preceding paragraphs, and contracts in breach with the provisions of this Article shall be deemed null and void.

CHAPTER III RIGHTS AND OBLIGATIONS

Article 28 (Rights and obligations of licensees)

Licensees shall enjoy the following rights:

(a) To carry out, by itself or by third parties, the works set out in the prospecting license;

(b) To carry out, by itself or by third parties, the infra-structures necessary for the carrying out of the works referred to in paragraph (a) ;

(c) To occupy, in compliance with the law and existing rights, the areas necessary for the execution of prospecting operations, as well accommodation in the field for personnel assigned to such operations;

(d) To import consumable or durable goods intended for the execution of the works set out in the prospecting license.

Licensees shall have the duties referred to in sub-paragraphs (b) , (f) , (g) , (h) , (i) and (k) of Article 30, paragraph 1.

Article 29 (Rights of the National Concessionaire)

Subject to the specific regulatory provisions related to each of the situations hereinafter described, and in addition to the mining rights of which it is the titleholder, the National Concessionaire shall also have, amongst others, the following rights:

(a) To carry out, by itself or by third parties, the activities related to petroleum operations;

(b) To carry out, by itself or by third parties, the infrastructure work required to perform, under the normal economic conditions of the oil industry, the petroleum operations, including the transport of materials, equipment and extracted products;

(c) To occupy, with due respect of the law and existing rights, the land which is necessary to carry out the petroleum operations and for accommodation, in the camp, of the personnel engaged in such operations;

(d) To import consumable or durable goods intended for the performance of the Petroleum Operations;

(e) To take, transport, store, sell, load and export its share of the production, under the terms and conditions of the concession;

(f) With due respect for applicable law, and the national interests and security, to be assisted by the Angolan authorities in the entry, stay and departure from the Republic of Angola, of the workers of any nationality of the National Concessionaire, its associates or any entities which cooperate with them in the carrying out of petroleum operations.

The facilities referred to in sub-paragraph f) of the preceding paragraph shall apply to the members of the relevant employee's family, including spouse, minor children and those children who, though adults, are living under the same roof as the employee.

Article 30 (Duties of the National Concessionaire)

Without prejudice to its duties under Angolan law, this law and the concession decree, in relation to Petroleum Operations the National Concessionaire shall:

(a) be subject to the guidelines of the Government in respect of the trade policy for import and export, taking into consideration at all times, in the performance of its business, the higher interests of the Republic of Angola;

(b) carry out the obligatory work programs and other approved work plans within the time frames established therein, under sound technical rules and in accordance with the oil industry practice;

(c) when petroleum shows occur in any drill hole, carry out the relevant tests in accordance with the approved programs, and to inform the supervising Ministry, without delay, of the results of the same, to enable it to form an opinion on the value of the discoveries and the viability of their exploitation;

(d) submit proposals for the establishment of petroleum storage and transport facilities to the approval of the supervising Ministry;

(e) to provide the relevant State authorities with all the data which they deem necessary for the effective control of petroleum operations, and allow their representatives free access to all sites, facilities and equipment relating to petroleum operations, so that such representatives may perform their duties of supervision, inspection and verification;

(f) submit to all supervision, inspection and verification activities which the State may wish to carry out;

(g) prepare and submit to the supervising Ministry monthly reports on the Petroleum Operations, including all technical and economic data related to the operations carried out during the month to which the report relates, and also quarterly and annual operations reports, including a statement of results and an analysis comparing these with the forecast results for the respective periods.

(h) keep in Angola all books and accounting records kept under the commercial law in force, the original accounting documents justifying expenses incurred in relation with the petroleum operations, as well as a complete and updated record of all technical operations conducted under the terms of the relevant concession decree;

(i) keep in the best storage conditions possible, significant portions of each cutting sample and each core obtained in drill holes, together with all and any data, namely geological and geophysical reports, well logs, magnetic tapes, tests, production and reservoir reports, information and interpretation of said data;

(j) submit to open tender, save in cases authorized by the supervising Ministry and under terms to be regulated, the execution of works provided for in the approved work programs and budgets;

(k) grant to the representatives of the relevant State authorities and other official organizations the same conditions granted in the camp to its own employees of equivalent professional rank;

1. The reports referred in sub-paragraph 1(g) shall also be sent to the Ministry of Finance.
2. The National Concessionaire shall comply in full with any obligations which may result

from liabilities arising from risks for which it has not obtained insurance coverage.

Article 31 (Rights and duties of associates of the National Concessionaire)

1. In order to pursue the objectives established in the relevant contracts entered into with the National Concessionaire, the associates of the National Concessionaire shall have, amongst others, the rights set out in Article 29 herein, with the limitations established in the main body of the same Article.
2. The associates of the National Concessionaire shall be subject to the general obligations set forth in Angolan law regarding companies which invest and operate in Angola, the terms herein, the concession statutes, the obligations set out in Article 30, paragraph 1, the obligations contained in the relevant contracts entered into with the National Concessionaire and, furthermore, the following obligations:

(a) to participate in the efforts made towards the integration, training and professional promotion of Angolan citizens under Article 86 and applicable law;

(b) without prejudice to Article 30, subparagraph 1(e) , to keep, under the terms of the law and of the contracts entered into with the National Concessionaire, strictly confidential any technical or economic information obtained in the course of the petroleum operations;

(c) to adopt the accounting procedures and rules established in Angolan legislation and in the contracts entered into with the National Concessionaire;

(d) to submit all accounting books and records to an annual audit to be conducted by the Ministry of Finance.

The national associates shall enjoy the special facilities and the consequent special rights and duties set forth in this law and in the laws on promotion of Angolan private business community, provided that such associates fulfill and maintain the special legal requirements for national companies set forth in such legislation for the purposes of promotion of the business community, as well as in the relevant regulatory legislation.

Article 32 (Guaranty of performance of duties)

1. The licensees and the associates of the National Concessionaire shall provide a bank guarantee to guarantee the performance of their work obligations under the license or the contract entered into with the National Concessionaire.
2. The guarantee mentioned in the previous paragraph shall be provided within thirty days of the date of issue of the prospecting license or the date of signing of the contract between the National Concessionaire and its associates.
3. The value of the guarantee for the prospecting license shall be equivalent to fifty percent of the work budgeted.
4. The value of the guarantee required from the associates of the National Concessionaire shall be equal to the value which is agreed for the obligatory work program for the petroleum concession.
5. The amount of the bank guarantee referred to in paragraphs 3 and 4 above shall be reduced in the extent of the work obligations set forth therein are complied as provided for in the prospecting license and the agreements mentioned in paragraph 2 above.
6. In the event that the National Concessionaire so requires, and within a period of not less than sixty days as from the date of the signing of the agreements referred to in paragraph 2, the National Concessionaire's associates shall also submit a business guarantee in the form defined thereby.

CHAPTER IV PROSPECTING LICENSE Article 33 (Issuing of license)

In order to facilitate the acquisition and processing of information which might allow for a better assessment and technical back-up of the applications for mining rights or for the status of associate of the National Concessionaire, the supervising Minister may issue a prospecting license, under Article 8 and by means of an Executive Decree, which shall be governed by the provisions of the following Articles.

Article 34 (License holders)

Any Angolan or foreign company of recognized capacity, technical knowledge, and financial capability may apply to the supervising Minister for a prospecting license in order to evaluate the petroleum potential of a given area.

Article 35 (Object, area and nature of license)

1. The prospecting license shall cover the activities referred to in Article 2, paragraph 19.
2. The area covered by a prospecting license shall be defined in the relevant title.
3. A prospecting license does not confer upon the holder any exclusive right to carry out the activities for which it is granted in the area defined in the relevant title.
4. A prospecting license does not confer upon the holder any right of first refusal to become associate of the National Concessionaire in the area to which it relates.

Article 36 (Ownership of data)

1. The data and information acquired in the course of the petroleum operations covered by the prospecting license shall be the property of the State, notwithstanding the rights of the licensees and the National Concessionaire to use such data and information.
2. The supervising Ministry may authorize the licensee to sell the data and information referred to in paragraph 1, once the National Concessionaire has been consulted.

3. In the event that the licensee sells the data and information under the preceding paragraph, the net proceeds from such sale shall be shared equitably between the National Concessionaire and the licensee.

Article 37 (License applications)

1. Applications for prospecting licenses shall be submitted to the supervising Ministry, accompanied by documentation showing the capacity and the technical and financial capability of the applicant, under the provisions of Article 45, duly adapted.
2. The application shall clearly state the objectives, the intended area, technical and financial resources and the provisional budget, in addition to other information which the applicant deems relevant for the purpose.
3. The application shall trigger payment of a fee to be set by the relevant body pursuant to applicable law.

Article 38 (Approval of applications and award of licenses)

1. Applications shall be reviewed by the supervising Ministry, after receiving the recommendation of the National Concessionaire, which may request the applicant to provide further information on the terms of his application.
2. After reviewing the application and hearing the applicant, the supervising Minister shall decide on the application.
3. When the Minister has issued his consent order, the supervising Ministry shall issue the prospecting license and the relevant fee shall be paid under applicable law.
4. The supervising Ministry shall duly publicize the prospecting licenses awarded by it, together with the contents of the same.

Article 39 (Contents of license)

Issued licenses shall contain, namely, the following information:

(a) full identification of the licensee;

(b) area and duration of license;

(c) rights and duties of the licensee;

(d) description of the operations to be undertaken, and the respective schedule and budget;

(e) definition of the regime governing ownership of the data obtained from the prospecting, as set forth in Article 36.

Article 40 (Causes of extinguishment of prospecting licenses)

Prospecting licenses may be extinguished for the following reasons:

(a) Termination;

(b) Waiver;

(c) Expiration.

Article 41 (Termination of licenses)

Prospecting licenses shall be terminated whenever:

(a) The licensee fails to perform his obligations under the license or applicable law;

(b) Cases of force majeure of a definitive nature occur which make it impossible for the licensee to fulfill its obligations in full.

The supervising Minister shall be responsible for terminating prospecting licenses after consulting with the National Concessionaire.

Article 42 (Waiver of license)

A prospecting license may lapse on waiver by the licensee provided that he has performed his legal duties and the duties imposed by the license in full by the date on which such waiver becomes effective.

Article 43 (Expiration of licenses)

Prospecting licenses may expire in the following cases:

(a) expiry of the term of the license;

(b) extinction of the license holder;

(c) accomplishment of an expiration condition provided for in the license.

CHAPTER V PETROLEUM CONCESSIONS

SECTION I CONCESSIONS AND THE STATUS OF ASSOCIATE OF THE NATIONAL CONCESSIONAIRE

Article 44 (Granting of concessions and the status of associate of the National Concessionaire)

1. In the event that the National Concessionaire does not wish to associate itself with any other entity in order to carry out petroleum operations in a given area, the Government may, at the request of the National Concessionaire, award it directly the concession by publication, in the Official Gazette, of the relevant concession decree.
2. In the event that the National Concessionaire wishes to associate itself with third parties in order to carry out petroleum operations in a given area jointly, the concession shall be granted by means of a concession decree and shall be deemed effective on the date referred to in Article 12, sub-paragraph 7(b) .
3. To ends established in the previous paragraph, the National Concessionaire shall apply to the supervising Ministry for due authorization to carry out an open tender to define the entities with which it shall associate, whose application for authorization shall be accompanied by the draft terms of reference for the tendering process.
4. The status of associate of the National Concessionaire may be awarded through direct negotiation with the interested companies, but only in the following cases:

(a) Immediately following an open tender procedure which has not resulted in the awarding of the status of associate of the National Concessionaire because of the lack of bids;

(b) Immediately following an open tender procedure which has not resulted in the awarding of the status of associate of the National Concessionaire due to the supervising Ministry, after consulting with the National Concessionaire, considered the submitted bids unsatisfactory in view of the adopted criteria for the award.

1. In the event of receiving a proposal for direct negotiations under the preceding paragraph, the National Concessionaire, if the supervising Ministry decides to go ahead with the award of the petroleum concession, shall declare the same through a public notice, and may commence direct negotiations with the company involved if, within fifteen days from the date of the notice, no other entity declares an interest in the area in question.
2. If other entities declare an interest in the same concession area, a tender shall be held limited to the interested companies.
3. The Government may cancel the status of associate of the National Concessionaire granted to any entity which seriously or repeatedly fails to fulfill the obligations deriving from this law.

Article 45 (Requirements of associates of the National Concessionaire)

1. The status of Operator associate of the National Concessionaire in a Petroleum concession may only be awarded to corporations which can show they have the technical and financial capacity and capability to carry out Petroleum Operations in the relevant concession area.
2. The status of non-operator associates of the National Concessionaire may only be awarded to corporations which show capacity and financial capability.
3. The requirements regarding evidence of the technical and financial capacity and capability referred to in the preceding paragraphs shall be established in the regulations referred to in Article 46.

SECTION II OPEN TENDER PROCEDURE AND DIRECT NEGOTIATION

Article 46 (Open tender procedures)

The open tender procedures for the award of the status of associate of the National Concessionaire shall be established by regulations to be approved by the Government within sixty days from the effective date of this law.

Article 47 (Direct negotiation regime)

1. In the cases referred to in Article 44, paragraph 4, any entity of proven capacity and technical and financial capability may apply to the National Concessionaire for the award of the status of associate of the National Concessionaire, through direct negotiation.
2. The application referred to in the preceding paragraph shall be drawn up under Article 44, paragraph 3 *in fine*, and shall be submitted by the National Concessionaire, which shall issue its own recommendation to the supervising Minister, for the purpose of deciding whether or not to start the relevant negotiations.
3. If the supervising Ministry, after complying with the provisions of Article 44, paragraph 5, finds that there is still only one entity interested in acquiring the status of associate of the National Concessionaire, it may decide to start the direct negotiation process.

SECTION III CONCESSION DECREE

Article 48 (Contents)

1. The concession decree is the formal instrument of the Government whereby it awards a given petroleum concession to the National Concessionaire.
2. The Concession Decree shall cover the following issues, amongst others:

(a) award of mining rights;

(b) definition and description of the concession area;

(c) duration of the concession and the different phases and periods;

(d) identity of the operator.

Article 49 (Approval of contract)

In the event of the National Concessionaire associating with third parties for the purpose of carrying out Petroleum Operations, the concession decree shall contain the following:

(a) the authorization for the National Concessionaire to enter into such association;

(b) the identity of its associates;

(c) the approval of the relevant contract.

The contract approved under the terms of the preceding paragraph shall be executed within thirty days from the date the concession decree is published in the Official Gazette.

Article 50 (Amendments to contract)

Any amendments which the parties may wish to make to the contract referred to in the preceding Article may only be made by means of approval by decree of the Government.

SECTION IV EXTINGUISHMENT AND REVERSION OF CONCESSIONS

Article 51 (Extinguishment of concessions)

Concessions may be extinguished in any of the following cases:

(a) agreement between the State and the National Concessionaire;

(b) termination;

(c) relinquishment by the National Concessionaire;

(d) redemption;

(e) expiration.

Article 52 (Agreement between the State and the National Concessionaire)

1. Mining rights shall be extinguished by agreement between the State and the National Concessionaire, on the application of the latter stating the duly substantiated grounds which determine that petroleum production is technically or economical unfeasible in the concession area.
2. In the event that the National Concessionaire has entered into an association with third parties under the terms herein, the application referred to in the preceding paragraph shall also be subscribed by the associates.

Article 53 (Termination of concession)

Concessions may be terminated on the following grounds:

(a) unjustified failure to carry out petroleum operations under the terms of the approved plans and projects;

(b) abandonment of any petroleum deposit without the prior consent of the supervising Minister under Article 75;

(c) serious or repeated breach, whilst carrying out Petroleum Operations, of this law, the concession decree or the legislation in force;

(d) willful extraction or production of any mineral not covered by the concession, except when such extraction or production is inevitable as the result of operations conducted in accordance with the common practice in the oil industry.

The Government shall be responsible for terminating concessions following a duly substantiated proposal from the supervising Ministry.

Article 54 (Relinquishment by the National Concessionaire)

1. The National Concessionaire may relinquish all or part of the concession area at any time during the production period provided it has fully performed its legal and contractual duties up to the effective date of the relinquishment.
2. Notice of a relinquishment under the preceding paragraph shall be given to the supervising Ministry at least one year prior to its effective date.
3. Relinquishment under this Article shall cause the extinguishment of mining rights relating to the area in question.
4. Notice of relinquishment under this Article shall also be signed by the associates of the National Concessionaire, if any.

Article 55 (Redemption of concession)

1. Concessions may be redeemed by the State, in whole or in part, for reasons of public interest, against payment of fair compensation.
2. The Government shall have powers to redeem concessions, on the proposal of the supervising Minister.

3. The compensation referred to in paragraph 1 shall be negotiated between the State and the National Concessionaire and, if the latter has associated itself with other entities under this law, such associates shall also take part in the negotiations.
4. Should no agreement be reached as to the value of compensation referred to in paragraph 1 above, such value shall be fixed by arbitration conducted in accordance with the

principles established in Article 89, duly adapted.

Article 56 (Expiration of concession)

The following shall cause concessions to expire:

(a) expiry of the exploration period or extensions thereof, except for areas where Petroleum Operations are still being carried out under the contractually agreed or duly authorized terms, or for which a declaration of commercial discovery was made;

(b) expiry of the production period or any extension thereof;

(c) extinction of the National Concessionaire;

(d) accomplishment of an expiration condition provided for in the concession decree, if any.

Article 57 (Reversion of concession)

Upon extinguishment of a concession in any of the cases provided for in Article 51, and without prejudice to the provisions of Article 75, the equipment, instruments, facilities and any other goods acquired for carrying out the Petroleum Operations, together with all information of a technical and economic nature obtained during such operations shall revert to the National Concessionaire, at no charge to the same.

CHAPTER VI PETROLEUM OPERATIONS

SECTION I PROSPECTING, EXPLORATION AND APPRAISAL

Article 58 (Approval of annual work plans)

1. The work referred to in Article 2 shall be described in an annual plan, drawn up in due detail and with the respective budget, to be prepared by the National Concessionaire and its associates which must be submitted by the former to the supervising Ministry for review and approval.
2. The deadline for submittal of the annual plan referred to in the previous paragraph shall be set by the supervising Ministry.
3. The annual work plan shall be reviewed by the supervising Ministry, which may only order it not to be implemented if it fails to comply with the provisions of the law or of the Concession Decree.
4. In the event of all or part of the annual plan being refused, the supervising Ministry shall notify the National Concessionaire of the fact within fifteen days of receiving the plan, indicating the reasons for the refusal.

5. In the event of refusal under the preceding paragraph, the National Concessionaire and its associates shall draw up a new plan, or rectify the previous plan, which shall be submitted to the supervising Ministry by the National Concessionaire.
6. If the plan is not refused within the period referred to in paragraph 4, the plan may be freely implemented.
7. The National Concessionaire, after consulting its associates may submit addenda to the annual work plan to the supervising Ministry provided they are justified on technical grounds.

Article 59 (Prospecting and exploration activities)

1. During the exploration period, the National Concessionaire shall carry out prospecting operations and exploration drilling throughout the concession area on a regular basis, in accordance with the annual plans and relevant work programs.
    1. The National Concessionaire shall notify the supervising Ministry immediately of the discovery of any petroleum deposit, and keep such Ministry regularly informed of the plans
    2. for future studies and of the findings of such studies.
2. The National Concessionaire shall also notify the supervising Ministry of the existence of beds of other mineral resources, including fresh water and salts.
3. After completing the drilling of any exploration well, the National Concessionaire shall submit to the supervising Ministry a full report on said well within the established legal deadline.

Article 60 (Appraisal activities)

1. In the event of discovery of a commercial well, the National Concessionaire shall carry out the appraisal of the petroleum deposit.
2. After completion of the appraisal, the National Concessionaire shall submit to the supervising Ministry a detailed report on technical and commercial aspects of the petroleum deposit.

Article 61 (Prospecting in adjacent areas)

Whenever the carrying out of prospecting operations in an area adjacent to a concession is of recognized interest to the study of the petroleum potential of the said concession, whether or not the adjacent area is covered by a concession, the supervising Ministry may, on receipt of a duly justified request from the National Concessionaire, authorize the latter, for a given period of time, to carry out such operations; however, the National Concessionaire's activities shall not jeopardize petroleum operations in the adjacent area, if it is included in a petroleum concession.

SECTION II DEVELOPMENT AND PRODUCTION

Article 62 (Commercial discoveries and commencement of the production period)

1. The National Concessionaire may declare a commercial discovery when it deems that, in the course of prospecting, exploration and appraisal activities, there exists an economically exploitable petroleum deposit.
2. The deadline for making a declaration of commercial discovery shall be provided for in the relevant contract.

3. In the event of the National Concessionaire being associated with third parties through a production sharing agreement or if it carries out petroleum operations through a risk services agreement, the declaration referred to in paragraph 1 shall only be signed, respectively, by its associates or by the contractor.
4. Following the declaration of a commercial discovery the National Concessionaire shall then proceed to prepare a preliminary demarcation of the deposit in question, and to prepare the plan referred to in Article 63.
5. A Commercial Discovery shall be communicated to the supervising Ministry, marking the beginning of the production period.

Article 63 (Approval of the general development and production plan)

The National Concessionaire and its associates shall draw up a general development and production plan, which shall be submitted by the National Concessionaire to the supervising Ministry for review and approval within the following deadlines:

(a) three or twelve months from the date of declaration of a Commercial Discovery of crude oil or natural gas, respectively;

(b) three or twelve months from the date of the award of the concession in the case of a concession with a sole period for production of crude oil or natural gas, respectively;

(c) a longer deadline if such is granted by the supervising Ministry.

1. In the event of the occurrence of any of the situations provided for in paragraph 6 of the following Article, the deadline for submission of the plan referred to in the preceding paragraph shall be determined by the supervising Ministry after conclusion of the respective unitization process and after consulting the National Concessionaire and its associates.
2. The information to be included in the general development and production plan shall be defined by the supervising Ministry by means of special regulations.
3. Within ninety days of receiving the plan referred to in paragraph 1, the supervising Ministry shall review and approve the same, being applicable Article 58, paragraphs 4, 5 and 6, duly adapted.
4. The general development and production plan may, at any time, be amended on the express and duly substantiated request of the National Concessionaire to the supervising Ministry after consulting its affiliates; the deadline provided for in paragraph 4 shall apply to the review and approval of requests for amendments.
5. The general development and production plan may not be implemented before approval by the supervising Ministry.
6. The supervising Ministry may exceptionally authorize the National Concessionaire to start certain activities provided for in the general development and production plan before the plan is formally approved.

Article 64 (Unitization and joint development)

The National Concessionaire shall immediately notify the supervising Ministry as soon as:

(a) it discovers in the concession area a petroleum deposit capable of commercially viable development which extends beyond the area of the said concession;

(b) it discovers in the concession area a petroleum deposit which can only be commercially developed when in conjunction with a petroleum deposit existing in an area adjacent to the said concession;

(c) it considers that a commercial discovery in the concession should, for technical and economic reasons, be developed jointly with a commercial discovery in an area adjacent to the concession in question.

1. In the event of the two areas being covered by petroleum concessions, the supervising Ministry may, by means of written notice addressed to the National Concessionaire and its associates, determine that the Petroleum discovered be developed and produced on a joint basis.
2. Should the supervising Ministry exercise the rights referred to in the preceding paragraph, the entities involved shall cooperate in the preparation of a plan for the joint development and production of the petroleum in question.
3. The plan provided for in the previous paragraph shall be presented to the supervising Ministry for review and approval within one hundred and eighty days of the date the National Concessionaire received the notice referred to in the preceding paragraph, or such longer period as the supervising Ministry may grant.
4. Should the general development and production plan not be submitted within the period established in the preceding paragraph, the supervising Ministry may arrange for an independent consultant to prepare the said plan in accordance with generally accepted practice in the international petroleum industry and at the expense of the National Concessionaire and/or its associates.
5. The consultant provided for in the previous paragraph shall consult with and keep all the parties informed of his work at all times.
6. The National Concessionaire and its associates shall execute the general development and production plan drawn up under the terms of the preceding paragraph, on the penalty of the deposit or deposits in question reverting to the State.
7. In the event of unitization under paragraph 1 in respect of an area for which a Petroleum concession has not been granted, or of a neighboring country, the supervising Ministry, by means of a proposal by the National Concessionaire shall submit the strategy to be pursued in order to render the production of the Petroleum in question possible to the approval of the Government.

Article 65 (Approval of annual development and production work plans)

1. The development and production work foreseen for each year shall be stated in annual plans, drawn up in due detail and with the respective budgets, to be submitted by the National Concessionaire to the supervising Ministry for approval and decision, under the provisions of Article 58, paragraphs 4, 5, 6 and 7, duly adapted, applying.
2. The annual development and production plans may be altered, upon request of the National Concessionaire, under Article 58, paragraph 7.

Article 66 (Definitive demarcation of Petroleum deposits)

1. Except in the concessions which cover only the production period, the demarcation of Petroleum areas in which the commercially exploitable Petroleum deposits are located, shall be deemed definitive with the approval of the general development and production plan referred to in Article 63.

2. At the end of the exploration period any areas which have not been definitively demarcated shall cease to be part of the concession area and shall be deemed relinquished in favor of the State.

Article 67 (Right of way and comissioning of facilities)

1. The supervising Ministry may authorize the laying of pipelines, gas transmission lines, cables of all kinds, facilities and other equipment of a petroleum concession throughout another concession, provided that this does not hinder progress in the work of the latter and after consulting the National Concessionaire.
2. The provisions of the preceding paragraph shall also apply to all prospecting made on the relevant area prior to the installation of the referred facilities.

Article 68 (Right to use the facilities of third parties)

1. The supervising Ministry may determine that in a given petroleum concession the facilities and other equipment of another concession be used, if such use contributes to more efficient and economic management of the existing resources and provided this does not imply reducing production levels or disrupting the satisfactory progress of Petroleum Operations in the concession to which such facilities and equipment are allocated.
2. The decision of the supervising Ministry provided for in the previous paragraph, shall be taken after consulting the National Concessionaire and its associates in each of the concessions involved.
3. The amount to be paid for use of the facilities and equipment referred to in the paragraph 1 shall be agreed between the National Concessionaire and its associates, and shall be submitted to the supervising Ministry for homologation.
4. Should no such agreement be reached within a period which the supervising Ministry deems adequate, the Ministry shall set the price for such use.

Article 69 (Commencement of commercial production)

1. No later than ninety days prior to the commencement of commercial production from a
2. petroleum deposit, the National Concessionaire shall apply to the supervising Ministry for commencement of commercial production, submitting for this purpose a report on the execution of the general development and production plan referred to in Article 63.
2. Commercial production from a petroleum deposit may only commence after authorization has been granted by the supervising Ministry, when it has ascertained that the tasks detailed in the general development and production plan have been carried out.

Article 70 (Annual production plans)

1. By the end of October each year, the National Concessionaire and its associates shall prepare annual production plans in respect of each petroleum deposit which shall be submitted by the National Concessionaire to the supervising Ministry for approval.
2. For purposes of Article 21, the National Concessionaire, after consulting its associates, shall, when necessary, submit to the supervising Ministry for review and approval alternative production plans, including possible injection methods

and respective recovery factors, together with secondary and tertiary recovery plans.

3. Any amendment to the production plans established shall require the prior review and approval of the supervising Ministry which, on its own initiative and provided such is justified by the national interest, to ensure the efficient use of reservoirs, facilities and/or transport systems, may determine an increase, reduction or maintenance of the scheduled production volumes and shall, in such cases, give the National Concessionaire a reasonable period for submittal of additional production plans.

Article 71 (Metering and records)

The National Concessionaire shall meter and record all petroleum extracted and recovered on a daily basis, using for such purpose methods and instruments certified under the legal standards in force, in strict compliance with the rules of good technical standards and the practice in the petroleum industry, and shall inform the supervising Ministry of the volumes produced in each development area on a weekly basis.

Article 72 (Transportation and storage)

1. Projects relating to the installation and functioning of oil pipelines, gas pipelines and petroleum storage facilities, prepared in accordance with international oil industry practice, shall observe the provisions set forth in applicable law and are subject to approval and licensing by the supervising Ministry.
2. The transport and storage equipment referred to in the preceding paragraph may, depending on the available capacity be used by other petroleum concessions, as set forth in Article 68.

Article 73 (Natural Gas)

1. The natural gas produced from any petroleum deposit shall be exploited, and flaring of the same is expressly forbidden, except flaring for short periods of time when required for purpose of testing or other operating reasons.
2. The development plans for Petroleum deposits shall always be devised in such a way as to allow for the use, preservation or commercial exploitation of associated gas.
3. In the case of marginal or small deposits, the supervising Ministry may authorize the flaring of associated gas in order to make its exploitation viable.
4. The authorization referred to in the preceding paragraph may only be granted on submission of a duly substantiated technical and economic and environmental impact evaluation report evidencing that it is not feasible to exploit or preserve the natural gas.
    1. The provisions of Article 64 relating to unitization and joint development shall apply, duly
    2. adapted, to the exploitation of natural gas.
5. When gas flaring is authorized, the supervising Ministry may determine that a relevant fee be charged in accordance with the quantity and quality of the gas flared and with its location.

Article 74 (Definitive plugging of a producing well)

For additional analytical, business and investment opportunities information, please contact Global Investment & Business Center, USA at (202) 546-2103. Fax: (202) 546-3275. E-mail: rusric@erols.com

The definitive plugging of any producing well requires the prior submittal of the plan therefore to the supervising Ministry for review and approval.

Article 75 (Abandonment or continuation of Petroleum Operations)

1. At least one year prior to termination of the concession or the date of abandonment of any area included therein, the National Concessionaire shall prepare and deliver to the supervising Ministry a plan providing for the cases of decommissioning the wells, facilities, equipment for the rehabilitation of the landscape and continuation of the Petroleum Operations.
2. The plan provided for in the previous paragraph shall provide the supervising Ministry with sufficient information in order to assess the future purpose of facilities from a technical, financial, safety and environmental standpoint.
3. The National Concessionaire shall inform the supervising Ministry, in the plan referred to above, of which of the two options referred to in paragraph 1 above it intends to adopt.
4. In the event the abandonment is decided, the National Concessionaire shall proceed to correctly abandon the well or wells in question, and shall also take other measures to decommission the facilities and other assets and proceed to rehabilitate the landscape, in accordance with the applicable law and, secondarily, with the normal practice in the oil industry.
5. The measures provided for in the previous paragraph shall be taken in accordance with a detailed plan to be drawn up by the National Concessionaire and approved by the supervising Ministry.
6. Should the plan indicated in paragraph 1 not be delivered within the prescribed period, or if the plan referred to in paragraph 5 is not carried out within the time frame provided for therein, the supervising Ministry may take the measures needed to ensure that they are prepared and executed at the expense and risk of the National Concessionaire.

CHAPTER VII INSPECTION OF PETROLEUM OPERATIONS

Article 76 (Monitoring and inspection)

1. The supervising Ministry shall be responsible for monitoring and inspecting all activities undertaken by the licensees, the National Concessionaire and its associates, under the scope of the petroleum operations.
2. For the purposes of the preceding paragraph, the licensees, the National Concessionaire and its associates shall send to the supervising Ministry the information and operating reports the contents and frequency of which are provided for in the prospecting license or the concession decree.
3. Regardless of the provisions of the preceding paragraph, the licensees, the National Concessionaire and its associates shall provide the relevant State authorities with all data and information which they deem necessary for the effective technical, economical and administrative control of their activity, and they shall allow free access to the representatives of such authorities to the locations and facilities where they carry out their operations, in order to allow them to perform their duties of inspection, supervision and verification in all matters of a technical, economical and administrative nature.
4. In the exercise of the powers referred to in this Article, and without prejudice to the duty of confidentiality in respect of the information transmitted to it, the supervising Ministry may arrange to be assisted by qualified entities which it appoints.

5. Without prejudice to the provisions of the previous paragraphs, the licensees, the National Concessionaire and its associates shall cooperate in all matters as requested by the supervising Ministry within the scope of its powers of supervision.

6. If it is determined that a given petroleum operation may endanger the lives of persons or the preservation of the environment, the supervising Minister, after consulting the licensees, the National Concessionaire and its associates, may:

(a) order such petroleum operation to be suspended;

(b) order the withdrawal of all persons from the locations deemed dangerous, in coordination with the relevant State authorities;

(c) order the suspension of the use of any machine or equipment which may jeopardize the said values.

Article 77 (Duty of confidentiality)

1. The supervising Ministry, as well as the persons or entities which cooperate with it, shall keep confidential all data or information of a technical, economic, accounting or other nature supplied by licensees, the National Concessionaire and its associates.

2. The licensees, the National Concessionaire and its associates, as well as the persons or entities which cooperate with them, shall keep confidential all data or information supplied by the supervising Ministry.

3. The duty of confidentiality in respect of the information referred to in this Article shall expire after the period set forth in the relevant license or Concession Decree.

4. The provisions of this Article shall not be applicable whenever such data or information is to be provided to other entities as a requirement of the law, namely for budget and statistical purposes.

CHAPTER VIII ADDITIONAL PROVISIONS

Article 78 (Satisfaction of domestic consumption requirements)

1. At any time, by giving prior notice of at least ninety days, the Government may request the National Concessionaire and its associates, to supply to an entity appointed by the same at the delivery point, from their respective share in output, with a quantity of petroleum aimed at satisfying the domestic consumption requirements of the Republic of Angola.

2. For the purposes of the preceding paragraph, delivery point shall mean the

F.O.B. point of the Angolan loading facility at which the Petroleum reaches the inlet flange of the loading pipe of the means of lifting transport, or any other point which may be agreed between the supervising Ministry, the National Concessionaire and its associates.

1. The participation of the National Concessionaire and its associates in the satisfaction of the country's domestic consumption requirements shall not exceed the proportion between the annual output derived from the concession area and the total annual output of petroleum in the Republic of Angola nor exceed forty percent of the total output from the relevant concession area.

2. The value of the petroleum acquired under the provisions of paragraph 1 shall be calculated in accordance with the rules on the valuation of Petroleum for fiscal purposes and shall be paid in internationally convertible currency within thirty days of the end of the month during which the petroleum is lifted.

Article 79 (Government's right of requisition)

1. In the event of a national emergency, such as armed conflict, natural disaster or the imminent expectation of the same, the Government may requisition, to take effect only as long as the state of emergency lasts, all or part of the output of any petroleum concession, net of operational consumption, and require that the National Concessionaire and its associates increase such output to the technically viable maximum limit. Under the same circumstances the Government may also requisition petroleum facilities of any petroleum concession.
2. The requisition of output shall be effected by order of the Government by means of an Executive Decree from the supervising Minister, but when petroleum facilities are requisitioned, it shall be effected by resolution of the Government.
3. In the event of requisition as provided in the preceding paragraphs above, the Government shall compensate the National Concessionaire and its associates in full for the period during which the requisition is maintained, including:

(a) the value of all direct losses and damage directly arising from the requisition;

(b) the value of the entire output requisitioned each month.

. The value of losses and damage caused by acts of war carried out by enemy forces shall not be included in the compensation referred to in the preceding paragraph.

5. The value of output requisitioned by the Government under the terms provided in the preceding paragraphs shall be calculated in accordance with the rules for valuation of petroleum for fiscal purposes, and shall be paid in internationally convertible currency within thirty days of the end of the month in which the output is lifted.

Article 80 (Reservation of rights to other substances)

1. The extraction or production of substances other than those which are the object of mining rights granted hereunder is forbidden, except when such extraction or production has been expressly authorized.
2. In the areas of prospecting and concession licenses, the Government reserves the right to authorize the prospecting and production of any other substances, apart from those exclusively permitted hereunder.
3. The execution of the activities arising from the right referred to in the preceding paragraph shall not jeopardize or interfere with the petroleum operations carried out in the in the respective area.

Article 81 (Disposal of Petroleum produced)

1. The associates of the Concessionaire shall dispose freely of their share of the petroleum produced under this law and other applicable legislation.
2. The National Concessionaire shall dispose of its share of the petroleum produced in accordance with the rules set forth by the Government for this purpose.

3. The provisions of the preceding paragraphs shall be applied without prejudice to the provisions of Articles 78 and 79

Article 82 (Ownership of Petroleum produced)

The point of transfer of ownership of the petroleum produced shall be situated at all times outside or beyond the wellhead, and the metering point for petroleum produced shall be located prior to the point where ownership is transferred.

Article 83 (Management and support services)

The National Concessionaire, when it is not itself carrying out the petroleum activities, shall ensure that the Operator has a system of organizational and support services in Angola which allows it to manage the Petroleum Operations independently and to carry them out efficiently, without prejudice to the Operator's right to use the services of affiliates or third parties, when duly authorized by the National Concessionaire.

Article 84 (Bonus)

1. Bonuses paid to the National Concessionaire resulting from agreements entered into with its associates shall fully revert to the State by way of the unique Treasury account.
2. A portion of the bonuses referred to in the previous paragraph shall be spent in projects of regional and local development and promotion of Angolan private business community, under terms to be regulated by the Government.

Article 85 (Recourse to third party funding)

Recourse by the National Concessionaire or its associates to third party funding for the purpose of investment in the petroleum operations which involves the assignment of rights over the petroleum production shall only be possible with the prior consent of the Minister of Finance and the supervising Minister by means of a joint executive decree.

Article 86 (Recruitment, integration and training of Angolan personnel)

1. Entities that carry out in national territory the activities set forth in Article 1 hereunder shall be required to employ only Angolan citizens in all categories and functions, except if there are no Angolan citizens in the national market with the required qualifications and experience, under terms to be regulated.
2. National and foreign workers employed by the entities referred to in the preceding paragraph who occupy identical professional categories and carry out identical functions shall enjoy the same rights of remuneration and the same working and social conditions, without any type of discrimination.
3. The duties of recruitment, integration and training of Angolan personnel that fall upon the entities referred to in paragraph 1 shall be established by Government decree.

Article 87 (Technical standards)

The supervising Minister, by means of an executive decree, may establish technical standards applicable to the carrying out of Petroleum Operations provided for herein.

Article 88 (Infractions and penalties)

The following practices shall be deemed infractions to the provisions herein, and be subject to penalties:

(a) carrying out petroleum operations without submittal and approval of the respective plans and projects;

(b) refusal to deliver information gathered in the course of petroleum operations and other available data, when requested by the relevant State bodies;

(c) breach of the duty of confidentiality provided for in Article 77;

(d) Failure to provide the bank guarantee within the specified time frames;

(e) Failure to deliver, within the relevant time frame, the plans referred to in Articles 58, 63 and 70;

(f) Non-compliance with the provisions of Article 69 and 73;

(g) Failure to adopt the preventive measures in respect of the safety and hygiene of personnel and facilities, as provided for in Article 23 herein.

1. The penalties due for the infractions provided in the previous paragraph shall be regulated by decree law.
2. The application and payment of fines shall not release the offender from his liability to perform the duties and obligations which gave rise to such fines.
3. The supervising Ministry shall have the powers to take the initiative of commencing and conducting the procedures for charging offenders and applying the respective fines.
4. The proceeds of fines shall revert as follows: sixty percent to the State and forty percent to the supervising Ministry.
5. The provisions of Article 89 shall not apply to this Article, and any appeals against penalties applied shall be decided under the terms of the legislation in force.

Article 89 (Dispute Resolution)

1. Any disputes that may arise between the supervising Ministry and licensees, or between the National Concessionaire and its associates, which relate to strictly contractual issues shall be resolved by agreement between the parties, according to the principles of good faith and of equity and balance between the interests of the parties.
2. Should no agreement be reached between the parties, disputes shall be resolved by resorting to arbitration, under the terms set forth in the prospecting licenses and agreements entered into under Article 14.
3. The arbitral tribunal shall have its seat in Angola and apply Angolan law, and arbitration shall be conducted in the Portuguese language.
4. The provisions set forth in the preceding paragraphs shall not prejudice the application of and respect for the legal provisions in force, notably with regard to the security of the maritime and concessionary public domain, taxation, environment and supervision of petroleum operations.

Article 90 (Suspension of Petroleum Operations)

Whenever reasons of safety or national interest so require, the Government may on an exceptional basis order, by means of a decree, that the petroleum operations be restricted or suspended.

Article 91 (Challenge)

The decisions to suspend, terminate and redeem licenses and concessions may be challenged in accordance with the law.

CHAPTER IX FINAL PROVISIONS

Article 92 (Transitional regime)

1. Rights acquired under petroleum concessions and temporary prospecting licenses, as well as under agreements relating to existing or future petroleum concessions and temporary prospecting licenses, which have been validly entered into by the National Concessionaire and are effective at the date of entry into force of this law, shall continue to be fully valid and effective, so as to protect contractual stability, without prejudice to the provisions of the following paragraphs.
2. In cases where such is deemed necessary and convenient, valid and effective contracts pursuant to the preceding paragraph may be renegotiated between the parties according to the principle of equity and balance of interests, but only in order to gradually adapt contractual provisions deemed incompatible with this law and ancillary regulations.
3. The provisions set forth in the preceding paragraphs shall not prejudice the application of the legal provisions in force, provided for in Article 89, paragraph 4.

Article 93 (Special regimes)

The fiscal, foreign exchange and customs regimes applicable to Petroleum Operations shall be contained in specific statutes.

Article 94 (Applicable law)

Angolan law shall be applicable to the Petroleum operations carried out pursuant to the terms set forth in this law.

Article 95 (Regulations)

This law shall be regulated by the Council of Ministers within 180 days.

Article 96 (Interpretation and insertion of omissions)

Any doubts or omissions arising from the interpretation and application of this law shall be resolved by the National Assembly.

Article 97 (Revocation)

Without prejudice to the provisions of Article 92, all legislation which is inconsistent with the provisions of this law, in particular Law No. 13/78, of 26 August 1978, is hereby revoked.

Seen and approved by the National Assembly in Luanda, on 11 August 2004.

The President of the National Assembly, *Roberto António Victor Francisco de Almeida*. Promulgated on 4 October 2004. Be it published. The President of the Republic, *José Eduardo dos Santos*.

LAW ON TAXATION OF PETROLEUM ACTIVITIES

TITLE I GENERAL PROVISIONS

Article 1 (Purpose)

The purpose of this Law is to establish the tax regime applicable to the entities referred to in Article 3, which carry out activities of exploration, development, production, storage, sale, exportation, treatment and transportation of crude oil and natural gas, as well as of naphtha, ozocerite, sulphur, helium, carbon dioxide and saline substances, provided they result from petroleum operations.

Article 2 (Definitions)

For the purposes of this Law, and unless otherwise expressly stated in the text, the words and expressions used herein are defined as follows, with definitions in the singular applying to those in the plural, and vice versa:

Administration and services, the series of activities carried out to support petroleum operations,

including, but not limited to, all general administration and support activities to petroleum operations, such as management, supervision and functions related to generally overseeing such activities, and also including, but not limited to, accommodation and meals for employees, transportation, storage, emergency security and medical assistance programs, social services, accounting and record keeping. Affiliate:

(a) a company or any other entity in which the taxpayer, directly or indirectly, holds the absolute majority of votes at the General Shareholders' Assembly or equivalent body, or is the holder of more than 50% of the rights and interests which confer the power of management on said company or entity, or has the power of management and control over said company or entity;

(b) a company or any other entity which, directly or indirectly, holds the absolute majority of votes at the taxpayer's General Shareholders' Assembly or equivalent body, or holds the power of management and control over said taxpayer;

(c) a company or any other entity in which the absolute majority of votes at its General Shareholders' Assembly or equivalent body, as well as the rights and interests which confer the power of management on said company or entity are held, directly or indirectly, by a company or any other entity which, directly or indirectly, holds the absolute majority of votes at the General Shareholders' Assembly or equivalent body of the taxpayer, or has the power of management and control over it.

Development area, in petroleum concessions where this concept applies, the entire area, within the area of the petroleum concession, capable of production from the deposit or deposits identified by a commercial discovery, and defined in accordance with the rules governing the petroleum concession in question.

Associates of the State Concessionaire, those entities which, under the Petroleum Activities Law, enter into association with the State Concessionaire, with a view to jointly carrying out petroleum operations.

Petroleum concession or concession, an area in which the exercise of mining rights has been authorized under the Petroleum Activities Law.

State Concessionaire, Sociedade Nacional de Combustíveis de Angola, Empresa Pública (Sonangol – E.P.) , as the title holder of the mining rights.

Tax costs, expenses or charges which are essential to carry out petroleum operations as provided for in Article 21.

Commercial discovery, the discovery of a petroleum deposit which the State Concessionaire or its associates consider to be worth developing;

Development, activities performed subsequent to the declaration of a commercial discovery, including, but not limited to:

(a) geophysical, geological and reservoir studies and surveys;

(b) drilling of production and injection wells;

(c) design, construction, installation, connection and initial testing of equipment, pipelines, systems, facilities, machinery and related activities which are required to produce and operate said wells, and to secure, collect, process, handle, store, transport and deliver petroleum, or to undertake repressurization, recycling and other secondary or tertiary recovery projects.

Mining rights, the series of powers granted to the State Concessionaire in order to carry out petroleum operations in the area of a given petroleum concession.

Tax charges, any charges of a tax nature imposed by law which are owed due to the carrying out of any activities of an economic nature.

Gas or natural gas, a mixture, which is essentially made up of methane and other hydrocarbons and which is found in a petroleum deposit in a gaseous state or which becomes gaseous when produced under normal conditions of pressure and temperature.

Petroleum Transaction Tax, the tax provided for in Title III, Chapter III of this Law. *Petroleum Production Tax*, the tax provided for herein, which is calculated based on the quantity of crude oil or natural gas, as well as on the other substances referred to in Article 1 of this Law.

Petroleum Income Tax, the tax provided for herein which is levied on the profit or net income assessed as taxable income.

Capital gains, revenues or earnings realized on the disposal, for consideration, for whatever reason, of fixed assets or of goods or securities held as reserve or for enjoyment.

Tax obligations, the obligations of a tax nature set forth by this Law, which are owed due to the carrying out of exploration, development, production, storage, sales, exportation, transportation and processing activities involving crude oil or natural gas as well as naphtha, ozocerite, suplhur, helium, carbon dioxide and saline substances when resulting from petroleum operations.

Petroleum operations, all exploration, appraisal, development, production, storage, sales, exportation, treatment and transportation activities involving petroleum which are carried out under the Petroleum Activities Law.

Operator, the entity which performs petroleum operations within a given petroleum concession.

Exploration, the activity carried out with a view to discovering petroleum, including, namely, geological, geophysical and geochemical surveys and studies; aerial surveys and other surveys as may be included in exploration work programs and budget; and the drilling of shot holes, core holes, stratigraphic tests, wells to discover petroleum and other related holes and wells, the purchase and acquisition of the corresponding supplies, materials and equipment which may be included in said work programs and budget.

Petroleum. crude oil, natural gas and all other hydrocarbon substances which may be found in and extracted from a petroleum concession area, or otherwise obtained and saved therefrom.

Crude oil, a mixture of liquid hydrocarbons from any petroleum concession area which are in a liquid state at the wellhead or in the separator, under conditions of normal pressure and temperature; including distillates and condensates as well as liquids extracted from natural gas.

Profit petroleum, in production sharing agreements, all petroleum produced and saved from each development area, and which is not used in petroleum operations, minus the petroleum for cost recovery from said development area.

Cost recovery petroleum, in production sharing agreements, the share of petroleum produced and saved from the development areas which is required to recover exploration, development, production and administration and services expenditures.

Production, includes, but is not limited to, the running, servicing, maintenance and repair of completed wells, and equipment, pipelines, systems, facilities and plants completed during development. It shall also include all activities related to the planning, scheduling, controlling, measuring, testing and carrying out the flow, gathering, treating, storing and dispatching of crude oil and gas from underground petroleum reservoirs to designated exporting and lifting locations and all other operations necessary for the production of petroleum. Production further includes the operations to transfer and abandon petroleum facilities and fields.

State Concessionaire receipts, the share of profit oil belonging to the State Concessionaire, as provided for in subparagraph 1 (b) of Article 19 of this Law, except for petroleum lifted under sole risk operations.

Surface fee, the fee of a tax nature which is calculated on the basis of the surface area on which development and production operations may be carried out.

Arm's length sales to third parties, impartial and non preferential sales between independent entities on a term or spot basis of petroleum by sellers to unaffiliated buyers, but excluding sales involving processing deals, barter and offset agreements, and any sales made by governments or state-owned companies to other state-owned companies or governments, unless such sales are accepted to be true commercial agreements.

Article 3 (**Scope**)

This Law applies to all entities, whether Angolan or foreign, performing petroleum operations in Angolan territory, as well as in other territorial or international areas within the tax levying jurisdiction of the Republic of Angola, as recognized by international law or agreements.

Article 4 (**Tax Charges**)

1. 1. The tax charges applying to the entities referred to in Article 3 are the following:
   1. 2. The tax charges referred to in paragraph 1 of this Article do not exempt the entities referred to in the preceding Article from other taxes or fees nor from duties and other customs charges which are due under the law as a result of carrying out acts which are supplemental or incidental to the activities provided for in Article 1 of this Law, unless they have been specifically exempted from them.
      1. Petroleum Production Tax;
      2. Petroleum Income Tax;
      3. Petroleum Transaction Tax;
      4. Surface Fee;
      5. Levy for the training of Angolan personnel.

Article 5 (**Ring-fencing of Tax Charges and Obligations**)

1. 1. In corporations, unincorporated joint ventures or any other type of business
2. association, and in risk service contracts, the assessment of taxable income and the computation of tax charges for each petroleum concession shall be carried out on a completely independent basis, with the tax obligations pertaining to a given petroleum concession being entirely independent from the obligations pertaining to any other concessions.
2. 2. In production sharing agreements, the assessment of taxable incomeand the tax computation for each development area shall be carried out on a completely independent basis, with the tax obligations pertaining to a given development area being entirely independent from the obligations pertaining to any other areas, except for the expenses provided for in Article 23, subparagraph 2 (b) to which the preceding paragraph shall apply.

TITLE II COMMON PROVISIONS

Article 6 (Determination of the Price of Crude Oil and of Other Substances)

1. For the purposes of assessing the taxable income relating to the tax charges referred to in this Law, excluding the Surface Fee, the crude oil produced shall be valued at the market price calculated on the basis of the actual FOB prices obtained through arm's length sales to third parties in accordance with the rules set forth in the following subparagraphs:

(a) The State Concessionaire and each of its associates shall separately submit to the Ministry of Petroleum, at least 15 days prior to the beginning of each quarter, an informative report addressing their forecasts for world supply and consumption of petroleum, and their estimates of the market prices which can be obtained for the crude oil to be produced in their respective concession during the quarter in question;

For additional analytical, business and investment opportunities information, please contact Global Investment & Business Center, USA at (202) 546-2103. Fax: (202) 546-3275. E-mail: rusric@erols.com

(b) Within 15 days following the end of each quarter, or by another subsequent date as may be determined by the Ministry of Petroleum, the State Concessionaire and each of its associates shall separately submit to said Ministry formal reports including the actual prices obtained in their respective arm's length sales to third parties, distinguishing between term sales and spot sales. Said reports shall provide a detailed account of sales volumes, buyers, prices received, credit terms and density adjustments. They shall also include the actual calculations of volumetrically weighted average prices on a comparable basis of density and terms of credit. The State Concessionaire and its associates may also provide any further market-related informative data they consider relevant to substantiate the veracity of the information provided;

(c) The Ministry of Petroleum shall examine the data provided, as well as any other trustworthy data which reflect market conditions and which the Ministry considers may be useful in determining a suitable market price for the crude oil sold during the quarter in question. If necessary, the Ministry can meet separately with the State Concessionaire and each of its associates in order to discuss all relevant information which has been provided or which is otherwise available. The data provided, as well as any trustworthy additional data reflecting market conditions, if the latter exists, shall be the sole criteria used to determine market price;

(d) The Ministry of Petroleum and the Ministry of Finance shall analyze the data referred to in the preceding subparagraphs and shall jointly determine the market price, which must be communicated to the State Concessionaire and its associates within 15 days following the presentation of the reports mentioned in subparagraph (b) above;

(e) In the event that neither the State Concessionaire nor its associates have made arm's length sales to third parties during the quarter, the reports of the State

Concessionaire and its associates shall be limited to the data relevant to market conditions. The aforementioned Ministries shall in this case determine the market price using the same method described in subparagraph *(c)* above;

(f) In the event that the State Concessionaire or any of its associates considers that the

market price determined under the terms of the preceding subparagraphs does not reflect relevant market conditions, they may individually or jointly, within 20 days of being notified of the determined market price, request a second separate meeting with the Ministries of Petroleum and Finance and submit any additional information which they may consider relevant to the matter in question. Within 10 days of having received the aforementioned additional information, and having taken said data into consideration, the Ministries of Petroleum and Finance shall either revise the determined market price, or shall confirm the previously determined market price, providing a duly substantiated explanation;

(g) Should the State Concessionaire or any of its associates consider that the price determined by way of the analysis provided for in the preceding subparagraph still does not reflect market conditions, the matter may be submitted to an independent expert, to be appointed within 15 days, under the terms of subparagraph (i) below;

(h) The expert must prepare and submit a report on the market values for the quarter in question. This report shall include the determination of a fair market value for the crude oil produced in the area in question, and said determination shall be presented to the Ministries of Petroleum and Finance for forwarding to the State Concessionaire and its associates. Within 10 days of having received said report, the State Concessionaire and its associates shall meet jointly with the Ministries of Petroleum and Finance in order to discuss this new information with a view to agreeing upon a mutually acceptable price. In the event they are unable to reach such an agreement, the aforementioned ministries, taking into account the report of the independent expert, shall either proceed to revise the determined price, or confirm the previously determined price, providing a duly substantiated explanation;

(i) The expert shall be an independent and impartial individual or entity, and be appointed by agreement between the State Concessionaire and its associates or, in the absence of such an agreement, shall be appointed within a period of 20 days by a qualified official of a specialized international institution, at the request of the State Concessionaire or any of its associates. The terms of reference provided to the expert shall be such as to require him to submit his report to the Ministries of Petroleum and Finance within 20 days of receiving the matter for consideration. The expert shall take into account all relevant information which may be provided to him by the State Concessionaire, by its associates, or by the Ministries of Petroleum and Finance, as well as information that he may reasonably request from the State Concessionaire or its associates, to be provided to him from their records, or which he may obtain from other available trustworthy sources. Any fees and expenses of the international institution or the expert shall be borne by whosoever submits the case to the latter.

1. In order to assess the taxable income on substances other than crude oil which are produced within the area of each concession, such substances shall be evaluated at their actual price of sale, unless the Ministries of Petroleum and Finance determine that the procedures set forth in the preceding paragraph are to be followed, in which case the special nature of such substances, as well as the particular conditions under which they are sold, shall be given due consideration.

2. The procedures provided for in the preceding paragraphs shall not suspend any obligations of the State Concessionaire and its associates to the State, and these obligations shall be fulfilled on the basis of the price determined under paragraph 1, subparagraph (d) , of this Article. In the event that the market price determined in accordance with said subparagraph is revised, the revision shall take effect retroactively for the entire quarter in question, and the obligations of the State Concessionaire and its associates shall be revised accordingly. If, as a consequence of such a decision, overpayments have been made, said payments shall be credited against the obligations of the State Concessionaire and its associates for subsequent quarters. Conversely, if underpayments have occurred, the shortfall must be made up for at the tax office which has computed the tax in question by the last day of the month following the month in which the revision of the market price was made.

    1. All reports prepared under this Article, as well as the data and information contained
    2. therein, shall be treated as confidential and property of the State. With the exception of information of the public domain, the aforementioned reports may only be disclosed to third parties with the written consent of the Government.

3. Once the market price has been determined for the concession area or for each development area, if any, said price shall be uniformly applied to all petroleum produced therein during the quarter in question.

Article 7 (Accounting Rules)

1. The accounting system to be used by the State Concessionaire and its associates to record their operations and tax relevant acts must conform to the rules and methods of the General Accounting Plan.

2. The Minister of Finance has the power to issue rules so that the taxpayers subject to this Law may settle their asset and liability accounts, and profit and loss accounts —

whenever these accounts are affected by a currency devaluation — using the standard petroleum industry reference currency as the benchmark.

Article 8 (Mandatory Language and Currency)

Tax returns and all attached documents must always be written in Portuguese, with amounts given in Angolan currency.

Article 9 (Attestation of Signatures)

Whenever taxpayers do not authenticate their tax returns with a stamp using oil-based ink, or with embossed company seal, they must have the authenticity of their signatures attested to.

Article 10 (Fiscal Year)

1. 1. The fiscal year used by the taxpayers subject to this Law shall coincide with the calendar year, and accounts shall be closed at 31 December of each year.
2. 2. Approval of the accounts referred to in the preceding paragraph shall take place by 31 March of the year following that to which such accounts refer, as set forth in Articles 294 and 396 of Law No. 1/04, of 13 February 2004, the Commercial Companies Law.

Article 11 (Exemptions)

1. The assignment of interests made by the entities subject to this Law shall be exempt from any taxes or charges of a tax nature, directly related to the implementation or to the transfer thereof, with the realized profits or capital gains, whether or not entered into the accounts, being included in the overall calculation of profits subject to taxation, as set forth in this Law.
2. No tax, fee, contribution of a tax nature, premium or charge shall be levied on the shares or any other securities representative of the capital stock of the taxpayers to whom this Law applies, nor on the transfer of profits outside of Angola, nor on the payment of dividends in any way related to said shares, debentures or securities representing capital stock.
3. Subject to legislative authorization by the National Assembly, the Government may also grant exemption from the tax charges provided herein, the reduction of rates thereof or any other alterations to the rules applying to said charges, for crude oil and natural gas (including its liquefaction and/or processing) projects when the economic conditions of their exploitation so justify.
4. On the basis of a duly justified application from the State Concessionaire, the Government may grant, subject to legislative authorization by the National Assembly, a

reduction in the rate of, or exemption from, taxes or fees, as well as customs duties and other customs charges, payable by law, for acts that are supplemental or incidental to the activities referred to in Article 1 herein.

TITLE III TAX CHARGES

CHAPTER I PETROLEUM PRODUCTION TAX

Article 12 (Scope)

1. Petroleum Production Tax shall be levied on quantities of crude oil and natural gas measured at the wellhead and on the other substances mentioned in Article 1, deducted from the quantities consumed *in natura* by petroleum operations.
2. The deduction of the quantities consumed *in natura* by petroleum operations shall only be accepted upon favorable opinion from the State Concessionaire.
3. When, as a result of negligence or serious fault by the operator in carrying out petroleum operations, an operational accident or deficiency occurs, the quantities which technically could have been produced if such an accident or deficiency had not occurred, shall be considered as having been produced for the purposes of this tax.
4. Petroleum and other substances referred to in Article 1 produced under Production Sharing Agreements shall not be subject to Petroleum Production Tax provided for herein.

Article 13 (**Tax Return**)

1. Taxpayers subject to Petroleum Production Tax shall submit a tax return in quintuplicate, as per attached Form 1, to the relevant tax office.
2. The copies of the tax return referred to in the preceding paragraph, once verified and received by the relevant tax office, shall be distributed as follows:

(a) 2 for the files of the relevant tax office;

(b) 1 for the National Directorate of Taxes;

(c) 1 for the Ministry of Petroleum;

(d) 1 for the taxpayer.

1. Taxpayers shall submit the tax return referred to in this Article within the following time frames:
2. If no petroleum or other substances - as described in Article 1 - are produced, the taxpayer shall be required to report such fact under the terms and within the time frames provided above.

a) In the case of provisional computation, as provided for in Article 59, paragraph 2; b) In the case of final computation, during the month of March each year.

Article 14 (**Rate**)

1. The Petroleum Production Tax is levied at a rate of 20%.
2. The rate referred to in the preceding paragraph may be reduced to as little as 10% in the following cases:

(a) Petroleum exploitation in marginal fields;

(b) Petroleum exploitation in offshore depths exceeding 750 meters;

(c) Petroleum exploitation in onshore areas which the Government has previously defined as difficult-to-reach.

3. It is for the Government to decide, upon receiving a duly justified request from the State Concessionaire, whether to grant the reduction referred to in the preceding paragraph.

Article 15 (Form of payment)

The Petroleum Production Tax shall either be paid in kind or in cash, as per the State's option.

Article 16 (Payment in cash)

1. If the Petroleum Production Tax is paid in cash, the corresponding rate shall apply to:

(a) The value calculated under Article 6:

(a.1) Of the quantities of petroleum which are produced and measured at the wellhead using a method approved by the relevant departments;

(a.2) Of the quantities of petroleum which could have been produced, as referred to in Article 12, paragraph 3, calculated in accordance with the following formula:

$P = (T / 3) - M$: Where: P = quantities of petroleum which could have been produced; T = total output of the three preceding months; M = output of the month in which the accident or deficiency occurred.

(b) quantities produced of substances other than petroleum referred to in Article 1 measured at the inspection point using a method approved by relevant departments, and valued at the price obtained upon being sold.

2. Payment of the Petroleum Production Tax in cash shall be made as per Article 59 herein.

Article 17 (Payment in kind)

1. If the State chooses to receive the Petroleum Production Tax in kind, with regard to petroleum, the requirement to deliver the corresponding revenue to the safes of the National Treasury of Angola shall be the responsibility of the State Concessionaire, which shall be in charge of receiving, giving the relevant receipt and administering those substances given as payment by the taxpayer.
2. The State Concessionaire is required to deliver to the safes of the National Treasury of Angola, by the deadline set forth in Article 59, paragraph 2, the revenue earned by selling petroleum. If no sales have been made, the State Concessionaire is required to communicate such fact, by the same deadline.
3. If the Petroleum Production Tax is paid in accordance with this Article, the State Concessionaire must file a tax return in accordance with the provisions of Article 13.
4. The State Concessionaire, in addition to being subject to the inspections provided for in the regulations of the Ministry of Finance pertaining to Petroleum Production Tax, is required to present yearly accounts to the Audit Court for the receipt of those items referred to in paragraph 1 of this Article.
5. If the receipt in kind involves those substances referred to in Article 1 herein and which are other than petroleum, the State must determine the entity to which such substances are to be delivered, and said entity must carry out the other procedures set forth in this Article.

For additional analytical, business and investment opportunities information, please contact Global Investment & Business Center, USA at (202) 546-2103. Fax: (202) 546-3275. E-mail: rusric@erols.com

6. The relevant tax office, on submittal by the taxpayer of the receipt subscribed by the State Concessionaire, referred to in paragraph 1, or by the entity appointed by the Government under paragraph 5, shall issue the taxpayer with a certificate evidencing that it has fulfilled its tax obligation.

CHAPTER II PETROLEUM INCOME TAX

Section I Scope

Article 18 (Scope)

1. The Petroleum Income Tax is levied on the taxable income assessed as set forth in this Law, generated by any of the following activities:

(a) Exploration, development, production, storage, sales, exportation, treatment and transportation of petroleum;

(b) Wholesale trading of any other products resulting from the operations referred to in subparagraph (a) ;

(c) Other activities of the entities primarily engaged in carrying out the operations referred to in subparagraph (a) , resulting from occasional or merely incidental actions, provided that such activities do not take the form of an industry or business.

2. The tax referred to in this Chapter does not apply to the receipts of the State Concessionaire, premiums, bonuses and the price cap excess fee received by the State Concessionaire under the terms contractually agreed upon.

Section II Assessment of Taxable Income

Article 19 (Taxable Income)

1. Taxable income shall be the profit assessed at the end of each fiscal year, consistent with accounting principles, subject to adjustment under this Law, and shall consist of one of the following methods:

(a) In each petroleum concession, with regard to business corporations, unincorporated joint ventures or any other form of association and risk service agreements, taxable income shall be the result of the difference between all revenues or earnings obtained, and the expenses or losses attributable to the same fiscal year, respectively determined under Articles 20, 21, 22 and Article 23, paragraph 1, of this Law;

(b) In each development area, with regard to production sharing agreements, taxable income shall be the profit petroleum resulting from the deduction — from the total

amount of petroleum produced — of the cost recovery petroleum and of the receipts of the State Concessionaire, in accordance with the provisions of the relevant production sharing agreement, and in compliance with the rules stated in Articles 20, 21, 22 and Article 23, paragraph 2, of this Law.

1. Unless otherwise provided for herein, revenues or earnings and costs or losses common to more than one development area in the case of production sharing agreements and more than one petroleum concession in the case of corporations, unincorporated joint ventures or any other forms of association, and for risk service contracts, shall be shared, respectively, between such development areas and petroleum concessions in proportion to the annual production of each development area and petroleum concession, respectively, or by any other method accepted by the tax authorities.

2. The fiscal year referred to in this Article corresponds to the calendar year stated in Article 10 of this Law.

Article 20 (**Revenues or Earnings**)

1. Revenues or earnings for the fiscal year shall be deemed to be those resulting from any transactions or operations performed as a result of an action which is either normal or occasional, basic or merely incidental, namely resulting from:

(a) the basic activity, such as revenues or earnings resulting from the sale of petroleum, other substances referred to in Article 1, goods and services, from allocating products in kind, including as taxes, as well as bonuses and discounts obtained, commissions and brokerage fees;

(b) supplementary or incidental activities, including social and welfare activities;

(c) income from goods or securities kept as reserves or for enjoyment, including rents;

(d) operations of a financial nature, such as interest, dividends, corporate profit, discounts, premiums, transfers, exchange rate fluctuations, and premiums on bond issues;

(e) remuneration relating to offices held in other companies;

(f) income from intellectual property or similar forms of property;

(g) the provision of administrative, commercial, technical and research services.

2. The following shall also qualify as revenues or earnings:

(a) the value of buildings, equipment or other capital goods produced and used in the company itself insofar as their corresponding charges are considered to be costs for the fiscal year;

(b) indemnification which in any way, represents compensation for revenues or earnings which have ceased to be obtained, as well as realized capital gains, whether or not entered into the accounts, and profit from assignment of interests, and any positive variations in asset worth which are not reflected in the accounting profits;

(c) deferred revenues related to badwill between the acquisition value and the value of recoverable costs plus the net value of the remaining assets. This revenue shall be taxed to the extent of, and in exact proportion to, the recovery of the costs related thereto.

3. Under this Article, the following are also considered to be revenues for tax purposes:

(a)

gross revenue from any indemnification paid by insurers;

(b) any adjustments or discounts made by manufacturers, suppliers or their agents, received by taxpayers and their affiliates, for defective material, the cost of which has previously been considered as a tax cost under Article 21;

(c) revenue received from third parties for the use of goods and assets acquired by taxpayers for exclusive use in petroleum operations;

(d) rents, reimbursements and other credits, as well as indemnification resulting from any court ruling or arbitration award, which are received by taxpayers.

Article 21 (Deductible Costs and Losses)

1. Costs or losses which may be deducted for the fiscal year shall be deemed those which, within the limits considered reasonable by the Ministry of Finance, taking into account standard practice of the international petroleum industry and applicable Angolan legislation, had necessarily to be incurred in order to obtain the revenues or earnings subject to tax and to maintain the source of production, including, namely, the following:

(a) Charges from basic, incidental or supplementary activities, and which relate to the production or acquisition of any goods or services, such as:

(I) personnel expenses, including:

(i) the total amount of salaries and wages, including gratifications and bonuses for taxpayers' employees who are directly engaged in petroleum operations, provided that this is evidenced by job allocation sheets which shall record the time spent by personnel on petroleum operations, whether full- or part-time, and broken down by project;

(ii) expenses involving vacations, public holidays, overtime, and sickness and disability payments, and which are applicable to salaries and wages which may be chargeable under the preceding number;

(iii) contributions and other charges of a social nature which are applicable to salaries and wages chargeable under number (i) above, which under applicable law are owed by the entities subject to this tax;

(iv) expenditure on welfare schemes benefiting the taxpayer's employees, provided such schemes are approved by the Ministry of Petroleum;

(v) expenses incurred by the taxpayers for training programs for Angolan personnel engaged in petroleum operations, and for other training projects, provided that they are approved by the Ministry of Petroleum;

(vi) expenses relating to established plans for life assurance, medical assistance, pensions, and other related employee privileges or benefits, provided that they are granted to the taxpayers' employees in general, under their internal policies approved by the Ministry of Petroleum and the applicable Angolan legislation;

(vii) reasonable travel, accommodation and living expenses and personal expenses of employees including those which are incurred as a result of travel by and relocation of nonresident employees who are assigned to petroleum operations carried out by taxpayers within the Republic of Angola, provided that such expenses are in keeping with standard practice in the international petroleum industry and in accordance with applicable Angolan legislation;

(viii) travel expenses for employees' families which taxpayers pay for in accordance with their internal personnel transportation policies and practices, which must be in keeping with standard practice in the international petroleum industry and in accordance with applicable Angolan legislation;

(ix) travel expenses which are directly incurred by the return of non-resident employees and their families to their countries of origin.

(II) The costs of material, in accordance with the following rules:

(i) new or used material acquired for use in petroleum operations, valued at the invoice price minus all commercial discounts and rebates, expenses incurred for insurance, freight and handling between the point of supply and the point of delivery, and customs duties, taxes, fees and other impositions which are applicable to imported goods.

§ 1 – The value of material acquired from third parties shall not exceed prevailing prices on the open market for impartial transactions, devoid of favoritism, involving timely available material of the same quality, and taking into account freight and other related costs.

§ 2 - The value of material acquired from affiliates of the State Concessionaire or of taxpayers must be the lower of the price paid by said affiliates, or the prevailing price on the open market for comparable material obtained through impartial transactions devoid of favoritism.

(ii) new or used material for use in petroleum operations shall only be considered tax costs to the extent that they are consistent with prudent, efficient and economical operations, that they are reasonably necessary in the foreseeable future, and provided that surplus stocks are avoided.

(III) Charges for services, including:

(i) contracts with third parties, meaning the actual cost of technical service contracts and other contracts entered into within the scope of petroleum operations between taxpayers and third parties other than affiliates of the taxpayers or of the State Concessionaire, provided that the prices paid by the taxpayers are competitive with those which generally prevail on the international or local marketplace for similar work and services;

(ii) technical and administrative assistance services which are within the scope of petroleum operations, and which are provided by an affiliate of the State Concessionaire or of a taxpayer under the terms set forth in the relevant contract;

(iii) other services provided by taxpayers or their affiliates, provided that the prices paid are no higher than the most favorable prices charged by third parties for similar services.

(IV) Transportation expenses for material and supplies required to carry out petroleum operations.

(b) charges of an administrative nature involving general and administrative expenses incurred in Angola by taxpayers, acting as operators, pertaining to the maintenance of their offices, support installations for petroleum operations and housing connected with these operations;

(c) depreciation and amortization of costs under Article 23;

(d) rents paid to third parties in exchange for the occupation of real property required to carry out petroleum operations;

(e) costs of petroleum operations risk management services contracted under Decree No. 39/01, of 22 June 2001, its regulations and the applicable Angolan legislation. These costs include all expenditures on financing risks, funding pension funds and abandonment funds.

§ 1 – Only the part of costs or losses incurred as a consequence of accidents or damages occurring during petroleum operations, and not covered by insurance contracts entered into as indicated, shall be tax deductible.

§ 2 – Should the risk management activities not be implemented as per the above-mentioned terms, all costs borne to pay for any losses, claims, damages or awards, as well as any expenses, including legal services, shall not be considered tax costs.

(f) expenses arising from litigation, legal services and other related services which are required or appropriate for obtaining, maintaining and protecting the concession area, as well as legal services and other related services for prosecuting or defending oneself against lawsuits or claims relating to the petroleum operations;

Sole § – Where the legal services relating to the matters referred to in subparagraph (f) are provided by in-house or regularly retained attorneys of an affiliate of the taxpayer, the corresponding costs shall fall within the sphere of technical and administrative assistance as indicated in paragraph 1, subparagraph (a) , (III) , (ii) of this Article;

(g) losses or damage sustained during the fiscal year which may not have been covered or compensated by insurance or in any other way, provided that they are not the result of serious fault, gross negligence or willful misconduct on the part of the taxpayer or anyone acting on its behalf;

(h) environmental clean-up and restoration expenses provided that they are not the result of serious fault, gross negligence or willful misconduct on the part of the taxpayer or anyone acting on its behalf, and are incurred in accordance with legislation in force;

(i) all taxes, levies, charges, fees or any other liabilities of a tax nature relating to petroleum operations which the taxpayer owes and pays, with the exception of Petroleum Income Tax;

(j) losses resulting from indemnity claims against the taxpayer, notably destruction of or changes to inventory which occur during the fiscal year, and which result from random events involving uninsurable risk which are not the result of serious fault, gross negligence or willful misconduct on the part of the taxpayer or anyone acting on its behalf;

(k)

uncollectible debts resulting from the normal activity of the taxpayer, provided that they are recognized as such by a court having jurisdiction.

1. Interest and other charges pertaining to loans and finance which have been actually paid,
2. which are allocated for petroleum production and development operations, and which have been obtained from banks or credit institutions within Angolan territory may also, with prior authorization from the Ministers of Finance and Petroleum, be considered as tax costs.

2. With the exception of that which is provided for in Article 22, the following may also be considered as tax costs under terms to be regulated by the Ministries of Finance and Petroleum:

(a) donations for social, educational, cultural and scientific purposes;

(b) expenses related to social events promoted by the taxpayer;

(c) expenses incurred prior to the date of signature of the contract entered into between the State Concessionaire and its associates;

(d) promotional and advertising expenses;

(e) costs resulting from contracts for the supply of material and equipment or the provision of services which are entered into by the operator over and above the limits of its delegated authority under the relevant contract, and which have not received prior authorization from the State Concessionaire;

(f) costs resulting from the implicit renewal of the contracts referred to in the preceding subparagraph without prior authorization from the State Concessionaire;

(g) expenses for demurrage of oil tankers;

(h) general and administrative expenses of non-operator taxpayers, for the setting up and operating of their offices in Angola;

(i) the taxpayer's own costs or expenses, which are incurred outside of Angola.

1. The reductions or deductions to which this Article refers, which involve annual charges, shall be taken only in the year to which the accounts refer. Sole § – Reductions or deductions which are allowed for the calculation of cost recovery petroleum shall be excluded from this rule in the event that, due to the limit set forth in the relevant production sharing agreement, said costs cannot be wholly recovered during the year in which they occurred.
2. Tax deductions which constitute a duplication of other deductions already addressed in the preceding subparagraphs of this Article shall in no event be permitted.

Article 22 (Non-deductible costs or losses)

1. The following costs or losses shall not be considered deductible:

(a) expenses incurred due to serious fault, gross negligence or willful misconduct on the part of the taxpayer or anyone acting on its behalf;

(b) commissions paid to intermediaries;

(c) expenses for marketing or transporting petroleum beyond the point of delivery;

(d) expenses for any guarantee which is provided under the contract entered into with the State Concessionaire;

(e) indemnification, fines or penalties for breach of legal or contractual obligations;

(f) expenses incurred in arbitration procedures, unless undertaken in order to defend petroleum operations;

(g) expenses for the independent expert who may be consulted to determine the price of petroleum;

(h) Petroleum Income Tax;

(i) offers or donations, except for those made to the State or to other entities, provided that they pursue the aims referred to in Article 21, paragraph 3, subparagraph *(a)* herein;

(j) interest and other charges pertaining to loans and finance with the exception of those entered into under the conditions referred to in paragraph 2 of the preceding Article;

(k) expenses incurred for legal services, except for those specifically provided for in Article 21, paragraph 1, subparagraph *(f)* ;

(l) costs and losses which result from failure to implement risk management activities as per Decree No. 39/01, of 22 June 2001, the regulations thereof and the applicable Angolan legislation;

(m) expenses for training expatriate personnel and for training programs which do not comply

with the terms required by applicable legislation;

(n) costs and losses resulting from the inadequate observance of warranty conditions, as well as those resulting from the acquisition of material which are not guaranteed against defective workmanship by the suppliers, manufacturers or agents, in accordance with generally accepted practices within the petroleum industry;

(o) costs and losses resulting from the depreciation of materials which are not used in petroleum operations;

(p)

general and administrative expenses incurred outside of Angola which do not fall within the sphere of technical and administrative assistance as referred to in Article 21, paragraph 1, subparagraph *(a)* , *(III)* , *(ii)* ;

(q) any taxes and contributions owed by employees, whether or not they are residents of Angola;

(r) travel and other expenses incurred for moving employees beyond their country of origin, or for their use in other operations outside of Angola;

(s) payments to the State or the State Concessionaire in return for the awarding of the status of associate of the State Concessionaire.

2. The following costs or losses shall also be considered non-deductible:

(a) amounts entered into the accounts as funds, provisions or reserves, unless any such funds, provisions or reserves have been authorized by the Government;

(b) amortization and depreciation which exceed the limits set forth in Article 23;

(c) debts considered uncollectable, if no final judgment has been passed whereby the insolvency or bankruptcy of the corresponding debtors has been declared;

(d) Customs duties and other customs charges on imports owed for sold items, and which were exempt on their importation;

(e) personal income tax and other income taxes levied on any type of remuneration paid to administrators, directors, managers, members of the statutory audit board, employees and others serving the taxpayer, if such taxpayer pays said taxes in their stead;

(f) the costs of legal expenses incurred in arbitration proceedings involving any dispute between the State Concessionaire and its associates;

(g) costs resulting from damage caused by serious fault, gross negligence or willful misconduct on the part of the taxpayer or anyone acting on its behalf;

(h) indemnification paid to the State Concessionaire as liquidated damages;

(i) interest paid to shareholders, even for a loan to the company;

(j) any part of bonuses, gifts, privileges, wages or fees granted to shareholders or stockholders of the taxpayer which is greater than the highest remuneration granted to employees who are not shareholders or stockholders;

(k) personal expenses of the taxpayer's shareholders or stockholders;

(l) entertainment expenses, even when entered into the accounts under a different heading and duly documented, to the extent that the tax administration judges them to be excessive.

Article 23 (Assessment of Tax Costs)

1. Assessment of tax costs in order to determine the taxable income of corporations, unincorporated joint ventures or any other type of association, as well as risk service contracts, shall be undertaken in accordance with the following rules:

For additional analytical, business and investment opportunities information,
please contact Global Investment & Business Center, USA
at (202) 546-2103. Fax: (202) 546-3275. E-mail: rusric@erols.com

(a) The following costs shall be amortized or depreciated at a uniform rate of 16.666% as of the beginning of the year in which they were incurred, or the year in which petroleum is first commercially produced, whichever occurs later:

(i) costs incurred for exploration operations, including the cost of drilling dry or productive wells, of crude oil or natural gas, and the cost of services provided by third parties;

(ii) costs incurred for the drilling of development wells, including those for services provided by third parties;

(iii) costs incurred for production, transportation and storage facilities and facilities used in support of said activities, including services provided by third parties.

§ 1 – The value of the movable and immovable property for which the amount of deductions for wear and tear or obsolescence is calculated, and the amount of deductions for destroyed immovable property which is not covered by insurance, shall be their original cost, plus the amount of subsequent acquisitions of the same nature, including major repairs, but minus losses, damage or destruction sustained, as well as wear and tear, depreciation and obsolescence previously accepted and taken into consideration in previous years.

§ 2 – If at any time the State Concessionaire assumes ownership free of charge of any assets which were jointly owned with its associates and which are not fully amortized, it shall continue with the amortization of said assets, but only in proportion to its previous participation in the ownership of same and in relation to the non-amortized value as of the date of acquisition.

(iv) charges borne by the associates of the State Concessionaire with the assignment of participating interests, in relation to the difference between the acquisition price and the value of the capitalized costs plus the net value of the remaining assets (goodwill) , provided that the assignor has been taxed for such difference.

(b) charges borne in the period prior to the year in which production begins shallaccrue to, and shall be capitalized in, said year, and depreciated at a flat rate of 25% per year over a 4-year period as from 1 January of said year.

(c) when, upon closing the accounts for each year, it is shown that the total of all expenditures and expenses which, under this Article, are allowed to be deducted when assessing the net taxable income for the year, exceeds the gross annual income generated by way of the operations mentioned in Article 20, said excess amount shall be carried forward to subsequent years and considered in each year as an additional deduction when assessing the net taxable income. Any such additional deduction must be taken into account during the first subsequent fiscal year, inasmuch as this is possible. However, if this is not possible during said year, it must occur during the following or subsequent fiscal year, but for no more than five years. Moreover, said deduction may only be taken upon verification, by way of the accounting system used, that such amounts have not already been deducted in some other way.

2. The assessment of tax costs, for the purpose of assessing taxable income involving production sharing agreements, shall be undertaken in accordance with the following rules:

(a) lifting and the right to freely dispose of cost recovery petroleum is limited each year to a maximum percentage of the total amount of petroleum produced and saved in each development area, as set forth in the corresponding production sharing agreement;

(b) exploration expenses shall be recoverable from the unused balance of cost recovery petroleum within each development area after recovery of expenses for production, development, and administration and services, subject to the maximum amount of cost recovery petroleum indicated in the preceding subparagraph. Each year, such exploration expenses shall be recoverable first from any balance of cost recovery petroleum from the development area in which the most recent commercial discovery has occurred. Any remaining exploration expenses shall be recovered from the development areas in which the next most recent commercial discoveries have occurred. Exploration expenses shall not be entered into the accounts as fixed assets, and therefore shall not be amortized;

(c) development expenses shall be entered into the accounts in the following manner:

(i) development expenses in each development area shall only be recovered using cost recovery petroleum produced in the same area. These expenses shall be entered into the accounts as fixed assets and, once the investment allowance set forth in the relevant production sharing agreement has been added, shall be amortized at an annual rate of 25%, beginning with

the year in which they are incurred or the year in which the exportation of petroleum from the development area commences, whichever occurs later;

(ii) with regard to development expenses involving the construction or execution of specific work or projects which take longer than one year, the amortization of such costs shall only begin during the year of completion, at which time they shall be classified as fixed assets;

(iii) development expenses which are common to more than one development area shall be shared among said development areas in proportion to the annual output of each development area, following the allocation of expenses for administration and services as set forth in subparagraph (e) of this Article;

(d) production expenses shall be entered into the accounts in the following manner:

(i) production expenses in each development area shall only be recoverable using cost recovery petroleum produced in the same development area and shall be entered into the accounts as expenses for the year;

(ii) production expenses common to more than one development area shall be shared among the various development areas in proportion to the annual output of each development area, once the corresponding allocation of expenses for administration and services has been made under subparagraph

(e) of this Article; (iii) production expenses may also include a provision for abandonment costs, the limits of which shall be calculated and entered into the accounts in accordance with the rules set forth in the agreements entered into between the State Concessionaire and its associates;

(e) Administration and service expenses shall be entered into the accounts in the following manner:

(i) in the case of those administration and service expenses pertaining to the construction or acquisition of facilities or any tangible assets for the general logistical and administrative support of exploration, development and production activities, those expenses which may be capitalized due to their specific nature, high value or prolonged extinguishment shall be entered into the accounts as fixed assets;

(ii) the expenses referred to in the preceding paragraph shall be amortized at an annual rate of 25%, beginning with the year in which they are incurred or the year in which the exportation of petroleum from the concession area commences, whichever occurs later;

(iii) with regard to administration and service expenses involving the construction or execution of specific work or projects which take more than one year, the amortization of such expenses shall only begin during the year of completion, at which time they shall be classified as fixed assets;

(iv) administration and service expenses which cannot be entered into the accounts as fixed assets due to their value, intangibility, or rapid extinguishment through consumption, shall be entered into the accounts as expenses for the year;

(v) for the purposes of assessing deductible tax costs in order to determine taxable income, administration and service expenses shall be allocated each year to the expenses for exploration, development and production, as follows:

(vi) the annual amount of amortization of administration and service expenses classified as fixed assets under this paragraph shall be allocated to expenses for exploration, development and production, in proportion to the annual direct expenses incurred for each of these activities;

(vii) the amount of administration and service expenses entered into the accounts as expenses for the year, as per item (iv) of this subparagraph, shall be allocated to expenses for exploration, development and production using the method indicated in the preceding paragraph; (viii) the administration and service expenses allocated under the terms of the preceding paragraphs shall be considered an indirect expense of exploration, development and production activities;

(ix) for the purpose of tax deducting development expenses, the allocation of the amortization of those administration and service expenses which are entered into the accounts as fixed assets shall be added to direct development expenses, and the total shall be multiplied by the investment allowance referred to in subparagraph 2 (c) (i) of this Article.

(f) the material which the taxpayer acquires in order to carry out its work program and budget for each year, and which are not immediately used in petroleum operations in the corresponding concession area, shall be entered into the accounts under the heading of stock, and shall only be allocated to exploration, development, production, and administration and service activities in proportion to the extent of their actual utilization or consumption in petroleum operations;

(g) material classified by the taxpayer as strategic spare parts, constituting a safety provision guaranteeing the proper running of petroleum operations, shall be allocated to exploration, development, production, and administration and service expenses in accordance with the terms set forth in the relevant production sharing agreement;

(h) charges borne by the associates of the State Concessionaire with the assignment of participating interests, in relation to the difference between the acquisition price and the value of recoverable costs plus the net value of the remaining assets (goodwill) shall be deemed development expenses and accounted for as such, provided that the assignor has been taxed for such difference; however, such expenses shall not qualify for any investment allowance set forth in the corresponding production sharing agreement;

(i) in the event that the maximum amount of cost recovery petroleum for a given year is insufficient to enable the complete deduction of the recoverable costs for the year in question, as

For additional analytical, business and investment opportunities information,
please contact Global Investment & Business Center, USA
at (202) 546-2103. Fax: (202) 546-3275. E-mail: rusric@erols.com

per the corresponding production sharing agreement, then the unrecovered part of the costs pertaining to said year shall be carried forward to the following years;

(j) if the amount of crude oil for the recovery of expenses incurred in a given concession is revealed to be insufficient, said expenses shall remain unrecovered;

(k) if at any time the State Concessionaire assumes ownership free of charge of any assets which were jointly owned with its associates and which are not fully amortized, it shall continue with the amortization of said assets, but only in proportion to its previous participation in the ownership of same and in relation to the non-amortized value as of the date of acquisition.

Article 24 (**Books**)

1. Taxpayers subject to this Law are required to keep their accounting records as per commercial law and applicable accounting legislation.
2. Entries into the above accounting records are not allowed to be delayed for longer than ninety days.
3. Taxpayers may be exempted from the obligation to keep the books required under this Article, provided that they submit adequate accounting documents, dated and signed by two responsible individuals, to the relevant tax office for authentication.
4. Authenticated accounting documents, as per the preceding paragraph, shall be archived by the taxpayers and shall have the same worth as the books they replace for the purposes set forth in this Law.
5. If the authentication of accounting documents is the accepted procedure used, then there shall be no need to pay stamp duty.
6. The taxpayer must organize and maintain its records so that taxable income may be clearly assessed and monitored in strict observance of the provisions of this Law.
7. The Minister of Finance, by way of executive decree, may make it obligatory to keep certain books, documents or other accounting items, as well as to observe certain standards in the way they are arranged.

Article 25

(Centralization of Bookkeeping)

Taxpayers shall be required to centralize accounting at their head offices or actual management in Angola for all operations carried out by their head offices, subsidiaries, branches, or divisions, while always observing the principle of ring-fencing tax charges and obligations set forth in Article 5 of this Law.

Article 26 (**Tax Return**)

1. For the purposes of assessing the taxable income for Petroleum Income Tax, taxpayers shall be required to file a tax return in sixtuplicate with the relevant tax office as per the attached Forms 1, 2, 3, 4 and 5, within the deadlines set forth herein, for the computation of the tax charges provided for in this Law, except for the Levy for the Training of Angolan Personnel.

(a) in the case of final computation, during the month of March each year;

(b) in the case of provisional computation, as provided for in Article 59, paragraph 2.

2. The copies of the tax return referred to in the preceding paragraph, once verified and received by the relevant tax office, shall be distributed as follows:

(a) 2 for the files of the relevant tax office;

(b) 1 for the National Directorate for Taxes;

(c) 1 for the Ministry of Petroleum;

(d) 1 for the State Concessionaire;

(e) 1 for the taxpayer.

1. The tax return referred to in the preceding paragraph must be signed by the taxpayer and by the corresponding accountant, registered with the Accountants' and Accounting Experts Society, both of whom shall initial any supporting documentation, and such return shall be authenticated with the taxpayer's stamp or embossed seal.
2. Any tax return which is not signed or initialed as stated above shall be rejected, without prejudice to any sanctions established for failure to file such return.
3. In the event that the tax return and its supporting documentation are deemed to be insufficiently clear, the relevant tax office shall notify the taxpayer to provide any necessary clarification in writing by a set deadline of a maximum of 15 days as from the date of notification.

Article 27 (Attachments to the Tax Return)

1. The tax return referred to in the preceding Article shall be accompanied by the following documents:

(a) financial statements prepared pursuant to the General Accounting Plan, duly audited by an accounting expert, registered with the Accounting Experts Society;

(b) the list of permanent representatives, directors, managers, and members of the statutory audit board;

(c) a copy of the minutes of the general shareholders' assembly or meeting approving the annual accounts or, if approval needs to be granted differently, a document proving such approval;

(d) trial balances for the general ledger, before and after correction and adjustment entries have been made and the annual income has been assessed;

(e) an up-to-date, itemized list of movable and immovable property, indicating the initial cost thereof, any subsequent cost increases, and devaluation due to wear and tear, depreciation and obsolescence already taken into account in preceding years, as well as for the year addressed by the tax return, all of which shall be clearly distinguished;

(f) a report, broken down by product, of each and every export and domestic sale during the year addressed by the tax return, including columns for the following:

(i) the date the sale was entered into the books;

For additional analytical, business and investment opportunities information,
please contact Global Investment & Business Center, USA
at (202) 546-2103. Fax: (202) 546-3275. E-mail: rusric@erols.com

(ii) the month during which the sale occurred; (iii) the monthly amount of the product which was sold (in the metric decimal system) ; (iv) the unit price of the sale (in Angolan currency and US dollars, and expressed in decimal numbers) ;

(v) the amount of the sale (in Angolan currency and US dollars) ;

(vi) an itemized list of amounts and their designation, considered to be expenses in the taxpayer's accounts, but which, in accordance with Article 22, were not deducted from the gross revenue stated in the tax return which was filed;

(g) a technical report, based on detailed tables, which must succinctly relate the following:

(i) The depreciation and amortization which have been entered into the accounts, indicating the method used, the rate applied, and the initial and current values of the various items to which they apply;

(ii) The changes in every category of stock and the criteria used to measure their value; (iii) Constituted provisions and any changes occurring in them; (iv) Confirmed bad debts;

(v) Capital gains realized or entered into the accounts and the profit generated by the assignment of interests;

(vi) General administration overheads, with particular reference made to any type of remuneration paid to management bodies, as well as any entertainment expenses incurred during the fiscal year;

(vii) Changes in the criteria used to allocate costs or revenues to the different activities or establishments of the taxpayer;

(viii) The remaining expenditures incurred by the taxpayer for petroleum operations, as well as for its overall operations, especially liabilities incurred outside of Angola;

(ix) Other items deemed relevant to the fair determination of the taxable income and to the clarification of the balance sheet and the profit and loss account for the fiscal year, especially if the latter does not include the accounts required for a proper analysis of revenues or earnings, and costs or losses.

2. In the event that the accounts are not approved, the taxpayer may submit a request to the head of the relevant tax office for an extension of no more than 30 days to remedy such situation, indicating why the approval was not granted. If account approval is handled through the courts, the taxpayer shall attach a document evidencing this fact.

Article 28 (Assessment of Taxable Income)

1. The assessment of taxable income for the purposes of Petroleum Income Tax shall be made by the Assessment Committee referred to in the following Article on the basis of the taxpayer's return and accompanying documentation.
2. The Assessment Committee referred to in the preceding paragraph shall be formed within the relevant tax office.

Article 29 (Assessment Committee)

Taxable income for Petroleum Income Tax shall be mandatorily assessed by 30 June of the second year following the fiscal year in question. This shall be done by an Assessment Committee consisting of the following:

(a) the head of the relevant tax office, who shall preside and have the casting vote;

(b) a senior accounting inspector, who shall be the delegate of the Minister of Finance, and be designated by the Minister of Finance on the nomination of the National Inspector of Finance;

(c) a representative of the taxpayer, who shall be the delegate thereof, and whom such taxpayer shall nominate upon filing its tax return.

Article 30 (Authority of the Assessment Committee)

1. When performing its functions and analyzing the tax returns and documents filed by the taxpayer, the Assessment Committee, on the basis of an auditing report on the tax returns, shall assess the taxpayer's taxable income, and shall verify, among other aspects, the following:

(a) with regard to gross annual income:

(i) whether the reported gross annual income from export sales is based on the market price calculated under this Law. In the event that the income reported is based on prices lower than the market price, the Assessment Committee shall rectify said income, bringing it into line with the income that would have resulted had the aforementioned market price been used;

(ii) whether the gross annual income from domestic sales exceeds the maximum allowed 10% deviation between the value of the substances on the domestic market, in terms of current bulk prices, and the value entered into the taxpayer's accounts. The Committee shall take into account the current bulk prices for the substances on the domestic market, their quantity and quality, the duration of the sales contract and other related conditions, and accordingly make any adjustments to the taxpayer's tax return.

(b) with regard to deductions from gross annual income, the Committee shall verify whether the deductions made from the gross annual income are strictly in line with the provisions of Articles 22 and 23, and cancel any deductions made by the taxpayer which, for the purposes of assessing the taxable income, are not legally acceptable.

3. Once the operations referred to in the preceding paragraph have been carried out, and the amounts reported by the taxpayer have been adjusted, the Assessment Committee shall assess the net taxable income subject to tax.

4. Article 31 (Functions of the Chairman of the Assessment Committee)

1. The head of the relevant tax office, in his capacity as chairman of the Assessment Committee, shall convene its meetings and shall oversee its work.
2. Minutes shall be taken at all meetings, in an appropriate book, by an official to be designated by the relevant tax office.

Article 32 (Resolutions of the Assessment Committee)

1. The resolutions of the Assessment Committee shall be passed by way of a majority vote.
2. The members shall always be given at least 20 days' notice in writing to attend meetings, indicating the day and time of said meetings.
3. If any of the members is absent at the indicated time, the meeting shall be adjourned for an hour later. In the event that the meeting takes place in the absence of the member, the resolutions taken may not be challenged due to such absence.

Article 33 (Notification of the Resolutions of the Assessment Committee)

The head of the relevant tax office shall notify the taxpayer of its taxable income assessment within 15 days of the conclusion of the Assessment Committee's work.

Article 34 (Reviewing Committee)

1. The taxpayer has 30 days, from the date of receipt of the notice of the Committee's resolution regarding its assessed taxable income, referred to in the preceding Article, to file a petition with a Reviewing Committee.
2. The Reviewing Committee shall consist of the following:

(a) The National Director for Taxes, who shall preside and shall have the casting vote;

(b) A representative of the Ministry of Petroleum, acting as its delegate;

(c) Two representatives of the taxpayer, acting as its delegates, to be indicated by it in its petition.

3. The Reviewing Committee shall meet at the National Directorate for Taxes and shall be assisted by an official, designated by the National Director for Taxes, who shall fulfill the duties of secretary and who shall be responsible for taking minutes and prepare all the documentation for the business of the committee, which shall be considered confidential.

Article 35 (Filing Petition)

1. The petition must be filed with the tax office where the relevant Assessment Committee's resolution was reached and said office shall forward it on a confidential basis, within eight days, to the National Director for Taxes, accompanied by all data pertaining to the assessment.
2. The petition and all supporting documentation are subject to Stamp Duty and shall be signed by the petitioner himself.

Article 36 (Convening the Reviewing Committee)

1. Once the petition has been received, the chairman of the Reviewing Committee shall set the date and time for a meeting and shall provide the members with all necessary communications by means of an official letter.
2. Article 32, paragraphs 2 and 3, shall apply to the Reviewing Committee.

Article 37 (Authority of the Reviewing Committee)

1. The Reviewing Committee has the authority to review and make decisions regarding challenged facts, to correct or confirm them, and to rule decisively on the taxable income of the petitioner.
2. The resolutions of the Reviewing Committee shall comply with the provisions of Article 32, paragraph 1.

Article 38 (Decision-making period of the Reviewing Committee)

Petitions filed with the Reviewing Committee shall be ruled upon thereby no later than 31 December of the second year following the fiscal year to which such petitions refer.

Article 39 (**Notification of the Resolutions of the Reviewing Committee**)

1. The National Director for Taxes shall notify the taxpayer of the ruling issued within 10 days of the date the resolution was adopted.
2. In order to cover administrative costs, the taxpayer shall pay up to 5 % of the challenged value in the event that its request for review is completely dismissed.

Article 40

(Court Appeal)

1. No petition or appeal may be filed with regard to the amount of the taxable income assessed by the Reviewing Committee referred to in the preceding Articles. However, in the event of failure to comply with legal formalities, or errors in the interpretation of legal provisions resulting in harm to the State or to the taxpayer, the Public Prosecutor's Office or the taxpayer may appeal to the relevant court within thirty days. If such appeal is granted, said court shall be able to order a repeat of the assessment process, but without changing the amount which was determined.
2. The time allowed for filing such an appeal shall be counted as of the date of notification referred to in Article 39.
3. The complete dismissal of said appeal by the court shall cause the appellant to be liable for the payment of court costs amounting to the equivalent of 5 percent of the disputed amount, without prejudice to any other legal costs which may be owed under the Law.
4. Court appeals do not suspend the tax liabilities of the taxpayer.
5. If a new assessment is made as a result of the taxpayer's appeal, an annulment shall be issued in favor of the taxpayer, or an additional tax computation shall be made, as the case may be.

SECTION III TAX RATE

Article 41 (**Tax Rates**)

The rates of Petroleum Income Tax are as follows:

(a) In the event that the National Concessionaire does not enter into association with any entity, and for business corporations, unincorporated joint ventures or any other type of association, and risk service contracts entered into with the National Concessionaire, the rate is 65.75%;

(b) For production sharing agreements, the rate is 50%.

SECTION IV TAX COMPUTATION

Article 42 (**Tax Computation**)

Computation of Petroleum Income Tax shall be made as per Article 59 hereof.

SECTION V TAX INCENTIVES

Article 43 (**Investment Allowances**)

1. In addition to the incentive referred to in Article 23, subparagraph 2 (c) (I), the Government may, on the basis of a duly justified application from the Ministries of Petroleum and Finance, approve the granting of investment allowances, the amounts and regulation of which shall be included in each of the respective concession statutes.
2. The incentives proposed by the Ministries of Petroleum and Finance which are referred to in the preceding paragraph shall be submitted to the Ministries by the State Concessionaire and shall obey the following criteria:

(a) Economic terms of the agreement;

(b) Geological potential of the concession.

CHAPTER III PETROLEUM TRANSACTION TAX

Article 44 (**Scope**) The Petroleum Transaction Tax shall be levied on the taxable income calculated as set forth in Article 23, subparagraphs 1 *(a)* and 1 *(b)*, and shall also be subject to the rules set forth in the following Articles.

Sole § – Petroleum produced under Production Sharing Agreements shall not be subject to the Petroleum Transaction Tax set forth in this Law.

Article 45 (Deductible Charges)

1. In addition to the deductible costs or losses provided for in Article 21, the following deductions shall be allowed in calculating the taxable income:

(a) a production allowance, on the volume of crude oil and liquefied gas which was taken into account in calculating gross income;

(b) an investment allowance, which shall correspond to a certain percentage of the amounts invested and capitalized in each fiscal year, as from 1 January of the year of commencement of production.

2. The production allowance and the investment allowance shall be set forth in the relevant concession statutes.

Article 46 (**Non-Deductible Costs**) In addition to the non-deductible costs and losses provided for in Article 22, the following charges shall not be deductible in calculating taxable income:

(a) petroleum production tax;

For additional analytical, business and investment opportunities information,
please contact Global Investment & Business Center, USA
at (202) 546-2103. Fax: (202) 546-3275. E-mail: rusric@erols.com

(b) petroleum transaction tax;

(c) surface fee;

(d) levy for the training of Angolan personnel;

(e) financing costs, including interest and other charges.

Article 47 (**Tax Return**)

1. Taxpayers subject to Petroleum Transaction Tax must file a tax return in sixtuplicate with the relevant tax office, as per Form 3 attached hereto.
2. The copies of the tax return referred to in the preceding paragraph, once verified and received by the relevant tax office, are distributed as follows:

(a) 2 for the files of the relevant tax office;

(b) 1 for the National Directorate for Taxes;

(c) 1 for the Ministry of Petroleum;

(d) 1 for the State Concessionaire;

(e) 1 for the taxpayer.

3. Taxpayers must file the tax return referred to in this Article within the following deadlines:

(a) in the case of provisional computation, as provided for in Article 59, paragraph 2;

(b) in the case of final computation, during the month of March of each year.

Article 48 (**Rate**)

The Petroleum Transaction Tax is levied at a rate of 70%.

Article 49 (*Tax Computation*)

The computation of Petroleum Transaction Tax shall be made in accordance with Article 59 of this Law.

CHAPTER IV SURFACE FEE

Article 50 (**Scope**)

The Surface Fee applies to the concession area or to the development areas in the event that the agreement entered into under the Petroleum Activities Law provides for same.

Article 51 (**Tax return**)

For additional analytical, business and investment opportunities information,
please contact Global Investment & Business Center, USA
at (202) 546-2103. Fax: (202) 546-3275. E-mail: rusric@erols.com

1. Taxpayers subject to the Surface Fee must file a tax return in sixtuplicate with the relevant tax office, as per Form 4 attached hereto.
2. The copies of the tax return referred to in the preceding paragraph, once verified and received by the relevant tax office, shall be distributed as follows:

(a) 2 for the files of the relevant tax office;

(b) 1 for the National Directorate for Taxes;

(c) 1 for the Ministry of Petroleum;

(d) 1 for the State Concessionaire;

(e) 1 for the taxpayer.

1. Taxpayers must file the tax return referred to in this Article within the payment deadline set forth in Article 53.
2. Attached to the tax return provided for in paragraph 2 of this Article, taxpayers shall file a document issued by the State Concessionaire certifying the size of the area subject to the Surface Fee.

Article 52 (**Computation**)

The rate of the Surface Fee shall be the equivalent in Angolan currency to 300 US dollars per square kilometer, and shall be due by the associates of the State Concessionaire.

Article 53 (**Payment**)

The Surface Fee shall be paid on a yearly basis to the relevant tax office and within the following deadlines:

month following .(a) in concessions where no development areas are provided for, during the the month in which the relevant concession is granted;

.(b) in concessions where development areas are provided for, during the month following the month in which each commercial discovery is declared.

TITLE IV OTHER TAX CHARGES

CHAPTER I STATE CONCESSIONAIRE REGIME

Article 54

(Receipts of State Concessionaire)

1. The State Concessionaire must deliver the revenues derived from its receipts to the General State Budget.
2. The State Concessionaire may retain up to 10% of the revenues referred to in the preceding paragraph in order to cover expenses relating to supervision and control of its associates and of petroleum operations.

3. For the purposes set forth in the preceding paragraph, the State Concessionaire shall file a tax return, in quintuplicate, with the relevant tax office, as per Form 5 attached. Said tax return concerns the profit oil received, as well as the breakdown of expenses which are absolutely required to efficiently inspect and monitor its associates and petroleum operations.

4. The copies of the tax return referred to in the preceding paragraph, once verified and received by the relevant tax office, shall be distributed as follows:

(a) 2 for the files of the relevant tax office;

(b) 1 for the National Directorate for Taxes;

(c) 1 for the Ministry of Petroleum;

(d) 1 for the State Concessionaire.

5. The State Concessionaire shall file the tax return referred to in this Article within the following deadlines:

(a) in the case of provisional computation, as provided for in Article 59, paragraph 2;

(b) in the case of final computation, during the month of March of each year.

1. The computation of the receipts of the State Concessionaire shall be made in accordance with Article 59 hereof.

2. The State Concessionaire, in addition to being subject to the inspections provided for in the regulations of the Ministry of Finance related with the revenues referred to in this Article, shall be required to file with the Audit Court its financial statements on a yearly basis.

Article 55 (Contractual Bonuses and Price Cap Excess Fee)

1. The bonuses received by the State Concessionaire under agreements entered into pursuant to the Petroleum Activities Law, as well as the price cap excess fee provided in some Production Sharing Agreements, shall not be subject to the regime set forth in this Law.

2. The bonus and the price cap excess fee paid to the State Concessionaire referred to in the preceding paragraph shall revert in their entirety to the State through the Unique Treasury Account.

Article 56 (Other Revenues)

All revenues of the State Concessionaire, except for those referred to in the Articles of this Chapter, shall be subject to the tax charges provided herein.

CHAPTER II LEVY FOR THE TRAINING OF ANGOLAN PERSONNEL

Article 57 (Levy for the Training of Angolan Personnel)

1. The State Concessionaire's associates shall be required to pay a levy to the State for the training of Angolan personnel.

2. The Government shall define, by Decree-Law, within a period of 180 days, the amount of the levy for the training of Angolan personnel, as well as other rules, including collection thereof.

3. The above mentioned statute may also provide for its application to other entities directly or indirectly involved in petroleum operations.

TITLE V TAX COMPUTATION ARTICLE 58 (EXPECTED REVENUE)

1. By 30 November of each year, taxpayers subject to the tax charges provided for herein, with the exception of the levy for training of Angolan personnel, shall file with the relevant tax office a tax return, in sixtuplicate, as per the attached Forms 1, 2, 3, 4 and 5, regarding the payments they expect to make during the following fiscal year.

2. The copies of the tax return referred to in the preceding paragraph, once verified and received by the relevant tax office, shall be distributed as follows:

(a) 2 for the files of the relevant tax office;

(b) 1 for the National Directorate for Taxes;

(c) 1 for the Ministry of Petroleum;

(d) 1 for the State Concessionaire;

(e) 1 for the taxpayer.

1. The tax return referred to in the preceding paragraph shall be accompanied by essential supporting data provided by the operator, namely, forecasts on the volume of production, exportation, domestic sales, stock, production costs, sale prices and stock evaluation values, as well as any additional data considered necessary.

2. The submitted forecasts shall be deemed to have been accepted if, by the following first of January, the relevant tax office has not required them to be corrected.

3. The filing of the tax return provided for in this Article shall always be the responsibility of the taxpayer, which may delegate this duty to the operator provided it notifies the relevant tax office of this fact at least 15 days prior to the deadline stated in paragraph 1 of this Article.

4. The forecasts referred to in the preceding paragraphs must be revised and confirmed on a quarterly basis in accordance with the values generated, market outlook and other data considered relevant.

Article 59 (Tax Computation)

1. The computation of the tax charges provided for in this Law shall be handled by the relevant tax office, with the exception of the Levy for the Training of Angolan Personnel.

2. The provisional computation of the Petroleum Production Tax, the Petroleum Income Tax and the Petroleum Transaction Tax shall be made by the taxpayers on the basis of the revenue forecast as provided in the preceding Article. This computation shall take place up to the last day of the month following the month in which the substances referred to in Article 1 were produced, in the case of Petroleum Production Tax, or lifted in the other cases, and it shall be adjusted for the actual values occurring during the period to which the tax computation pertains.

For additional analytical, business and investment opportunities information, please contact Global Investment & Business Center, USA at (202) 546-2103. Fax: (202) 546-3275. E-mail: rusric@erols.com

3. The final computation of the tax charges referred to in the preceding paragraph shall be made in the month following the month in which the tax return referred to in Article 26, subparagraph 1 *(a)* was filed.

Article 60 (**Tax Credits**)

The costs listed in the subparagraphs below, which are paid by .1.

the taxpayer during the fiscal year, shall be credited against the tax liability computed by applying the rate set forth in Article 41, provided that they are not included among the deductions allowed in Article 21:

costs incurred from accommodation, meals, travel and other .

(a) costs of customs officials and officials of the Ministry of Petroleum when carrying out inspections, as well as expenses for the setting up and upkeep of taxation offices, and expenses incurred in hiring tax inspection, auditing and consulting services provided by the Ministry of Finance to the taxpayer and the State Concessionaire, whether directly or indirectly related to them;

any costs or expenses incurred from activities of a technical, .(b)

social or assistance-related nature which are performed by the taxpayer at the request of the relevant authority, duly approved by joint dispatch of the Ministers of Petroleum and Finance.

2. 2. In the event that the costs provided for in subparagraphs *(a)* and *(b)* above cannot be credited due to an overly low tax liability for the year in which they were incurred, they shall be credited against the tax liability for subsequent years, provided such amounts were not already deducted in some other manner, to be verified through the accounting system used.

Article 61 (**Relevant Tax Office**)

The computation of the tax and quasi-tax charges provided for herein shall be made at the tax office where the taxpayer's registered offices, actual management or main establishment are located.

TITLE VI TAX COMPLIANCE

CHAPTER I COMPLIANCE AND DEADLINES

Article 62 (**Payment**)

1. The taxpayers subject to the tax charges provided for in this Law, with the exception of the Levy for the Training of Angolan Personnel and the Surface Fee, shall pay said charges within the deadline set forth for the provisional tax computation, as provided for in Article 59, paragraph 2, herein.
2. The payment resulting from the final computation of the charges referred to in the preceding paragraph shall be made within 30 days from the notice on the final tax computation.
3. In the event of additional tax computation, the taxpayer shall pay the relevant tax within 15 days from the notice of the additional tax computation.

Article 63 (**Public Notices**)

Public notices or announcements regarding the collection of tax charges provided for in this Law shall not be required.

Article 64 (**Files and their Confidentiality**)

1. A file on each taxpayer subject to this Law shall be maintained at the relevant tax office, and all documents and data relating to the assessment of taxable income for the purposes of computing tax charges provided for herein shall be archived in said file.
2. Revenue Collection Documents ("*Documentos de Arrecadação de Receitas*") , which are the receipts of payment of the tax charges provided for herein, shall also be kept in the files referred to in the preceding paragraph.
3. Any civil servant who reveals or relays any data contained in the files referred to in the preceding paragraph 1 shall be held liable, in disciplinary terms, for breach of secrecy, without prejudice to any other liabilities provided for by Law.

Article 65 (**Annual Records**)

The tax charges applicable to each taxpayer shall be filed in annual electronic records, which shall show the monthly amounts of taxes collected for each type of charge and the respective accrued values thereof.

CHAPTER II INSPECTION

Article 66

(Inspection)

1. The entities referred to in Article 3 shall be subject to inspection as set forth in Law No. 1/04, of 13 February 2004, the Commercial Companies Law, Decree No. 38/00, of 6 October 2000, and other applicable legislation.
2. For the purposes of inspecting the tax charges addressed by this Law, all public departments and economic coordination bodies shall be required to provide the relevant tax office and the National Directorate for Taxes with all data, information or clarification within their power which is requested from them concerning the periods pertaining to taxpayers' tax returns.
3. The National Director for Taxes shall supervise compliance with the deadlines set forth in this Law, as well as the proper functioning of the Assessment Committees, as set forth in Article 65 of the General Tax Code .

Article 67 (Audit of Accounts)

1. For the purposes of taxation, the relevant tax office shall determine audits of the accounts of the taxpayers subject to this Law.
2. Such audits, provided they are judged to be absolutely necessary, may be extended to the accounts of any companies or entities which have connections to the taxpayers.

Article 68 (Confidentiality)

1. All data relating to tax charges dealt with by this Law shall be considered confidential.

2. The taxpayers may request certificates on data regarding their own tax.

TITLE VII PENALTIES

Article 69

(Failure to File a Tax Return)

1. The failure of a taxpayer to file a tax return as required by this Law, as well as omissions or inaccuracies occurring therein or in the documents that should accompany such return, shall be punished by a fine denominated in Angolan currency, equivalent in value to between 50,000 and 500,000 US dollars. However, in the event of willful misconduct, the fine shall be equal to twice the amount of the non-computed tax, to a minimum value equivalent to 500,000 US dollars, denominated in Angolan currency.
2. The failure to submit supporting data as required by Law or requested by the tax administration, as well as omissions or inaccuracies occurring therein, shall be punished by a fine denominated in Angolan currency, equivalent to 100,000 US dollars.

Article 70 (**Refusal to Reveal Accounts**)

1. The refusal to reveal accounts and their related documents, as well as the concealment, destruction, obsolescence or falsification thereof, shall be punished in accordance with the seriousness of the act with a fine denominated in Angolan currency, equivalent to between 500,000 and 5,000,000 US dollars, without prejudice to any criminal proceedings which may be brought against the directors, administrators, managers, audit board members, liquidators or accounting experts responsible for such actions.
    1. The same penalties shall be applied in the event that the accounting books or any other
    2. record approved by the tax administration and related documents are not archived or registered in a suitable or timely manner.
2. Taxpayers that do not observe the accounting organization provisions set forth by the Ministry of Finance, or which obstruct or in any way render difficult the inspection duties of the agents of the tax administration, or those acting in their name, shall be punished with a fine denominated in Angolan currency, equivalent to 800,000 US dollars.
3. Taxpayers that allow their accounts to fall more than 90 days behind shall be punished with a fine denominated in Angolan currency, equivalent to 800,000 US dollars.
4. If, during the course of any audit, any accounting data are not made available, or if any necessary clarification of same is not provided, the Public Prosecutor's Office may order the detention of the administrators, directors or managers responsible for such data and clarification until the completion of the audit, and authorize the seizure of documents wherever they may be located.

Article 71 (**Liability of Civil Servants**) Any civil servants who fail to fulfill any of their obligations, as set forth herein, shall be held liable in disciplinary terms without prejudice to any other liability provided for by law.

Article 72 (Liability of Accountants and Auditors) Accountants or auditors who act on behalf of the tax administration, and who, through their actions or omissions, fail to fulfill their legal or contractual obligations, shall be punished, depending on the seriousness of such failure, with a fine denominated in Angolan currency, equivalent to between 5,000 and 50,000 US dollars, without prejudice to any other liabilities provided for by law.

Article 73 (**Breach of Secrecy**)

Civil servants and accountants or auditors who commit a breach of secrecy shall be levied a fine denominated in Angolan currency, equivalent to between 5,000 and 50,000 US dollars, without prejudice to any other liabilities provided for by law.

Article 74 (**Fines for Voluntary Reporting**) Fines which, independently of infraction notice, are applied in the event of voluntary reporting of transgressors, shall be subject to the provisions set forth in the General Tax Code.

Article 75 (**Infractions by Legal Entities**) In the event that the infractions provided for herein are committed by legal entities, the provisions of the General Tax Code relative to liability for the payment of the fine shall apply.

TITLE VIII PETITIONS AND APPEALS

Article 76 (Petitions and Appeals) The taxpayers subject to the tax charges provided for in this Law may challenge and appeal the practices of the tax administration, as provided for in the law.

TITLE IX FINAL AND TRANSITIONAL PROVISIONS

Article 77 (**Subsidiary Law**)

The General Tax Code and other tax or administrative laws shall be applied as subsidiary law to all situations not covered herein.

Article 78 (**Authority to Compute Taxes and Payment**)

1. 1. The Special Tax Regimes Department of the National Directorate for Taxes shall replace the relevant tax offices for purposes of the provisional and final computation of the tax charges referred to in paragraph 1 of Article 59 until otherwise decided by the Minister of Finance.
2. 2. For as long as the tax computation is made in accordance with paragraph 1 of this Article, the National Directorate for Taxes shall designate the tax office at which the payments of the tax charges provided for in Article 62 shall be made.

Article 79 (**Surface Fee**)

The Surface Fee, which was paid to the State Concessionaire up to the effective date hereof, shall hereafter be paid into the National Treasury single account, subject to the procedures set forth in Chapter IV, Title III hereof.

Article 80 (**Tax Return**)

The Minister of Finance may, by means of Executive Decree, amend the attached tax return forms 1, 2, 3, 4 and 5, as well as approve new tax return forms.

Article 81 (**Legal Effect**)

This statute shall only be applicable to petroleum concessions which are granted after the effective date hereof, with the exception of the following matters, which shall also be applicable to the concessions existing on such date:

(a) Capital gains realized or accounted for and the profit obtained with the assignment of interests, pursuant to Article 20, subparagraph 2(b) for capital gains and Article 20, subparagraph 2(c) ; Article 23, subparagraph 1 (a) IV; and Article 23, subparagraph 2 (h) ;

(b) Books, pursuant to Article 24;

(c) Centralization of bookkeeping, pursuant to Article 25;

(d) Tax return, pursuant to Articles 26 and 27;

(e) Taxable income, assessment and review, pursuant to Articles 28, 29, 30, 31, 32, 33, 34, 35, 36, 37, 38 and 39;

(f) Court appeal, pursuant to Article 40;

(g) National Concessionaire regime, pursuant to Articles 54, 55 and 56;

(h) Levy for the training of Angolan personnel, pursuant to Article 57;

(i) Tax computation, pursuant to Articles 58, 59, 60 and 61;

(j) Compliance with tax obligations, pursuant to Articles 62, 63, 64 and 65;

(k) Inspection, pursuant to Articles 66, 67 and 68;

(l) Penalties, pursuant to Articles 69, 70, 71, 72, 73, 74 and 75;

(m) Petitions and appeals, pursuant to Article 76; and

(n) Final and transitional provisions, pursuant to Articles 77, 78, 79 and 80. Article 82 (**Revocation**)

Save as provided in the preceding Article, all statutory provisions which are inconsistent with the provisions of this Law are hereby revoked.

Article 83 (Doubts and Omissions)

Doubts and omissions that may arise in the interpretation and application of this Law shall be resolved by the National Assembly.

Article 84 (**Effective Date**)

This Law shall become effective on 1 January 2005. Seen and approved by the National Assembly, in Luanda, on 11 August 2004.

REPUBLIC OF ANGOLA LAW NO. 11/2004 CUSTOMS REGIME APPLICABLE TO PETROLEUM OPERATIONS IN THE AREAS UNDER THE JURISDICTION OF THE REPUBLIC OF ANGOLA.

Article 1 (Purpose)

This law sets forth the customs regime applicable to petroleum operations in the areas under the jurisdiction of the Republic of Angola.

Article 2 (Scope) The National Concessionaire, its associates and the entities which carry out petroleum operations on their behalf are subject to the regime provided in this law.

Article 3 (Definitions)

For the purposes of this law and unless otherwise expressly stated in the text, certain words and expressions used herein shall have the following meanings, it being understood that reference to the singular includes reference to the plural, and vice versa:

National Concessionaire -the entity which holds the mining rights pursuant to the Petroleum Regulatory Law;

(b) Associates of the National Concessionaire - the entities which associate with the National Concessionaire pursuant to the Petroleum Regulatory Law;

(c) Mining rights -the powers granted to the National Concessionaire in order to carry out petroleum operations in any petroleum concession;

(d) Natural gas or gas -a mixture mainly composed of methane and other hydrocarbons, which exists in a petroleum deposit in a gaseous state or which changes into such state when produced under normal conditions of pressure and temperature;

(e) Petroleum operations -the operations of survey, exploration, appraisal, development and production of petroleum, as well as the treatment, transportation and storage of the various types of gas, carried out pursuant to the Petroleum Regulatory Law;

(f) Operator -the entity which carries out the petroleum operations in a certain petroleum concession;

(g) Petroleum -the crude-oil, natural gas and any other hydrocarbon substances which may be found in, and extracted or otherwise obtained and saved from, the petroleum concession area;

(h) Crude oil -a mixture of hydrocarbons originating from a petroleum concession area which are in a liquid state at the wellhead or separator under normal pressure and temperature conditions, including distillates and condensates, as well as those liquids extracted from the natural gas;

(i) Goods – the generic word used for designating and classifying for customs purposes the goods under any customs regime, that is equipments, machines, devices, instruments, utensils, other crafts, raw materials and products used in the petroleum operations, which are described in the list attached to this law.

For additional analytical, business and investment opportunities information,
please contact Global Investment & Business Center, USA
at (202) 546-2103. Fax: (202) 546-3275. E-mail: rusric@erols.com

Article 4 (Exemptions on importation)

The importation of goods to be exclusively and directly used in carrying out petroleum operations and which are included on the list attached to this law is exempt from duties and general customs service fee, except for Stamp Duty, the statistical tax of one per thousand and "ad valorem" and other fees for the provision of services associated with the import and export of goods. Upon proposal of the Ministry of Petroleum and after the Ministry of Finance has given its opinion on such request, other goods to be exclusively and directly used in carrying out petroleum operations may be added to the attached list referred to in the preceding paragraph by means of a Government decree.

Article 5 (Exclusivity)

1. On the importation of the goods referred to in Article 4 of this law, a statement legalized by the Ministry of Petroleum shall be submitted to the customs authority, pledging that such goods shall be exclusively used in petroleum operations.
2. The document referred to in the preceding paragraph may only be legalized by an official of the Ministry of Petroleum whose signature is recognized by the National Directorate of Customs and who is also responsible for monitoring said pledge.
3. Without prejudice to that set forth in the following paragraph, the use of such goods for purposes other than those foreseen and declared shall constitute customs duty evasion, foreseen and punishable by the Customs Code in force and other applicable legislation.
4. Any departure from the rule concerning the exclusive use in petroleum operations, as well as their disposal, of goods imported with exemption of customs charges, shall be applied for in advance from the Minister of Finance, and if such application is accepted, said goods shall be subject to the payment of all charges due in accordance with the general legislation in force.

Article 6 (Protection of the national market) The exemption provided for in Article 4 of this law shall not apply in the event that the goods referred to herein exist in Angola with the same or similar quality and are available for sale and delivery in good time, at a price which does not exceed by more than ten percent (10%) the cost of the imported item excluding customs duties but including transportation and insurance costs, pursuant to the GATT method for assessing customs values.

Article 7 (Importation for sale to or use or consumption by workers) The exemption referred to in Article 4 of this law shall not apply to goods imported by the National Concessionaire, its associates and entities that carry out petroleum operations on their behalf, which are for sale to their workers or for the use or individual or collective consumption by same.

Article 8 (Exportation of petroleum) The exportation of petroleum produced in each petroleum concession, either in its natural state or after having been processed, is exempt from duties and general customs service fee, except for Stamp Duty on customs clearance documents, the statistical tax of one per thousand "ad valorem" and other fees for services rendered associated with the import and export of goods, provided that such exportation is made under a purchase and sales agreement and has been duly registered pursuant to the legislation in force.

Article 9 (Customs inspection) The Concession Areas are considered to be under the permanent inspection of Customs; therefore, access to all places of the Concession Area without any kind of restrictions shall be permitted to customs agents, so as to allow them to fully comply with their duties, namely the sealing and unsealing of storage tanks, the calculation of the quantities of oil stored and exported, measured at the established checking point by a method approved by the relevant authorities, as well as the reading of temperatures, densities and automatic meters.

Article 10 (Customs control) The goods included in the attached list, when imported by the National Concessionaire, by its associates and by the entities which carry out petroleum operations on their behalf shall be subject to inspection for purposes of confirming their quantity, quality, price and customs classification and the customs duties to which such goods would be subject to under the general regime, as per the terms to be established by the Minister of Finance by means of an Executive Decree after consulting the Ministry of Petroleum.

Article 11 (Temporary importation) Temporary importation is permitted without the need to deposit a guarantee for the goods included on the list attached hereto, such temporary importation and subsequent re-exportation being exempt from customs charges, including general customs service fee, with the exception of Stamp Duty on customs clearance documents and other fees for services rendered associated with the import and export of goods.

Article 12 (Temporary exportation) Temporary exportation is permitted without the need to deposit a guarantee for those goods included on the attached list that are sent abroad for repair, improvement or refitting, such temporary exportation and subsequent re-importation being exempt from customs charges, including general customs service fee, with the exception of Stamp Duty on customs clearance documents and other fees for services rendered.

Article 13 (Deadlines for temporary importation and re-importation of goods)

1. Goods imported on a temporary basis shall be re-exported within a maximum of two years after the date of filing the relevant import clearance application. Such deadline may be extended in exceptional cases when duly verified by the Ministry of Petroleum by means of an Order from the Minister of Finance.
2. The re-importation of goods exported on a temporary basis shall be made within one year. Such deadline may be extended as provided in the preceding paragraph.

Article 14 (Urgent clearance)

1. In the case of goods which by their very nature require urgent customs clearance, the Angolan customs authorities shall authorize their immediate delivery after adequate interim measures, but the importer shall within no more than 90 working days complete the relevant customs clearance bill.
2. In order to enjoy the system of urgent customs clearance referred to in the preceding paragraph, the Concessionaire, its Associates and the entities that carry out petroleum operations on their behalf may provide a guarantee, should the National Directorate of Customs so decide, which shall cover other customs charges due under this special customs regime, as well as any fines and costs of proceedings that may arise from failure to comply with the deadline set forth in the preceding paragraph and other customs procedures.

Article 15 (Revocation)

1. All provisions regarding customs contained in existing concession decrees and decree-laws are hereby repealed.
2. Except for the exemptions referring to the goods mentioned in Article 7 of this law, the rights acquired by the concessionaire and its associates deriving from the application of

existing contracts entered into between the concessionaire and its associates shall not be affected by the revocation referred to in the precedent paragraph.

Article 16 (Interpretation) Any doubts and omissions that may arise in the interpretation and application of this law shall be resolved by the National Assembly.

GENERAL REGULATORY FRAMEWORK FOR THE CONTRACTING OF GOODS AND SERVICES FROM NATIONAL COMPANIES BY COMPANIES IN THE OIL SECTOR

CHAPTER I GENERAL PROVISIONS

Article 1 Scope

1. **This general regulatory framework aims to establish the basic rules to be complied with**
2. **for the contracting from national companies suppliers of goods and services by companies in the Oil Sector.**
2. **First of all it guarantees the protection of the insertion of the national business community and the use of national goods and services in the activities which support the oil operations.**

CHAPTER II BUSINESS OPPORTUNITIES

Article 2 Systems

The business relationships to be established between national companies suppliers of goods and services and companies in the Oil Sector are based on the following systems:

1. Rule on exclusivity for the Angolan business initiative.

1.1 All activities which do not require a high capital value and basic average and in-depth non-specialised know-how in which the participation of foreign companies has to take place only on the initiative of Angolan companies come under this system.

1. The following business opportunities are covered by this system: Pressure tests on oil and/or gas storage tanks and pipelines. Transportation of equipment materials and foodstuffs or sounding and production platforms. Supply of industrial and drinking water. Catering Supply of technical material General cleaning and gardening General maintenance of equipment and vehicles. Operators and managers or supply points (air ports ports and service stations) . Inspection of the quality of products distributed and sold (oil products and derivatives) . Retailers of lighting oil gas and lubricants. Transport of products from the terminals to the supply points.
2. System of semi-compliance

2.1 All areas which require a reasonable level of capital in the oil industry and in-depth not always specialist know-how where the participation of foreign companies has to be permitted only in association with national companies or on their initiative come under this system

2.2 The following business opportunities are covered by this system:

For additional analytical, business and investment opportunities information,
please contact Global Investment & Business Center, USA
at (202) 546-2103. Fax: (202) 546-3275. E-mail: rusric@erols.com

Purchase and/or processing of geographical data;

Geographical or geodesic surveying.

Vertical directional and/or horizontal drilling of wells;

Geological control of drilling (mud logging)

Production tests.

Laboratories for geological geochemical and fluid analyses.

Specialist consultancy in engineering and management of geological geophysical and

geochemical sciences as well as tanks oil operations installations analysis and interpretation of

data Operation and maintenance of production installations including oil and gas pipelines. Calibration of storage tanks and measurement instruments.

Construction and assembly of mechanical electrical structures and production and drilling installations. Inspection and supervision of consignments of oil or natural gas Cargo transport of oil or natural gas. Cement and drilling sludge products Supply of drilling sludge Supply of seismic materials including explosives.

Drilling production materials and equipment. Cleaning and maintenance works on wells. Cementation and/or completion of wells. Transport of crude oil to the refinery.

Electricity and instrumentation.

Operators and managers of terminals.

Pressure tests on storage tanks and measurement instruments.

Maintenance engineering of terminals and supply points.

Inspection of distribution installations and supplies Manufacture and assembly of braziers and lamps Manufacture and assembly of electricity generating sets.

Assembly of selected makes of vehicles for the oil industry.

Manufacture of plastic for the oil industry as well as synthetic fibres and rubbers.

Manufacture of fertilisers.

Production of detergents.

3. Competition system Not excluding the possibility of partnerships between Angolan companies and foreign companies the competition system means all oil activities (offshore and onshore) not described in the systems above and which require a high level of capital in the oil industry and in-depth specialist know-how.

CHAPTER III CONTRACTING AND SUB-CONTRACTING

Article 3 National private companies

1. In order to be able to participate in the public tendering to be carried out by companies in the Oil Sector private national companies must have the majority of their respective share capital subscribed and paid up by Angolan citizens.
2. The companies referred to in the paragraph above must also:

2.1 Record in their company object the "provision of support services to the oil activities";

2.2 Proceed with up-dating the share capital in accordance with the requirements to be established by the Oil Ministry;

2.3 Be registered and certified by the Oil Ministry and by the Chamber of Commerce and Industry of Angola in accordance with the requirements to be established by those organisations.

Article 4 State companies

Angolan state companies compete for the supply of national goods and services to support the oil activities in equal circumstances and with the same rights and obligations as national private companies.

Article 5 Form of contract

1. The companies in the Oil Sector are obliged to put out to public tendering for the contracting and sub-contracting of Angolan private and/or state companies for the supply of goods and for the provision of support services to the oil activities in accordance with the provisions of this general regulatory framework.
2. However companies in the Oil Sector may have recourse to direct contracting from Angolan private and/or state companies or companies under foreign law provided that urgent technical reasons are confirmed or the insufficiency on the Angolan market is certified for that purpose they must apply in advance for authorisation from the Oil Ministry.

Article 6 Preferential rights

In the contracting and sub-contracting for the supply of goods and provision of support services to the oil activities Angolan state and/or private companies enjoy preferential rights provided that the amount of the respective proposal is not more than 10% higher than that proposed by other companies.

CHAPTER IV GOODS OF NATIONAL PRODUCTION AND SERVICES

For additional analytical, business and investment opportunities information,
please contact Global Investment & Business Center, USA
at (202) 546-2103. Fax: (202) 546-3275. E-mail: rusric@erols.com

Article 7 Goods of national production

Consumer goods of national production to be used in the services which support the oil activities are recorded in the "List of Available Capacities of Industrial Companies" published annually by the Ministry of Industry of the Republic of Angola which must also contain the respective location in the country.

Article 8 National companies' services

1. 1. The support services to the oil activities are amongst others those which may be carried out by national state and/or private companies in the areas which come under the systems described in article 2 of this regulatory framework.
2. 2. The areas of services referred to above are up-dated annually under the cover of the co-operation protocol to be entered into between the Oil Ministry and the Chamber of Commerce and Industry of Angola.

CHAPTER V OIL SECTOR COMPANIES ARTICLE 9 THE USE OF GOODS AND SERVICES OF NATIONAL COMPANIES

Companies in the Oil Sector undertake to:

1.1 Purchase on the Angolan market the consumer goods necessary for carrying out their activities such as food consumables equipment machinery and other goods of national production;

1. **To contract and sub-contract preferentially national private and/or state companies for the provision of support services to the oil activities.**
2. **Through the national system of concessions companies in the Oil Sector must send the Oil Ministry for confirmation all applications for requests for authorisations and all types of contracts accompanied by the respective documents an essential condition for the contract to come into force.**

CHAPTER VI FINAL AND TRANSITIONAL PROVISIONS

Article 10 Doubts and omissions Any doubts and omissions arising out of the interpretation and application of this general regulatory framework shall be resolved by order of the Oil Minister. The Minister *Desidério da Graça Veríssimo e Costa*. m² Km²

TRAVEL TO ANGOLA

US STATE DEPARTMENT RECCOMENDATIONS

WARNING: The Department of State warns U.S. citizens against travel to Angola because of renewed military conflict and continuing violent crime. Travel within Angola remains unsafe due to bandit attacks, undisciplined police and military personnel, sporadic high-intensity military actions in interior provinces, and unexploded land mines in rural areas. Foreign nationals, especially independent entrepreneurs, are subject to arbitrary detention and/or deportation by immigration and police authorities. Americans who find travel to Angola unavoidable are strongly urged to contact the U.S. Embassy for up-to-date information. Travel outside Luanda, the capital, is inadvisable. American citizens traveling outside Luanda despite this Warning should always contact the U.S. Embassy for the latest information on security conditions in the provinces to which visits are planned.

COUNTRY DESCRIPTION: Angola is a large, developing African country that has been engulfed in war and civil strife since independence from Portugal in 1975. A peace accord signed in 1994 brought a temporary halt to Angola's civil war, but unsettled political-military conditions and renewed fighting continue to make travel to and within Angola extremely unsafe. Facilities for tourism are non-existent. Severe shortages of lodging, transportation, food, water, medicine and utilities plague Luanda and other cities. Shortages cause unsanitary conditions in many areas, including Luanda.

ENTRY REQUIREMENTS: A passport and visa, which must be obtained in advance, and an International Certificate of Vaccination, are required. Persons arriving without visas are subject to possible arrest and/or deportation. Travelers whose international immunization cards do not show inoculations against yellow fever and cholera may be subject to involuntary vaccinations and/or heavy fines. Visitors remaining in Angola beyond their authorized visa duration are subject to fines and possible arrest. Current information on entry requirements may be obtained from the Embassy of the Republic of Angola at 1615 M Street, N.W., Suite 900, Washington, D.C. 20036, (202) 785-1156.

SAFETY/SECURITY: The security situation in Angola remains extremely volatile. Large crowds and demonstrations should be avoided. Travel in the interior is unsafe because of high-intensity military actions, bandit attacks in villages and on major highways, and land mines. The Government of Angola and the National Union for the Independence of Angola (UNITA) resumed armed conflict in late 1998. There has been heavy fighting in many provinces and a heightened potential for increased military action in all provinces.

CRIME INFORMATION: Violent crime occurs regularly throughout Angola. Street crime is common in all areas of Luanda, at all hours. Foreigners, including U.S. citizens, have been the targets of violent robberies in their homes and hotel rooms. Because of the high incidence of armed robberies and carjackings, travelers are cautioned against airport arrivals after dark. Before arrival, ensure that you have arranged for reliable transportation from the airport. Only unregulated taxis are available at the airport and in Luanda. They are unsafe, a high crime risk and should not be used.

City streets are patrolled by soldiers and police who normally carry automatic weapons. The soldiers and police are unpredictable and their authority should not be challenged. All motorists should stop at nighttime police checkpoints if so ordered. Police officers, often while still in uniform, frequently participate in shakedowns, muggings, carjackings and murders.

For additional analytical, business and investment opportunities information, please contact Global Investment & Business Center, USA at (202) 546-2103. Fax: (202) 546-3275. E-mail: rusric@erols.com

There have been police operations against illegal aliens and private companies that have resulted in the deportation of foreign nationals and the loss of personal and company property. Some foreign businesspersons have been forced to sign statements renouncing property claims in Angola before being deported. Independent entrepreneurs in Angola should carry all relevant immigration and business documents at all times.

Travelers should be alert to a number of scams perpetrated by Luanda airport personnel. Immigration and customs officials sometimes detain foreigners without cause, demanding gratuities before allowing them to enter or depart Angola. Airport health officials sometimes threaten arriving passengers with "vaccinations" with unsterilized instruments if gratuities are not paid.

The loss or theft abroad of a U.S. passport should be reported immediately to local police and to the nearest u.s. embassy or consulate. The pamphlets *A Safe Trip Abroad* and *Tips for Travelers to Sub-Saharan Africa* provide useful information on personal security while traveling abroad and on travel in the region in general. Both are available from the Superintendent of Documents, U.S. Government Printing Office, Washington, D.C. 20402, via the Internet at http://www.access.gpo.gov/su_docs, or via the Bureau of Consular Affairs home page at http://travel.state.gov.

MEDICAL FACILITIES: Adequate medical facilities are virtually non-existent throughout Angola, and most medicine is not available. Chloroquine-resistant and cerebral malaria are endemic to the region.

MEDICAL INSURANCE: Health providers often expect immediate cash payment for health services. U.S. medical insurance is not always valid outside the United States. The Medicare/Medicaid program does not provide for payment of medical services outside the United States. U.S. medical insurance is not always valid outside the United States. U.S. Medicare and Medicaid programs do not provide payment for medical services outside the United States. Uninsured travelers who require medical care overseas may face extreme difficulties. Check with your own insurance company to confirm whether your policy applies overseas, including provision for medical evacuation. Ascertain whether payment will be made to the overseas hospital or doctor or whether you will be reimbursed later for expenses you incur. Some insurance policies also include coverage for psychiatric treatment and for disposition of remains in the event of death. Useful information on medical emergencies abroad, including overseas insurance programs, is provided in the Department of State's Bureau of Consular Affairs brochure *Medical Information for Americans Traveling Abroad*, available via the Bureau of Consular Affairs home page or autofax: (202) 647-3000.

OTHER HEALTH INFORMATION: Travelers should consider taking prophylaxis against malaria. Information on vaccinations and other health precautions may be obtained from the Centers for Disease Control and Prevention's international traveler's hotline at telephone 1-877-FYI-TRIP (1-877-394-8747) ; fax, 1-888-CDC-FAXX (1-888-232-3299) ; or by visiting the CDC Internet home page at http://www.cdc.gov.

TRAFFIC SAFETY AND ROAD CONDITIONS: While in a foreign country, U.S. citizens may encounter road conditions which differ significantly from those in the United States. The information below concerning Angola is provided for general reference only, and may not be totally accurate in a particular location or circumstance.

Safety of Public Transportation: Poor
Urban Road Conditions/Maintenance: Poor

Rural Road Conditions/Maintenance: Poor
Availability of Roadside Assistance: Poor

Destinations in the interior are accessible safely only by private or chartered aircraft. Civilians have been killed by bandits or land mines exploding while traveling overland. Overland routes to neighboring countries are generally not open.

CIVIL AVIATION OVERSIGHT: As there is no direct commercial air service by local carriers at present, or economic authority to operate such service, between the U.S. and Angola, the U.S. Federal Aviation Administration (FAA) has not assessed Angola's civil aviation authority for compliance with international aviation safety standards for oversight of Angola's air carrier operations. For further information, travelers may contact the Department of Transportation within the U.S. at 1-800-322-7873, or visit the FAA Internet home page at http://www.faa.gov/avr/iasa/index.htm. The U.S. Department of Defense (DOD) separately assesses some foreign air carriers for suitability as official providers of air services. For information regarding the DOD policy on specific carriers, travelers may contact DOD at 618-256-4801.

CUSTOMS RESTRICTIONS: U.S. dollars can be converted to local currency at exchange houses authorized by the Angolan government. Rapid fluctuations in the value of the Angolan Kwanza and shortages of U.S. dollars are widespread. Currency conversions on the parallel (black) market are illegal and participants are subject to arrest. In general, only the newer series US 100 dollar bills are accepted due to widespread counterfeiting of the older style.

CRIMINAL PENALTIES: While in a foreign country, a U.S. citizen is subject to that country's laws and regulations, which sometimes differ significantly from those in the United States and may not afford the protections available to the individual under U.S. law. Penalties for breaking the law can be more severe than in the United States for similar offenses. Persons violating Angolan laws, even unknowingly, may be expelled, arrested or imprisoned. Penalties for possession, use, or trafficking in illegal drugs in Angola are strict and convicted offenders can expect jail sentences and heavy fines.

CHILDREN'S ISSUES: For information on international adoption of children, international parental child abduction, and international child support enforcement issues, please refer to our Internet site at http://travel.state.gov/children's_issues.html or telephone (202) 736-7000.

REGISTRATION/EMBASSY LOCATION: U.S. citizens are encouraged to register with and obtain updated information on travel and security from the Consular Section of the U.S. Embassy in Luanda located at the Casa Inglesa Complex, Rua Major Kanhangula No. 132/135, tel. 244-2-396-727; fax 244-2-390-515. The Embassy is located on Rua Houari Boumedienne in the Miramar area of Luanda, P.O. Box 6468, tel. 244-2-347-028/(345-481) /(346-418) ; (24-hour duty officer 244-9-501-343) ; fax 244-2-346-924.

HIGHWAYS

The roadway network covers about 75,000 km., 7,955 of which are paved. The main axis links the capital with the interior (East to West) . At the same time there are a series of branches that connect the main roadways and allow communication with neighboring countries, specifically with Namibia, the Democratic Republic of Congo and the Republic of Congo. Small and medium sized enterprises could be established to build and run hotels, inns, motels, car rental agencies, foreign exchange agencies, restaurants, tour vehicles, as well as in other sectors of the economy such as distribution of gas and linked services, health care units, commercial activity in general, etc.

Main Road Links	Distance in kms
Luanda-Malange-Saurimo	900
Luanda-Lobito-Benguela	600
Lobito-Benguela-Kuito	500
Cabinda-Lema	60
Lubango-Santa Clara	140

RAILWAYS

The country has a 2,750 km railway network, divided in three main axis, that are inter communicated: two inter-provincial and one intercontinental.

Route	Company	Extension
Lobito, Zambia, D.R. of Congo Inter-continental	Benguela Railways (CFB)	1,305 km
Namibe, Menongue Inter-provincial	Namibe Railways (CFN)	907 km
Luanda, Malange Inter-provincial	Luanda Railways (CFL)	538 km

MARITIME TRANSPORTATION

This is Angola's most important foreign trade route. The maritime infrastructure in general is in acceptable condition, and this has allowed Angola to meet the very heavy traffic needs.

The country has three large commercial ports and hundreds of smaller ones basically used for fisheries and the oil industry.

Main Commercial Ports	Volume of Cargo	Volume of Traffic
Luanda	10,000 m^2	+710,000 MT
Lobito	n/a	600,000 MT
Namibe	n/a	+115,000 MT

The most important carriers are CABOTANG, ANGONAVE, SECIL MARITIMA, EMPROMAR and NDS.

The area of maritime transportation also offers opportunities for tourism in ferry boats, etc.

AIR TRANSPORTATION

Mostly aimed at passenger traffic, both international and national. There is a network of airports and airfields distributed over the whole country that allows immediate access to every point in the national territory as well as to other countries from the 4 de Fevereiro International Airport in the capital.

TAAG (Angolan Airlines) is the flag airline that operates in the country as a whole and links it with several capitals in the world.

Apart from TAAG other foreign companies operate in the country such as: TAP, AIR FRANCE, AEROFLOT, SABENA, LAC (R. of Congo) , LINA-CONGO (Congo-Brazzaville) , AIR GABON, AIR NAMIBIA, SAA, ETHIOPIAN AIRLINES.

There are also smaller companies and charter companies that transport people and cargo such as SAL (light aviation) , AAC (Angola Air Charter LTD.) , Transafrica, etc.

Continent	Capitals
Africa	Johannesburg Windhoek Harare São Tomé Kinshasa Brazzaville, Point Noire Lusaka Sal
Europe	Lisbon Moscow Paris
America	Rio de Janeiro Havana

RIVER TRANSPORTATION

Angolan rivers offer excellent opportunities for transportation businesses both for tourism or a mix of trade and tourism.

There is a fluvial network made up of large rivers with several falls, rapids, and lakes, some of which are navigable over dozens of kilometers and also appropriate for bathing and water sports. Some of those rivers are the Kwanza, Zaire, Kuando and Cunene

Name	Length	Fluvial Network	Navigability
Zaire	150 km	30,050 km^2	150 km
Kwanza	1,000 km	147,690 km^2	240 km
Cunene	800 km	940,400 km^2	n/a
Kubango	975 km	153,400 km^2	n/a

MOUNTAINS AND WATERFALLS

The unexpected and diversified landscape that traces its identity to the heart of Africa includes areas such as the famous gorge of Tundavala and the Leba mountain range in the province of

Huila, the Calandula Falls and the Pungo a N'dondo rocks in Malange, the Moon lookout (Luanda) and the Kanda Mountains in the province of Zaire.

The falls of the rivers Cunene, Kwanza (in Barra do Kwanza) and Chiloango (in Cabinda) were chosen for the development of hotels and resorts because of the beauty of the landscape and their potential for Eco-tourism. Their development should aim at a providing several levels of quality, in keeping with the highest standards that are universally demanded.

TRAVEL AGENCIES

The large numbers of foreign travelers that have visited the country in the last few years, has given rise to a dynamic increase in the number of travel agencies. These are basically concentrated in the capital and some in provinces such as Benguela and Huila. The following are some of those agencies:

ZEPA, SECIL VIAGENS, EXPRESSO, ANGOTUR, RENOVAR, INTOUR'S, CHARME TOURS, FERTUR, EQUADOR, AUSTRAL VIAGENS E CARAVELA.

Because of the new outlook in the country offered by the establishment of peace and the development of tourist activities, this market sector will need new investment flows. They are specifically needed in the area of transport, communications, and modern equipment needed to replace the old. New agencies need to be established to give adequate coverage to international routes and visitors.

WORKING HOURS

HEALTH

The state of Angola's healthcare is very poor. HIV prevalence stands at around 2.78 per cent of the population aged 15-49 years (2000) . Around 160,000 people have HIV/AIDS, 7,900 are children under 15 years old (2000) . There are around 98,000 Angolan children who are orphaned due to the the pandemic (1999) . In the late 1980s, the government instituted a strategic plan to counter the spread of the disease, involving high profile political figures. A National Strategic Plan was formulated in 1999, but without adequate healthcare facilities its effects are limited.

MAIN CITIES

Luanda, capital (population 2.2 million in 1998) , Huambo (120,000) , Lobito, Benguela, Lubango, Soyo, Malanje

LANGUAGES SPOKEN

Local languages: principally Ovimbundu, Kimbundu (the language of the Mbundu) , Bakongo and Chokwe.
In July 1996 Portugal and six of its former colonies (Angola, Brazil, Cape Verde, Guinea-Bissau, Mozambique and São Tomé & Príncipe) launched the Community of Portuguese Speaking Countries (CPLP) to protect their common language.

OFFICIAL LANGUAGE

Portuguese

MEDIA

PRESS

Angola's only national daily newspaper is *O Jornal de Angola (JA)* . *Diário da República* (government news sheet) is published daily. Regional newspapers are published in several towns. *El Moujahid* is also circulated here. A few periodicals are also available. *Correio da Semana* is the Sunday newspaper.

BROADCASTING

Radio: National radio service with broadcasts in Portuguese, English, French, Spanish and vernacular languages, operated by the state-owned Radio Nacional de Angola. The Black Cock of Unita, a US-backed station broadcasting on behalf of Unita, is also permitted to operate.

Television: Limited TV service operated by Televisão Popular de Angola (TPA) . There are only 0.6 television sets per 100 inhabitants.

BUSINESS TRAVEL TO ANGOLA

TRAVEL ADVISORY AND VISAS

The following Travel Warning was issued by the Department of State on July 15, 1998: The Department of State warns U.S. citizens against travel to Angola because of continued unsettled conditions, violent crime, and the heightened potential for political-military instability due to the lack of progress in the
peace process since April, 1998. Travel within Angola remains unsafe due to bandit attacks, undisciplined police and troops, low intensity military actions in several interior provinces, and unexploded land mines in rural areas. Foreign nationals, especially independent entrepreneurs, are subject to arbitrary
detention and/or deportation by immigration and police
authorities.

Americans who find travel to Angola unavoidable are strongly urged to contact the U.S. Embassy for up-to-date information. Travel outside Luanda should not be initiated without contacting the U.S. Embassy for the latest information on
security conditions in the provinces they plan to visit. For further information on Angola, see the Department of State's latest Consular Information Sheet on Angola.

U.S. citizens are required to obtain Angolan visas and must present an international immunizations record on arrival or face the prospect of mandatory inoculations at the airport.

HOLIDAYS

Angola's official 1998 holidays are as follows:
January 1 (New Year's Day) ,
January 4 (Martyr's Day) ,
February 4 (Beginning of the Armed Fight Day) ,
February 24 (Carnival Day-- varies by year) ,
March 8 (Women's Day) ,
March 27 (Holy Friday - varies by year) ,
May 1 (Labor Day) ,
June 1 (Children's Day) ,
November 2 (Memorial Day) ,
November 11 (Veteran's Day) ,
and December 25 (Christmas Day) .

BUSINESS INFRASTRUCTURE

The U.S. Embassy in Luanda has an economic and commercial officer, who is available to discuss recent economic and business developments. All commercial services are coordinated by a full-time Foreign Service National employee, Maria Josefa Dos Santos, who is an expert in commercial and business affairs in Angola. She is well informed on all commercial and economic matters, and is an excellent source of valuable insights into doing business in Angola. Agricultural exports are supported by another Foreign Service National employee, Raul Danda, who is trained and experienced in promoting U.S. agricultural exports and who is in frequent contact with exporters, importers, and the U.S. Department of Agriculture.

GROUND TRANSPORTATION

The general condition of roads and related infrastructure is extremely poor, even within Luanda. Many roads are unpaved and impassible in the rainy season. Others are impassible due to landmines or banditry. Gasoline is available in most urban areas.

Rental cars are available for hire in Luanda and Cabinda. Hiring a driver is recommended. Driving at night is unsafe. Driving in areas outside of major metropolitan areas is unsafe due to unexploded mines, undisciplined police and troops, and groups of armed bandits. The embassy strongly recommends that
anyone planning surface travel in Angola register with the consular section and receive a briefing on personal security. In a few isolated areas of Angola, notably in the Cabinda enclave, foreigners may be the targets of political violence, including seizure and burning of vehicles by insurgent groups. Angola has
few public busses or other public transport.

AIR TRANSPORTATION

Air France, Air Namibe, Angolan Airlines (TAAG) , Sabena, South African Airways, TAP (Portugal) and several regional carriers provide international service to Luanda. No U.S. flag airlines service Angola, and no direct service exists between the U.S. and Angola. Internally, TAAG, SAL, and several smaller
charter or air taxi companies provide domestic flights. Given the difficulties and dangers in surface travel, air travel is often the only viable alternative when traveling to the interior of Angola.

As of June 1998, there is no airport departure tax for Angolans or foreign nationals.

RAIL TRANSPORTATION

Angola's three major rail lines (Luanda-Malange, Benguela-DROC, and Namibe-Menongue) are all not operative, either as a result of war-damage or neglect. Of the three, only the Benguela Railroad is currently being considered for
rehabilitation. Efforts have yet to get underway, and many observers doubt the viability of the project. Rail traffic for both passengers and cargo is currently limited to the 35 kilometers of line between the cities of Lobito and Benguela.

BOAT TRANSPORTATION

International shipping reaches Angola via the ports of Luanda, Lobito, and Namibe.

LANGUAGES

Portuguese is the official language of Angola. English or French is spoken by many business persons.

COMMUNICATIONS FACILITIES

With one telephone per 250 people, Angola ranked 18th out of 22 African countries ranked by the United Nations for number of telephones per capita. Angola's telecommunications infrastructure is overburdened, and service is deteriorating. Both domestic and international telecommunications are difficult. Most corporate offices and tourist class hotels have telephones; many have
faxes. The cellular phone system is oversubscribed and frequently inaccessible during business hours. Many large international corporations rely on high frequency radio transmissions for routine communication. There are two local Internet providers. The international country code for Angola is 244; the city code
for Luanda is 2, and the cellular code is 9.

HOUSING

Short-term visitors normally stay in tourist-class hotels located in major urban areas. Selection is limited and expensive. Due to security considerations, accommodation in rural areas is generally not recommended. Resident expatriates generally live in rehabilitated housing in the major urban centers, though the market for such housing is tight and growing worse. Prices are correspondingly high, with rents of $5,000 to $8,000 per month being paid for residences in the 1500-2000 square foot range. Power and water are generally available in major cities, but supply interruptions, lasting from hours to days, are common.

HEALTH

With a life expectancy of 47 years, Angola ranks near the bottom in a 1997 World Bank survey of African nations. Official Angolan studies place life expectancy at 42 years. Infant mortality is 124 per 1000 and 274 per thousand by age five. Only
16 percent of Angolan children have received basic vaccinations. Diseases thought to have been largely under control in Angola, including polio and sleeping sickness, have reemerged. World Health Organization estimates show an HIV infection rate of between 1.5 and 8 percent, varying by province.

Surveillance of tuberculosis and sexually transmitted diseases is insufficient to
generate meaningful statistics, but surveys of hospitals and clinics have shown that infection rates continue to climb. Choloraquin-resistant malaria and other tropical diseases are prevalent throughout the country. Just under three percent of Angolans suffer from physical or mental deficiency, and 53 percent suffer from chronic malnutrition, according to Angolan Government statistics.

Angola's national health facilities are below acceptable standards. Several private clinics in Luanda provide acceptable levels of care. Full immunizations and malaria prophylaxis are recommended. Water quality in major urban areas is poor. Boiling or drinking domestically produced bottled water may be
insufficient to guard against illness. The embassy recommends only imported bottled water. Raw, unpeeled fruits and vegetables should be avoided.

FOOD

A variety of foods are normally available in Angola's urban areas, although expensive. Several stores carry imported goods. There are few western standard restaurants and prices are high.

SUPPLEMENTS

US COMPANIES OPERATING IN OR INTERESTED IN PURSUING BUSINESS OPPORTUNITIES IN ANGOLA

"No southern African country more than Angola has the potential to emulate the explosive economic growth of the Asian 'Tigers'. U.S. companies have and will continue to excel in Angola's expansive oil and extractive minerals sectors. In the coming years, increasing numbers of U.S. companies will employ their comparative advantages in other promising Angolan sectors such as telecommunications, agriculture and infrastructure development. They will help Angola assume the vanguard of the young African 'Lions'."

Edmund De Jarnette
Executive Director, US-Angola Chamber of Commerce

A.A.D.L. (Texas)
ABB Lummus Global Inc. (Texas)
AM General Corp. (Georgia)
Africa One (New Jersey)
AVE Trading, Inc. (Florida)
Aero Industrial Sales Co. (New Jersey)
Amer-Con Corp. (Florida)
American Manufacturing & Trading, Inc. (Georgia)
Amoco Overseas Exploration Co. (Texas)
Arko Engineers Corp. (Maryland)
Caterpillar (Illinois)
British Petroleum America (Texas)
Chevron Overseas Petroleum, Inc. (California)
Citibank (New York)
Citizens Energy Corp. (Massachusetts)
EDI Architecture (Texas)
McDermott (Texas)
Equator Bank Limited (Connecticut)
ENRON Development Corp. (Texas)
Exxon Exploration Co. (Texas)
FH International Financial Services, Inc. (New York)
Global Industries (Louisiana)
Global Marine Drilling Co. (Texas)
Halliburton/Brown & Root (Texas or Oklahoma)
Ingersoll-Rand Corp. (New Jersey)
Inter-Continental Trade Associates (Maryland)
International Strategy Services (New York)
Lazare Kaplan International (New York)
MPS of America Corp. (Florida)
The MW Kellogg Co. (Florida)
Mampeza International (California)
Maywood Holdings International (New Mexico)
Mobil Oil Corp. (Texas)
Morgan Guaranty Trust Co. (New York)
Motorola, Inc. (Illinois)
Occidental International Exploration & Production (Louisiana)
Odebrecht of America, Inc. (California)
Ordsafe, Inc. (Maryland)
Panalpina, Inc. (New Jersey)

Pecten International Co. (Texas)
Schaffer/Serv-Tech (Louisiana)
Seaboard Corp. (Kansas)
Target Shipping Inc. (New York)
Texaco (New York)
Yankee Exports (Maine)

CONTACT AND RELATED INFORMATION ON THE HOTEL AND TOURISM INDUSTRIES IN ANGOLA

USEFUL CONTACT INFORMATION AT THE MINISTRY OF HOTELS AND TOURISM

Ministry of Hotels and Tourism
Largo 4 de Fevereiro - Palácio de Vidro
Luanda
Tel/Fax: 011-244-2-33-82-11

Minister for Hotels and Tourism
Dr.Jorge Alicerces Valentim
Tel/Fax: 011-244-233-82-11

Vice Minister for Hotels and Tourism
Dr. Paulino Domingos Baptista
Tel/Fax: 011-244-2-33-13-23

For Technical Help:

Legal office of the Ministry
Director: Dr. Francisco Barbosa da Silva Sobrinho
Tel/Fax: 011-244-2-33-99-25

Secretary General
Sr. Lourençao Miguel Neto
Tel/Fax: 011-244-2-3375-59

Office of Studies, Planning and Statistics
Director: Dr. Ambrósio Garcia Kadiamoniko
Tel/Fax: 011-244-2-33-78-02

Inspector's Office
Director: Sr. Domingos Francisco Kamavo
Tel/Fax: 011-244-2-33-68-92

For General Assistance:

Office of the Minister
Chief of Staff: Sr. Victorino Augusto da Salva
Tel/Fax: 011-244-2-33-96-34

Office of the Vice Minister
Chief of Staff: Dr. Rui Lopes Teixeira
Tel/Fax: 011-244-2-3376-24

Office of International Exchanges
Director: Dr. Mateus Filipe Martins
Tel/Fax: 011-244-233-67-70

Press office
Sr. Jorge Manuel Luceu Calado
Tel/Fax: 011-244-2-33-82-11

OTHER USEFUL CONTACTS

National Direcorate of Hotel Infrastructures
Director: Dr. José Apolinário de Oliveira Diogo
Tel/Fax: 011-244-2-33-92-45

National Directorate of Tourist Activities
Director: Dr. Januário Francisco Marra
Tel/Fax: 011-244-2-33-72-51

National Directorate for Hotel and Tourism Development
Director: Dr.ª Amélia Cecília Domingas Carlos Cazalma
Tel/Fax: 011-244-2-33-62-40

Angola is a member of the following International Hotel and Tourism Institutions:

- Angola became a member of the **WTO (World Tourism Organization)** in 1989, during the 8th Session of the General Assembly held in Paris. Its contributions to the organization are up to date.
- The corporation MABOQUE (a private entity) became a member of the WTO in 1996, during the general assembly held in Tunisia.
- Angola has been a member of **RETOSA (Regional Tourism Organization of the SADC)** since its inception.
- **Main professional associations for hotel and tourism industries in Angola:**
- **HORESIL** - Association of hotel owners and similar organizations in Luanda
- **AADHA** - Association of travel agents and tour operators in Angola

TIPS FOR TRAVELERS TO SUB-SAHARAN AFRICA
General Information

Your trip to Africa will be an adventure off the beaten path. The estimated 325,000 U.S. citizens who travel to Africa each year are only a fraction of the more than 44 million Americans who go overseas annually.

The Department of State seeks to encourage international travel. Conditions and customs in sub-Saharan Africa, however, can contrast sharply with what you are accustomed. These pages contain advice to help you avoid inconvenience and difficulties as you go. Take our advice seriously but do not let it keep you at home. Africans are happy to share not just their scenery,

For additional analytical, business and investment opportunities information, please contact Global Investment & Business Center, USA at (202) 546-2103. Fax: (202) 546-3275. E-mail: rusric@erols.com

but their culture and traditions as well. This brochure should be used in conjunction with the Consular Information Sheets and Travel Warnings.

Before you go, learn as much as you can about your destination. Your travel agent, local bookstore, public library and the embassies of the countries you plan to visit are all useful sources of information. Another source is the Department of State's Background Notes series which include a pamphlet for each country in Africa. To obtain specific pamphlet prices and information, contact the Superintendent of Documents, U.S. Government Printing Office, Washington, D.C. 20402; tel: (202) 738-3238. You may also obtain select issues by fax by calling (202) 736-7720 from your fax machine.

This brochure covers all of Africa except the five nations bordering the Mediterranean. Sub-Saharan Africa includes 48 nations. Forty two of these nations are on the mainland. In addition, four island nations in the southwest Indian Ocean (Madagascar, Comoros, Mauritius, and Seychelles) and two island nations in the Atlantic Ocean (Cape Verde and Sao Tome and Principe) are considered part of Africa. For convenience, we will often use the word "Africa" to refer to the sub-Saharan region. For travel tips for the five northern African nations of Tunisia, Algeria, Morocco, Libya, and Egypt see Tips for Travelers to the Middle East and North Africa.

Consular Information Program

Before traveling, obtain the Consular Information Sheet for the country or countries you plan to visit. You should also check to see if the Department of State has issued a Travel Warning for the country or countries you will be visiting. Warnings are issued when the State Department decides, based on all relevant information, to recommend that Americans avoid travel to a certain country. Consular Information Sheets are available for every country of the world. They include such information as the location of the U.S. embassy or consulate in the subject country, unusual immigration practices, health conditions, minor political disturbances, unusual currency and entry regulations, crime and security information, and drug penalties. If an unstable condition exists in a country that is not severe enough to warrant a Warning, a description of the condition(s) may be included under an optional section entitled "Areas of Instability." On limited occasions, we also restate in this section any U.S. embassy advice given to official employees. Consular Information Sheets generally do not include advice, but present information on factual matters so travelers can make knowledgeable decisions concerning travel to a particular country. Countries where avoidance of travel is recommended will have Travel Warnings as well as Consular Information Sheets.

How to Access Consular Information Sheets and Travel Warnings

Consular Information Sheets and Travel Warnings may be heard any time by dialing the Citizens Emergency Center at (202) 647-5225 from a touchtone phone. The recording is updated as new information becomes available. They are also available at any of the 13 regional passport agencies, field offices of the U.S. Department of Commerce, and U.S. embassies and consulates abroad, or, by writing or sending a self-addressed, stamped envelope to the Office of Overseas Citizens Services, Bureau of Consular Affairs, Room 4811, U.S. Department of State, Washington, D.C. 20520-4818.

By Fax

From your fax machine, dial (202) 647-3000, using the handset as you would a regular telephone. The system will instruct you on how to proceed.

Consular Affairs Bulletin Board - CABB

If you have a personal computer, modem and communication software, you can access the Consular Affairs Bulletin Board (CABB) . This service is free of charge.

To view documents from a computer and modem, dial the CABB on (301) 946-4400. The login is **travel**; the password is **info**.

As you travel, keep abreast of local news coverage. If you plan a long stay in one place or if you are in an area where communications are poor or that is experiencing civil unrest or some natural disaster, you are encouraged to register with the nearest U.S. embassy or consulate. Registration takes only a few moments, and it may be invaluable in case of an emergency. Remember to leave a detailed itinerary and the numbers of your passport or other citizenship documents with a friend or relative in the United States.

Health

Health problems affect more visitors to Africa than any other difficulty. Information on health precautions can be obtained from local health departments, private doctors, or travel clinics. General guidance can also be found in the U.S. Public Health Service book, Health Information for International Travel, available for $7.00 from the Superintendent of Documents, U.S. Government Printing Office, Washington, D.C. 20402, or the Centers for Disease Control's international travelers hotline at (404) 332-4559. Depending on your destination, immunization may be recommended against cholera, diphtheria, tetanus, hepatitis, meningitis, polio, typhoid, and yellow fever. These diseases are transmitted by insects, contaminated food and water, or close contact with infected people. Travelers should take the proper precautions before leaving for sub-Saharan Africa to reduce the risk of infection.

Diseases transmitted by insects

Many diseases are transmitted through the bite of infected insects such as mosquitoes, flies, fleas, ticks, and lice. Travelers must protect themselves from insect bites by wearing proper clothing, using bed nets, and applying the proper insect repellent. Mosquito activity is most prominent during the hours between dusk and dawn. Malaria is a serious parasitic infection transmitted to humans by the mosquito. Symptoms range from fever and flu-like symptoms, to chills, general achiness, and tiredness. Travelers at risk for malaria should take Mefloquine to prevent malaria. This drug should be taken one week before leaving, while in the malarious area, and for a period of four weeks after leaving the area.

Travelers are advised to consult their personal physicians on the possible side effects of the malaria medication they choose. Yellow Fever is a viral disease transmitted to human by a mosquito bite. Symptoms range from fever, chills, headache, and vomiting to jaundice, internal bleeding, and kidney failure. Some sub-Saharan countries require yellow fever vaccination for entry. Dengue Fever is primarily an urban viral infection transmitted by mosquito bites. The illness is flu-like and characterized by the sudden onset of a high fever, severe headaches, joint and muscle pain, and rash. Prevention is important since no vaccine or specific treatment exists.

Diseases Transmitted Through Food and Water

Food and waterborne diseases are one of the major causes of illness to travelers, the most frequent being diarrhea. It can be caused by viruses, bacteria, or parasites which are found universally throughout the region. Typhoid Fever is a bacterial infection transmitted throughout contaminated food and/or water, or directly between people. Symptoms of typhoid include fever, headaches, tiredness, loss of appetite, and constipation more often then diarrhea. Typhoid fever can be treated effectively with antibiotics. Drinking only bottled or boiled water and eating only thoroughly cooked food reduces the risk of infection. Cholera is an acute intestinal infection caused by a bacterium. Infection is acquired by ingesting contaminated water or food.

Symptoms include an abrupt onset of voluminous watery diarrhea, dehydration, vomiting, and muscle cramps. The best method of prevention is to follow the standard food and water precautions. Individuals with severe cases should receive medical attention immediately. Hepatitis A is a viral infection of the liver transmitted by the fecal oral; through direct person to person contact; from contaminated water, ice or shellfish; or from fruits or uncooked vegetables contaminated through handling. Symptoms include fatigue, fever, loss of appetite, nausea, dark urine, jaundice, vomiting, aches and pains, and light stools. No specific therapy is available. The virus is inactivated by boiling or cooking to 85 degrees centigrade for one minute. Travelers should eat thoroughly cooked foods and drink only treated water as a precaution.

Diseases Transmitted Through Intimate Contact with People

Human immunodeficiency virus (HIV) which causes acquired immunodeficiency syndrome or AIDS is found primarily in blood, semen, and vaginal secretions of an infected person. HIV is spread by contact with an infected person, by needle sharing among injecting drug users, and through transfusions of infected blood and blood clotting factors. Treatment has prolonged the survival of some HIV infected persons, but there is no known cure or vaccine available. International travelers should be aware that some countries serologically screen incoming travelers (primarily those with extended visits, such as for work or study) and deny entry to persons with AIDS and those whose test results indicate infection with HIV.

Persons who are intending to visit a country for substantial periods or to work or study may wish to consult the embassy of that country concerning the policies and requirements on HIV testing. Hepatitis B is a viral infection of the liver. Primarily, Hepatitis B is transmitted through activities which result in the exchange of blood or blood derived fluids and/or through sexual activity with an infected person. The primary prevention consists of either vaccination and/or reducing intimate contact with those suspected of being infected. Meningococcal Disease (bacterial meningitis) is a bacterial infection in the lining of the brain or spinal cord. Early symptoms are headache, stiff neck, a rash, and fever. This is spread by repository droplets when an infected person sneezes or coughs on you. A one dose vaccine called Menomune (TM) is available.

Other Diseases

Schistosomiasis is an infection that develops after the larvae of a flatworm have penetrated the skin. Water treated with chlorine or iodine is virtually safe, and salt water poses no risk. The risk is a function of the frequency and degree of contact with contaminated fresh water for bathing, wading, or swimming. It is often difficult to distinguish between infested and non-infested water; therefore, swimming in fresh water in rural areas should be avoided. Rabies is a viral infection that affects the central nervous system. The virus is introduced by an animal bite. The best prevention is not to handle animals. Any animal bite should receive prompt attention.

Some countries have shortages of medicines; bring an adequate supply of any prescription and over-the-counter medicines that you are accustomed to taking. Keep all prescriptions in their original, labeled containers.

Medical facilities may be limited, particularly in rural areas. Should you become seriously ill or injured abroad, contact the nearest U.S. embassy or consulate. A U.S. consular officer can furnish you with a list of recommended local hospitals and English-speaking doctors. Consular officers can also inform your family or friends in the United States of your condition. Because medical coverage overseas can be quite expensive, prospective travelers should review their health insurance policies. Doctors and hospitals expect immediate payment in full for health services in many sub-Saharan countries. If your policy does not provide medical coverage overseas, consider buying supplemental insurance. It is also advisable to obtain insurance to cover the exorbitant cost of medical evacuation in the event of a medical emergency.

Except in first-class hotels, drink only boiled water or bottled beverages. Avoid ice cubes. Unless you are certain they are pasteurized, avoid dairy products. Vegetables and fruits should be peeled or washed in a purifying solution. A good rule of thumb is, "If you can't peel it or cook it, don't eat it."

Crime

Crime is a worldwide problem, particularly in urban populated areas. In places where crime is especially acute, we have noted this problem under the specific geographic country section. Travelers should, however, be alert to the increasing crime problem throughout sub-Saharan Africa.

Weather

Sub-Saharan Africa is tropical, except for the high inland plateaus and the southern part of South Africa. Within 10 degrees of the Equator, the climate seldom varies and is generally hot and rainy. Further from the Equator, the seasons become more apparent, and if possible, you should plan your trip in the cooler months. If traveling to rural areas, avoid the rainy months which generally run from May through October north of the equator and November through April south of the equator. Roads may be washed out during these times.

Visa and Other Entry Requirements

A U.S. passport is required for travel to all countries in Africa. In addition, most countries in sub-Saharan Africa require U.S. citizens to have a visa. If visas are required, obtain them before you leave home. If you decide to visit additional countries en route, it may be difficult or impossible to obtain visas. In most African countries, you will not be admitted into the country and will have to depart on the next plane, if you arrive without a visa. This can be inconvenient if the next plane does not arrive for several days, the airport hotel is full, and the airport has no other sleeping accommodations.

The best authority on a country's visa and other entry requirements is its embassy or consulate. The Department of State publication, Foreign Entry Requirements, gives basic information on entry requirements and tells where and how to apply for visas. You can order a copy for 50 cents from the Consumer Information Center, Pueblo, Colorado 81009.

Allow plenty of time to apply for visas. An average of two weeks for each visa is recommended. When you inquire, check the following:

- visa price, length of validity, and number of entries;

- financial data required

- proof of sufficient funds, proof of onward/return ticket;

- immunizations required;

- currency regulations;

- import/export restrictions; and

- departure tax. If required, be sure to keep sufficient hard currency so that you may leave the country on schedule.

- HIV clearance certification. Some countries require travelers to submit certification or be tested upon arrival for HIV.

In the past, some African countries refused to admit travelers who had South African visas or entry and exit stamps in their passports. The situation has improved.

Restricted Areas

A visa is good only for those parts of a country that are open to foreigners. Several countries in Africa have areas of civil unrest or war zones that are off-limits to visitors without special permits. Others have similar areas that are open but surrounded by security checkpoints where travelers must show their passport, complete with valid visa. When traveling in such a country, keep your passport with you at all times. No matter where you travel in Africa, do not overstay the validity of your visa; renew it if necessary.

If stopped at a roadblock, be courteous and responsive to questions asked by persons in authority. In areas of instability, however, try to avoid travel at night. If you must travel at night, turn on the interior light of the car. For information on restricted or risky areas, consult Department of State Consular Information Sheets or, if you are already in Africa, the nearest U.S. embassy or consulate.

In some areas, when U.S. citizens are arrested or detained, police or prison officials have failed to inform the U.S. embassy or consulate. If you are ever detained for any reason, it is your right to speak with a U.S. consular officer immediately.

U.S. Citizens Married to Foreign Nationals

Women who travel to Africa should be aware that in some countries, either by law or by custom, a woman and her children need the permission of her husband to leave the country. If you or your children travel, be aware of the laws and customs of the places you visit. Do not visit or allow your children to visit unless you are confident that you will be permitted to leave. Once overseas, you are subject to the laws of the country you visit; U.S. law cannot protect you.

Currency Regulations

The amount of money, including traveler's checks, which may be taken into or out of African countries varies. In general, visitors must declare all currency and travelers checks upon arrival. Do not exchange money on the black market. Use only banks and other authorized foreign exchange offices and retain receipts. You may need to present the receipts as well as your original currency declaration when you depart. Currency not accounted for may be confiscated, and you may be fined or detained. Many countries require that hotel bills be paid in hard currency. Some require that a minimum amount of hard currency be changed into the local currency upon arrival. Some countries prohibit the import or export of local currency. Also, some countries prohibit the destruction of local currency, no matter how small the denomination.

U.S. Wildlife Regulations

The United States prohibits the import of products from endangered species, including the furs of any spotted cats. Most African countries have enacted laws protecting wildlife, but poaching and illegal trafficking in wildlife are still commonplace. Importing products made from endangered species, may result in the seizure of the product and a possible fine. African ivory cannot generally be imported legally into the United States.

The import of most types of parrots and other wild birds from Africa is now restricted and subject to licensing and other controls. There are also restrictions which require the birds to be placed in quarantine upon arrival to ensure they are free from disease. For further information on the import of wildlife and related products, consult the U.S. Fish and Wildlife Service or TRAFFIC U.S.A., World Wildlife FundÑU.S., 1250 24th Street, N.W., Washington, D.C. 20037.

Air Travel

If you are flying to places in Africa other than the major tourist destinations, you may have difficulty securing and retaining reservations and experience long waits at airports for customs and immigration processing. If stranded, you may need proof of a confirmed reservation in order to obtain food and lodging vouchers from some airlines. Flights are often overbooked, delayed, or cancelled and, when competing for space on a plane, you may be dealing with a surging crowd rather than a line. Traveling with a packaged tour may insulate you from some of these difficulties. All problems cannot be avoided, but you can:

 - Learn the reputation of the airline and the airports you will use to forestall problems and avoid any unpleasant surprises.

 - Reserve your return passage before you go; reconfirm immediately upon arrival.

 - Ask for confirmation in writing, complete with file number or locator code, when you make or confirm a reservation.

 - Arrive at the airport earlier than required in order to put yourself at the front of the line - or the crowd, as the case may be.

 - Travel with funds sufficient for an extra week's subsistence in case you are stranded.

Photography

Africa is filled with photogenic scenery, and photography is generally encouraged. However, most governments prohibit photography of military installations or locations having military significance, including airports, bridges, tunnels, port facilities, and public buildings. Visitors can seek guidance on restrictions from local tourist offices or from the nearest U.S. embassy or consulate. Taking such photographs without prior permission can result in your arrest or the confiscation of your film and/or equipment.

Shortages, High Prices, and Other Problems

Consumer goods, gas, and food are in short supply in some African countries and prices for these commodities may be high by U.S. standards. Shortages of hotel accommodations also exist so confirm reservations well in advance. Some countries experience disruptions in electricity and water supply or in services such as mail and telecommunications.

Local Transportation

Rental cars, where available, may be expensive. Hiring a taxi is often the easiest way to go sight-seeing. Taxi fares should be negotiated in advance. Travel on rural roads can be slow and difficult in the dry season and disrupted by floods in the rainy season.

COUNTRY INFORMATION

Angola

Angola is a developing country which has experienced war and civil strife since before independence from Portugal in 1975. In 1993, the U.S. recognized the Angolan government and a U.S. Embassy was established in Luanda. Facilities for tourism are virtually nonexistent. Visas are required. Persons arriving without visas are subjected to possible arrest or deportation. Travel in many parts of the city is considered unsafe at night because of the increased incidence of armed robberies and carjackings. Violent crime exists throughout the country. Adequate medical facilities are scarce in Angola, and most medicine is not available. Travelers are advised to purchase medical evacuation insurance.

Benin

Benin is a developing West African country. Its capital is Porto Novo; however the adjoining city of Cotonou is the main port and site of most government and tourist activity. Tourist facilities in Cotonou are available, but are not fully developed elsewhere in Benin. U.S. citizens are required to have a visa. Because of security concerns in remote areas, especially the northern region of Atacora, travel can be dangerous. Medical facilities in Benin are limited. Crime rates are rising, particularly in Cotonou.

Botswana

Botswana is a developing southern African nation. Facilities for tourism are available. No visa is necessary for stays of less than 90 days. Medical facilities in Botswana are limited. Some petty crime, such as pickpocketing and purse snatching is common in the capital city of Gaborone. Travel by automobile outside of large towns may be dangerous. Although major roads are generally in good condition, the combination of long stretches of two-lane highway, high speed limits, and the occasional presence of large animals on the roads makes accidents a frequent occurrence.

Burkina Faso

Burkina Faso, previously known as Upper Volta, is a developing West African country which borders the Sahara Desert. The official language is French. Facilities for tourism are not widely available. A visa is required. Cholera and yellow fever immunizations is recommended. Medical facilities in Burkina Faso are limited and medicine is in short supply. Some petty crime occurs. There are restrictions on photography and a valid photo permit must be obtained from the Ministry of Tourism. The Ministry maintains a list of photo restrictions that are expected to be observed by visitors. The U.S. Embassy in Ouagadougou can provide information on specific photography regulations. Credit cards are rarely accepted. Travelers checks can be cashed at local banks. Local telephone service is excellent but expensive.

Burundi

Burundi is a small, inland African nation passing through a period of instability following a coup attempt in October 1993. Facilities for tourism, particularly in the interior, are limited. A passport is required. Medical facilities are limited. Street crime poses a high risk for visitors. Burundi has a good network of roads between the major towns and border posts. Travel on other roads is difficult, particularly in the rainy season. Public transportation to border points is often difficult and frequently unavailable. At the time of publication, the Department of State warned U.S. citizens to avoid travel due to continuing unstable conditions throughout the country.

Cameroon

Cameroon is a developing African country. Facilities for tourism are limited. A visa and proof of innoculation against yellow fever are required. Obtain a visa before arrival to avoid difficulty at the airport. Airport security is stringent and visitors may be subject to baggage searches. Medical facilities are limited. Armed banditry is an increasing problem in the extreme north and petty crime is common throughout the country. Persons traveling at night on rural highways are at extreme risk. While photography is not officially forbidden, security officials are extremely sensitive about the photographing of government buildings and military installations, many of which are unmarked. Photography of these subjects may result in seizure of photographic equipment by Cameroonian authorities.

Cape Verde

The Republic of Cape Verde consists of several rugged volcanic islands off the west coast of Africa. The climate is warm and dry. Tourist facilities are limited. A visa is required. Evidence of immunization against yellow fever (if arriving from an infected area) is required. Medical facilities in Cape Verde are extremely limited. Some petty theft is common.

Central African Republic

The Central African Republic is a developing African country. Facilities for tourism are limited. A passport and visa are required. Medical facilities in the Central African Republic are limited. Petty crime such as pickpocketing can occur throughout the country, especially in the urban areas. Foreigners have been victims of assault on the streets of Bangui, the capital. Walking at night in Bangui is unsafe; caution should be displayed in the market areas at all times. Endemic banditry in the northern strip of the country which borders Chad sometimes affects foreign travelers. Taking photographs of police or military installations, as well as government buildings, is prohibited.

Chad

Chad is a developing country in north central Africa which has experienced sporadic armed disturbances over the past several years. Facilities for tourism are limited. Visitors to Chad must have a visa before arrival. Evidence of a yellow fever vaccination must be presented. Medical facilities are extremely limited. Medicines are in short supply. Pickpocketing and purse snatching are endemic in market and commercial areas. A permit is required for all photography. Even with a permit, there are prohibitions against taking pictures of military establishments and official buildings. At the time of publication, the U.S. Embassy advised U.S. citizens that travel across the southwestern border into Cameroon was hazardous because of highway banditry and other violence in northern Cameroon.

Comoros

Comoros is a developing island nation located in the Indian Ocean, off the east coast of Africa. Facilities for tourism are limited. A visa is required. Visas for stays of three weeks or less can be issued at the airport upon arrival, provided an onward/return ticket is presented. Medical facilities in Comoros are limited. Petty thievery is common.

Congo

Congo is a developing nation in central Africa. Facilities for tourism are limited. A visa is required. Medical facilities in Congo are limited. Some medical supplies are in short supply. Street crime, including mugging and purse snatching, is common in Brazzaville, as well as in parts of the countryside. Driving may be hazardous, particularly at night, and travelers should be alert to possible roadblocks. Travelers may wish to contact the U.S. Embassy in Brazzaville for the latest information on conditions on the Congo.

Cote d'Ivoire

Cote d'Ivoire is also known as the Ivory Coast. It is a developing West African nation. Tourism facilities in the capital city of Abidjan include some luxury hotels. Other accommodations, especially outside the capital, may be limited in quality and availability. A visa is not required for a stay of up to 90 days. All travelers arriving in Cote d'Ivoire must be in possession of a World Health Organization (W.H.O.) vaccination card reflecting a current yellow fever inoculation. The W.H.O. card is inspected is inspected by Ivorian Health officials at the airport before admittance into the country. Medical facilities are adequate in Abidjan but may be limited elsewhere. Not all medicines are available. Street crime of the "grab and run" variety, as well as pickpocketing in crowded areas, has increased. Automobile accidents are one of the greatest threats to Americans in Cote d'Ivoire. Night driving is particularly hazardous due to poorly lit roads and vehicles. Airline travel in Cote d'Ivoire and many other parts of West Africa is routinely overbooked; schedules are limited, and airline assistance is of varying quality.

Djibouti

Djibouti is a developing African country. Facilities for tourism are limited. Visitors to Djibouti must obtain a visa before arrival. Evidence of yellow fever immunization must be presented. Medical facilities are limited. Medicine is often unavailable. Petty crime occurs in Djibouti City and elsewhere in the country.

Equatorial Guinea

Equatorial Guinea is a developing country in West Africa. Tourism facilities are minimal. A visa is required and must be obtained in advance. Medical facilities are extremely limited. Many medicines are unavailable. Petty crime is common. The government of Equatorial Guinea has established stringent currency restrictions, applied both on arrival and departure from the country.

Special permits may be needed for some types of photography. Permits are also required to visit certain areas of the country.

Eritrea

Eritrea is a poor but developing East African country. Formerly a province of Ethiopia, Eritrea became an independent country in 1993, following a 30-year long struggle for independence. Tourism facilities in Eritrea are very limited. A visa is required as well as evidence of yellow fever immunization. Airport visas are unavailable. Flights between Asmara and Addis Ababa, the capital of Ethiopia, are heavily booked and advance reservations are recommended. Medical facilities in Eritrea are extremely limited. Travelers must bring their own supplies of prescription drugs and preventative medicines. Street crime such as theft and robbery is on the increase, particularly in the capital of Asmara. While travel throughout Eritrea is relatively safe, visitors may wish to exercise normal safety precautions with regard to what valuables are carried and what environs are visited. The government of Eritrea continues to use the Ethiopian birr as a currency. Credit cards are not accepted in Eritrea. Foreigners must pay bills in U.S. dollars or U.S. dollar denomination travelers checks.

Ethiopia

Ethiopia is a developing East African country. Tourism facilities, although available in larger cities, are limited. A visa is required, as well as evidence of yellow fever immunization. Travelers must enter Ethiopia by air, either at Addis Ababa or Dire Dawa. Individuals entering overland risk being detained by immigration authorities and/or fined. Airport visas may be obtained if 48 hours advance notice has been provided by the traveler's sponsoring organization to proper authorities within Ethiopia. Visitors must declare hard currency upon arrival and may be required to present this declaration when applying for an exit visa. Upon departure, travelers should remember that antiquities and religious artifacts require export permission. There is a functioning black market for hard currency, although the official and unofficial exchange rates continue to converge. Black market exchanges remain illegal and visitors are encouraged to exchange funds at banks or hotels. Domestic and international air services generally operate on schedule, although flights between Addis Ababa and Asmara, Eritrea are heavily booked and may be canceled without prior warning. Internal travel is usually safe along major arteries. However, in rural areas and at night, bandit attacks are common. Additionally, not all land mines have been disabled and cleared, especially in rural and isolated areas. Pickpocketing is rampant, and there have been numerous reports of thieves snatching jewelry. Although physicians are well trained, medical facilities are minimal. Hospitals in Addis Ababa suffer from inadequate facilities, antiquated equipment and shortages of supplies, particularly medications. Certain buildings and public places may not be photographed.

Gabon

Gabon is a developing West African nation. French is the official language. Facilities for tourism are limited, especially outside the capital city. A visa is required. Evidence of a yellow fever vaccination must be submitted. Medical facilities in Gabon are limited. Some medicines are not available. Petty crime, such as robbery and mugging, is common, especially in urban areas.

Gambia

The Gambia is a developing West African nation. Facilities for tourists are among the most extensive in West Africa, including one five star hotel and several other hotels of acceptable quality near the coast. In inland areas there are few tourist facilities. Health facilities and services do not meet U.S. standards and there is a limited selections of medicines available. A visa is required. Malaria is common. Evidence of yellow fever immunization must be submitted with one's visa application. Petty street crime is common such as pickpocketing and purse snatching is common in some urban areas. All international travelers must pay $20 (U.S.) at the airport upon departure.

Ghana

Ghana is a developing country on the west coast of Africa. A visa is required. Evidence of immunization for yellow fever is also required. Medical facilities in Ghana are limited, particularly outside the capital city of Accra. Malaria is common, as are other tropical diseases. Petty crime, such as pickpocketing, is common. Robberies often occur in public places and at the beach. In order to comply with Ghanaian law, currency transactions must be conducted with banks or foreign exchange bureaus. Visitors arriving in Ghana with electronic equipment, particularly video cameras and laptop computers, may be required to pay a refundable deposit of 17.5 per cent of the value of the item prior to entry into the country.

In some areas, possession of a camera is considered to be suspicious. Individuals have been arrested for taking pictures near sensitive installations. The government of Ghana does not recognize dual nationality except for minors under 21 years of age. The wearing of any military apparel, such as camouflage jackets or pants, or any clothing or items which may appear military in nature is strictly prohibited.

Guinea

Guinea is a developing coastal West African country. Facilities for tourism are minimal. A visa is required. Evidence of yellow fever immunization is required, and the Guinean government recommends taking of malarial suppressants. Medical facilities are limited. Diseases such as malaria, including cerebral malaria, hepatitis and intestinal hepatitis disorders are endemic. Street crime is very common. Criminals particularly target visitors at the airport in Conakry. Pickpockets or persons posing as officials sometimes offer assistance and then steal bags, purses or wallets.

Travelers may wish to be met at the airport by travel agents, business contacts, family members or friends to avoid this possibility. Permission from the Guinean governmentÕs security personnel is required for photographing government buildings, airports, bridges or official looking buildings. Credit cards are rarely accepted in Guinea. Inter-bank fund transfers are frequently difficult, if not impossible, to accomplish. The communication system is poor. The limited telephone and fax lines are usually available only between 6:00 pm and 6:00 am local time.

Guinea-Bissau

Guinea-Bissau is a developing nation on the west coast of Africa. Portuguese is the official language; French is also widely spoken. Facilities for tourism are minimal, particularly outside the capital city of Bissau. A visa must be obtained in advance; recent visitors arriving without visas via land or air have been turned back. Visa applications must be accompanied by two photos and evidence of yellow fever immunization. Medical facilities in Guinea-Bissau are extremely limited. Medicines often are not available. Malaria is common, as are other tropical diseases. Petty thievery and pickpocketing are increasingly common, particularly at the airport, in markets and at public gatherings. Thieves have occasionally posed as officials and stolen bags and other personal items. Visitors should request permission from security personnel before photographing military or police installations. Small U.S. currency denominations are most useful for exchange into Guinea-Bissau pesos. Credit cards and travelers checks are rarely accepted in Guinea-

Bissau. Inter-bank fund transfers are frequently difficult and time-consuming to accomplish. Taking pesos out of the country is prohibited. Travelers may have difficulty finding public phones and receiving international calls. Telephone services are expensive.

Kenya

Kenya is a developing East African country known for the wildlife in its national park system. Tourist facilities are widely available in Nairobi, on the coast, and in the game park and reserves. A visa is required. Visas may be obtained in advance at any Kenyan embassy or consulate, or upon arrival at a Kenyan port of entry. Evidence of yellow fever immunization may be requested. Adequate medical services are available in Nairobi. There is a high rate of street crime against tourists in downtown Nairobi, Mombasa and at the coastal beach resorts. Pickpockets and thieves are also involved in "snatch and run" crimes near crowds. While traveling in wildlife areas, visitors should use reputable travel firms and knowledgeable guides and avoid camping alone. Water in Nairobi is potable. In other parts of the country, water must be boiled or bottled. Travel by passenger train in Kenya may be unsafe, particularly during the rainy season, because of the lack of routine maintenance and safety checks.

Lesotho

Lesotho is a developing country in southern Africa. Facilities for tourists are limited. Visas are required and should be obtained at a Lesotho diplomatic mission abroad. However, Americans have obtained visas without difficulties at the immigration office in Maseru after entering the country. Basic medical facilities are available, although many medicines are unavailable. Lesotho has experienced varying degrees of political and military instability since January 1994; during such periods the U.S. Embassy advises American citizens to avoid public demonstrations and travelling at night. Armed robberies, break-ins, and auto thefts are common in Maseru and can occur elsewhere in the country.

Liberia

Liberia is a West African country which has suffered internal strife for the past several years. Tourism facilities are poor, and in some cases, non-existant. At the time of publication, U.S. citizens were warned to avoid travel due to unsettled security conditions. Travelers are required to have a visa prior to arrival. Evidence of yellow fever vaccinations are required. An exit permit must be obtained from Liberian immigration authorities upon arrival. Medical facilities have been disrupted. Medicines are scarce. Monrovia's crime rate is high. Foreigners have been targets of street crime. Lodging, water, electricity, fuel, transportation, telephone and postal services continue to be uneven in Monrovia.

Madagascar

Madagascar is an island nation off the east coast of Africa. Facilities for tourism are available, but vary in quality. Visas are required. Evidence of yellow fever immunizations must be submitted. Medical facilities are minimal. Many medicines are unavailable. Street crimes poses a risk for visitors, especially in the capital of Antananarivo. Reported incidents include muggings and purse snatching. These crimes generally occur in or near public mass transit systems, and against individuals walking at night in the Antananarivo city center. Foreigners who remain near or photograph political gatherings or demonstrations, especially in towns outside Antananarivo, may be at risk.

Malawi

Malawi is a developing African nation. In May 1994, it established its first democratically elected government in thirty years, following peaceful and universally supported elections. Facilities for tourists exist in major cities, resort areas, and game parks, but are limited and vary in quality. Visas are not required for a stay of up to three months. Medical facilities are limited and not up to U.S. standards. Medicines and medical equipment are in short supply. The dress code restrictions which applied to all visitors in Malawi (no slacks or short skirts for women and no long hair or flared slacks for men) are no longer in effect. Travelers may wear comfortable clothes, but may wish to dress modestly, especially when visiting remote areas. Lake Malawi is not bilharzia-free. Petty crime including pickpocketing and purse snatching occurs in urban areas. Residential crime and vehicle thefts are on the increase. Road travel at night, particularly outside the three major cities is not recommended due to the high number of serious road accidents. Hotel bills must be paid in U.S. currency, but major credit cards are generally accepted. It is forbidden to take more than 200 kwacha (Malawi currency) out of the country.

Mali

Mali is a West African nation with a new democratically elected system of government. Facilities for tourism are limited. A visa is required. Medical facilities are limited. Many medicines are unavailable. Petty crime, including pickpocketing and purse snatching, is common. Incidents of banditry and vehicle theft have been reported along major travel routes, near the principal cities and in smaller towns. Victims have included foreigners. The roads from Bamako to Mopti, Douentza, Koutiala, Sikasso, and Bougouni, and a few other roads are paved. Road conditions are poor, particularly in the rainy season from mid-June to mid-September. Driving is hazardous after dark, and nighttime travel may be dangerous. Photography of military subjects is restricted. However, interpretation of what may be considered off limits varies. Other subjects may be considered sensitive from a cultural or religious viewpoint, and it is helpful to obtain permission before taking pictures. The Malian currency is the CFA franc which is exchangeable for French francs at a fixed rate. Exchange of dollars in cash or travelers checks is slow and often involves out-of-date rates. Use of credit cards is limited to payments for services at only two hotels in Bamako. Cash advances on credit cards are performed by one bank in Mali, the BMCD Bank in Bamako, and only with a "VISA" credit card. International calls are expensive and difficult to make outside of Bamako. Collect calls cannot be made from Mali. Calls to the United States cost approximately ten dollars a minute.

Mauritania

Mauritania is located in northwestern Africa. A visa is required. Evidence of yellow fever immunization and proof of sufficient funds are required. Medical facilities in Mauritania are limited. Medicines are difficult to obtain. Petty crime exists. Local currency may not be imported or exported. Credit cards, other than American Express, are not acceptable in Mauritania. American Express cards can only be used at a few hotels in Nouakchott and Nouadhibou. The land border with neighboring Senegal, closed as a result of a 1989 crisis, was reopened in 1992. Overland travel is now possible between the two countries.

Mauritius

The Republic of Mauritius has a stable government and growing economy. Facilities for tourism are largely available. Although the spoken languages are French and Creole, English is the official language. An onward/return ticket and evidence of sufficient funds are required for entrance to Mauritius. U.S. citizens do not need visas for a stay of three months or less for business or tourism. Petty crime is common in Mauritius.

Mozambique

Mozambique, a less developed country in southern Africa, ended a 17-year civil war in October 1992 with the signing of a peace agreement between the government and the rival rebel group. Facilities for tourism are severely limited outside of Maputo. Travel by road outside of the major urban areas is possible; however, road conditions vary greatly. A visa is required. Visas must be obtained in advance. Medical facilities are minimal. Many medicines are unavailable. MaputoÕs special clinic, which requires payment in hard currency, can provide general non-emergency services. Economic conditions in the country, spotty police protection, and years of war have caused an increase in violent and armed robberies, break-ins, and auto thefts. Victims, including members of the foreign community, have been killed. Traveling alone or at night is particularly risky. Currency can be converted at locations authorized by the Mozambican government. Currency conversions on the black market are illegal and very risky. Credit cards are not widely accepted in Mozambique. Some merchants prefer to be paid in U.S. dollars.

Namibia

Namibia is a southern African country with a moderately developed economy. Facilities for tourism are available. An onward/return ticket and proof of sufficient funds are required for entrance into Namibia. A visa is not required for tourist or business visits. Medical facilities are relatively modern, especially in the city of Windhoek. Some petty crime occurs.

Niger

Niger is an inland African nation whose northern area includes a part of the Sahara Desert. Tourism facilities are minimal, particularly outside of Niamey. A visa is required to enter Niger. Visas are valid for a period of one week to three months from the date of issuance, depending on the type of visa and category of traveler. Yellow fever and cholera vaccinations are required for entry into Niger. Medical facilities are minimal in Niger, particularly outside the capital of Niamey. Some medicines are in short supply. Armed bandits operate in northern Niger, and a number of people have been killed. Thieves and pickpockets are especially active in tourist areas. Care must be taken in walking city streets anywhere at any time, but especially at night. There have been incidents of groups of men assaulting women who are, or appear to be, African, and who are wearing garments other than the traditional ankle-length wrap known as "pagnes." Tourists are free to take pictures anywhere in Niger, except near military installations, radio and television stations, the Presidency Building, and the airport. There are no laws restricting currency transactions in Niger. Local currency (the CFA Franc) or foreign currency, up to the equivalent of $4,000 (U.S.) , may be taken into or out of Niger. International telephones service to and from Niger is expensive and callers experience delays getting a line. Telefaxes are often garbled due to poor quality.

Nigeria

At the time of publication, Nigeria, with limited facilities for tourism, poses many risks for travelers. A visa is required for admission to the country, and no visas are issued at the airport. Evidence of yellow fever and cholera vaccinations are also required. Violent crime is a serious problem, especially in Lagos and the southern half of the country. Foreigners in particular are vulnerable to armed robbery, assault, burglary, carjackings and extortion. Disease is widespread and the public is not always informed in a timely manner about outbreaks of typhoid, cholera and yellow fever. Malaria, including potentially fatal cerebral malaria, and hepatitis are endemic. Medical facilities are limited; not all medicines are available. Permission is required to take photographs of government buildings, airports, bridges or official looking buildings. Permission may be obtained from Nigerian security personnel. Persons seeking to trade at lower rates on the "black market" could be arrested or shaken down. To avoid problems, dollars should be exchanged for naira (Nigerian currency) only at the official rate and at approved exchange facilities, including many major hotels. Credit cards are rarely accepted, and their use is generally ill advised because of the prevalence of credit card fraud in Nigeria and perpetrated by Nigerians in the United States. It is often necessary to bring travelers checks or currency in sufficient amounts to cover the trip. Interbank transfers are practically impossible to accomplish. Prospective visitors should consult the Consular Information Sheet for Nigeria. Because of the incidence of business scams and swindles, persons interested in doing business in Nigeria are advised to consult Tips for Business Travelers to Nigeria before providing any information or funds in response to an unverified business offer. This publication is available free of charge by sending a self addressed, stamped envelope to the Office of Overseas Citizens Services, Department of State, Washington, D.C. 20520-4818.

Rwanda

Rwanda is a central East African country torn by ethnic and political strife. A four year civil war resumed in April and ended in mid-July of 1994. Much of the country's basic infrastructure - telephones, water distribution, electricity, etc. - was destroyed in the war. Medical facilities are severely limited and extremely overburdened. Almost all medical facilities in the capital, Kigali, were destroyed during the civil war. Looting and street crime are common. Civilian law enforcement authorities may be limited or non-existant. Clean water and food are unavailable on a regular basis, and only rudimentary lodging can be found. At the time of publication, the Department of State warned U.S. citizens to avoid travel due to the unsettled conditions following the aftermath of the civil war.

Sao Tome and Principe

Sao Tome and Principe is a developing island nation off the west coast of Africa. Facilities for tourism are not widely available. A visa is required. Fees are charged for both business and tourist visas. Evidence of yellow fever immunization must be submitted. Medical facilities in Sao Tome and Principe are limited. Some crime occurs.

Senegal

Senegal is a French speaking West African country. Facilities for tourists are widely available although of varying quality. Visas are not required for stays of less than 90 days. Medical facilities are limited, particularly in areas outside the capital, Dakar. Street crime in Senegal poses moderate risks for visitors. Most reported incidents involve pickpockets, purse snatchers and street scam artists.

Seychelles

Seychelles is a tropical island nation in the Indian Ocean off the east coast of Africa. The principle island of Mahe has a population of about 50,000. The two other islands with significant permanent populations are Praslin and La Digue. Facilities for tourism are generally well developed. A visa is required and may be issued on arrival for a stay of up to one month. There is no charge. The visa may be extended for a period of up to one year. Medical facilities in Seychelles are limited, especially in the isolated outer islands, where doctors are often unavailable. Petty crime occurs, although violent crime against tourists is considered to be rare. Keep valuables in hotel safes; close and lock hotel windows at night, even while the room is occupied to minimize the risk of crime.

Sierra Leone

Sierra Leone is a developing country which has few facilities for tourism and poses considerable risks for travelers. Military activity and banditry affect large parts of the country outside Freetown. Telephone service is unreliable. A visa is required. Airport visas are not available upon arrival in Sierra Leone. Yellow fever immunizations are required. Malaria suppressants are recommended. Travelers must declare foreign currency being brought into Sierra Leone. Declaration is made on an exchange control form which must be certified and stamped at the port of entry. Medical facilities are limited and medicines are in short supply. Sterility of equipment is questionable, and treatment is often unreliable. Petty crime and theft of wallets and passports are common. Requests for payments at military roadblocks are common. Permission is required to photograph government buildings, airports, bridges or official-looking buildings. Areas forbidding photography are not marked or defined.

Somalia

At the time of publication, U.S. citizens were warned not to travel to Somalia. The Liaison Office in Mogodishu ceased operations in September 1994. No visas are required because there is no functioning government. Anyone entering Somalia must receive immunization against cholera, typhoid, and yellow fever, and obtain a doctor's advice regarding any other immunizations that might be necessary. There are virtually no health facilities or medicines available in Somalia. Looting, banditry, and all forms of violent crime are common in Somalia, particularly in the capital city of Mogodishu. Electricity, water, food, and lodging are unobtainable on a regular basis.

South Africa

Although South Africa is in many respects a developed country, much of its population, particularly in rural areas, lives in poverty. The political situation in South Africa remains unsettled as the country continues its transition to a non-racial democracy. There are adequate facilities in all urban centers, game parks and areas most commonly visited by tourists. Food and water are generally safe, and a wide variety of consumer goods and pharmaceuticals are readily available. Road conditions are generally good, but there is a very high incidence of highway casualties, especially over holiday weekends. A passport valid for at least six months is required, but a visa is not required for visits for holiday, business or transit purposes. Visas are required, however, for extended stays, employment, study and for diplomatic and official passport holders. Evidence of a yellow fever vaccination is necessary if arriving from an infected area. Medical facilities are good in urban areas and in the vicinity of game parks and beaches, but may be limited elsewhere. There is continuing and significant street crime such as muggings, pickpocketing, and random street violence, which affects foreigners as well as local residents, especially in the center of major cities such as Johannesburg

Sudan

Sudan is a large under-developed country in northeastern Africa. Tourism facilities are minimal. A visa is required to enter Sudan. The Sudanese government recommends that malarial suppressants be taken, and that yellow fever, cholera and meningitis vaccinations be in order. Visas are not granted in passports showing Israeli visas. Travelers are required to register with police headquarters within three days of arrival. Travelers must obtain police permission before moving to another location in Sudan and must register with police within 24 hours of arrival at the new location.

The exchange of money at other than an authorized banking institution may result in arrest and loss of funds though unscrupulous black marketeers. A permit must be obtained before taking photographs anywhere in Khartoum, as well as in the interior of the country. Photographing military areas, bridges, drainage stations, broadcast stations, public utilities, and slum areas or beggars is prohibited. Disruption of water and electricity is frequent. Telecommunications are slow and often not possible. Unforeseen circumstances such as sandstorms and electrical outages may cause flight delays.

Swaziland

Swaziland is a small developing nation in southern Africa. Facilities for tourism are available. Visas are not required of tourists planning to stay less than 60 days. Temporary residence permits are issued in Mbabane, the capital. For longer stays, visitors must report to immigration authorities or to a police station within 48 hours of arrival, if they are not lodged in a hotel. Yellow fever and cholera immunizations are required for visitors arriving from an infected area. Anti-malarial treatment is recommended. Medical facilities are limited. Petty street crime, primarily theft of money and personal property occurs with some frequency.

Tanzania

Tanzania is an East African nation. Tourist facilities are adequate in major cities, but limited in remote areas. A visa is required for entrance into the country. Visas for mainland Tanzania are also valid for Zanzibar. Airport visas may be obtained only in Zanzibar; they are not available at mainland airports. Yellow fever and cholera immunizations are required if arriving from an affected area. Airport officials often require current immunizations records from travelers arriving from non-infected areas as well.

Medical facilities are limited. Some medicines are in short supply or unavailable. Malaria is endemic in Tanzania and anti-malarial prophylaxis are advisable. Numerous cases of meningococcal meningitis and cholera have been reported throughout the country. Crime is a concern in both urban and rural areas of Tanzania. Incidents include muggings, vehicle thefts and residential break-ins. Valuables such as passports, travelers checks, cameras and jewelry are particular targets for thieves, and are easily stolen if left in luggage at airline check-ins or hotel lobbies. Photography of military installations is forbidden. Individuals have been detained and/or had their cameras and film confiscated for taking pictures of hospitals, schools, bridges, industrial sites and airports.

Togo

Togo is a small West African nation with a developing economy. Tourism facilities are limited, especially outside the capital city. No visa is required for a stay of less than three months. Yellow fever immunizations are required. Medical facilities in Togo are limited under normal conditions and have degraded because of a long general strike, the departure of medical personnel and the closure or reduction of service in clinics and hospitals. Some medicines are available through local pharmacies. Petty crime, including pickpocketing, has increased.

Uganda

Uganda is an East African nation. Tourism facilities are adequate in Kampala; they are limited, but are improving in other areas. A visa is not required for U.S. citizens. Evidence of immunization for yellow fever, cholera and typhoid is often requested. Medical facilities in Uganda are limited. Medical supplies, equipment and medication are often in short supply or not available.

For additional analytical, business and investment opportunities information, please contact Global Investment & Business Center, USA at (202) 546-2103. Fax: (202) 546-3275. E-mail: rusric@erols.com

Incidents of armed vehicle hijacking and armed highway robbery occur throughout the country with varying frequency. Many roads in Uganda are poor, and bandit activity in some areas is both frequent and unpredictable. Insurgent activities have made travel to the northern area of the country risky. Highway travel at night is particularly dangerous. Photographing security forces or government installations is prohibited.

Zaire

Zaire is the largest sub-Saharan African country. Although Zaire has substantial human and natural resources, in recent years, the country has suffered a profound political and economic crisis. This has resulted in the dramatic deterioration of the physical infrastructure of the country, insecurity and an increase in crime in urban areas (including occasional episodes of looting and murder in Kinshasa's streets) . There have also been occasional official hostility to U.S. citizens and nationals of European countries, periodic shortages of basic needs such as gasoline, chronic shortages of medicine and supplies for some basic medical care, hyperinflation, and corruption. In some urban areas, malnutrition and starvation are acute.

Tourism facilities are minimal. A visa and vaccination certificate showing valid yellow fever and cholera immunizations are required for entry. Medical facilities are extremely limited. Medicine is in short supply. Most intercity roads are difficult or impassable in the rainy season. While the U.S. dollar and travelers checks can, in theory, be exchanged for local currency (zaires) at banks in Kinshasa, banks often do not have sufficient new Zaire cash on hand to make transactions. Credit cards are generally not accepted, except by a few major hotels and restaurants. Photography of public buildings and/or military installations is forbidden, including photography of the banks of the Congo River. Offenders may to be arrested, held for a minimum of several hours, fined and the film and camera may also be confiscated.

Zambia

Zambia is a developing African country. Tourist facilities outside of well-known game parks are not fully developed. Visa are required prior to entering the country. Medical facilities are limited. Cholera and yellow fever are endemic. Crime is prevalent in Zambia. Muggings and petty theft are commonplace, especially in Lusaka in the vicinity of Cairo Road and in other commercial areas.

Zimbabwe

Zimbabwe is a landlocked southern African nation with extensive tourist facilities. Although no visa is required to enter Zimbabwe, immigration authorities require a firm itinerary, sufficient funds for the visit, and a return ticket to the United States. Onward tickets to non-U.S. destinations may not suffice. If these requirements are not met, immigration authorities may order departure by the next available flight. Medical facilities in Zimbabwe are limited. Some medicine is in short supply. Muggings, purse snatching and break-ins are an increasing problem in Harare, Bulawayo and tourist resorts areas. Thieves often operate in downtown Harare, especially in crowded areas, and on public transportation. Bus travel can be dangerous due to overloaded buses, inadequate maintenance, unskilled drivers and occasional cases of drivers operating buses while intoxicated. Zimbabwean authorities are extremely sensitive about photographing certain locations and buildings, including government offices, airports, military installations, official residences and embassies.

U.S EMBASSIES AND CONSULATES IN AFRICA

Note: The workweek is Monday-Friday except where noted. Mail to APO and FPO addresses must originate in the United States; the street address must not appear in an APO or FPO address.

ANGOLA
American Embassy
Rua Houari Boumedienne
P.O. Box 6468
Luanda
Tel: (244-2) 34-54-81

BENIN
American Embassy
Rue Caporal Anani Bernard
B.P. 2012
Cotonou
Tel: (229) 30-06-50

BOTSWANA
American Embassy
P.O. Box 90
Gaborone
Tel: (267) 353-982

BURKINO FASO
American Embassy
B.P. 35
Ouagadougou
Tel: (226) 306-723

BURUNDI
American Embassy
B.P. 34 1720
Bujumbura
Tel: (257) (2) 23454

CAMEROON
American Embassy
Rue Nachtigal, B.P. 817
Yaounde
Tel: (237) 23-40-14

CAPE VERDE
American Embassy
Rua Abilio Macedo 81
C.P. 201
Praia
Tel: (238) 61-56-16

CENTRAL AFRICAN REPUBLIC
American Embassy
Avenue David Dacko
B.P. 924
Bangui
Tel: (236) 61-02-00

CHAD
American Embassy
Avenue Felix Eboue
B.P. 413
N'Djamena
Tel: (235) 516-218

COMOROS
Services provided by the American Embassy in Port Louis, Mauritius.

CONGO
American Embassy
Avenue Amilcar Cabral
B.P. 1015, Box C
Brazzaville
Tel: (242) 83-20-70

COTE d'IVOIRE
American Embassy
5 Rue Jesse Owens 01
B.P. 1712
Abidjan
Tel: (225) 21-09-79

DJIBOUTI
American Embassy
Plateau du Serpent, Blvd. Marechal Joffre
B.P. 185
Djibouti
Tel: (253) 353-995

EQUATORIAL GUINEA
American Embassy
Calle de Los Ministros
P.O. Box 597
Malabo
Tel: (240-9) 2406

For additional analytical, business and investment opportunities information, please contact Global Investment & Business Center, USA at (202) 546-2103. Fax: (202) 546-3275. E-mail: rusric@erols.com

ERITREA
American Embassy
34 Zera Yacob St.
P.O. Box 211
Asmara
Tel: (291-1) 12-00-04

ETHIOPIA
American Embassy
Entoto St., P.O. Box 1014
Addis Ababa
Tel: (251-1) 550-666, ext. 316/336

GABON
American Embassy
Blvd. de la Mer
B.P. 4000
Libreville
Tel: (241) 762-003, 743-492

THE GAMBIA
American Embassy
Kairaba Ave.
P.M.B. No. 19
Banjul
Tel: (220) 392856, 392858, 391970/1

GHANA
American Embassy
Ring Road East
P.O. Box 194
Accra
Tel: (223-21) 775-347

GUINEA
American Embassy
2d Blvd. and 9th Ave
B.P. 603
Conakry
Tel: (224) 441-520

GUINEA-BISSAU
American Embassy
C.P. 297
1067 Codex
Bissau Tel: (245) 25-2273

KENYA
American Embassy
Moi and Haile Selassie Ave.
P.O. Box 30137

Nairobi
Tel: (254) (2) 334-141

LESOTHO
American Embassy
254 Kingsway
P.O. Box 333, Maseru 100
Maseru
Tel: (266) 312-666

LIBERIA
American Embassy
111 United Nations Dr.
P.O. Box 10-0098, Mamba Point
Monrovia
Tel: (231) 222-991

MADAGASCAR
American Embassy
14 and 16 Rue Rainitovo, Antsahavola
B.P. 620
Antananarivo
Tel: (261) (2) 21257, 20089

MALAWI
American Embassy
P.O. Box 30016
Lilongwe
Tel: (265) 783-166

MALI
American Embassy
Rue de Rochester N.Y.
B.P. 34
Bamako
Tel: (223) 223-678, 225-470

MAURITANIA
American Embassy
B.P. 222
Nouakchott
Tel: (222) (2) 52660
Workweek: Sunday-Thursday

MAURITIUS
American Embassy
Rogers Bldg. (4th Fl.)
John F. Kennedy Street
Port Louis
Tel: (230) 208-9764

**For additional analytical, business and investment opportunities information,
please contact Global Investment & Business Center, USA
at (202) 546-2103. Fax: (202) 546-3275. E-mail: rusric@erols.com**

MOZAMBIQUE
American Embassy
Avenida Kaunda 193
Maputo
Tel: (258) (1) 49-27-97

NAMIBIA
American Embassy
Private Bag 12029
Windhoek 9000
Tel: (264-61) 22-1601

NIGER
American Embassy
B.P. 11201
Niamey
Tel: (227) 722-661

NIGERIA
American Embassy
2 Eleke Crescent
Victoria Island, Lagos
Tel: (234) (1) 261-0050

RWANDA
American Embassy
Blvd. de la Revolution
B.P. 28
Kigali
Tel: (205) 75601

SAO TOME AND PRINCIPE
Falls under the jurisdiction of American
Embassy in Libreville, Gabon

SENEGAL
American Embassy
Avenue Jean XXIII
B.P. 49
Dakar
Tel: (221) 23-42-96

SEYCHELLES
American Embassy
Box 148, Unit 62501
Victoria
Tel: (248) 225-256

SIERRA LEONE
American Embassy
Corner Walpole and Siaka Stevens St.
Freetown
Tel: (232-22) 226-481

SOMALIA
U.S. Liaison Office ceased operation
September 1994; services provided through
the U.S. Embassy in Nairobi, Kenya

SOUTH AFRICA
American Embassy
887 Pretorius St.
Pretoria
Tel: (27) (12) 342-1048

American Consulate General
Broadway Industries Center
Heerengracht
Foreshore
Cape Town
Tel: (27) (21) 214-280

American Consulate General
Durban House, 29th Fl.
333 Smith St.
Durban 4001
Tel: (27) (31) 304-4737

American Consulate General
Kine Center, 11th Fl.
141 Commissioner St.
Johannesburg
Tel: (27) (11) 331-1681

SUDAN
American Embassy
Sharia Ali Abdul Latif
P.O. Box 699
Khartoum
Tel: 74700, 74611
Workweek: Sunday-Thursday

SWAZILAND
American Embassy
Central Bank Bldg.
Warner Street
P.O. Box 199
Mbabane
Tel: (268) 464-41/5

TANZANIA
American Embassy
30 Laibon Rd. (off Ali Hassan Mwinyi Rd.)
P.O. Box 9123
Dar Es Salaam
Tel: (255) (51) 66010/4

For additional analytical, business and investment opportunities information,
please contact Global Investment & Business Center, USA
at (202) 546-2103. Fax: (202) 546-3275. E-mail: rusric@erols.com

TOGO
American Embassy
Rue Pelletier Caventou & Rue Vauban
B.P. 852
Lome
Tel: (228) (21) 29-91

UGANDA
American Embassy
Parliament Ave.
P.O. Box 7007
Kampala
Tel: (256) (41) 259-792, 259-795

ZAIRE
American Embassy
310 Avenue des Aviateurs

Unit 31550
Kinshasa
Tel: (243) (12) 21523

ZAMBIA
American Embassy
Independence and United Nations Aves.
P.O. Box 31617
Lusaka
Tel: (260) (1) 250-955

ZIMBABWE
American Embassy
172 Herbert Chitepo Avenue
P.O. Box 3340
Harare
Tel: (263) (4) 794-521

BASIC TITLES FOR ANGOLA

IMPORTANT!
All publications are updated annually!
Please contact IBP, Inc. at ibpusa3@gmail.com for the latest ISBNs and additional information

Title
Angola Business and Investment Opportunities Yearbook
Angola Business and Investment Opportunities Yearbook
Angola Business and Investment Opportunities Yearbook Volume 1 Strategic Information and Opportunities
Angola Business Intelligence Report - Practical Information, Opportunities, Contacts
Angola Business Intelligence Report - Practical Information, Opportunities, Contacts
Angola Business Law Handbook - Strategic Information and Basic Laws
Angola Business Law Handbook - Strategic Information and Basic Laws
Angola Business Law Handbook - Strategic Information and Basic Laws
Angola Business Law Handbook - Strategic Information and Basic Laws
Angola Company Laws and Regulations Handbook
Angola Constitution and Citizenship Laws Handbook - Strategic Information and Basic Laws
Angola Country Study Guide - Strategic Information and Developments
Angola Country Study Guide - Strategic Information and Developments
Angola Country Study Guide - Strategic Information and Developments Volume 1 Strategic Information and Developments
Angola Customs, Trade Regulations and Procedures Handbook
Angola Customs, Trade Regulations and Procedures Handbook
Angola Diplomatic Handbook - Strategic Information and Developments
Angola Diplomatic Handbook - Strategic Information and Developments
Angola Ecology & Nature Protection Handbook
Angola Ecology & Nature Protection Handbook
Angola Ecology & Nature Protection Laws and Regulation Handbook
Angola Energy Policy, Laws and Regulation Handbook
Angola Energy Policy, Laws and Regulations Handbook

Title
Angola Energy Policy, Laws and Regulations Handbook
Angola Energy Sector Handbook
Angola Energy Sector Handbook
Angola Export-Import Trade and Business Directory
Angola Export-Import Trade and Business Directory
Angola Foreign Policy and Government Guide
Angola Foreign Policy and Government Guide
Angola Immigration Laws and Regulations Handbook - Strategic Information and Basic Laws
Angola Industrial and Business Directory
Angola Industrial and Business Directory
Angola Insolvency (Bankruptcy) Laws and Regulations Handbook - Strategic Information and Basic Laws
Angola Internet and E-Commerce Investment and Business Guide - Strategic and Practical Information: Regulations and Opportunities
Angola Internet and E-Commerce Investment and Business Guide - Strategic and Practical Information: Regulations and Opportunities
Angola Investment and Business Guide - Strategic and Practical Information
Angola Investment and Business Guide - Strategic and Practical Information
Angola Investment and Business Guide - Strategic and Practical Information
Angola Investment and Business Guide - Strategic and Practical Information
Angola Investment and Trade Laws and Regulations Handbook
Angola Labor Laws and Regulations Handbook - Strategic Information and Basic Laws
Angola Land Ownership and Agriculture Laws Handbook
Angola Mineral & Mining Sector Investment and Business Guide - Strategic and Practical Information
Angola Mineral & Mining Sector Investment and Business Guide - Strategic and Practical Information
Angola Mining Laws and Regulations Handbook
Angola Oil & Gas Laws and Regulations Handbook
Angola Oil & Gas Sector Business & Investment Opportunities Yearbook
Angola Oil and Gas Exploration Laws and Regulation Handbook
Angola Oil Explorations and Concessions Regulations Handbook
Angola President Jose Eduardo dos Santos Handbook
Angola President José Eduardo dos Santos Handbook
Angola Privatization Programs and Regulations Handbook
Angola Privatization Programs and Regulations Handbook
Angola Recent Economic and Political Developments Yearbook
Angola Recent Economic and Political Developments Yearbook
Angola Recent Economic and Political Developments Yearbook
Angola Starting Business (Incorporating) in....Guide
Angola Taxation Laws and Regulations Handbook
Angola Telecom Laws and Regulations Handbook
Angola Telecommunication Industry Business Opportunities Handbook
Angola Telecommunication Industry Business Opportunities Handbook
Angola: How to Invest, Start and Run Profitable Business in Angola Guide - Practical Information,

For additional analytical, business and investment opportunities information,
please contact Global Investment & Business Center, USA
at (202) 546-2103. Fax: (202) 546-3275. E-mail: rusric@erols.com

Title
Opportunities, Contacts

**For additional analytical, business and investment opportunities information,
please contact Global Investment & Business Center, USA
at (202) 546-2103. Fax: (202) 546-3275. E-mail: rusric@erols.com**

INFORMATION STRATEGY, INTERNET AND E-COMMERCE DEVELOPMENT HANDBOOKS LIBRARY

Price: $99.95 Each

World Business Information Catalog: http://www.ibpus.com

TITLE
Albania Information Strategy, Internet and E-Commerce Development Handbook - Strategic Information, Programs, Regulations
Algeria Information Strategy, Internet and E-Commerce Development Handbook - Strategic Information, Programs, Regulations
Angola Information Strategy, Internet and E-Commerce Development Handbook - Strategic Information, Programs, Regulations
Argentina Information Strategy, Internet and E-Commerce Development Handbook - Strategic Information, Programs, Regulations
Armenia Information Strategy, Internet and E-Commerce Development Handbook - Strategic Information, Programs, Regulations
Australia Information Strategy, Internet and E-Commerce Development Handbook - Strategic Information, Programs, Regulations
Austria Information Strategy, Internet and E-Commerce Development Handbook - Strategic Information, Programs, Regulations
Azerbaijan Information Strategy, Internet and E-Commerce Development Handbook - Strategic Information, Programs, Regulations
Bangladesh Information Strategy, Internet and E-Commerce Development Handbook - Strategic Information, Programs, Regulations
Belarus Information Strategy, Internet and E-Commerce Development Handbook - Strategic Information, Programs, Regulations
Belgium Information Strategy, Internet and E-Commerce Development Handbook - Strategic Information, Programs, Regulations
Bermuda Information Strategy, Internet and E-Commerce Development Handbook - Strategic Information, Programs, Regulations
Bolivia Information Strategy, Internet and E-Commerce Development Handbook - Strategic Information, Programs, Regulations
Bosnia and Herzegovina Information Strategy, Internet and E-Commerce Development Handbook - Strategic Information, Programs, Regulations
Botswana Information Strategy, Internet and E-Commerce Development Handbook - Strategic Information, Programs, Regulations
Brazil Information Strategy, Internet and E-Commerce Development Handbook - Strategic Information, Programs, Regulations
Bulgaria Information Strategy, Internet and E-Commerce Development Handbook - Strategic Information, Programs, Regulations
Cambodia Information Strategy, Internet and E-Commerce Development Handbook - Strategic Information, Programs, Regulations
Cameroon Information Strategy, Internet and E-Commerce Development Handbook - Strategic Information, Programs, Regulations
Canada Information Strategy, Internet and E-Commerce Development Handbook - Strategic Information, Programs, Regulations
Chile Information Strategy, Internet and E-Commerce Development Handbook - Strategic Information, Programs,

TITLE
Regulations
China Information Strategy, Internet and E-Commerce Development Handbook - Strategic Information, Programs, Regulations
Colombia Information Strategy, Internet and E-Commerce Development Handbook - Strategic Information, Programs, Regulations
Cook Islands Information Strategy, Internet and E-Commerce Development Handbook - Strategic Information, Programs, Regulations
Costa Rica Information Strategy, Internet and E-Commerce Development Handbook - Strategic Information, Programs, Regulations
Croatia Information Strategy, Internet and E-Commerce Development Handbook - Strategic Information, Programs, Regulations
Cuba Information Strategy, Internet and E-Commerce Development Handbook - Strategic Information, Programs, Regulations
Cyprus Information Strategy, Internet and E-Commerce Development Handbook - Strategic Information, Programs, Regulations
Czech Republic Information Strategy, Internet and E-Commerce Development Handbook - Strategic Information, Programs, Regulations
Denmark Information Strategy, Internet and E-Commerce Development Handbook - Strategic Information, Programs, Regulations
Dominican Republic Information Strategy, Internet and E-Commerce Development Handbook - Strategic Information, Programs, Regulations
Dubai Information Strategy, Internet and E-Commerce Development Handbook - Strategic Information, Programs, Regulations
Ecuador Information Strategy, Internet and E-Commerce Development Handbook - Strategic Information, Programs, Regulations
Egypt Information Strategy, Internet and E-Commerce Development Handbook - Strategic Information, Programs, Regulations
El Salvador Information Strategy, Internet and E-Commerce Development Handbook - Strategic Information, Programs, Regulations
Equatorial Guinea Information Strategy, Internet and E-Commerce Development Handbook - Strategic Information, Programs, Regulations
Estonia Information Strategy, Internet and E-Commerce Development Handbook - Strategic Information, Programs, Regulations
Fiji Information Strategy, Internet and E-Commerce Development Handbook - Strategic Information, Programs, Regulations
Finland Information Strategy, Internet and E-Commerce Development Handbook - Strategic Information, Programs, Regulations
France Information Strategy, Internet and E-Commerce Development Handbook - Strategic Information, Programs, Regulations
Georgia Republic Information Strategy, Internet and E-Commerce Development Handbook - Strategic Information, Programs, Regulations
Germany Information Strategy, Internet and E-Commerce Development Handbook - Strategic Information, Programs, Regulations
Greece Information Strategy, Internet and E-Commerce Development Handbook - Strategic Information, Programs, Regulations
Guatemala Information Strategy, Internet and E-Commerce Development Handbook - Strategic Information, Programs, Regulations
Guernsey Information Strategy, Internet and E-Commerce Development Handbook - Strategic Information, Programs, Regulations
Guyana Information Strategy, Internet and E-Commerce Development Handbook - Strategic Information, Programs, Regulations
Haiti Information Strategy, Internet and E-Commerce Development Handbook - Strategic Information, Programs, Regulations
Honduras Information Strategy, Internet and E-Commerce Development Handbook - Strategic Information, Programs, Regulations
Hungary Information Strategy, Internet and E-Commerce Development Handbook - Strategic Information, Programs, Regulations
Iceland Information Strategy, Internet and E-Commerce Development Handbook - Strategic Information, Programs, Regulations
India Information Strategy, Internet and E-Commerce Development Handbook - Strategic Information, Programs, Regulations

TITLE
Indonesia Information Strategy, Internet and E-Commerce Development Handbook - Strategic Information, Programs, Regulations
Iran Information Strategy, Internet and E-Commerce Development Handbook - Strategic Information, Programs, Regulations
Iraq Information Strategy, Internet and E-Commerce Development Handbook - Strategic Information, Programs, Regulations
Ireland Information Strategy, Internet and E-Commerce Development Handbook - Strategic Information, Programs, Regulations
Israel Information Strategy, Internet and E-Commerce Development Handbook - Strategic Information, Programs, Regulations
Italy Information Strategy, Internet and E-Commerce Development Handbook - Strategic Information, Programs, Regulations
Jamaica Information Strategy, Internet and E-Commerce Development Handbook - Strategic Information, Programs, Regulations
Japan Information Strategy, Internet and E-Commerce Development Handbook - Strategic Information, Programs, Regulations
Jordan Information Strategy, Internet and E-Commerce Development Handbook - Strategic Information, Programs, Regulations
Kazakhstan Information Strategy, Internet and E-Commerce Development Handbook - Strategic Information, Programs, Regulations
Kenya Information Strategy, Internet and E-Commerce Development Handbook - Strategic Information, Programs, Regulations
Korea, North Information Strategy, Internet and E-Commerce Development Handbook - Strategic Information, Programs, Regulations
Korea, South Information Strategy, Internet and E-Commerce Development Handbook - Strategic Information, Programs, Regulations
Kuwait Information Strategy, Internet and E-Commerce Development Handbook - Strategic Information, Programs, Regulations
Kyrgyzstan Information Strategy, Internet and E-Commerce Development Handbook - Strategic Information, Programs, Regulations
Laos Information Strategy, Internet and E-Commerce Development Handbook - Strategic Information, Programs, Regulations
Latvia Information Strategy, Internet and E-Commerce Development Handbook - Strategic Information, Programs, Regulations
Lebanon Information Strategy, Internet and E-Commerce Development Handbook - Strategic Information, Programs, Regulations
Libya Information Strategy, Internet and E-Commerce Development Handbook - Strategic Information, Programs, Regulations
Lithuania Information Strategy, Internet and E-Commerce Development Handbook - Strategic Information, Programs, Regulations
Macao Information Strategy, Internet and E-Commerce Development Handbook - Strategic Information, Programs, Regulations
Macedonia, Republic Information Strategy, Internet and E-Commerce Development Handbook - Strategic Information, Programs, Regulations
Madagascar Information Strategy, Internet and E-Commerce Development Handbook - Strategic Information, Programs, Regulations
Malaysia Information Strategy, Internet and E-Commerce Development Handbook - Strategic Information, Programs, Regulations
Malta Information Strategy, Internet and E-Commerce Development Handbook - Strategic Information, Programs, Regulations
Mauritius Information Strategy, Internet and E-Commerce Development Handbook - Strategic Information, Programs, Regulations
Mauritius Information Strategy, Internet and E-Commerce Development Handbook - Strategic Information, Programs, Regulations
Mexico Information Strategy, Internet and E-Commerce Development Handbook - Strategic Information, Programs, Regulations
Micronesia Information Strategy, Internet and E-Commerce Development Handbook - Strategic Information, Programs, Regulations
Moldova Information Strategy, Internet and E-Commerce Development Handbook - Strategic Information, Programs, Regulations
Monaco Information Strategy, Internet and E-Commerce Development Handbook - Strategic Information,

TITLE
Programs, Regulations
Mongolia Information Strategy, Internet and E-Commerce Development Handbook - Strategic Information, Programs, Regulations
Morocco Information Strategy, Internet and E-Commerce Development Handbook - Strategic Information, Programs, Regulations
Myanmar Information Strategy, Internet and E-Commerce Development Handbook - Strategic Information, Programs, Regulations
Namibia Information Strategy, Internet and E-Commerce Development Handbook - Strategic Information, Programs, Regulations
Netherlands Information Strategy, Internet and E-Commerce Development Handbook - Strategic Information, Programs, Regulations
New Zealand Information Strategy, Internet and E-Commerce Development Handbook - Strategic Information, Programs, Regulations
Nicaragua Information Strategy, Internet and E-Commerce Development Handbook - Strategic Information, Programs, Regulations
Nigeria Information Strategy, Internet and E-Commerce Development Handbook - Strategic Information, Programs, Regulations
Norway Information Strategy, Internet and E-Commerce Development Handbook - Strategic Information, Programs, Regulations
Opportunities
Pakistan Information Strategy, Internet and E-Commerce Development Handbook - Strategic Information, Programs, Regulations
Panama Information Strategy, Internet and E-Commerce Development Handbook - Strategic Information, Programs, Regulations
Peru Information Strategy, Internet and E-Commerce Development Handbook - Strategic Information, Programs, Regulations
Philippines Information Strategy, Internet and E-Commerce Development Handbook - Strategic Information, Programs, Regulations
Poland Information Strategy, Internet and E-Commerce Development Handbook - Strategic Information, Programs, Regulations
Portugal Information Strategy, Internet and E-Commerce Development Handbook - Strategic Information, Programs, Regulations
Romania Information Strategy, Internet and E-Commerce Development Handbook - Strategic Information, Programs, Regulations
Russia Information Strategy, Internet and E-Commerce Development Handbook - Strategic Information, Programs, Regulations
Saudi Arabia Information Strategy, Internet and E-Commerce Development Handbook - Strategic Information, Programs, Regulations
Scotland Information Strategy, Internet and E-Commerce Development Handbook - Strategic Information, Programs, Regulations
Serbia Information Strategy, Internet and E-Commerce Development Handbook - Strategic Information, Programs, Regulations
Singapore Information Strategy, Internet and E-Commerce Development Handbook - Strategic Information, Programs, Regulations
Slovakia Information Strategy, Internet and E-Commerce Development Handbook - Strategic Information, Programs, Regulations
Slovenia Information Strategy, Internet and E-Commerce Development Handbook - Strategic Information, Programs, Regulations
South Africa Information Strategy, Internet and E-Commerce Development Handbook - Strategic Information, Programs, Regulations
Spain Information Strategy, Internet and E-Commerce Development Handbook - Strategic Information, Programs, Regulations
Sri Lanka Information Strategy, Internet and E-Commerce Development Handbook - Strategic Information, Programs, Regulations
Sudan Information Strategy, Internet and E-Commerce Development Handbook - Strategic Information, Programs, Regulations
Suriname Information Strategy, Internet and E-Commerce Development Handbook - Strategic Information, Programs, Regulations
Sweden Information Strategy, Internet and E-Commerce Development Handbook - Strategic Information, Programs, Regulations
Switzerland Information Strategy, Internet and E-Commerce Development Handbook - Strategic Information,

TITLE
Programs, Regulations
Syria Export Import &Business Directory
Taiwan Information Strategy, Internet and E-Commerce Development Handbook - Strategic Information, Programs, Regulations
Tajikistan Information Strategy, Internet and E-Commerce Development Handbook - Strategic Information, Programs, Regulations
Thailand Information Strategy, Internet and E-Commerce Development Handbook - Strategic Information, Programs, Regulations
Tunisia Information Strategy, Internet and E-Commerce Development Handbook - Strategic Information, Programs, Regulations
Turkey Information Strategy, Internet and E-Commerce Development Handbook - Strategic Information, Programs, Regulations
Turkmenistan Information Strategy, Internet and E-Commerce Development Handbook - Strategic Information, Programs, Regulations
Uganda Information Strategy, Internet and E-Commerce Development Handbook - Strategic Information, Programs, Regulations
Ukraine Information Strategy, Internet and E-Commerce Development Handbook - Strategic Information, Programs, Regulations
United Arab Emirates Information Strategy, Internet and E-Commerce Development Handbook - Strategic Information, Programs, Regulations
United Kingdom Information Strategy, Internet and E-Commerce Development Handbook - Strategic Information, Programs, Regulations
United States Information Strategy, Internet and E-Commerce Development Handbook - Strategic Information, Programs, Regulations
Uruguay Information Strategy, Internet and E-Commerce Development Handbook - Strategic Information, Programs, Regulations
US Information Strategy, Internet and E-Commerce Development Handbook - Strategic Information, Programs, Regulations
Uzbekistan Information Strategy, Internet and E-Commerce Development Handbook - Strategic Information, Programs, Regulations
Venezuela Information Strategy, Internet and E-Commerce Development Handbook - Strategic Information, Programs, Regulations
Vietnam Information Strategy, Internet and E-Commerce Development Handbook - Strategic Information, Programs, Regulations